OXFORD SHAKESPEARE CONCORDANCES

OXFORD SHAKESPEARE CONCORDANCES

KING JOHN

A CONCORDANCE TO THE TEXT
OF THE FIRST FOLIO

OXFORD
AT THE CLARENDON PRESS
1970

Oxford University Press, Ely House, London W. 1

GLASGOW NEW YORK TORONTO MELBOURNE WELLINGTON
CAPE TOWN SALISBURY IBADAN NAIROBI DAR ES SALAAM LUSAKA ADDIS ABABA
BOMBAY CALCUTTA MADRAS KARACHI LAHORE DACCA
KUALA LUMPUR SINGAPORE HONG KONG TOKYO

FILMSET BY COMPUTAPRINT LIMITED
AND PRINTED IN GREAT BRITAIN
AT THE UNIVERSITY PRESS, OXFORD
BY VIVIAN RIDLER
PRINTER TO THE UNIVERSITY

GENERAL INTRODUCTION

IN this series of Oxford Shakespeare Concordances, a separate volume is devoted to each of the plays. The text for each concordance is the one chosen as copy-text by Dr. Alice Walker for the Oxford Old Spelling Shakespeare now in preparation.

Each concordance takes account of every word in the text, and represents their occurrence by frequency counts, line numbers, and reference lines, or a selection of these according to the interest of the particular word. The number of words which have frequency counts only has been kept as low as possible. The introduction to each volume records the facsimile copy of the text from which the concordance was prepared, a table of Folio through line numbers and Globe edition act and scene numbers, a list of the misprints corrected in the text, and an account of the order of printing, and the proof-reading, abstracted from Professor Charlton Hinman's *The Printing and Proof-Reading of the First Folio of Shakespeare* (Oxford, 1963).

The following notes on the main features of the concordances may be helpful.[1]

A. *The Text*

The most obvious misprints have been corrected, on conservative principles, and have been listed for each play in the introduction to the corresponding concordance. Wrong-fount letters have been silently corrected.

Obvious irregularities on the part of the original compositor—for example the anomalous absence of full stops after speech prefixes—have been normalized and noted. Colons, semicolons, exclamation and interrogation marks after italicized words have been modernized to roman fount after current practice, since this aspect of

---

[1] An account of the principles and methods by which the concordances were edited appears in *Studies in Bibliography*, vol. 22, 1969.

compositorial practice would not normally be studied from a concordance. The spacing of words in the original printed texts, particularly in 'justified' lines, is extremely variable; spacing has been normalized on the basis of the compositor's practice as revealed in the particular column or page.

For ease of reference, the contractions *S., L., M.,* and forms such as *Mist.* and tildes, have been expanded when the compositor's own preferred practice is clear, and the expansion has been noted in the text. For M^r, the superior character has been lowered silently. Superior characters like the circumflex in *baâ* and those in $\overset{\iota}{y}$, $\overset{e}{y}$, $\overset{u}{y}$, and $\overset{c}{w}$, have been ignored. The reader should find little difficulty in distinguishing the original form of the pronominal contractions when they are encountered in the text. They are listed under Y and W respectively.

B. *Arrangement of entries*

The words in the text are arranged alphabetically, with numerals and & and &c listed at the end. Words starting with I and J, and U and V, will be found together under I and V respectively. The reader should note that the use of U for the medial V (and I for J) leads in some cases to an unfamiliar order of entry. For example, ADUISED is listed before ADULTERY. The reader will usually find the word he wants if he starts his inquiry at the modern spelling, for when the old spelling differs considerably from the modern spelling, a reference such as 'ENFORCE *see* inforce' will direct the reader to the entry in the concordance.

In hyphenated compounds where the hyphen is the second or third character of the heading-word (as in A-BOORD), the hyphenated form may be listed some distance from other occurrences of the same word in un-hyphenated form. In significant cases, references are given to alert the user.

Under the heading-word, the line numbers or lines of context are in the order of the text. The heading-word is followed by a frequency count of the words in short and long (that is, marked with an asterisk) lines, and the reference lines. When a word has been treated as one to have a frequency count only, or a list of the line numbers and count, any further count which follows will refer to the reference lines listed under the same heading. Where there are two counts but no reference lines (as with AN), the first count refers to the speech prefix.

C. *Special Forms*

(*a*) The following words have not been given context lines and line references but are dealt with only by the counting of their frequency:

A AM AND ARE AT BE BY HE I IN IS IT OF ON SHE THE THEY TO WAS WE WITH YOU

These forms occur so often in most texts that the reader can locate them more easily by examining the text of the play than he could by referring to an extensive listing in the concordance.

Homographs of these words (for example I = *ay*) have been listed in full and are given separate counts under the same heading-word.

(*b*) A larger number of words, consisting mainly of variant spellings, have been given line references as well as frequency counts.

These words are: ACTUS AN AR ART ATT AU BEE BEEING BEEN BEENE BEING BENE BIN BUT CAN CANST CE COULD COULDST DE DECIMA DES DID DIDD DIDDEST DIDDST DO DOE DOES DOEST DOETH DONE DOO DOOE DOOES DOOEST DOOING DOON DOONE DOOS DOOST DOOTH DOS DOST DOTH DU E EN EST ET ETC FINIS FOR FROM HA HAD HADST HAH HAS HAST HATH HAUE HEE HEEL HEELE HEL HELL HER HIM HIR HIS IE IF IL ILL ILLE INTO LA LE LES MA MAIE MAIEST MAIST MAY ME MEE MIGHT MIGHTEST MIGHTST MINE MOI MOY MY NE NO NOE NON NONA NOR NOT O OCTAUA OFF OH OR OU OUR OUT PRIMA PRIMUS QUARTA QUARTUS QUE QUINTA QUINTUS SCAENA SCENA SCOENA SECUNDA SECUNDUS SEPTIMA SEPTIMUS SEXTA SHAL SHALL SHALT SHEE SHOLD SHOLDE SHOLDST SHOULD SHOULDE SHOULDST SIR SO SOE TE TERTIA TERTIUS THAT THEE THEIR THEIRE THEM THEN THER THERE THESE THEYR THIS THOSE THOU THY TIS TU VN VNE VOS VOSTRE VOUS VS WAST WEE WER WERE WERT WHAT WHEN WHER WHERE WHICH WHO WHOM WHOME WHY WIL WILL WILT WILTE WOLD WOLDE WOLDST WOULD WOULDE WOULDEST WOULDST YE YEE YF YOUE YOUR YT & &c 1 2 3 4.

Homographs of words on this list (e.g. *bee* = n.) have been listed in full, and also have separate counts.

(*c*) All speech prefixes, other than *All.*, *Both.*, and those which represent the names of actors, have been treated as count-only words. In some cases, however, where a speech prefix corresponds to a form already on the count-only list (e.g. *Is.*), a full entry has been given. In some other cases, when two counts are given for the same heading-word for no apparent reason, the count which does not correspond to the following full references or to the list of line references is that of the speech prefix form (for example AN in *The Tempest*).

(*d*) Hyphenated compounds such as *all-building-law* have been listed under the full form, and also under each main constituent after the first. In this example there are entries under ALL-BUILDING-LAW, BUILDING, and LAW. When, however, one of the constituents of the compound is a word on the count- or location-only list ((*a*) or (*b*) above), it is dealt with in whichever of these two lists applies. References such as 'AT *see also* bemock't-at-stabs' are given to assist the reader in such cases.

Simple or non-hyphenated compounds such as *o'th'King* have been listed only under the constituent parts—in this example under OTH and KING.

(*e*) 'Justified' lines where the spellings *may* have been affected by the compositor's need to fit the text to his measure are distinguished by an asterisk at the beginning of the reference line. If only location is being given, the asterisk occurs before the line reference. If only frequency counts are being given, the number *after* the asterisk records the frequency of forms occurring in 'justified' lines. Lines which do not extend to the full width of the compositor's measure have not been distinguished as 'justified' lines, even though in many cases the shorter line may have affected the spelling.

D. *Line Numbers*

The lines in each text have been numbered from the first *Actus Primus* or stage direction and thereafter in normal reading order, including all stage directions and act and scene divisions. Each typographical line has been counted as a unit when it contains matter for inclusion in the concordance. Catchwords are not included in the count. The only general exception is that turn-overs are regarded as belonging to their base-lines; where a turn-over occurs on a line by itself, it has been reckoned as part of the base-line, and the line containing only the turn-over has not been counted as a separate line. Turn-overs may readily be distinguished by vertical stroke and single bracket after the last word of the base-line; for example *brought with* | (*child,*.

When two or more lines have been joined in order to provide a fuller context, the line-endings are indicated by a vertical stroke |, and the line reference applies to that part of the line before the vertical stroke. For the true line-numbers of words in the following part of the context line, the stated line-number should be increased by one each time a vertical stroke occurs, save when the next word is a turn-over.

The numbering of the quarto texts has been fitted to that of the corresponding Folio texts; lines in the Quarto which do not occur in the Folio are prefixed by +. The line references are similarly specified. The line references of these concordances therefore provide a consistent permanent numbering of each typographical line of text, based on the First Folio.

PROGRAM CHANGES

Preparation of concordances to the first few texts, and the especial complexity of *Wiv.*, have enabled some improvements to be made to the main concordance program. For texts other than *Tmp.*, *TGV*, *MM*, and *Err.*, the concordances have been prepared with the improved program.

Speech-prefixes now have separate entries under the appropriate heading-word and follow any other entry under the same heading-word. Entries under AN in *Wiv.*, AND and TO in *TN*, and AD in *AYL* offer examples. This alteration provides a clearer record of the total number of occurrences of words which occur both as speech-prefixes and also as forms on the 'count only' or 'locations only' lists.

Another modification supplies a more precise reference to the location of words such as BEENE for which line numbers but no full lines are given. When a 'location only' word is encountered to the right of the 'end-of-line' bar (which shows that lines of text have been joined together in order to provide a sufficient context), the line number is now adjusted to supply the exact reference. In the concordances to the texts listed above, users will find that in some instances the particular occurrence of a 'location only' word which they wish to consult in the text is to be found in the line after the one specified in the concordance; this depends on whether lines have been joined in the computer-readable version of the text from which the concordance was made. It is not expected that readers will be seriously inconvenienced by this. Should a concordance to the First Folio be published, it will, of course, incorporate all improvements.

KING JOHN

THE concordance to *Jn.* was made from the Lee facsimile of the First Folio (Oxford, 1902). Professor Charlton Hinman (*Printing and Proof-Reading*, Oxford, 1963. V. 1, p. 266) records that only a3ᵛ shows sign of proof-correction but the variant which the Lee facsimile shows does not affect the text. He gives (v. 2, p. 515) the following order of printing for this section of the Folio:

By By a3ᵛ:4	By By a3:4ᵛ	Cy Cy a2ᵛ:5	Cy Cy a2:5ᵛ	‖	Cy Cy a1ᵛ:6	Cy Cy a1:6ᵛ	Cy Cy b3ᵛ:4

By By b3:4ᵛ	By By b2ᵛ:5	By By b2:5ᵛ	By By b1ᵛ:6	By By b1:6ᵛ	[Here a jump back to quire

Y, but no delay is in evidence.]

TABLE OF LINE AND ACT/SCENE NUMBERS

Page	Col.	Comp.	F line nos.	Globe act/scene nos.
a1	a	C	1–48	1.1.1–1.1.42
	b	C	49–96	1.1.88
a1ᵛ	a	C	97–162	1.1.154
	b	C	163–227	1.1.217
a2	a	C	228–90	1.1.276
	b	C	291–351	2.1.57
a2ᵛ	a	C	352–414	2.1.117
	b	C	415–80	2.1.178
a3	a	B	481–545	2.1.239
	b	B	546–611	2.1.301
a3ᵛ	a	B	612–75	2.1.361
	b	B	676–741	2.1.426
a4	a	B	742–807	2.1.491
	b	B	808–73	2.1.552
a4ᵛ	a	B	874–933	3.1.12
	b	B	934–96	3.1.74
a5	a	C	997–1058	3.1.132
	b	C	1059–124	3.1.196
a5ᵛ	a	C	1125–90	3.1.259
	b	C	1191–256	3.1.323
a6	a	C	1257–315	3.3.17
	b	C	1316–80	3.3.74
a6ᵛ	a	C	1381–441	3.4.57
	b	C	1442–507	3.4.122

Page	Col.	Comp.	F line nos.	Globe act/scene nos.
b1	a	B	1508–68	3.4.183
	b	B	1569–630	4.1.54
b1^v	a	B	1631–96	4.1.117
	b	B	1697–756	4.2.39
b2	a	B	1757–822	4.2.104
	b	B	1823–88	4.2.167
b2^v	a	B	1889–954	4.2.229
	b	B	1955–2014	4.3.17
b3	a	B	2015–80	4.3.80
	b	B	2081–146	4.3.141
b3^v	a	C	2147–206	5.1.38
	b	C	2207–65	5.2.14
b4	a	C	2266–331	5.2.78
	b	C	2332–97	5.2.143
b4^v	a	B	2398–457	5.3.17
	b	B	2458–519	5.4.58
b5	a	B	2520–74	5.6.18
	b	B	2575–635	5.7.28
b5^v	a	B	2636–82	5.7.72
	b	B	2683–729	5.7.118

The following misprints, etc. in the text have been corrected:

Col.	Line	Text
a1	23	with-held,
	69	cerraine
a1^v	131	kept.
a2^v	410	beast
a3	521	yours
	558	th'involuerable
a3^v	616	earrh,
	638	yonr
	652	with
	676	Speeke
	716	Townc:
a4	768	ftom . . . moiion,
	787	vnsur∧d
	852	daughtet
	869	turn∧d
a4	959	heue
a5	984	Euvenom
a5^v	1070	Arſhbiſhop
	1137	that∧s
	1174	onr
a6	1280	le'ts
a6^v	1481	Remembets
b1	1606	Arthnr.
b2	1761	reform'd.
b2^v	1986	incensəd
b3	2086	your
b4	2304	wirh
	2380	hee∧ll
b4^v	2406	you
	2430	Lcgate
	2449	rhe
b5	2575	Brcefe

December, 1969   T. H. H.

KING JOHN

A = 320*12, 4

1

ABSENT = 1
   Con. Greefe fils the roome vp of my absent childe: 1478
ABSEY = 1
   And then comes answer like an Absey booke: 206
ABSTRACT = 1
   This little abstract doth containe that large,   398
ABUNDANCE = 1
   With this abundance of superfluous breath?   448
ACCENT = 2
   The accent of his tongue affecteth him: 94
   That any accent breaking from thy tongue,   2569
ACCOMPT = *1
   Ioh. Oh, when the last accompt twixt heauen & earth   1941
ACCORDING = 1
   Bast. According to the faire-play of the world,   2372
ACCORDINGLY = 1
   Which trust accordingly kinde Cittizens,   537
ACCOUNTS = 1
   In this which he accounts so clearely wonne: 1507
ACCOUTREMENT = 1
   Exterior forme, outward accoutrement;   221
ACE = 1
   An Ace stirring him to bloud and strife,   357
ACHE *see* ake
ACKNOWLEDGE = 1
   Iohn. Acknowledge then the King, and let me in.   575
ACQUAINT = 1
   To acquaint you with this euill, that you might   2582
ACQUAINTANCE = 1
   Should scape the true acquaintance of mine eare.   2570
ACQUAINTED = 1
   Acquainted me with interest to this Land,   2342
ACT = 6
   The better Act of purposes mistooke,   1205
   Though that my death were adiunct to my Act, | By heauen I would doe
   it.   1356
   This Act so euilly borne shall coole the hearts   1534
   Bast. If thou didst but consent | To this most cruell Act: do but
   dispaire,   2129
   Hub. If I in act, consent, or sinne of thought,   2139
   Be great in act, as you haue beene in thought: 2213
ACTE = 2
   This acte, is as an ancient tale new told,   1735
   And consequently, thy rude hand to acte   1965
ACTION = 5
   Fore-wearied in this action of swift speede,   539
   Of any kindred-action like to this?   1396
   Whilst he that heares, makes fearefull action   1916
   The gracelesse action of a heauy hand,   2057
   To vnder-prop this Action? Is't not I   2352
ACTIONS = 1*1
   Dol. Strong reasons makes strange actions: let vs go,   1567
   And on our actions set the name of right | With holy breath.   2319
ACTS = 1
   At your industrious Scenes and acts of death.   690
ACTUS *l.*1 920 997 1569 2165 = 5

ADDE = 3

    Or adde a royall number to the dead: 661

    Adde thus much more, that no *Italian* Priest   1080

    To smooth the yce, or adde another hew   1730

ADDITION = 1

    With her to thee, and this addition more,   849

ADIEU = 3

    Bast. Brother adieu, good fortune come to thee,   189

    Bla. The Sun's orecast with bloud: faire day adieu,   1259

    Hub. Peace: no more. Adieu,   1707

ADIUNCT = 1

    Though that my death were adiunct to my Act, | By heauen I would doe

    it.   1356

ADMIT = 2

    Whose title they admit, *Arthurs* or *Iohns.*   503

    Iohn. Whose party do the Townesmen yet admit?   675

ADUANCED = 1

    These flagges of France that are aduanced heere   513

ADUANTAGE *see also* vantage = 8

    Th'aduantage of his absence tooke the King,   110

    Iohn. For our aduantage, therefore heare vs first: 512

    Bast. Speed then to take aduantage of the field.   605

    Till this aduantage, this vile drawing byas,   898

    And with aduantage meanes to pay thy loue: 1321

    That none so small aduantage shall step forth   1536

    The rich aduantage of good exercise,   1777

    As I vpon aduantage did remoue,   2672

ADUANTAGES = 1

    To cull the plots of best aduantages: 333

ADUENTURE = 1

    To try the faire aduenture of to morrow. *Exeunt*   2548

ADUERSE = 2

    Hath put himselfe in Armes, the aduerse windes   351

    When aduerse Forreyners affright my Townes   1894

ADUICE = 1

    So hot a speed, with such aduice dispos'd,   1393

ADUISD = 2

    Be well aduis'd, tell ore thy tale againe.   926

    More vpon humor, then aduis'd respect.   1939

ADULTERATES = 1

    Sh'adulterates hourely with thine Vnckle *Iohn,*   977

AERY *see* ayery

AFEARD *see* a-feard

AFFAIRES = 2

    To treat of high affaires touching that time: 109

    Why may not I demand of thine affaires, | As well as thou of mine? 2557

AFFECTETH = 1

    The accent of his tongue affecteth him: 94

AFFECTIONS = 1

    And great affections wrastling in thy bosome   2292

AFFLICTED = 1

    In the vilde prison of afflicted breath: 1402

AFFLICTION = 1

    Fra. O faire affliction, peace.   1420

AFFRAID = 1

    He is affraid of me, and I of him: 1594

AFFRIGHT = 1
  When aduerse Forreyners affright my Townes   1894
AFRAIDE = 1
  I am afraide, and yet Ile venture it.   2001
AFTER = 11
  Chat. Thus (after greeting) speakes the King | of France,   6
  Your fathers wife did after wedlocke beare him: 125
  Heere after excursions, Enter the Herald of France | with Trumpets to
  the gates.   608
  Then after fight who shall be king of it?   714
  Nay, after that, consume away in rust,   1642
  Go after him: for he perhaps shall neede   1900
  After they heard yong *Arthur* was aliue?   2206
  Wherein we step after a stranger, march   2278
  After yong *Arthur*, claime this Land for mine,   2347
  Like *Amazons*, come tripping after drummes: 2409
  After such bloody toile, we bid good night,   2530
AFTERNOONE = 1
  If you thinke meete, this afternoone will poast   2704
AGAIN = 1*1
  Is to mistake again, though indirect,   1206
  * *Pem.* This once again (but that your Highnes pleas'd)   1720
AGAINE = 28*1
  Bast. Now by this light were I to get againe,   272
  We will beare home that lustie blood againe,   561
  And part your mingled colours once againe,   703
  And she againe wants nothing, to name want,   750
  Coole and congeale againe to what it was.   795
  Be well aduis'd, tell ore thy tale againe.   926
  Then speake againe, not all thy former tale,   946
  That faith would liue againe by death of need: 1145
  As now againe to snatch our palme from palme: 1175
  And will againe commit them to their bonds,   1459
  If that be true, I shall see my boy againe;   1463
  And so hee'll dye: and rising so againe,   1471
  And I did neuer aske it you againe: 1620
  * *Iohn.* Heere once againe we sit: once against crown'd   1718
  Vnder the tide; but now I breath againe   1859
  I haue a way to winne their loues againe: 1889
  And flye (like thought) from them, to me againe.   1897
  And didst in signes againe parley with sinne,   1963
  Bast. Your sword is bright sir, put it vp againe.   2079
  Pan. Take againe | From this my hand, as holding of the Pope   2169
  My tongue shall hush againe this storme of warre,   2187
  Iohn. Would not my Lords returne to me againe   2205
  Returne the president to these Lords againe,   2254
  Pem. Vp once againe: put spirit in the French,   2461
  And welcome home againe discarded faith,   2473
  I say againe, if *Lewis* do win the day,   2491
  By his perswasion, are againe falne off,   2537
  And instantly returne with me againe.   2686
  Now, these her Princes are come home againe,   2726
AGAINST *see also* 'gainst = 26*1
  Against whose furie and vnmatched force,   278
  Against the browes of this resisting towne,   331
  And stirre them vp against a mightier taske: 349
  Against th'involnerable clouds of heauen,   558

AGAINST *cont.*

Which heere we came to spout against your Towne,	562
Haue we ramm'd vp our gates against the world.	578
As we will ours, against these sawcie walles,	718
Arme, arme, you heauens, against these periur'd Kings,	1032
Why thou against the Church, our holy Mother,	1068
Against the Pope, and count his friends my foes.	1098
Thy tongue against thy tongue. O let thy vow	1196
What since thou sworst, is sworne against thy selfe,	1199
But thou hast sworne against religion:	1211
By what thou swear'st against the thing thou swear'st,	1212
Against an oath the truth, thou art vnsure	1214
Therefore thy later vowes, against thy first,	1219
Against these giddy loose suggestions:	1223
Against the blood that thou hast married?	1234
Vpon my knee I beg, goe not to Armes | Against mine Vncle.	1241
Holding th'eternall spirit against her will,	1401
Iohn. Heere once againe we sit: once against crown'd	1718
Witnesse against vs to damnation.	1943
Hub. Arme you against your other enemies:	1974
My innocent life against an Emperor.	2089
That so stood out against the holy Church,	2324
Against the winde, the which he prickes and wounds	2623
Vpon a Parchment, and against this fire | Do I shrinke vp.	2640

AGE = 1

Ar. Ah, none but in this Iron Age, would do it:	1637

AGENT = 1

Whiles we Gods wrathfull agent doe correct	384

AGES = 1

Sweet, sweet, sweet poyson for the ages tooth,	223

AGO = 1

Are wrack'd three nights ago on *Goodwin* sands.	2451

AGUES = 1

As dim and meager as an Agues fitte,	1470

AH = 3

But (ah) I will not, yet I loue thee well,	1353
Ar. Ah, none but in this Iron Age, would do it:	1637
Dol. Ah fowle, shrew'd newes. Beshrew thy very | (hart:	2540

AID *see* ayd
AIME *see* ayme
AIRE *see* ayre
AKE = 1

Art. Haue you the heart? When your head did but | ake,	1616

AL = 2

Though you, and al the rest so grossely led,	1095
With al true duetie: On toward *Callice*, hoa. | *Exeunt.*	1379

ALACK = 1

K.Iohn. Alack thou dost vsurpe authoritie.	415

ALACKE = 1

O husband heare me: aye, alacke, how new	1238

ALARUMS = 1*1

Alarums, excursions, Retreat. Enter Iohn, Eleanor, Arthur| Bastard,	
Hubert, Lords.	1297
Alarums. Enter Iohn and Hubert.	2439

ALAS = 2

Art. Alas, what neede you be so boistrous rough?	1652
Art. Alas, I then haue chid away my friend,	1663

ALBEIT = 1
And Noble Dolphin, albeit we sweare   2260
ALCHYMIST = 1
Stayes in his course, and playes the Alchymist,   1003
ALCIDES = 1
As great *Alcides* shooes vpon an Asse: 444
ALIKE = 2
Both are alike, and both alike we like: 643
ALIUE = 2
Yong *Arthur* is aliue: This hand of mine   1976
After they heard yong *Arthur* was aliue?   2206
ALL *see also* all-changing-word = 87*3
Till she had kindled *France* and all the world,   39
Of that I doubt, as all mens children may.   71
With halfe that face would he haue all my land,   101
Which fault lyes on the hazards of all husbands   127
This Calfe, bred from his Cow from all the world: 132
And to his shape were heyre to all this land,   152
For thou wast got i'th way of honesty. | *Exeunt all but bastard.*   190
Legitimation, name, and all is gone;   261
With all my heart I thanke thee for my father: 283
To land his Legions all as soone as I: 353
And all th'vnsetled humors of the Land,   360
King *Iohn*, this is the very summe of all: 451
All punish'd in the person of this childe,   492
And all for her, a plague vpon her.   493
All preparation for a bloody siedge   519
And King ore him, and all that he enioyes: 546
Saue in aspect, hath all offence seal'd vp: 556
With vnhack'd swords, and Helmets all vnbruis'd,   560
Though all these English, and their discipline   567
*Iohn. Then God forgiue the sinne of all those soules,   590
In best appointment all our Regiments.   604
Hither returne all gilt with Frenchmens blood: 627
Our lustie English, all with purpled hands,   633
Fra. A greater powre then We denies all this,   682
And all that we vpon this side the Sea,   804
That all I see in you is worthie loue,   834
Iohn. We will heale vp all,   871
That dayly breake-vow, he that winnes of all,   890
Makes it take head from all indifferency,   900
From all direction, purpose, course, intent.   901
But they will quake and tremble all this day.   939
Then speake againe, not all thy former tale,   946
As it makes harmefull all that speake of it.   962
This day all things begun, come to ill end,   1019
So tell the Pope, all reuerence set apart | To him and his vsurp'd
authoritie.   1086
*Iohn. Though you, and all the Kings of Christendom   1089
With all religous strength of sacred vowes,   1160
Pand. All forme is formelesse, Order orderlesse,   1184
Is all too wanton, and too full of gawdes   1335
Pand. Courage and comfort, all shall yet goe well.   1386
Con. No, I defie all Counsell, all redresse,   1406
But that which ends all counsell, true Redresse: 1407
Remembers me of all his gracious parts,   1481
My life, my ioy, my food, my all the world: 1489

ALL *cont.*

On their departure, most of all shew euill:	1500
Dol. All daies of glory, ioy, and happinesse.	1502
Pan. Your minde is all as youthfull as your blood.	1510
May then make all the claime that *Arthur* did.	1528
Dol. And loose it, life and all, as *Arthur* did.	1529
Of all his people, and freeze vp their zeale,	1535
Of all his people shall reuolt from him,	1550
Me thinkes I see this hurley all on foot;	1554
That I might sit all night, and watch with you.	1603
All things that you should vse to do me wrong	1697
For all the Treasure that thine Vnckle owes,	1702
Art. O now you looke like *Hubert*. All this while | You were disguis'd.	1705
That *Hubert* for the wealth of all the world, | Will not offend thee.	1711
To ouer-beare it, and we are all well pleas'd,	1754
Since all, and euery part of what we would	1755
To sound the purposes of all their hearts,	1765
Both for my selfe, and them: but chiefe of all	1766
That blood which ow'd the bredth of all this Ile,	1817
To all our sorrowes, and ere long I doubt. *Exeunt*	1820
Poure downe thy weather: how goes all in France?	1827
The tydings comes, that they are all arriu'd.	1833
And be thou hee. | *Mes.* With all my heart, my Liege.	1902
The angry Lords, with all expedient hast,	1993
Pem. All murthers past, do stand excus'd in this:	2050
Away with me, all you whose soules abhorre	2114
And it shall be as all the Ocean,	2136
How easie dost thou take all *England* vp,	2147
The life, the right, and truth of all this Realme	2149
And from his holinesse vse all your power	2173
Bast. All Kent hath yeelded: nothing there holds out	2198
As *Lewis* himselfe: so (Nobles) shall you all,	2313
Bast. By all the bloud that euer fury breath'd,	2381
That shall reuerberate all, as lowd as thine.	2426
Since I must loose the vse of all deceite?	2488
Euen with a treacherous fine of all your liues:	2499
Awakes my Conscience to confesse all this.	2504
I will vpon all hazards well beleeue	2561
Hub. Why know you not? The Lords are all come | backe,	2590
And they are all about his Maiestie.	2594
Hen. It is too late, the life of all his blood	2605
That all my bowels crumble vp to dust:	2638
And all the shrowds wherewith my life should saile,	2663
And then all this thou seest, is but a clod, | And module of confounded royalty.	2667
Were in the *Washes* all vnwarily,	2673
To whom with all submission on my knee,	2714

ALLARUMS = *1

Allarums, Excursions: Enter Bastard with Austria's | head.	1283

ALLAY = 2

That nothing can allay, nothing but blood,	1275
It would allay the burning qualitie	2613

ALLEGEANCE = 1

From his Allegeance to an heretique,	1102

ALLEGIANCE = 1

Swearing Allegiance, and the loue of soule	2177

7

ALL-CHANGING-WORD = 1
  This Bawd, this Broker, this all-changing-word,   903
ALMOST = 4
  By heauen *Hubert*, I am almost asham'd   1326
  Or do you almost thinke, although you see,   2042
  Last in the field, and almost Lords of it.   2532
  I left him almost speechlesse, and broke out   2581
ALOFT = 1
  Aloft the flood, and can giue audience   1860
ALONE = 10
  And not alone in habit and deuice,   220
  And a may catch your hide and you alone: 436
  And leaue those woes alone, which I alone | Am bound to vnder-beare.   985
  Where we doe reigne, we will alone vphold   1084
  Yet I alone, alone doe me oppose   1097
  Without a tongue, vsing conceit alone,   1349
  Hub. Go stand within: let me alone with him.   1661
  In spight of spight, alone vpholds the day.   2464
ALONG = 1
  With him along is come the Mother Queene,   356
ALOUD = 1
  I tore them from their bonds, and cride aloud,   1455
ALPES = 1
  And talking of the Alpes and Appenines, | The Perennean and the riuer
  Poe,   212
ALREADIE = 1
  If that yong *Arthur* be not gone alreadie,   1548
ALREADY = 2
  Already smoakes about the burning Crest   2495
  Sal. Nay, 'tis in a manner done already,   2699
ALTAR = 2
  Vpon the Altar at S.(aint) *Edmondsbury*,   2479
  Euen on that Altar, where we swore to you | Deere Amity, and
  euerlasting loue.   2480
ALTER = 1
  Alter not the doome fore-thought by heauen.   1245
ALTHOUGH = 2
  Good Lords, although my will to giue, is liuing,   1801
  Or do you almost thinke, although you see,   2042
AM = 40
AMAZD = 4
  Behold the French amaz'd vouchsafe a parle,   532
  Iohn. Beare with me Cosen, for I was amaz'd   1858
  I am amaz'd me thinkes, and loose my way   2145
  Startles mine eyes, and makes me more amaz'd   2302
AMAZED = 1
  Why stand these royall fronts amazed thus: 670
AMAZEMENT = 1
  And wilde amazement hurries vp and downe   2203
AMAZONS = 1
  Like *Amazons*, come tripping after drummes: 2409
AMBITION = 1
  Marke how they whisper, vrge them while their soules | Are capeable of
  this ambition,   791
AMBITIOUS = 2
  How that ambitious *Constance* would not cease   38
  If loue ambitious, sought a match of birth,   745

AMEN = 3
    Fran. Amen, Amen, mount Cheualiers to Armes.   594
    Good Father Cardinall, cry thou Amen   1109
AMENDS = 1
    And for amends to his posteritie,   299
AMIABLE = 1
    Death, death, O amiable, louely death,   1408
AMISSE = 2
    For that which thou hast sworne to doe amisse,   1201
    Is not amisse when it is truely done: 1202
AMITIE = 2
    Let in that amitie which you haue made,   857
    The grapling vigor, and rough frowne of Warre | Is cold in amitie, and
    painted peace,   1029
AMITY = 2
    Was deepe-sworne faith, peace, amity, true loue   1162
    Euen on that Altar, where we swore to you | Deere Amity, and
    euerlasting loue.   2480
AMONG = 3
    Among the high tides in the Kalender?   1011
    Bast. How I haue sped among the Clergy men,   1862
    Among the thornes, and dangers of this world.   2146
AMPLE = 1
    As to my ample hope was promised,   2365
AN *l.*34 107 206 337 357 444 599 613 1078 1102 1194 1213 1214 1296 1470
    1518 1520 1645 1735 1836 1958 1977 1984 2089 2107 2208 2261 2277
    2293 2299 2316 2399 2403 2424 2503 2543 *2675 2693 = 37*1
ANATOMY = 1
    And rowze from sleepe that fell Anatomy   1424
ANCIENT = 1
    This acte, is as an ancient tale new told,   1735
AND *see also* &. = 655*28, 6
    Bast. Madam, and if my brother had my shape   146
    It cannot be, and if thou wert his mother.   428
    And a may catch your hide and you alone: 436
    Ile smoake your skin-coat and I catch you right,   439
    Bast. And if thou hast the mettle of a king,   715
    Art. And if you do, you will but make it blush,   1692
ANGELL = 2
    And if an Angell should haue come to me,   1645
    And euen there, methinkes an Angell spake,   2316
ANGELLS = 1
    Of hoording Abbots, imprisoned angells   1306
ANGELS = 1
    When his faire Angels would salute my palme,   911
ANGERLY = 1
    Nor looke vpon the Iron angerly: 1658
ANGIERS = 12*3
    Enter before Angiers, Philip King of France, Lewis, Daul-| phin,
    Austria, Constance, Arthur.   292
    Lewis. Before *Angiers* well met braue *Austria,*   294
    Welcome before the gates *Angiers* Duke.   310
    Till *Angiers,* and the right thou hast in *France,*   315
    England and *Ireland, Angiers, Toraine, Maine,*   452
    These men of Angiers, let vs heare them speake,   502
    Iohn. England for it selfe: | You men of Angiers, and my louing
    subiects.   508

ANGIERS *cont.*

Fra. You louing men of Angiers, *Arthurs* subiects,	510
F.Her. You men of ·Angiers open wide your gates,	610
* E.Har. Reioyce you men of Angiers, ring your bels,	623
Lord of our presence Angiers, and of you.	681
* Bast. By heauen, these scroyles of Angiers flout you | (kings,	687
And lay this Angiers euen with the ground,	713
For *Angiers,* and faire *Toraine Maine, Poyctiers,*	803
Are we not beaten? Is not *Angiers* lost?	1388

ANGIRES = 1

Fra. Now Cittizens of Angires ope your gates,	856

ANGRY = 2

The angry Lords, with all expedient hast,	1993
Doth dogged warre bristle his angry crest,	2154

ANIOW = 1

Poyctiers and *Aniow,* these fiue Prouinces	848

ANIOWE = 1

To *Ireland, Poyctiers, Aniowe, Torayne, Maine,*	16

ANNOINTED = 1

Pan. Haile you annointed deputies of heauen;	1063

ANNOYANCE = 2

Any annoyance in that precious sense:	1672
To sowsse annoyance that comes neere his Nest;	2404

ANON = 3

There's toyes abroad, anon Ile tell thee more. | *Exit Iames.*	244
Anon becomes a Mountaine. O noble Dolphine,	1562
Still and anon cheer'd vp the heauy time;	1623

ANOTHER = 8

Which we God knowes, haue turn'd another way, | To our owne vantage.	869
To smooth the yce, or adde another hew	1730
And whisper one another in the eare.	1914
Another leane, vnwash'd Artificer,	1926
Forme such another? This is the very top,	2044
Sound but another, and another shall	2427
Behold another day breake in the East:	2493

ANSWER = 12

Controlement for controlement: so answer *France.*	25
And then comes answer like an Absey booke:	206
O sir, sayes answer, at your best command,	207
And so ere answer knowes what question would,	210
Con. Stay for an answer to your Embassie,	337
To draw my answer from thy Articles?	408
Const. Let me make answer: thy vsurping sonne.	418
France. When I haue saide, make answer to vs both.	541
Hub. Why answer not the double Maiesties,	796
Oh, answer not; but to my Closset bring	1992
And, as you answer, I doe know the scope	2376
Where heauen he knowes how we shall answer him.	2670

ANSWERD = 2

Blood hath bought blood, and blowes haue answerd | (blowes:	640
This must be answer'd either heere, or hence.	1807

ANSWERE = 2

To charge me to an answere, as the Pope:	1078
Con. O be remou'd from him, and answere well.	1149

ANSWERS = 1

Iohn. The king is moud, and answers not to this.	1148

ANTICKE = 1
   Sal. In this the Anticke, and well noted face   1738
ANUILE = 1
   The whilst his Iron did on the Anuile coole,   1919
ANY = 17
   It would not be sir nobbe in any case.   . 155
   Well, now can I make any *Ioane* a Lady,   194
   In any breast of strong authoritie,   410
   There stucke no plume in any English Crest,   628
   Holdes hand with any Princesse of the world.   810
   That any thing he see's which moues his liking,   829
   That I can finde, should merit any hate.   838
   That takes away by any secret course | Thy hatefull life.   1105
   Of any kindred-action like to this?   1396
   Any annoyance in that precious sense: 1672
   With any long'd-for-change, or better State.   1725
   Mes. From France to England, neuer such a powre | For any forraigne
   preparation,   1828
   To any tongue, speake it of what it will.   1861
   If that it be the worke of any hand.   2058
   Sal. If that it be the worke of any hand?   2059
   To any Soueraigne State throughout the world.   2335
   That any accent breaking from thy tongue,   2569
ANYTHING *see* thing
APACE = 1
   Looke where the holy Legate comes apace,   2317
APART = 1
   So tell the Pope, all reuerence set apart | To him and his vsurp'd
   authoritie.   1086
APISH = 1
   This apish and vnmannerly approach,   2385
APPARANT = 1
   Sal. It is apparant foule-play, and 'tis shame   1811
APPENINES = 1
   And talking of the Alpes and Appenines, | The Perennean and the riuer
   Poe,   212
APPOINTMENT = 1
   In best appointment all our Regiments.   604
APPROACH = 4
   That ere I heard: shall I produce the men? | *K.Iohn.* Let them approach: 53
   King *Iohn*, your king and Englands, doth approach,   624
   Pan. O Sir, when he shall heare of your approach,   1547
   This apish and vnmannerly approach,   2385
APPROACHING = *1
   *Approaching neere these eyes, would drinke my teares, 1639
APPROCH = 1
   And but for our approch, those sleeping stones,   522
APRILL = 1
   Mes. My Liege, her eare | Is stopt with dust: the first of Aprill di'de   1838
APT = 1
   Apt, liable to be employ'd in danger,   1951
AR = 7
ARBITRATE = 1
   With fearefull bloudy issue arbitrate.   44
ARCHBISHOP = 1
   Keepe *Stephen Langton* chosen Archbishop | Of *Canterbury* from that
   holy Sea: 1070

ARCH-HERETIQUE = 1
Let goe the hand of that Arch-heretique, 1120
ARE = 50*4
ARGUMENT = 1
To breake into this dangerous argument. 1771
ARGUMENTS = 1
This might haue beene preuented, and made whole | With very easie
arguments of loue, 41
ARISE = 2
Arise Sir *Richard*, and *Plantagenet*. 171
Arise forth from the couch of lasting night, 1410
ARMADO = 1
A whole Armado of conuicted saile 1384
* ARME = 6
Arme, arme, you heauens, against these periur'd Kings, 1032
Then arme thy constant and thy nobler parts 1222
Hub. Arme you against your other enemies: 1974
My arme shall giue thee helpe to beare thee hence, 2519
The better arme you to the sodaine time, 2583
ARMED = 3
Set armed discord 'twixt these periur'd Kings, 1036
Thinking this voyce an armed Englishman. 2399
Their thimbles into armed Gantlets change, 2410
ARMES = 24*1
My armes, such eele skins stuft, my face so thin, 149
Will I not thinke of home, but follow Armes. 324
Hath put himselfe in Armes, the aduerse windes 351
Wilt thou resigne them, and lay downe thy Armes? 454
And then our Armes, like to a muzled Beare, 555
Fran. Amen, Amen, mount Cheualiers to Armes. 594
Before we will lay downe our iust-borne Armes, 659
Wee'l put thee downe, 'gainst whom these Armes wee | (beare, 660
You came in Armes to spill mine enemies bloud, 1027
But now in Armes, you strengthen it with yours. 1028
Therefore to Armes, be Champion of our Church, 1186
Daul. Father, to Armes. | *Blanch*. Vpon thy wedding day? 1232
Vpon my knee I beg, goe not to Armes | Against mine Vncle. 1241
Were there in Armes, they would be as a Call 1559
Of murthers Armes: This is the bloodiest shame, 2046
Bast. Go, beare him in thine armes: 2144
Goe I to make the *French* lay downe their Armes. *Exit*. 2191
To Armes Inuasiue? Shall a beardlesse boy, 2238
And finde no checke? Let vs my Liege to Armes: 2242
*Enter (in Armes) Dolphin, Salisbury, Meloone, Pem-| broke, Bigot,
Souldiers*. 2250
That *Neptunes* Armes who clippeth thee about, 2285
He flatly saies, hee'll not lay downe his Armes. 2380
To whip this dwarfish warre, this Pigmy Armes 2389
No: know the gallant Monarch is in Armes, 2402
Come the three corners of the world in Armes, 2727
ARMIES = 2
Of both your Armies, whose equality 638
Where these two Christian Armies might combine 2288
ARMOR = 1
With burden of our armor heere we sweat: 389
ARMOUR = 1
And France, whose armour Conscience buckled on, 885

ARMOURS = 1
    Their Armours that march'd hence so siluer bright,   626
ARMS = *1
    *Iohn. No more then he that threats. To Arms let's hie. | Exeunt.   1280
ARMY = 2
    I am with both, each Army hath a hand,   1261
    That such an Army could be drawne in France, | And she not heare of
    it?   1836
ARRAS = 1
    Within the Arras: when I strike my foot   1572
ARRIUD = 3
    King. A wonder Lady: lo vpon thy wish | Our Messenger Chattilion is
    arriu'd,   344
    The tydings comes, that they are all arriu'd.   1833
    Hear'st thou the newes abroad, who are arriu'd?   1881
ART see also thou'rt l.63 65 240 270 391 404 434 955 972 1046 1047 1214
1279 1364 1428 1991 2090 2121 2125 2553 2562 2563 2661 2680 = 24
ART = 12*1
ARTH = 2
ARTHUR see also Ar., Art., Arth. = 30*2
    Arthur Plantaginet, laies most lawfull claime   14
    *Enter before Angiers, Philip King of France, Lewis, Daul-|phin,
    Austria, Constance, Arthur.   292
    Arthur that great fore-runner of thy bloud,   295
    In right of Arthur doe I claime of thee: 453
    Arthur of Britaine, yeeld thee to my hand,   456
    And let yong Arthur Duke of Britaine in,   611
    Arthur of Britaine, Englands King, and yours.   621
    For wee'l create yong Arthur Duke of Britaine   872
    Enter Constance, Arthur, and Salisbury.   921
    Enter Iohn, Arthur, Hubert.   1288
    *Alarums, excursions, Retreat. Enter Iohn, Eleanor, Arthur | Bastard,
    Hubert, Lords.   1297
    Arthur tane prisoner? diuers deere friends slaine?   1389
    Yong Arthur is my sonne, and he is lost: 1431
    Must I behold my pretty Arthur more.   1474
    O Lord, my boy, my Arthur, my faire sonne,   1488
    Are not you grieu'd that Arthur is his prisoner?   1508
    Iohn hath seiz'd Arthur, and it cannot be,   1516
    That Iohn may stand, then Arthur needs must fall, | So be it, for it
    cannot be but so.   1524
    May then make all the claime that Arthur did.   1528
    Dol. And loose it, life and all, as Arthur did.   1529
    If that yong Arthur be not gone alreadie,   1548
    Enter Arthur.   1579
    *Reade heere yong Arthur. How now foolish rheume?   1606
    Th'infranchisement of Arthur, whose restraint   1769
    He tels vs Arthur is deceas'd to night.   1803
    Of Arthur, whom they say is kill'd to night, on your | (suggestion. 1886
    Yong Arthur is aliue: This hand of mine   1976
    Iohn. Doth Arthur liue? O hast thee to the Peeres,   1985
    Enter Arthur on the walles.   1996
    Arthur doth liue, the king hath sent for you.   2075
    After they heard yong Arthur was aliue?   2206
    After yong Arthur, claime this Land for mine,   2347
ARTHUR = 1

ARTHURS = 10
ARTICLES = 1
ARTIFICER = 1
ARTILLERIE = 1
AS = 130*1

AS *cont.*

But for my hand, as vnattempted yet,	912
Sal. As true as I beleeue you thinke them false,	948
As doth the furie of two desperate men,	953
As it makes harmefull all that speake of it.	962
To charge me to an answere, as the Pope:	1078
But as we, vnder heauen, are supreame head,	1082
Canonized and worship'd as a Saint,	1104
Con. What should he say, but as the Cardinall?	1132
As now againe to snatch our palme from palme:	1175
And falshood, falshood cures, as fire cooles fire	1208
So heauy, as thou shalt not shake them off	1227
Is it as he will? well then, *France* shall rue.	1258
As deere be to thee, as thy father was.	1302
And busse thee as thy wife: Miseries Loue, | O come to me.	1418
As they haue giuen these hayres their libertie:	1457
And he will looke as hollow as a Ghost,	1469
As dim and meager as an Agues fitte,	1470
Fra. You are as fond of greefe, as of your childe.	1477
Fareyouwell: had you such a losse as I,	1484
Life is as tedious as a twice-told tale,	1493
Dol. As heartily as he is glad he hath him.	1509
Pan. Your minde is all as youthfull as your blood.	1510
Must be as boysterously maintain'd as gain'd.	1521
Dol. And loose it, life and all, as *Arthur* did.	1529
Were there in Armes, they would be as a Call	1559
Or, as a little snow, tumbled about,	1561
Ar. As little Prince, hauing so great a Title	1582
To be more Prince, as may be: you are sad.	1583
Yong Gentlemen would be as sad as night	1588
I should be as merry as the day is long:	1591
These eyes, that neuer did, nor neuer shall | So much as frowne on you.	1633
Hub. Come forth: Do as I bid you do.	1648
And I will sit as quiet as a Lambe.	1656
This acte, is as an ancient tale new told,	1735
As patches set vpon a little breach,	1749
Pem. Then I, as one that am the tongue of these	1764
Why then your feares, which (as they say) attend	1773
Your noble mother; and as I heare, my Lord,	1840
But as I trauail'd hither through the land,	1864
With eyes as red as new enkindled fire,	1884
As bid me tell my tale in expresse words:	1959
As good to dye, and go; as dye, and stay.	2004
Sal. Murther, as hating what himselfe hath done,	2036
By heauen, I thinke my sword's as sharpe as yours.	2082
Thou'rt damn'd as blacke, nay nothing is so blacke,	2124
As thou shalt be, if thou didst kill this childe.	2127
And it shall be as all the Ocean,	2136
As doth a Rauen on a sicke-falne beast,	2158
Pan. Take againe | From this my hand, as holding of the Pope	2169
Be great in act, as you haue beene in thought:	2213
Be stirring as the time, be fire with fire,	2216
Was borne to see so sad an houre as this,	2277
Come, come; for thou shalt thrust thy hand as deepe	2311
As *Lewis* himselfe: so (Nobles) shall you all,	2313
And such as to my claime are liable,	2354
Viue le Roy, as I haue bank'd their Townes?	2357

AS *cont.*

As to my ample hope was promised,	2365
And, as you answer, I doe know the scope	2376
That shall reuerberate all, as lowd as thine.	2426
(As lowd as thine) rattle the Welkins eare,	2428
Which bleeds away, euen as a forme of waxe	2485
As this hath made me. Who was he that said	2542
The day shall not be vp so soone as I,	2547
Why may not I demand of thine affaires, | As well as thou of mine?	2557
Thou maist be-friend me so much, as to thinke	2565
Is, as a fiend, confin'd to tyrannize,	2656
As I vpon aduantage did remoue,	2672
*Sal. You breath these dead newes in as dead an eare	2675
As it on earth hath bene thy seruant still.	2683
Sal. It seemes you know not then so much as we,	2691
As we with honor and respect may take,	2695

ASCEND = 1

If not, bleede *France*, and peace ascend to heauen.	383

ASCENSION = 3

That ere the next Ascension day at noone,	1872
Iohn. Is this Ascension day? did not the Prophet	2192
Say, that before Ascension day at noone,	2193

ASCENTION = 1

On this Ascention day, remember well,	2189

ASHAMD = 1

By heauen *Hubert*, I am almost asham'd	1326

ASHES = 2

To ashes, ere our blood shall quench that fire:	1278
And strew'd repentant ashes on his head.	1690

ASIDE = 1

Desiring thee to lay aside the sword	17

ASKE = 6

Dol. Nay aske me if I can refraine from loue,	845
And I did neuer aske it you againe:	1620
I shall indue you with: Meane time, but aske	1760
That you haue bid vs aske his libertie,	1780
Which for our goods, we do no further aske,	1781
And comfort me with cold. I do not aske you much,	2649

ASPECT = 3

Saue in aspect, hath all offence seal'd vp:	556
Liues in his eye: that close aspect of his,	1790
But taking note of thy abhorr'd Aspect,	1949

ASPIRING = 1

Shew boldnesse and aspiring confidence:	2224

ASSAULT = 1

Fra. Let it be so: say, where will you assault?	722

ASSAYLED = 1

My Mother is assayled in our Tent, | And tane I feare.	1291

ASSAYLETH = 1

Of that fell poison which assayleth him.	2614

ASSE = 2

As great *Alcides* shooes vpon an Asse:	444
But Asse, Ile take that burthen from your backe,	445

ASSEMBLE = 1

Lets kings assemble: for my greefe's so great,	993

ASSISTANCE = 2

Without th'assistance of a mortall hand:	1085

ASSISTANCE *cont.*
    If *Lewis,* by your assistance win the day.   2500
ASSURANCE = 1
    Thy now vnsur'd assurance to the Crowne,   787
ASSURD = 2
    Aust. And your lippes too, for I am well assur'd,   854
    That I did so when I was first assur'd.   855
ASSURED = 1
    Assured losse, before the match be plaid.   1269
ASUNDER *see* a-sunder
AT = 59*2
ATCHIEUD = 1
    No certaine life atchieu'd by others death: 1823
ATTEMPT = 1
    Till my attempt so much be glorified,   2364
ATTEND = 4
    Hubert shall be your man, attend on you   1378
    Why then your feares, which (as they say) attend   1773
    With our pure Honors: nor attend the foote   2023
    Dol. We will attend to neyther: 2419
ATTENDANTS = 2
    Enter France, Dolphin, Pandulpho, Attendants.   1382
    Enter King Iohn and Pandolph, attendants.   2166
ATTENDED = 2
    Attended with the pleasures of the world,   1334
    Iohn. It is the curse of Kings, to be attended   1933
AUANT = 1
    Auant thou hatefull villain, get thee gone.   2077
AUDIENCE = 3
    To giue me audience: If the mid-night bell   1336
    Aloft the flood, and can giue audience   1860
    Let me haue audience: I am sent to speake: 2373
AUGHT *see* ought
AUOID = 1
    Yet to auoid deceit I meane to learne;   225
AUS = 1*1
AUST = 12*2
AUSTRIA see also Aus., Aust. = 5
    **Enter before Angiers, Philip King of France, Lewis, Daul-|phin,*
    Austria, Constance, Arthur.   292
    Lewis. Before *Angiers* well met braue *Austria,*   294
    Austria and France shoot in each others mouth.   729
    **Enter King Iohn, France, Dolphin, Blanch, Elianor, Philip, | Austria,*
    Constance.   998
    O *Lymoges,* O *Austria,* thou dost shame   1040
AUSTRIAS = 1*1
    **Allarums, Excursions: Enter Bastard with Austria's | head.*   1283
    And pour's downe mischiefe. *Austrias* head lye there,   1287
AUTHORITIE = 5
    In any breast of strong authoritie,   410
    K.Iohn. Alack thou dost vsurpe authoritie.   415
    So tell the Pope, all reuerence set apart | To him and his vsurp'd
    authoritie.   1086
    And on the winking of Authoritie | To vnderstand a Law; to know the
    meaning   1936
    Your Soueraigne greatnesse and authoritie.   2171

AWAKE = 2
We must awake indeuor for defence,   376
He will awake my mercie, which lies dead: 1599
AWAKES = 1
Awakes my Conscience to confesse all this.   2504
AWAY = 24*1
When I was got, Sir *Robert* was away.   175
Iohn. France, hast thou yet more blood to cast away?   648
Ile stirre them to it: Come, away, away.   730
That takes away by any secret course | Thy hatefull life.   1105
Iohn. Cosen away for *England,* haste before,   1304
I prethee Lady goe away with me.   1403
But they will plucke away his naturall cause,   1541
Nay, after that, consume away in rust,   1642
Nay heare me *Hubert,* driue these men away,   1655
Thrust but these men away, and Ile forgiue you,   1659
Art. Alas, I then haue chid away my friend,   1663
Iohn. Hubert, away with him: imprison him,   1876
Ile finde a thousand shifts to get away;   2003
Away with me, all you whose soules abhorre   2114
Big. Away, toward *Burie,* to the Dolphin there.   2117
Hold out this tempest. Beare away that childe,   2161
By some damn'd hand was rob'd, and tane away.   2209
Away, and glister like the god of warre   2222
Bast. Away then with good courage: yet I know   2247
And with a great heart heaue away this storme: 2306
Which bleeds away, euen as a forme of waxe   2485
Right in thine eye. Away, my friends, new flight,   2521
Are cast away, and sunke on *Goodwin* sands.   2539
Away before: Conduct me to the king,   2601
AWHILE *see also* a-while = *1
Hub. Heare vs great kings, vouchsafe awhile to stay   731
AWLESSE = 1
The awlesse Lion could not wage the fight,   279
AY *see* I
AYD = 1
Hath drawne him from his owne determin'd ayd,   905
AYE = 3
May easily winne a womans: aye my mother,   282
O husband heare me: aye, alacke, how new   1238
Iohn. Aye me, this tyrant Feauer burnes mee vp,   2454
AYERIE = 1
And like an Eagle, o're his ayerie towres,   2403
AYERY = 1
Some ayery Deuill houers in the skie,   1286
AYME = 1
It ill beseemes this presence to cry ayme | To these ill-tuned repetitions: 499
AYRE = 3
Euen till vnfenced desolation | Leaue them as naked as the vulgar ayre: 700
Mocking the ayre with colours idlely spred,   2241
That being brought into the open ayre,   2612
A-FEARD = 1
Bast. But if you be a-feard to heare the worst,   1856
A-SUNDER = 1
They whurle a-sunder, and dismember mee.   1263
A-WHILE = 1
Be friends a-while, and both conioyntly bend   693

BA = *1
BABE = 1
  Or madly thinke a babe of clowts were he;   1442
BABY-EYES = 1
  Commend these waters to those baby-eyes   2307
BACK = *1
  *Bast. Bell, Booke, & Candle, shall not driue me back,   1310
BACKE = 9*1
  Whose foot spurnes backe the Oceans roaring tides,   317
  Bast. It lies as sightly on the backe of him   443
  But Asse, Ile take that burthen from your backe,   445
  Cry hauocke kings, backe to the stained field   671
  Let him come backe, that his compassion may | Giue life to yours.   1665
  Hub. Stand backe Lord Salsbury, stand backe I say   2081
  *Dol. Your Grace shall pardon me, I will not backe: 2331
  And now it is halfe conquer'd, must I backe,   2348
  Hub. Why know you not? The Lords are all come | backe,   2590
BACKS = 1
  Bearing their birth-rights proudly on their backs,   364
BACKWARD = 1
  When English measure backward their owne ground   2527
BAD = 1
  Three foot of it doth hold; bad world the while: 1818
BADLY = 1
  Hub. Badly I feare; how fares your Maiesty?   2441
BAGS = 1
  And ere our comming see thou shake the bags   1305
BAKD = 1
  Had bak'd thy bloud, and made it heauy, thicke,   1342
BALD = *1
  *Bast. Old Time the clocke setter, y bald sexton Time: 1257
BALLS = 1
  And put my eye-balls in thy vaultie browes,   1413
BANISHD = 1
  Const. O faire returne of banish'd Maiestie.   1254
BANKD = 1
  Viue le Roy, as I haue bank'd their Townes?   2357
BANKES = 1
  Do glorifie the bankes that bound them in: 757
BANNERS = 1
  Vpon the dancing banners of the French,   618
BARBAROUS = 1
  With barbarous ignorance, and deny his youth   1776
BARE-PICKT = 1
  Now for the bare-pickt bone of Maiesty,   2153
BARE-RIBD = 1
  A bare-rib'd death, whose office is this day   2433
BARGAINE = 1
  To clap this royall bargaine vp of peace,   1166
BARGAINES = 1
  No bargaines breake that are not this day made;   1018
BARRD = 1
  Our former scruple in our strong barr'd gates: 684
BARRE = 1
  Let it be lawfull, that Law barre no wrong: 1114
BARRES = 1
  A Will, that barres the title of thy sonne.   495

BASE = 2
To a most base and vile-concluded peace.   907
Send fayre-play-orders, and make comprimise, | Insinuation, parley, and
base truce   2236
BASILISCO-LIKE = 1
Bast. Knight, knight good mother, Basilisco-like: 257
BAST = 64*16
BASTARD see also Ba., Bast. = 13*2
For thou wast got i'th way of honesty. | *Exeunt all but bastard.*   190
For he is but a bastard to the time   217
With them a Bastard of the Kings deceast,   359
*Enter K.(ing) of England, Bastard, Queene, Blanch, Pembroke, | and
others.*   379
Queen. Out insolent, thy bastard shall be King,   419
My boy a bastard? by my soule I thinke | His father neuer was so true
begot,   426
Allarums, Excursions: Enter Bastard with Austria's | head.   1283
*Alarums, excursions, Retreat. Enter Iohn, Eleanor, Arthur | Bastard,
Hubert, Lords.*   1297
Then I haue nam'd. The Bastard *Falconbridge*   1556
Enter Bastard and Peter of Pomfret.   1851
Enter Bastard.   2018
Enter Bastard.   2197
Enter Bastard.   2371
Enter Bastard and Hubert, seuerally.   2550
Enter Bastard.   2658
BASTARDS = 2
Twice fifteene thousand hearts of Englands breed. | *Bast.* Bastards and
else.   582
Fran. As many and as well-borne bloods as those. | *Bast.* Some Bastards
too.   585
BASTARDY = 1
But once he slanderd me with bastardy: 82
BASTINADO = 1
He giues the bastinado with his tongue: 779
BATED = 1
And like a bated and retired Flood,   2514
BATTAILES = 1
Like Heralds 'twixt two dreadfull battailes set: 1796
BATTELMENTS = 1
And stand securely on their battelments,   688
BATTERIE = 1
This Vnion shall do more then batterie can   761
BATTERING = 1
Their battering Canon charged to the mouthes,   696
BAWD = 3
This Bawd, this Broker, this all-changing-word,   903
And made his Maiestie the bawd to theirs.   980
France is a Bawd to Fortune, and king *Iohn*,   981
BE *see also* shallbe = 164*6
BEADLE = 1
Her iniurie the Beadle to her sinne,   491
BEADS = 1
I, with these Christall beads heauen shall be brib'd   473
BEAME = 1
Will serue to strangle thee: A rush will be a beame   2133

BEARD = 1
Whose valour plucks dead Lyons by the beard;   438
BEARDLESSE = 1
To Armes Inuasiue? Shall a beardlesse boy,   2238
BEARE = 20
K.Iohn. Beare mine to him, and so depart in peace,   28
Your fathers wife did after wedlocke beare him: 125
K.Iohn. From henceforth beare his name | Whose forme thou bearest: 168
Some sinnes doe beare their priuiledge on earth,   274
And then our Armes, like to a muzled Beare,   555
We will beare home that lustie blood againe,   561
Wee'l put thee downe, 'gainst whom these Armes wee | (beare,   660
And beare possession of our Person heere,   680
And leaue those woes alone, which I alone | Am bound to vnder-beare.   985
Fra. Well could I beare that *England* had this praise,   1397
Exec. I hope your warrant will beare out the deed.   1576
To ouer-beare it, and we are all well pleas'd,   1754
Thinke you I beare the Sheeres of destiny?   1809
Iohn. Beare with me Cosen, for I was amaz'd   1858
Bast. Go, beare him in thine armes: 2144
Hold out this tempest. Beare away that childe,   2161
Would beare thee from the knowledge of thy selfe,   2286
In lieu whereof, I pray you beare me hence   2505
My arme shall giue thee helpe to beare thee hence,   2519
And tempt vs not to beare aboue our power.   2596
BEAREST = 1
K.Iohn. From henceforth beare his name | Whose forme thou bearest: 168
BEARING = 2
Bearing their birth-rights proudly on their backs,   364
Ore-bearing interruption spight of *France*?   1391
BEAST = 1
As doth a Rauen on a sicke-falne beast,   2158
BEAT = 2
When liuing blood doth in these temples beat   405
Fran. Excuse it is to beat vsurping downe.   416
BEATEN = 2*1
Are we not beaten? Is not *Angiers* lost?   1388
Bast. Indeede your drums being beaten, wil cry out;   2422
And so shall you, being beaten: Do but start   2423
BEATS = 2
Cuts off more circumstance, they are at hand, | *Drum beats.*   371
Their proud contempt that beats his peace to heauen.   385
BEAUTEOUS = 2
To seeke the beauteous eye of heauen to garnish,   1732
Which was embounded in this beauteous clay,   2141
BEAUTIE = 5
If lustie loue should go in quest of beautie,   741
Such as she is, in beautie, vertue, birth,   747
Can in this booke of beautie read, I loue: 801
In titles, honors, and promotions, | As she in beautie, education, blood, 808
Big. Or when he doom'd this Beautie to a graue,   2038
BEAUTY = 1
And chase the natiue beauty from his cheeke,   1468
BECAUSE = 5
Philip. Because he hath a half-face like my father?   100
But for because he hath not wooed me yet: 909
Because, | *Bast.* Your breeches best may carry them.   1129

BECAUSE *cont.*
Because my poore childe is a prisoner.   1460
Because that *Iohn* hath made his peace with *Rome?*   2349
BECKS = 1
When gold and siluer becks me to come on.   1311
BECOME = 3
Blan. O well did he become that Lyons robe,   441
Become thy great birth, nor deserue a Crowne.   971
When he intendeth to become the field: 2223
BECOMES = 3
Becomes a sonne and makes your sonne a shadow: 816
France friend with *England,* what becomes of me?   956
Anon becomes a Mountaine. O noble Dolphine,   1562
BED = 7
Vpon his death-bed he by will bequeath'd   117
To make roome for him in my husbands bed: 268
Con. My bed was euer to thy sonne as true   421
Shall gild her bridall bed and make her rich   807
Vn-sweare faith sworne, and on the marriage bed   1176
Lies in his bed, walkes vp and downe with me,   1479
I (by the honour of my marriage bed)   2346
BEDLAM = 1
Iohn. Bedlam haue done. | *Con.* I haue but this to say,   485
BEDS = 2
By this time from their fixed beds of lime   525
Rescue those breathing liues to dye in beds,   734
BEE *l.**836 990 = 1*1
BEENE *see also* bene, bin *l.*41 288 1051 1584 1945 2213 2230 2722 = 8
BEFORE *see also* 'fore = 31*2
Full fourteene weekes before the course of time: 121
**Elinor.* Nay, I would haue you go before me thither.   163
That will take paines to blow a horne before her?   229
**Enter before Angiers, Philip King of France, Lewis, Daul-|phin,*
Austria, Constance, Arthur.   292
Lewis. Before *Angiers* well met braue *Austria,*   294
Welcome before the gates *Angiers* Duke.   310
Wee'll lay before this towne our Royal bones,   334
Before the eye and prospect of your Towne,   514
Haue brought a counter-checke before your gates,   530
In warlike march, these greenes before your Towne,   548
Before the dew of euening fall, shall fleete   592
Before we will lay downe our iust-borne Armes,   659
And euen before this truce, but new before,   1164
Assured losse, before the match be plaid.   1269
Iohn. Cosen away for *England,* haste before,   1304
He lies before me: dost thou vnderstand me?   1363
Pand. Before the curing of a strong disease,   1497
Was once superfluous: you were Crown'd before,   1721
To guard a Title, that was rich before;   1727
Then did the fault before it was so patch'd.   1751
Sal. To this effect, before you were new crown'd   1752
Before the childe himselfe felt he was sicke: 1806
Three dayes before: but this from Rumors tongue   1842
Bring them before me. | *Bast.* I will seeke them out.   1891
Iohn. Nay, but make haste: the better foote before.   1892
Kneeling before this ruine of sweete life,   2064
Say, that before Ascension day at noone,   2193

BEFORE   *cont.*
 Before I drew this gallant head of warre,   2366
 Seeke out King *Iohn*, and fall before his feete: 2474
 King *Iohn* did flie an houre or two before   2543
 Away before: Conduct me to the king,   2601
 Since it hath beene before hand with our greefes.   2722
BEFRIEND   *see* be-friend
BEG = 1
 Vpon my knee I beg, goe not to Armes | Against mine Vncle.   1241
BEGET = 1
 If old Sir *Robert* did beget vs both,   88
BEGGE = 1
 I begge cold comfort: and you are so straight   2650
BEGGER = 2
 Like a poore begger, raileth on the rich.   913
 Well, whiles I am a begger, I will raile,   914
BEGGERIE = 1
 To say there is no vice, but beggerie: 917
BEGGERS = 1
 Of kings, of beggers, old men, yong men, maids,   891
BEGIN = 1
 Thus leaning on mine elbow I begin,   204
BEGINNING = 1
 Elea. A strange beginning: borrowed Maiesty?   10
BEGOT = 6
 But where I be as true begot or no,   83
 But that I am as well begot my Liege   85
 And I am I, how ere I was begot.   184
 And they shall say, when *Richard* me begot,   287
 My boy a bastard? by my soule I thinke | His father neuer was so true
 begot,   426
 What Cannoneere begot this lustie blood,   777
BEGUILD = 1
 Const. You haue beguil'd me with a counterfeit   1024
BEGUN = 2
 K.Iohn. What is thy name? | *Bast. Philip* my Liege, so is my name
 begun,   165
 This day all things begun, come to ill end,   1019
BEHALFE = 3
 Chat. Philip of *France*, in right and true behalfe   12
 Γo spread his colours boy, in thy behalfe,   301
 In that behalfe which we haue challeng'd it?   570
ΒEHΑUIOUR = 1
 In my behauiour to the Maiesty,   8
ΒEHAUIOURS = 1
 That borrow their behauiours from the great,   2219
ΒEHELD = 1*1
 Till now, infixed I beheld my selfe,   818
 Sal. Sir *Richard*, what thinke you? you haue beheld,   2040
BEHINDE = 2
 Iohn. So shall it be: your Grace shall stay behinde   1299
 Bast. Art thou gone so? I do but stay behinde,   2680
BEHOLD = 3*1
 Behold the French amaz'd vouchsafe a parle,   532
 Hubert. Heralds, from off our towres we might behold   636
 Must I behold my pretty *Arthur* more.   1474
 Behold another day breake in the East: 2493

BEHOLDING = 1
To whom am I beholding for these limmes?   252
BEING *l.*79 135 424 483 549 716 815 916 1025 1203 1437 1686 1737 2299
2421 *2422 2423 2612 = 16*2
BELDAMES = 1
Hub. Old men, and Beldames, in the streets   1910
BELEEFE = 1*1
And let beleefe, and life encounter so,   952
* *Pem.* His Highnesse yet doth speak, & holds beleefe,   2611
BELEEUD = *1
*I would not haue beleeu'd him: no tongue but *Huberts.*   1647
BELEEUE = 8
Beleeue me, I doe not beleeue thee man,   930
Sal. As true as I beleeue you thinke them false,   948
Con. Oh if thou teach me to beleeue this sorrow,   950
And I do fearefully beleeue 'tis done,   1792
To your proceedings: yet beleeue me Prince,   2262
Sal. We do beleeue thee, and beshrew my soule,   2510
I will vpon all hazards well beleeue   2561
BELL = 1*1
* *Bast.* Bell, Booke, & Candle, shall not driue me back,   1310
To giue me audience: If the mid-night bell   1336
BELS = *1
* *E.Har.* Reioyce you men of Angiers, ring your bels,   623
BELYE = 1
Con. Thou art holy to belye me so,   1428
BEND = 2*1
Be friends a-while, and both conioyntly bend   693
Bend their best studies, heartily request   1768
* *Ioh.* Why do you bend such solemne browes on me?   1808
BENE *l.*2683 = 1
BENT = 1*1
* *King.* Well, then to worke our Cannon shall be bent   330
Iohn. Speake on with fauour, we are bent to heare.   737
BEQUEATH = 2
Bequeath thy land to him, and follow me?   157
I do bequeath my faithfull seruices | And true subiection euerlastingly.   2715
BEQUEATHD = 1
Vpon his death-bed he by will bequeath'd   117
BESEECH = 2
I shall beseech you; that is question now,   205
Ar. I do beseech you Madam be content.   963
BESEEMES = 1
It ill beseemes this presence to cry ayme | To these ill-tuned repetitions: 499
BESHREW = 2
Sal. We do beleeue thee, and beshrew my soule,   2510
Dol. Ah fowle, shrew'd newes. Beshrew thy very | (hart: 2540
BESIDE = 1
Lord of thy presence, and no land beside.   145
BESIDES = 2
Besides I met Lord *Bigot,* and Lord *Salisburie*   1883
The loue of him, and this respect besides   2502
BESIEDGD = 1
(Except this Cittie now by vs besiedg'd)   805
BESMEARD = 1
Heauen knowes they were besmear'd and ouer-staind   1167

24

BEST = 12

O sir, sayes answer, at your best command,	207
To cull the plots of best aduantages:	333
In best appointment all our Regiments.	604
By our best eyes cannot be censured:	639
Because, | *Bast.* Your breeches best may carry them.	1129
(The best I had, a Princesse wrought it me)	1619
Exec. I am best pleas'd to be from such a deede.	1662
Bend their best studies, heartily request	1768
Bast. What ere you thinke, good words I thinke | were best.	2026
Haue I not heere the best Cards for the game	2358
For in a night the best part of my powre,	2671
With other Princes that may best be spar'd,	2707

BESTAINED = 1

We will not lyne his thin-bestained cloake	2022

BESTOW = 1

And tell me how you would bestow your selfe?	1156

BETHINKE = 1

Dolph. Bethinke you father, for the difference	1133

BETHUMPT = 1

Zounds, I was neuer so bethumpt with words,	782

BETIME = 1

Ile strike thee dead. Put vp thy sword betime,	2100

BETTER = 13*1

Bast. A foot of Honor better then I was,	192
Madam I would not wish a better father:	273
But buffets better then a fist of France:	781
The better Act of purposes mistooke,	1205
And better conquest neuer canst thou make,	1221
Vpon which better part, our prayrs come in,	1224
But I will fit it with some better tune.	1325
I could giue better comfort then you doe.	1485
And O, what better matter breeds for you,	1555
With any long'd-for-change, or better State.	1725
* *Pem.* When Workemen striue to do better then wel,	1745
Iohn. Nay, but make haste: the better foote before.	1892
Bast. Thou wer't better gaul the diuell Salsbury.	2097
The better arme you to the sodaine time,	2583

BETTERS = 1

Bast. Our Country manners giue our betters way.	164

BETWEEN = 1

Between compulsion, and a braue respect:	2295

BETWEENE = 6

Betweene my father, and my mother lay,	114
Betweene our kingdomes and our royall selues,	1163
Betweene his purpose and his conscience,	1795
Betweene my conscience, and my Cosins death.	1973
Ile make a peace betweene your soule, and you.	1975
Betweene this chastiz'd kingdome and my selfe,	2337

BETWIXT *see also* 'twixt = 1

Some Messenger betwixt me, and the Peeres,	1901

BEUTY = *1

* *P.* Oh death, made proud with pure & princely beuty,	2034

BEYOND = 1

Beyond the infinite and boundlesse reach of mercie,	2120

BE-FRIEND = 1

Thou maist be-friend me so much, as to thinke	2565

25

BLANCH cont.
**Enter K.(ing) of England, Bastard, Queene, Blanch, Pembroke,	and others.*	379
*Hub. That daughter there of Spaine, the Lady *Blanch*	738
Where should he finde it fairer, then in *Blanch*:	742
Where should he finde it purer then in *Blanch*?	744
Whose veines bound richer blood then Lady *Blanch*?	746
Drawne in the flattering table of her eie.	*Whispers with Blanch.*	819
**Enter King Iohn, France, Dolphin, Blanch, Elianor, Philip,	Austria, Constance.*	998
Pan. You, in the right of Lady *Blanch* your wife,	1527

BLANCH = 1
BLASPHEME = 1
Fra. Brother of *England*, you blaspheme in this.	1088

BLAUNCH = 1*2
**Shall *Lewis* haue *Blaunch*, and *Blaunch* those Prouinces?	924
Lewes marry *Blaunch*? O boy, then where art thou?	955

BLEAKE = 1
To make his bleake windes kisse my parched lips,	2648

BLEEDE = 1
If not, bleede *France*, and peace ascend to heauen.	383

BLEEDING = 1
Whose sonnes lye scattered on the bleeding ground:	614

BLEEDS = 1
Which bleeds away, euen as a forme of waxe	2485

BLESSED = 5
Now blessed be the houre by night or day	174
And with a blessed and vn-vext retyre,	559
He is the halfe part of a blessed man,	752
Fran. 'Tis true (faire daughter) and this blessed day,	1000
And blessed shall he be that doth reuolt	1101

BLESSING = 1
Ele. My blessing goe with thee.	1376

BLEST = 1
Some gentle order, and then we shall be blest	1182

BLEW = 1
Pand. It was my breath that blew this Tempest vp,	2184

BLINDE = 1
Vpon thy feature, for my rage was blinde,	1989

BLOOD = 30*1
When liuing blood doth in these temples beat	405
We will beare home that lustie blood againe,	561
And stalke in blood to our possession?	572
Hither returne all gilt with Frenchmens blood:	627
Blood hath bought blood, and blowes haue answerd	(blowes:	640
*Iohn. France, hast thou yet more blood to cast away?	648
Fra. England thou hast not sau'd one drop of blood	655
When the rich blood of kings is set on fire:	665
The others peace: till then, blowes, blood, and death.	674
Whose veines bound richer blood then Lady *Blanch*?	746
What Cannoneere begot this lustie blood,	777
In titles, honors, and promotions,	As she in beautie, education, blood,	808
False blood to false blood ioyn'd. Gone to be freinds?	923
Against the blood that thou hast married?	1234
That nothing can allay, nothing but blood,	1275
The blood and deerest valued bloud of *France*.	1276

BLOOD *cont.*

To ashes, ere our blood shall quench that fire:	1278
Pan. Your minde is all as youthfull as your blood.	1510
For he that steepes his safetie in true blood,	1532
That blood which ow'd the bredth of all this Ile,	1817
There is no sure foundation set on blood:	1822
A fearefull eye thou hast. Where is that blood,	1824
This kingdome, this Confine of blood, and breathe	1971
Not painted with the Crimson spots of blood,	1978
And foule immaginarie eyes of blood	1990
That leaues the print of blood where ere it walkes.	2024
Full warm of blood, of mirth, of gossipping:	2310
Hen. It is too late, the life of all his blood	2605
On vnrepreeuable condemned blood.	2657

BLOODED = 1

Vpon my partie: thou cold blooded slaue,	1049

BLOODIE = 1

Shall finde but bloodie safety, and vntrue.	1533

BLOODIEST = 1

Of murthers Armes: This is the bloodiest shame,	2046

BLOODS = 1

Fran. As many and as well-borne bloods as those. | *Bast.* Some Bastards too.	585

BLOODY = 12

All preparation for a bloody siedge	519
For bloody power to rush vppon your peace.	527
Turne face to face, and bloody point to point:	704
Of smiling peace to march a bloody hoast,	1177
Out of the bloody fingers ends of *Iohn.*	1553
Euen with the fierce lookes of these bloody men.	1650
Pem. This is the man should do the bloody deed:	1787
To breake within the bloody house of life,	1935
Finding thee fit for bloody villanie:	1950
Bast. It is a damned, and a bloody worke,	2056
Their Needl's to Lances, and their gentle hearts | To fierce and bloody inclination.	2411
After such bloody toile, we bid good night,	2530

BLOOD-SHED = 1

And proue a deadly blood-shed, but a iest,	2054

BLOOME = 1

The bloome that promiseth a mightie fruite.	789

BLOT = 1

Const. There's a good grandame boy | That would blot thee.	430

BLOTS = 2*1

To looke into the blots and staines of right,	411
Queen. Theres a good mother boy, that blots thy fa-|(ther	429
Full of vnpleasing blots, and sightlesse staines,	966

BLOUD = 13*2

K.Io. Heere haue we war for war, & bloud for bloud,	24
Arthur that great fore-runner of thy bloud,	295
Wade to the market-place in *French*-mens bloud,	335
Lest vnaduis'd you staine your swords with bloud,	338
And then we shall repent each drop of bloud,	341
An Ace stirring him to bloud and strife,	357
You came in Armes to spill mine enemies bloud,	1027
And shall these hands so lately purg'd of bloud?	1170
Bla. The Sun's orecast with bloud: faire day adieu,	1259

BLOUD *cont.*
The blood and deerest valued bloud of *France.* 1276
Had bak'd thy bloud, and made it heauy, thicke, 1342
To stranger-bloud, to forren Royalty; 2178
The bloud of malice, in a vaine of league, 2289
Bast. By all the bloud that euer fury breath'd, 2381
BLOUDY = 3*2
Chat. The proud controle of fierce and bloudy warre, 22
With fearefull bloudy issue arbitrate. 44
*That bloudy spoyle: thou slaue, thou wretch, y coward, 1041
And bloudy *England* into *England* gone, 1390
You bloudy Nero's, ripping vp the wombe 2406
BLOW = 2
That will take paines to blow a horne before her? 229
Shall blow each dust, each straw, each little rub 1513
BLOWES = 3
Blood hath bought blood, and blowes haue answerd | (blowes: 640
The others peace: till then, blowes, blood, and death. 674
BLOWNE = 4
And with the halfe-blowne Rose. But Fortune, oh, 975
The breath of heauen, hath blowne his spirit out, 1689
This showre, blowne vp by tempest of the soule, 2301
And now 'tis farre too huge to be blowne out 2339
BLUNT = *1
K.Iohn. A good blunt fellow: why being yonger born 79
BLUSH = 3
Art. And if you do, you will but make it blush, 1692
Of your deere Mother-England: blush for shame: 2407
But staid, and made the Westerne Welkin blush, 2526
BLUSHES = 1
Sal. Oh he is bold, and blushes not at death, 2076
BLUSTRING = 1
And make faire weather in your blustring land: 2188
BOAST = 1
Of Natures guifts, thou mayst with Lillies boast, 974
BODIE = 2
In peace: and part this bodie and my soule 2508
Hen. At Worster must his bodie be interr'd, | For so he will'd it. 2709
BODY = 4
Art. 'Mercie on me: | Me thinkes no body should be sad but I: 1585
Was leuied in the body of a land. 1830
Nay, in the body of this fleshly Land, 1970
His soule and body to their lasting rest. 2630
BOISTROUS = 1
Art. Alas, what neede you be so boistrous rough? 1652
BOLD = 1
Sal. Oh he is bold, and blushes not at death, 2076
BOLDNESSE = 1
Shew boldnesse and aspiring confidence: 2224
BONDS = 2
I tore them from their bonds, and cride aloud, 1455
And will againe commit them to their bonds, 1459
BONE = 1
Now for the bare-pickt bone of Maiesty, 2153
BONES = 3*1
(Faire fall the bones that tooke the paines for me) 86
Wee'll lay before this towne our Royal bones, 334

BONES *cont.*

And I will kisse thy detestable bones,	1412
*Heauen take my soule, and England keep my bones. *Dies*	2006

BOOKE = 2*1

And then comes answer like an Absey booke:	206
Can in this booke of beautie read, I loue:	801
Bast. Bell, Booke, & Candle, shall not driue me back,	1310

BORN = *1

K.Iohn. A good blunt fellow: why being yonger born	79

BORNE = 11*1

Borne in *Northamptonshire*, and eldest sonne | As I suppose, to *Robert Faulconbridge,*	59
That *Geffrey* was thy elder brother borne,	401
Fran. As many and as well-borne bloods as those. | *Bast.* Some Bastards too.	585
Before we will lay downe our iust-borne Armes,	659
A woman naturally borne to feares;	936
There was not such a gracious creature borne:	1466
This Act so euilly borne shall coole the hearts	1534
This must not be thus borne, this will breake out	1819
Was borne to see so sad an houre as this,	2277
I am too high-borne to be proportied	2332
Am I *Romes* slaue? What penny hath *Rome* borne?	2350
Sal. Be of good comfort (Prince) for you are borne	2631

BORROW = 1

That borrow their behauiours from the great,	2219

BORROWED = 2

The borrowed Maiesty of *England* heere.	9
Elea. A strange beginning: borrowed Maiesty?	10

BOSOM = 1

Vpon her gentle bosom, and fill vp	2279

BOSOME = 9

Iohn. We from the West will send destruction | Into this Cities bosome.	723
Liues in this bosome, deerely cherished.	1323
I would into thy bosome poure my thoughts:	1352
Vpon the bosome of the ground, rush forth	1573
Hub. His words do take possession of my bosome.	1605
Within this bosome, neuer entred yet	1979
And great affections wrastling in thy bosome	2292
There is so hot a summer in my bosome,	2637
Through my burn'd bosome: nor intreat the North	2647

BOTH = 16

If old Sir *Robert* did beget vs both,	88
France. When I haue saide, make answer to vs both.	541
We for the worthiest hold the right from both.	589
Of both your Armies, whose equality	638
Both are alike, and both alike we like:	643
We hold our Towne for neither: yet for both.	645
Be friends a-while, and both conioyntly bend	693
So newly ioyn'd in loue? so strong in both,	1171
I am with both, each Army hath a hand,	1261
And in their rage, I hauing hold of both,	1262
Must you with hot Irons, burne out both mine eyes?	1612
I will both heare, and grant you your requests.	1763
Both for my selfe, and them: but chiefe of all	1766
The deed, which both our tongues held vilde to name.	1966
Both they and we, perusing ore these notes	2256

BOTTOMES = 1
Then now the *English* bottomes haue waft o're,   367
BOUGHT = 2
Blood hath bought blood, and blowes haue answerd | (blowes: 640
Mel. Fly Noble English, you are bought and sold,   2471
BOUNCE = *1
*He speakes plaine Cannon fire, and smoake, and bounce,   778
BOUND = 6
I am a Souldier, and now bound to *France*.   158
Whose veines bound richer blood then Lady *Blanch*?   746
Do glorifie the bankes that bound them in: 757
Blan. That she is bound in honor still to do   841
And leaue those woes alone, which I alone | Am bound to vnder-beare.   985
For heauen sake *Hubert* let me not be bound: 1654
BOUNDEN = 1
Hub. I am much bounden to your Maiesty.   1328
BOUNDLESSE = 1
Beyond the infinite and boundlesse reach of mercie,   2120
BOUNDS = 3
Two such controlling bounds shall you be, kings,   759
Like a proud riuer peering ore his bounds?   944
Stoope lowe within those bounds we haue ore-look'd,   2516
BOW = 2
Heere is my Throne bid kings come bow to it.   996
Vnto the Raine-bow; or with Taper-light   1731
BOWELS = 3
The Canons haue their bowels full of wrath,   516
Whose Bowels sodainly burst out: The King   2587
That all my bowels crumble vp to dust: 2638
BOY = 25*3
Lady. Sir *Roberts* sonne, I thou vnreuerend boy,   238
To spread his colours boy, in thy behalfe,   301
Lewis. A noble boy, who would not doe thee right?   311
Salute thee for her King, till then faire boy   323
But we will make it subiect to this boy.   336
That Iudge hath made me guardian to this boy,   412
As thine was to thy husband, and this boy   422
My boy a bastard? by my soule I thinke | His father neuer was so true
begot,   426
Queen. Theres a good mother boy, that blots thy fa-|(ther   429
Const. There's a good grandame boy | That would blot thee.   430
Then ere the coward hand of *France* can win; | Submit thee boy.   458
Qu. Mo. His mother shames him so, poore boy hee | (weepes.   468
Of this oppressed boy; this is thy eldest sonnes sonne,   479
That yon greene boy shall haue no Sunne to ripe   788
Fra. What sai'st thou boy? looke in the Ladies face.   811
Lewes marry *Blaunch*? O boy, then where art thou?   955
But thou art faire, and at thy birth (deere boy)   972
Iohn. Hubert, keepe this boy: *Philip* make vp,   1290
On yon young boy: Ile tell thee what my friend,   1360
If that be true, I shall see my boy againe;   1463
O Lord, my boy, my *Arthur*, my faire sonne,   1488
And binde the boy, which you shall finde with me   1574
Hub. Yong Boy, I must. | *Art.* And will you? | *Hub.* And I will.   1613
Hub. Come (Boy) prepare your selfe.   1667
Hub. I can heate it, Boy.   1684
Hub. But with my breath I can reuiue it Boy.   1691

BOY *cont.*
Yet am I sworne, and I did purpose, Boy,	1703
To Armes Inuasiue? Shall a beardlesse boy,	2238

BOYES = 1
This Ship-boyes semblance hath disguis'd me quite.	2000

BOYISH = 1
This vn-heard sawcinesse and boyish Troopes,	2387

BOYSTEROUS = 1
Then feeling what small things are boysterous there,	1673

BOYSTEROUSLY = 1
Must be as boysterously maintain'd as gain'd.	1521

BRABLER = 1
We hold our time too precious to be spent | with such a brabler.	2415

BRACD = 1
And euen at hand, a drumme is readie brac'd,	2425

BRACE = 1
Art. Hubert, the vtterance of a brace of tongues,	1676

BRAG = 1
A ramping foole, to brag, and stamp, and sweare,	1048

BRAGGING = 1
Of bragging horror: So shall inferior eyes	2218

BRAINE = 1
Is touch'd, corruptibly: and his pure braine	2606

BRAUE = 5*2
Lewis. Before *Angiers* well met braue *Austria,*	294
By this braue Duke came early to his graue:	298
Big. Out dunghill: dar'st thou braue a Nobleman?	2087
A cockred-silken wanton braue our fields,	2239
Between compulsion, and a braue respect:	2295
Dol. There end thy braue, and turn thy face in peace,	2413
Haue done me shame: Braue Soldier, pardon me,	2568

BRAUED = 1
My Nobles leaue me, and my State is braued,	1968

BRAUELY = 1
In faint Retire: Oh brauely came we off,	2528

BRAUER = 1
In briefe, a brauer choyse of dauntlesse spirits	366

BRAULD = 1
Till their soule-fearing clamours haue braul'd downe	697

BRAYING = 1
Shall braying trumpets, and loud churlish drums	1236

BRAZEN = 1
Did with his yron tongue, and brazen mouth	1337

BREACH = 1
As patches set vpon a little breach,	1749

BREAK = *1
*Deepe shame had struck me dumbe, made me break off,	1960

BREAKE = 8*1
Lew. Women & fooles, breake off your conference.	450
Since Kings breake faith vpon commoditie,	918
No bargaines breake that are not this day made;	1018
To breake into this dangerous argument.	1771
His passion is so ripe, it needs must breake.	1797
This must not be thus borne, this will breake out	1819
To breake within the bloody house of life,	1935
If I get downe, and do not breake my limbes,	2002
Behold another day breake in the East:	2493

BREAKES = 2
That Broker, that still breakes the pate of faith,   889
Pem. And when it breakes, I feare will issue thence   1798
BREAKE-VOW = 1
That dayly breake-vow, he that winnes of all,   890
BREAKING = 1
That any accent breaking from thy tongue,   2569
BREAST = 2
In any breast of strong authoritie,   410
What meanes that hand vpon that breast of thine?   942
BREATH = 18*1
With this abundance of superfluous breath?   448
Least zeale now melted by the windie breath   793
Is but the vaine breath of a common man: 929
Can tast the free breath of a sacred King?   1075
The latest breath that gaue the sound of words   1161
In the vilde prison of afflicted breath: 1402
And stop this gap of breath with fulsome dust,   1415
Con. No, no, I will not, hauing breath to cry: 1421
For euen the breath of what I meane to speake,   1512
One minute, nay one quiet breath of rest.   1519
The breath of heauen, hath blowne his spirit out,   1689
Hub. But with my breath I can reuiue it Boy.   1691
Vnder the tide; but now I breath againe   1859
Be guiltie of the stealing that sweete breath   2140
Pand. It was my breath that blew this Tempest vp,   2184
And on our actions set the name of right | With holy breath.   2319
Your breath first kindled the dead coale of warres,   2336
But euen this night, whose blacke contagious breath   2494
*Sal. You breath these dead newes in as dead an eare   2675
BREATHD = 1*1
*We breath'd our Councell: but it pleas'd your Highnes   1753
Bast. By all the bloud that euer fury breath'd,   2381
BREATHE = 2
Or let the Church our mother breathe her curse,   1187
This kingdome, this Confine of blood, and breathe   1971
BREATHES = 1
While *Philip* breathes.   1289
BREATHING = 3
Rescue those breathing liues to dye in beds,   734
And breathing to his breathlesse Excellence   2065
Euen this ill night, your breathing shall expire,   2497
BREATHLESSE = 1
And breathing to his breathlesse Excellence   2065
BRED = 1
This Calfe, bred from his Cow from all the world: 132
BREDTH = 1
That blood which ow'd the bredth of all this Ile,   1817
BREECHES = 1
Because, | *Bast.* Your breeches best may carry them.   1129
BREED = 1
Twice fifteene thousand hearts of Englands breed. | *Bast.* Bastards and
else.   582
BREEDS = 1
And O, what better matter breeds for you,   1555
BREEFE = 3*1
Shall draw this breefe into as huge a volume: 400

BREEFE *cont.*

Cit. In breefe, we are the King of Englands subiects   573
I must be breefe, least resolution drop   1608
Bast. Breefe then: and what's the newes?   2575
BREEFELY = 1
What *England* saies, say breefely gentle Lord,   346
BREST = 1
Do shew the mood of a much troubled brest,   1791
BRIBD = 1
I, with these Christall beads heauen shall be brib'd   473
BRIDALL = 1
Shall gild her bridall bed and make her rich   807
BRIDE = 1
In likenesse of a new vntrimmed Bride.   1139
BRIEFE = 2
In briefe, a brauer choyse of dauntlesse spirits   366
A thousand businesses are briefe in hand,   2163
BRIGHT = 2
Their Armours that march'd hence so siluer bright,   626
Bast. Your sword is bright sir, put it vp againe.   2079
BRING = 5
My Lord *Chattilion* may from *England* bring   339
And if not that, I bring you Witnesses   581
But on my Liege, for very little paines | Will bring this labor to an
happy end. *Exit.*   1295
Bring them before me. | *Bast.* I will seeke them out.   1891
Oh, answer not; but to my Closset bring   1992
BRINGS = 3
What brings you heere to Court so hastily?   231
The yearely course that brings this day about,   1006
And brings from him such offers of our peace,   2694
BRISTLE = 1
Doth dogged warre bristle his angry crest,   2154
BRITAINE = 4
Arthur of *Britaine*, yeeld thee to my hand,   456
And let yong *Arthur* Duke of Britaine in,   611
Arthur of Britaine, Englands King, and yours.   621
For wee'l create yong *Arthur* Duke of Britaine   872
BROKE = 3
Vpon good Friday, and nere broke his fast: 248
I faintly broke with thee of *Arthurs* death: 1952
I left him almost speechlesse, and broke out   2581
BROKEN = 1
Sal. Vpon our sides it neuer shall be broken.   2259
BROKER = 2
That Broker, that still breakes the pate of faith,   889
This Bawd, this Broker, this all-changing-word,   903
BROODED = 1
Then, in despight of brooded watchfull day,   1351
BROOKE = 1
Fellow be gone: I cannot brooke thy sight,   957
BROTHER = 16*2
Of thy deceased brother, *Geffreyes* sonne,   13
Your brother did imploy my father much.   104
K.Iohn. Sirra, your brother is Legittimate,   124
That marry wiues: tell me, how if my brother   128
My brother might not claime him, nor your father   134

BROTHER *cont.*
And like thy brother to enioy thy land: 143
Bast. Madam, and if my brother had my shape   146
Bast. Brother, take you my land, Ile take my chance;   159
*Bast. Brother by th'mothers side, giue me your hand,   172
Bast. Brother adieu, good fortune come to thee,   189
*Lady. Where is that slaue thy brother? where is he?   233
Bast. My brother *Robert*, old Sir *Roberts* sonne: 235
Lady. Hast thou conspired with thy brother too,   254
Looke heere vpon thy brother *Geffreyes* face,   396
That *Geffrey* was thy elder brother borne,   401
Sonne to the elder brother of this man,   545
Brother of England, how may we content   867
Fra. Brother of *England*, you blaspheme in this.   1088
BROTHERS = 4
That is my brothers plea, and none of mine,   75
What doth moue you to claime your brothers land.   99
Insooth he might: then if he were my brothers,   133
Since I first cal'd my brothers father Dad.   783
BROUGHT = 9*1
Haue brought a counter-checke before your gates,   530
Whom zeale and charitie brought to the field,   886
And here's a Prophet that I brought with me   1868
*Pem. Who brought that Letter from the Cardinall?   2011
And brought in matter that should feed this fire;   2338
This newes was brought to *Richard* but euen now,   2452
And brought Prince *Henry* in their companie,   2592
That being brought into the open ayre,   2612
Hen. Let him be brought into the Orchard heere: 2615
Iohn brought in.   2634
BROW = 4*1
Hang'd in the frowning wrinkle of her brow,   822
And make a ryot on the gentle brow | Of true sincerity? O holy Sir   1178
Threaten the threatner, and out-face the brow   2217
Lift vp thy brow (renowned *Salisburie*)   2305
*Hub. Why heere walke I in the black brow of night | To finde you out. 2573
BROWES = 5*1
Against the browes of this resisting towne,   331
These eyes, these browes, were moulded out of his;   397
And put my eye-balls in thy vaultie browes,   1413
I knit my hand-kercher about your browes   1618
*Ioh. Why do you bend such solemne browes on me?   1808
With wrinkled browes, with nods, with rolling eyes.   1917
BUCKETS = 1
To diue like Buckets in concealed Welles,   2393
BUCKLED = 1
And France, whose armour Conscience buckled on,   885
BUD = 1
But now will Canker-sorrow eat my bud,   1467
BUFFETS = 1
But buffets better then a fist of France: 781
BULLETS = 1
Fran. Our Thunder from the South, | Shall raine their drift of bullets on
this Towne.   726
BULLETTS = 1
And now insteed of bulletts wrapt in fire   533

BULWARKE = 1
That Water-walled Bulwarke, still secure   320
BURDEN = 1
With burden of our armor heere we sweat: 389
BURIE = 1
Big. Away, toward *Burie*, to the Dolphin there.   2117
BURN = 1
Io. They burn in indignation: I repent: *Enter Mes.*   1821
BURND = 3
Within the scorched veines of one new burn'd: 1209
France, I am burn'd vp with inflaming wrath,   1273
Through my burn'd bosome: nor intreat the North   2647
BURNE = 3*1
Fra. Thy rage shall burne thee vp, & thou shalt turne   1277
Must you with hot Irons, burne out both mine eyes?   1612
And with hot Irons must I burne them out.   1636
With this same very Iron, to burne them out.   1704
BURNES = 1
Iohn. Aye me, this tyrant Feauer burnes mee vp,   2454
BURNING = 4
There is no malice in this burning cole,   1688
Figur'd quite ore with burning Meteors.   2304
Already smoakes about the burning Crest   2495
It would allay the burning qualitie   2613
BURNT = 1
The tackle of my heart, is crack'd and burnt,   2662
BURST = 1
Whose Bowels sodainly burst out: The King   2587
BURTHEN = 1
But Asse, Ile take that burthen from your backe,   445
BURTHENS = 1
Pray that their burthens may not fall this day,   1015
BUSINESSE = 2
Sweat in this businesse, and maintaine this warre?   2355
To consummate this businesse happily.   2705
BUSINESSES = 1
A thousand businesses are briefe in hand,   2163
BUSSE = 1
And busse thee as thy wife: Miseries Loue, | O come to me.   1418
BUT *l.*49 69 82 83 85 113 170 *178 191 193 215 217 222 227 259 284 309
324 336 391 445 480 483 486 488 522 528 535 564 576 736 765 781 815
893 909 912 915 917 927 929 937 939 947 960 972 975 994 1007 1017
1028 1035 1045 1082 1132 1141 1143 *1151 *1153 1164 1193 1211 1217
1225 1228 1275 1295 1325 1330 1332 1353 1407 1437 1447 1458 1465
1467 1496 1525 1526 1533 1537 1541 1546 1558 1586 1592 1616 1628
1637 1643 *1647 1659 1664 1669 1670 1681 1691 1692 1708 *1720 1734
*1753 1760 1766 1842 1856 1859 1864 1867 1892 1931 1949 *1956 1962
1992 1994 2029 2054 2088 2098 2122 2129 2130 2135 2186 2196 2199
2201 2212 2271 2273 2300 2353 2362 2423 2427 2452 2484 2494 2511
2526 2666 2667 2676 2680 2720 2721 2725 2729 = 144*7
BUTCHER = 1
Then to be butcher of an innocent childe.   1984
BUY = 1
Dreading the curse that money may buy out,   1091
BY = 93*6
BYAS = 3
Commoditie, the byas of the world,   895

36

BYAS *cont.*
 Till this aduantage, this vile drawing byas,   898
 And this same byas, this Commoditie,   902
CAINE = 1
 For since the birth of *Caine*, the first male-childe   1464
CALAMITIE = 2
 The different plague of each calamitie.   1444
 Like true, inseparable, faithfull loues, | Sticking together in calamitie. 1450
CALD = 1
 Since I first cal'd my brothers father Dad.   783
CALENDER *see* kalender
CALFE = 1
 This Calfe, bred from his Cow from all the world: 132
CALL = 10
 I am thy grandame *Richard*, call me so.   177
 And if his name be *George*, Ile call him *Peter*;   196
 Call for our cheefest men of discipline,   332
 Queen. Who is it thou dost call vsurper *France*?   417
 Call not me slanderer, thou and thine vsurpe | The Dominations,
 Royalties, and rights   477
 Then tell vs, Shall your Citie call vs Lord,   569
 We make him Lord of. Call the Lady *Constance*,   874
 And call them Meteors, prodigies, and signes,   1542
 Were there in Armes, they would be as a Call   1559
 And call it cunning. Do, and if you will,   1630
CALLD = 3
 How comes it then that thou art call'd a King,   404
 Our Trumpet call'd you to this gentle parle.   511
 And meritorious shall that hand be call'd,   1103
CALLICE = 1
 With al true duetie: On toward *Callice*, hoa. | *Exeunt.* 1379
CALME = 1
 They shoote but calme words, folded vp in smoake,   535
CALMELY = 1
 And calmely run on in obedience   2517
CALUES = 1*1
 And hang a Calues skin on those recreant limbes.   1055
 *Bast. Hang nothing but a Calues skin most sweet lout. 1151
CALUES-SKIN = 2*2
 *Phil. And hang a Calues-skin on those recreant limbs 1057
 *Phil. And hang a Calues-skin on those recreant limbs. 1059
 Bast. And hang a Calues-skin on his recreant limbs. 1127
 Bast. Wil't not be? | Will not a Calues-skin stop that mouth of thine? 1230
CAME = 9
 You came not of one mother then it seemes.   66
 And if he were, he came into the world   120
 By this braue Duke came early to his graue: 298
 Which heere we came to spout against your Towne,   562
 This widdow Lady? In her right we came,   868
 You came in Armes to spill mine enemies bloud,   1027
 Vnder whose conduct came those powres of France,   1848
 In faint Retire: Oh brauely came we off,   2528
 Who halfe an houre since came from the Dolphin,   2693
CAN *l.*76 194 458 494 566 576 761 763 801 830 838 *843 845 995 1075
 1113 1118 1275 1387 *1492 1610 1684 1691 1860 2160 = 23*2
CANDLE = *1
 *Bast. Bell, Booke, & Candle, shall not driue me back, 1310

CANKER = 1
And heale the inueterate Canker of one wound,   2265
CANKER-SORROW = 1
But now will Canker-sorrow eat my bud,   1467
CANKRED = 1
A womans will, a cankred Grandams will.   497
CANNON = 1*2
The thunder of my Cannon shall be heard.   31
*King. Well, then to worke our Cannon shall be bent   330
*He speakes plaine Cannon fire, and smoake, and bounce,   778
CANNONEERE = 1
What Cannoneere begot this lustie blood,   777
CANNONS = 1
Our Cannons malice vainly shall be spent   557
CANNOT = 14
Phil. Well sir, by this you cannot get my land,   105
It cannot be, and if thou wert his mother.   428
By our best eyes cannot be censured: 639
It cannot be, thou do'st but say 'tis so.   927
With my vext spirits, I cannot take a Truce,   938
Fellow be gone: I cannot brooke thy sight,   957
Law cannot giue my childe his kingdome heere;   1115
Husband, I cannot pray that thou maist winne: 1264
Which cannot heare a Ladies feeble voyce,   1425
Iohn hath seiz'd Arthur, and it cannot be,   1516
That Iohn may stand, then Arthur needs must fall, | So be it, for it
cannot be but so.   1524
Iohn. We cannot hold mortalities strong hand.   1800
Perchance the Cardinall cannot make your peace;   2243
We cannot deale but with the very hand   2273
CANON = 2
The Canon of the Law is laide on him,   482
Their battering Canon charged to the mouthes,   696
CANONIZD = 1
And thou shalt be Canoniz'd (Cardinall.)   1436
CANONIZED = 1
Canonized and worship'd as a Saint,   1104
CANONS = 1
The Canons haue their bowels full of wrath,   516
CANST l.30 1076 *1153 1221 2414 = 4*1
CANTERBURY = 1
Keepe Stephen Langton chosen Archbishop | Of Canterbury from that
holy Sea: 1070
CAP = *1
*K.Iohn. Why what a mad-cap hath heauen lent vs here?   92
CAPEABLE = 2
Marke how they whisper, vrge them while their soules | Are capeable of
this ambition,   791
For I am sicke, and capeable of feares,   933
CARDINALL = 11*1
I Pandulph, of faire Millane Cardinall,   1065
Thou canst not (Cardinall) deuise a name   1076
Good Father Cardinall, cry thou Amen   1109
Aust. King Philip, listen to the Cardinall.   1126
Iohn. Philip, what saist thou to the Cardinall?   1131
Con. What should he say, but as the Cardinall?   1132
And thou shalt be Canoniz'd (Cardinall.)   1436

CARDINALL *cont.*

And Father Cardinall, I haue heard you say   1461
Pem. Who brought that Letter from the Cardinall?   2011
Perchance the Cardinall cannot make your peace;   2243
The Cardinall *Pandulph* is within at rest,   2692
To the disposing of the Cardinall,   2702
CARDS = 1
Haue I not heere the best Cards for the game   2358
CARE = 2*1
I would not care, I then would be content,   969
Where hath it slept? Where is my Mothers care?   1835
Dol. Well: keepe good quarter, & good care to night,   2546
CARKASSE = 1
Bast. Heeres a stay, | That shakes the rotten carkasse of old death   771
CARRIAGES = 1
For many carriages hee hath dispatch'd   2700
CARRION = 1
And be a Carrion Monster like thy selfe;   1416
CARRY = 1
Because, | *Bast.* Your breeches best may carry them.   1129
CASE = 1
It would not be sir nobbe in any case.   155.
CASED = 1
A cased Lion by the mortall paw,   1190
CASKET = 1
An empty Casket, where the Iewell of life   2208
CAST = 2*2
Iohn. France, hast thou yet more blood to cast away?   648
Bast. They found him dead, and cast into the streets,   2207
Are cast away, and sunke on *Goodwin* sands.   2539
Ioh. Poyson'd, ill fare: dead, forsooke, cast off,   2643
CASTLE = 1
But Douer Castle: London hath receiu'd   2199
CATCH = 3
And haue is haue, how euer men doe catch: 182
And a may catch your hide and you alone: 436
Ile smoake your skin-coat and I catch you right,   439
CATECHIZE = 1
Why then I sucke my teeth, and catechize   202
CAUSE = 8
That giue you cause to proue my saying true.   949
Fra. By heauen Lady, you shall haue no cause   1021
Iohn. Good friend, thou hast no cause to say so yet,   1329
Such temperate order in so fierce a cause,   1394
But they will plucke away his naturall cause,   1541
Thy hand hath murdred him: I had a mighty cause   1930
Vpon the spot of this inforced cause,   2281
To the sea side, and put his cause and quarrell   2701
CEASE = 1
How that ambitious *Constance* would not cease   38
CENSURED = 1
By our best eyes cannot be censured: 639
CENTER = 1
Now happy he, whose cloake and center can   2160
CERTAIN = 1
Philip. Most certain of one mother, mighty King,   67

CERTAINE = 3
But for the certaine knowledge of that truth, 69
Be by some certaine king, purg'd and depos'd. 686
No certaine life atchieu'd by others death: 1823
CERTAINELY = 1
Pan. If you had won it, certainely you had. 1503
CHAIRE = 1
Fast to the chaire: be heedfull: hence, and watch. 1575
CHALLENGD = 1
In that behalfe which we haue challeng'd it? 570
CHAMBERS = 1
That in your Chambers gaue you chasticement? 2401
CHAMPION = 3
Thou Fortunes Champion, that do'st neuer fight 1044
Therefore to Armes, be Champion of our Church, 1186
That is, to be the Champion of our Church, 1198
CHANCE = 2*1
Bast. Brother, take you my land, Ile take my chance; 159
*Bast. Madam by chance, but not by truth, what tho; 178
Where but by chance a siluer drop hath falne, 1447
CHANGD = 1
She is corrupted, chang'd, and wonne from thee, 976
CHANGE = 4
Yea, faith it selfe to hollow falshood change. 1020
And kisse the lippes of vnacquainted change, 1551
With any long'd-for-change, or better State. 1725
Their thimbles into armed Gantlets change, 2410
CHANGER = 1
With that same purpose-changer, that slye diuel, 888
CHANGING = 1
This Bawd, this Broker, this all-changing-word, 903
CHANNELL = 1
Shall leaue his natiue channell, and ore-swell 651
CHAPPELL = 1
For at Saint Maries Chappell presently, 858
CHAPS = 1
Oh now doth death line his dead chaps with steele, 666
CHARGE = 5
This expeditions charge: what men are you? 56
Heauen lay not my transgression to my charge, 269
To charge me to an answere, as the Pope: 1078
What we so fear'd he had a charge to do. 1793
That vnder-goe this charge? Who else but I, 2353
CHARGED = 1
Their battering Canon charged to the mouthes, 696
CHARITABLE = 1
In such a iust and charitable warre. 329
CHARITIE = 1
Whom zeale and charitie brought to the field, 886
CHARITY = 1
Offending Charity: If but a dozen French 1558
CHASE = 2
That holds in chase mine honour vp and downe. 234
And chase the natiue beauty from his cheeke, 1468
CHASTICEMENT = 1
That in your Chambers gaue you chasticement? 2401

CHASTISE = 1
And by whose helpe I meane to chastise it. 414
CHASTIZD = 1
Betweene this chastiz'd kingdome and my selfe, 2337
CHAT = 1
Pembroke looke too't: farewell *Chattillion*. | *Exit Chat. and Pem.* 35
CHAT = 3*2
CHATILION = 1
We coldly pause for thee, *Chatilion* speake, 347
CHATILLION = *1
King Iohn. | *Now say *Chatillion,* what would *France* with vs? 4
CHATTILION see also Chat. = 3
My Lord *Chattilion* may from *England* bring 339
Enter Chattilion. 343
King. A wonder Lady: lo vpon thy wish | Our Messenger *Chattilion* is
arriu'd, 344
CHATTILLION = 1
Pembroke looke too't: farewell *Chattillion*. | *Exit Chat. and Pem.* 35
CHATTYLION = 1
**Enter King Iohn, Queene Elinor, Pembroke, Essex, and Sa-|lisbury,
with the Chattylion of France.* 2
CHAUNTS = 1
Who chaunts a dolefull hymne to his owne death, 2628
CHEAREFULL = 1
And look'd vpon, I hope, with chearefull eyes. 1719
CHEATS = 1
But the word Maid, cheats the poore Maide of that. 893
CHECKE = 4
That thou maist be a Queen, and checke the world. 420
Haue brought a counter-checke before your gates, 530
To checke his reigne, but they will cherish it. 1537
And finde no checke? Let vs my Liege to Armes: 2242
CHEEFEST = 1
Call for our cheefest men of discipline, 332
CHEEKE = 2
Aust. Vpon thy cheeke lay I this zelous kisse, 312
And chase the natiue beauty from his cheeke, 1468
CHEEKES = 4
To saue vnscratch'd your Citties threatned cheekes: 531
And straine their cheekes to idle merriment, 1345
That I haue seene inhabite in those cheekes? 1825
That siluerly doth progresse on thy cheekes: 2297
CHEERD = 1
Still and anon cheer'd vp the heauy time; 1623
CHERISH = 2
This iugling witchcraft with reuennue cherish, 1096
To checke his reigne, but they will cherish it. 1537
CHERISHED = 1
Liues in this bosome, deerely cherished. 1323
CHERRY = 1
Giue yt a plum, a cherry, and a figge, 463
CHESTS = 1
To lye like pawnes, lock'd vp in chests and truncks, 2395
CHEUALIERS = 1
Fran. Amen, Amen, mount Cheualiers to Armes. 594
CHID = 1
Art. Alas, I then haue chid away my friend, 1663

CHIEFE = 1
Both for my selfe, and them: but chiefe of all   1766
CHILD = 1
Queen. Come to thy grandame child.   460
CHILDE = 18
To dispossesse that childe which is not his.   139
Cons. Doe childe, goe to yt grandame childe,   461
Thy sinnes are visited in this poore childe,   481
All punish'd in the person of this childe,   492
In the releefe of this oppressed childe,   551
Or if it must stand still, let wiues with childe   1014
Law cannot giue my childe his kingdome heere;   1115
Because my poore childe is a prisoner.   1460
For since the birth of *Caine*, the first male-childe   1464
Fra. You are as fond of greefe, as of your childe.   1477
Con. Greefe fils the roome vp of my absent childe: 1478
And, pretty childe, sleepe doubtlesse, and secure,   1710
Before the childe himselfe felt he was sicke: 1806
And finde th'inheritance of this poore childe,   1815
Then to be butcher of an innocent childe.   1984
As thou shalt be, if thou didst kill this childe.   2127
Hold out this tempest. Beare away that childe,   2161
CHILDES = 1
The foule corruption of a sweet childes death.   1799
CHILDREN = 4
Of that I doubt, as all mens children may.   71
And leaue your children, wiues, and you in peace.   563
Make such vnconstant children of our selues   1174
That we, the sonnes and children of this Isle,   2276
CHOAKE = 1
Your tender kinsman, and to choake his dayes   1775
CHOSEN = 1
Keepe *Stephen Langton* chosen Archbishop | Of *Canterbury* from that
holy Sea: 1070
CHOYSE = 1
In briefe, a brauer choyse of dauntlesse spirits   366
CHRISTALL = 1
I, with these Christall beads heauen shall be brib'd   473
CHRISTENDOM = *1
Iohn. Though you, and all the Kings of Christendom   1089
CHRISTENDOME = 2
To doe offence and scathe in Christendome: 369
Onely for wantonnesse: by my Christendome,   1589
CHRISTIAN = 1
Where these two Christian Armies might combine   2288
CHURCH = 6
Why thou against the Church, our holy Mother,   1068
Therefore to Armes, be Champion of our Church,   1186
Or let the Church our mother breathe her curse,   1187
That is, to be the Champion of our Church,   1198
Is now in England ransacking the Church,   1557
That so stood out against the holy Church,   2324
CHURCH-YARD = 1
If this same were a Church-yard where we stand,   1339
CHURLISH = 2*1
The interruption of their churlish drums   370
*Though churlish thoughts themselues should bee your | Iudge,   836

CHURLISH *cont.*
Shall braying trumpets, and loud churlish drums   1236
CIRCLE = 2
    K.Iohn. Thus haue I yeelded vp into your hand | The Circle of my glory.   2167
    From out the circle of his Territories.   2390
CIRCUMFERENCE = 1
    Were harbour'd in their rude circumference: 568
CIRCUMSTANCE = 1
    Cuts off more circumstance, they are at hand, | *Drum beats.*   371
CIT = 3*1
CITIE = 5
    Craues harbourage within your Citie walles.   540
    Then tell vs, Shall your Citie call vs Lord,   569
    The flintie ribbes of this contemptuous Citie,   698
    Win you this Citie without stroke, or wound,   733
    In mortall furie halfe so peremptorie, | As we to keepe this Citie.   769
CITIES = 1
    Iohn. We from the West will send destruction | Into this Cities bosome.   723
CITIZEN see also Cit. = 1
    Trumpet sounds. | Enter a Citizen vpon the walles.   504
CITIZENS = 1
    Fra. Speake Citizens for England, whose your king.   676
CITTIE = 2
    To speake vnto this Cittie: what say you?   799
    (Except this Cittie now by vs besiedg'd)   805
CITTIES = 2
    Comfort your Citties eies, your winking gates: 521
    To saue vnscratch'd your Citties threatned cheekes: 531
CITTIZENS = 2
    Which trust accordingly kinde Cittizens,   537
    Fra. Now Cittizens of Angires ope your gates,   856
CIUILL = 2
    And like a ciuill warre setst oath to oath,   1195
    Hostilitie, and ciuill tumult reignes   1972
CLAIMD = 1
    Had of your father claim'd this sonne for his,   130
CLAIME = 9
    Arthur Plantaginet, laies most lawfull claime   14
    Doth he lay claime to thine inheritance?   80
    What doth moue you to claime your brothers land.   99
    My brother might not claime him, nor your father   134
    In right of *Arthur* doe I claime of thee: 453
    Fran. Stand in his face to contradict his claime.   587
    May then make all the claime that *Arthur* did.   1528
    After yong *Arthur,* claime this Land for mine,   2347
    And such as to my claime are liable,   2354
CLAMOR = 1
    An eccho with the clamor of thy drumme,   2424
CLAMORS = 1
    Clamors of hell, be measures to our pomp?   1237
CLAMOURS = 1
    Till their soule-fearing clamours haue braul'd downe   697
CLAP = 1
    To clap this royall bargaine vp of peace,   1166
CLAPD = 1
    Clap'd on the outward eye of fickle France,   904

CLAY = 2
Which was embounded in this beauteous clay,	2141
When this was now a King, and now is clay?	2679

CLEARELY = 1
In this which he accounts so clearely wonne:	1507

CLEARLY = 1
And woon'd our tott'ring colours clearly vp,	2531

CLEERES = 1
So foule a skie, cleeres not without a storme,	1826

CLERGY = 1
Bast. How I haue sped among the Clergy men,	1862

CLIMATE = 1
That swayes the earth this Climate ouer-lookes,	658

CLIPPETH = 1
That *Neptunes* Armes who clippeth thee about,	2285

CLOAKE = 2
We will not lyne his thin-bestained cloake	2022
Now happy he, whose cloake and center can	2160

CLOCKE = *1
Bast. Old Time the clocke setter, y bald sexton Time:	1257

CLOD = 1
And then all this thou seest, is but a clod, | And module of confounded royalty.	2667

CLODDY = 1
The meager cloddy earth to glittering gold:	1005

CLOSE = 1*1
Fra. It likes vs well young Princes: close your hands	853
Liues in his eye: that close aspect of his,	1790

CLOSED = 1
To our fast closed gates: for at this match,	762

CLOSELY = 1
Hub. Silence, no more; go closely in with mee,	1714

CLOSSET = 1
Oh, answer not; but to my Closset bring	1992

CLOUDS = 1
Against th'involnerable clouds of heauen,	558

CLOWTS = 1
Or madly thinke a babe of clowts were he;	1442

CLUTCH = 1
Not that I haue the power to clutch my hand,	910

COALE = 1
Your breath first kindled the dead coale of warres,	2336

COAT = 1
Ile smoake your skin-coat and I catch you right,	439

COCKRED-SILKEN = 1
A cockred-silken wanton braue our fields,	2239

COLBRAND = 1
Colbrand the Gyant, that same mighty man,	236

COLD = 6
The grapling vigor, and rough frowne of Warre | Is cold in amitie, and painted peace,	1029
Vpon my partie: thou cold blooded slaue,	1049
Dolph. I muse your Maiesty doth seeme so cold,	1250
Loe, by my troth, the Instrument is cold,	1682
And comfort me with cold. I do not aske you much,	2649
I begge cold comfort: and you are so straight	2650

COLDLY = 3
We coldly pause for thee, *Chatilion* speake,   347
Coldly embracing the discoloured earth,   616
The French fight coldly, and retyre themselues.   2453
COLE = 1
There is no malice in this burning cole,   1688
COLLECTED = 1
The summes I haue collected shall expresse: 1863
COLOUR = 1
Sal. The colour of the King doth come, and go   1794
COLOURS = 7
To spread his colours boy, in thy behalfe,   301
Our colours do returne in those same hands   630
And part your mingled colours once againe,   703
Mocking the ayre with colours idlely spred,   2241
And follow vnacquainted colours heere: 2283
Therefore thy threatning Colours now winde vp,   2326
And woon'd our tott'ring colours clearly vp,   2531
COMBAT = 1
Oh, what a noble combat hast fought   2294
COMBINE = 1
Where these two Christian Armies might combine   2288
COME = 42*2
Come from the Country to be iudg'd by you   52
Come Madam, and come *Richard*, we must speed   187
Bast. Brother adieu, good fortune come to thee,   189
Come Lady I will shew thee to my kinne,   286
At our importance hether is he come,   300
With him along is come the Mother Queene,   356
Queen. Come to thy grandame child.   460
And like a iolly troope of Huntsmen come   632
Ile stirre them to it: Come, away, away.   730
That heere come sacrifices for the field.   735
Heere is my Throne bid kings come bow to it.   996
This day all things begun, come to ill end,   1019
Vpon which better part, our prayrs come in,   1224
When gold and siluer becks me to come on.   1311
Ele. Come hether little kinsman, harke, a worde.   1317
Iohn. Come hether *Hubert*. O my gentle *Hubert*,   1318
Yet it shall come, for me to doe thee good.   1331
Come, grin on me, and I will thinke thou smil'st,   1417
And busse thee as thy wife: Miseries Loue, | O come to me.   1418
Yong Lad come forth; I haue to say with you.   1578
And if an Angell should haue come to me,   1645
Hub. Come forth: Do as I bid you do.   1648
Let him come backe, that his compassion may | Giue life to yours.   1665
Hub. Come (Boy) prepare your selfe.   1667
Sal. The colour of the King doth come, and go   1794
This murther had not come into my minde.   1948
That you shall thinke the diuell is come from hell.   2102
And grapple with him ere he come so nye.   2229
Come, come; for thou shalt thrust thy hand as deepe   2311
Himselfe to *Rome*, his spirit is come in,   2323
And come ye now to tell me *Iohn* hath made   2344
I come to learne how you haue dealt for him: 2375
Like *Amazons*, come tripping after drummes: 2409
I come one way of the *Plantagenets*.   2566

45

COME *cont.*

Bast. Come, come: sans complement, What newes | abroad?	2571
Hub. Why know you not? The Lords are all come | backe,	2590
I doubt he will be dead, or ere I come. *Exeunt*	2602
And none of you will bid the winter come	2644
Iohn. Oh Cozen, thou art come to set mine eye:	2661
Now, these her Princes are come home againe,	2726
Come the three corners of the world in Armes,	2727

COMES = 8

And then comes answer like an Absey booke:	206
But who comes in such haste in riding robes?	227
How comes it then that thou art call'd a King,	404
Fra. Heere comes the holy Legat of the Pope.	1062
Looke who comes heere? a graue vnto a soule,	1400
The tydings comes, that they are all arriu'd.	1833
Looke where the holy Legate comes apace,	2317
To sowsse annoyance that comes neere his Nest;	2404

COMFORT = 9*1

Comfort your Citties eies, your winking gates:	521
Pand. Courage and comfort, all shall yet goe well.	1386
Fra. Patience good Lady, comfort gentle *Constance.*	1405
I could giue better comfort then you doe.	1485
My widow-comfort, and my sorrowes cure. *Exit.*	1490
Being create for comfort, to be vs'd	1686
Mes. Be of good comfort: for the great supply	2449
Sal. Be of good comfort (Prince) for you are borne	2631
And comfort me with cold. I do not aske you much,	2649
I begge cold comfort: and you are so straight	2650

COMFORTLESSE = 1

Blacke, fearefull, comfortlesse, and horrible.	2577

COMMAND = 2*1

O sir, sayes answer, at your best command,	207
*Command the rest to stand, God and our right. *Exeunt*	607
Command thy sonne and daughter to ioyne hands.	852

COMMANDEMENT = 1

Haue I commandement on the pulse of life?	1810

COMMANDER = 1

Commander of this hot malicious day,	625

COMMANDING = 1

Subiected tribute to commanding loue,	277

COMMEND = 2

Commend these waters to those baby-eyes	2307
Commend me to one *Hubert*, with your King;	2501

COMMENT = 1

Forgiue the Comment that my passion made	1988

COMMENTS = 1

Doth by the idle Comments that it makes,	2608

COMMING = 1

And ere our comming see thou shake the bags	1305

COMMISSION = 1*1

K.Iohn. From whom hast thou this great commission | (*France*,	407
Vse our Commission in his vtmost force.	1309

COMMIT = 2

And will againe commit them to their bonds,	1459
Iohn. Let it be so: I do commit his youth	1785

COMMODITIE = 6

That smooth-fac'd Gentleman, tickling commoditie,	894

CONDUCT *cont.*
Vnder whose conduct came those powres of France,	1848
Away before: Conduct me to the king,	2601

CONFERENCE = *1
Lew. Women & fooles, breake off your conference.	450

CONFESSE = 3
Sir *Robert* could doe well, marrie to confesse	249
And though thou now confesse thou didst but iest	937
Awakes my Conscience to confesse all this.	2504

CONFIDENCE = 1
Shew boldnesse and aspiring confidence:	2224

CONFIDENT = 3
And confident from forreine purposes,	321
His forces strong, his Souldiers confident:	355
Lyons more confident, Mountaines and rockes	767

CONFIND = 1
Is, as a fiend, confin'd to tyrannize,	2656

CONFINE = 1
This kingdome, this Confine of blood, and breathe	1971

CONFINING = 1
With course disturb'd euen thy confining shores,	652

CONFIRM = 1
Then let confusion of one part confirm	673

CONFIRME = *1
Pem. Big. Our soules religiously confirme thy words.	2072

CONFIRMERS = 1
Be these sad signes confirmers of thy words?	945

CONFOUND = 1
They do confound their skill in couetousnesse,	1746

CONFOUNDED = 1
And then all this thou seest, is but a clod, | And module of confounded royalty.	2667

CONFRONTED = *1
*Strength matcht with strength, and power confronted | power,	641

CONFUSED = 1
Of sterne Iniustice, and confused wrong:	2274

CONFUSION = 2
Then let confusion of one part confirm	673
Meet in one line: and vast confusion waites	2157

CONGEALE = 1
Coole and congeale againe to what it was.	795

CONIOYNTLY = 1
Be friends a-while, and both conioyntly bend	693

CONIUNCTION = 1*1
Old Qu. Son, list to this coniunction, make this match	784
And the coniunction of our inward soules	1158

CONIURE = 1
I coniure thee but slowly: run more fast. *Exeunt.*	1994

CONQUERD = 1
And now it is halfe conquer'd, must I backe,	2348

CONQUEROR = 1
Lye at the proud foote of a Conqueror,	2724

CONQUERORS = 1
To enter Conquerors, and to proclaime	620

CONQUEST = 2
And better conquest neuer canst thou make,	1221
To out-looke Conquest, and to winne renowne	2368

CONS = 2
CONSCIENCE = 6
So much my conscience whispers in your eare,   48
And France, whose armour Conscience buckled on,   885
Betweene his purpose and his conscience,   1795
Made it no conscience to destroy a Prince.   1954
Betweene my conscience, and my Cosins death.   1973
Awakes my Conscience to confesse all this.   2504
CONSENT = 3
Yea, without stop, didst let thy heart consent,   1964
Bast. If thou didst but consent | To this most cruell Act: do but
dispaire,   2129
Hub. If I in act, consent, or sinne of thought,   2139
CONSEQUENTLY = 1
And consequently, thy rude hand to acte   1965
CONSIDERATION = 1
Startles, and frights consideration: 1742
CONSPIRE = 1
Iohn layes you plots: the times conspire with you,   1531
CONSPIRED = 1
Lady. Hast thou conspired with thy brother too,   254
CONST = 8*1
CONSTANCE *see also Con., Cons., Const.* = 11*1
How that ambitious *Constance* would not cease   38
*Enter before Angiers, Philip King of France, Lewis, Daul-| phin,
Austria, Constance, Arthur.*   292
Is not the Ladie *Constance* in this troope?   860
We make him Lord of. Call the Lady *Constance*,   874
Enter Constance, Arthur, and Salisbury.   921
*Enter King Iohn, France, Dolphin, Blanch, Elianor, Philip, | Austria,
Constance.*   998
Heare me, Oh, heare me. | *Aust.* Lady *Constance*, peace.   1037
Bla. The Lady *Constance* speakes not from her faith, | But from her
need.   1140
Enter Constance.   1399
Fra. Patience good Lady, comfort gentle *Constance*.   1405
My name is *Constance*, I was *Geffreyes* wife,   1430
The Lady *Constance* in a frenzie di'de   1841
CONSTANT = 1
Then arme thy constant and thy nobler parts   1222
CONSTRAINT = 2
Being no further enemy to you | Then the constraint of hospitable zeale,   549
I did suppose it should be on constraint,   2195
CONSUME = 1
Nay, after that, consume away in rust,   1642
CONSUMMATE = 1
To consummate this businesse happily.   2705
CONTAGIOUS = 1
But euen this night, whose blacke contagious breath   2494
CONTAINE = 1
This little abstract doth containe that large,   398
CONTAINING = 1
But for containing fire to harme mine eye: 1643
CONTEMND = 1
Should seeke a plaster by contemn'd reuolt,   2264
CONTEMPLATION = 1
With contemplation, and deuout desires.   2509

49

CONTEMPT = 1
Their proud contempt that beats his peace to heauen.   385
CONTEMPTUOUS = 1
The flintie ribbes of this contemptuous Citie,   698
CONTENT = 4
Brother of England, how may we content   867
Ar. I do beseech you Madam be content.   963
Con. If thou that bidst me be content, wert grim   964
I would not care, I then would be content,   969
CONTINUANCE = 1
In their continuance, will not feele themselues.   2620
CONTINUE = 1
To doe your pleasure, and continue friends.   1183
CONTRADICT = 1
Fran. Stand in his face to contradict his claime.   587
CONTRARIE = 1
I haue a Kings oath to the contrarie.   931
CONTRARY = 1
Had falsely thrust vpon contrary feete,   1923
CONTROLE = *1
Chat. The proud controle of fierce and bloudy warre,   22
CONTROLEMENT = 2
Controlement for controlement: so answer *France.*   25
CONTROLL = 1
To be a secondary at controll,   2333
CONTROLLING = 1
Two such controlling bounds shall you be, kings,   759
CONTROUERSIE = 1
Essex. My Liege, here is the strangest controuersie   51
CONUERSANT = 1
Nor conuersant with Ease, and Idlenesse,   2069
CONUERSION = 1
For your conuersion, now your traueller,   199
CONUERTITE = 1
But since you are a gentle conuertite,   2186
CONUICTED = 1
A whole Armado of conuicted saile   1384
COOLE = 3
Coole and congeale againe to what it was.   795
This Act so euilly borne shall coole the hearts   1534
The whilst his Iron did on the Anuile coole,   1919
COOLES = 1
And falshood, falshood cures, as fire cooles fire   1208
COOPES = 1
And coopes from other lands her Ilanders,   318
COPIE = 1
The Copie of your speede is learn'd by them: 1831
COPPIED = 1
Dol. My Lord *Melloone*, let this be coppied out,   2252
CORD = 1
And if thou want'st a Cord, the smallest thred   2131
CORDELION = 3
A Souldier by the Honor-giuing-hand | Of *Cordelion*, Knighted in the field.   61
Or the reputed sonne of *Cordelion*,   144
Lady. King Richard Cordelion was thy father,   266

CORDELIONS = 2
   Elen. He hath a tricke of *Cordelions* face,   93
   Arth. God shall forgiue you *Cordelions* death   305
CORNER = 1
   Euen till that vtmost corner of the West   322
CORNERS = 1
   Come the three corners of the world in Armes,   2727
CORRECT = 1
   Whiles we Gods wrathfull agent doe correct   384
CORRONATION = 1
   Ioh. Some reasons of this double Corronation   1757
CORRUPTED = 2
   She is corrupted, chang'd, and wonne from thee,   976
   Purchase corrupted pardon of a man,   1093
CORRUPTIBLY = 1
   Is touch'd, corruptibly: and his pure braine   2606
CORRUPTION = 1
   The foule corruption of a sweet childes death.   1799
COSEN = 7
   Iohn. Cosen, goe draw our puisance together,   1272
   So strongly guarded: Cosen, looke not sad,   1300
   Iohn. Cosen away for *England,* haste before,   1304
   Ele. Farewell gentle Cosen. | *Iohn.* Coz, farewell.   1315
   Iohn. For *England* Cosen, goe.   1377
   Iohn. Beare with me Cosen, for I was amaz'd   1858
   For I must vse thee. O my gentle Cosen,   1880
COSINS = 1
   Betweene my conscience, and my Cosins death.   1973
COUCH = 1
   Arise forth from the couch of lasting night,   1410
COUER = 1
   Is yet the couer of a fayrer minde,   1983
COUETOUSNESSE = 1
   They do confound their skill in couetousnesse,   1746
COULD *l.*249 250 279 1165 1372 1397 1398 1434 1456 1485 1836 2041
   2043 = 14
COULDST *l.*1347 2284 = 2
COUNCELL = *1
   *We breath'd our Councell: but it pleas'd your Highnes 1753
COUNFOUND = *1
   *Counfound themselues. 'Tis strange y death shold sing: 2626
COUNSELL = 3
   How like you this wilde counsell mighty States,   709
   Con. No, I defie all Counsell, all redresse,   1406
   But that which ends all counsell, true Redresse: 1407
COUNT = 3*1
   Against the Pope, and count his friends my foes.   1098
   Sal. The Count *Meloone,* a Noble Lord of France,   2012
   Pem. It is the Count *Meloone.* | *Sal.* Wounded to death. 2469
   **Mes.* The Count *Meloone* is slaine: The English Lords 2536
COUNTERFEIT = 1
   Const. You haue beguil'd me with a counterfeit   1024
COUNTER-CHECKE = 1
   Haue brought a counter-checke before your gates,   530
COUNTIES = 1
   Our discontented Counties doe reuolt: 2175

COUNTRIES = 1
My picked man of Countries: my deare sir,   203
COUNTRY = 2
Come from the Country to be iudg'd by you   52
Bast. Our Country manners giue our betters way.   164
COUNTS = 2
There is a soule counts thee her Creditor,   1320
Counts it your weale: he haue his liberty.   1783
COUPLED = 2
With slaughter coupled to the name of kings.   663
Married in league, coupled, and link'd together   1159
COURAGE = 3
For courage mounteth with occasion,   377
Pand. Courage and comfort, all shall yet goe well.   1386
Bast. Away then with good courage: yet I know   2247
COURSE = 9
Full fourteene weekes before the course of time: 121
With course disturb'd euen thy confining shores,   652
From all direction, purpose, course, intent.   901
Stayes in his course, and playes the Alchymist,   1003
The yearely course that brings this day about,   1006
That takes away by any secret course | Thy hatefull life.   1105
It makes the course of thoughts to fetch about,   1741
Leauing our ranknesse and irregular course,   2515
Nor let my kingdomes Riuers take their course   2646
COURT = 2
What brings you heere to Court so hastily?   231
When I shall meet him in the Court of heauen   1472
COW = 1
This Calfe, bred from his Cow from all the world: 132
COWARD = 1*1
Then ere the coward hand of *France* can win; | Submit thee boy.   458
*That bloudy spoyle: thou slaue, thou wretch, y coward,   1041
COYLE = 1
I am not worth this coyle that's made for me.   467
COYNE = 1
Full thirty thousand Markes of English coyne: 850
COZ = 1
Ele. Farewell gentle Cosen. | *Iohn.* Coz, farewell.   1315
COZEN = 1
Iohn. Oh Cozen, thou art come to set mine eye: 2661
CRACKD = 1
The tackle of my heart, is crack'd and burnt,   2662
CRACKE = 1
Or lay on that shall make your shoulders cracke.   446
CRACKER = *1
Aust. What cracker is this same that deafes our eares   447
CRAFTIE = 1
Nay, you may thinke my loue was craftie loue,   1629
CRAUES = 1
Craues harbourage within your Citie walles.   540
CREATE = 2
For wee'l create yong *Arthur* Duke of Britaine   872
Being create for comfort, to be vs'd   1686
CREATURE = 1
There was not such a gracious creature borne: 1466

CREATURES = 1
Creatures of note for mercy, lacking vses.   1700
CREDITOR = 1
There is a soule counts thee her Creditor,   1320
CREEPE = 1
But thou shalt haue: and creepe time nere so slow, 1330
CREST = 6
There stucke no plume in any English Crest,   628
The heighth, the Crest: or Crest vnto the Crest   2045
Doth dogged warre bristle his angry crest,   2154
Already smoakes about the burning Crest   2495
CRIDE = 1
I tore them from their bonds, and cride aloud,   1455
CRIES = 2
A widdow cries, be husband to me (heauens)   1033
Cries out vpon the name of *Salisbury*.   2270
CRIMSON = 1
Not painted with the Crimson spots of blood,   1978
CRIPPLE = 1
And cripple thee vnto a Pagan shore,   2287
CROOKED = 1
Lame, foolish, crooked, swart, prodigious,   967
CROST = 1
Lest that their hopes prodigiously be crost: 1016
CROW = 1
Euen at the crying of your Nations crow,   2398
CROWCH = 1
To crowch in litter of your stable plankes,   2394
CROWND = 2*1
Iohn. Heere once againe we sit: once against crown'd 1718
Was once superfluous: you were Crown'd before,   1721
Sal. To this effect, before you were new crown'd 1752
CROWNE = 9*1
Vpon the maiden vertue of the Crowne: 395
Which owe the crowne, that thou ore-masterest?   406
Iohn. Doth not the Crowne of England, prooue the | King? 579
Thy now vnsur'd assurance to the Crowne,   787
Finde liable to our Crowne and Dignitie,   806
Become thy great birth, nor deserue a Crowne.   971
Your Highnes should deliuer vp your Crowne.   1873
I shall yeeld vp my Crowne, let him be hang'd   1878
My Crowne I should giue off? euen so I haue: 2194
To winne this easie match, plaid for a Crowne?   2359
CRUELL = 2
Bast. If thou didst but consent | To this most cruell Act: do but
dispaire,   2129
For I do see the cruell pangs of death   2520
CRUMBLE = 1
That all my bowels crumble vp to dust: 2638
CRY = 4*1
It ill beseemes this presence to cry ayme | To these ill-tuned repetitions: 499
Cry hauocke kings, backe to the stained field   671
Good Father Cardinall, cry thou Amen   1109
Con. No, no, I will not, hauing breath to cry: 1421
Bast. Indeede your drums being beaten, wil cry out; 2422
CRYER = 1
Aust. Peace. | *Bast*. Heare the Cryer.   432

CRYING = 1
Euen at the crying of your Nations crow,   2398
CUDGELD = 1
Our eares are cudgel'd, not a word of his   780
CUDGELL = 1
To cudgell you, and make you take the hatch,   2392
CULL = 2
To cull the plots of best aduantages: 333
Then in a moment Fortune shall cull forth   705
CULLD = 1
And cull'd these fiery spirits from the world   2367
CUNNING = 2
And call it cunning. Do, and if you will,   1630
Sal. Trust not those cunning waters of his eyes,   2110
CURE = 3
Will giue her sadnesse very little cure: 866
My widow-comfort, and my sorrowes cure. *Exit.*   1490
Sal. Indeed we fear'd his sicknesse was past cure.   1804
CURES = 1
And falshood, falshood cures, as fire cooles fire   1208
CURING = 1
Pand. Before the curing of a strong disease,   1497
CURRANT = 1
Say, shall the currant of our right rome on,   649
CURRENTS = 1
O two such siluer currents when they ioyne   756
CURSE = 12*1
To curse the faire proceedings of this day: 1022
Dreading the curse that money may buy out,   1091
Con. O lawfull let it be | That I haue roome with *Rome* to curse a
while,   1107
There is no tongue hath power to curse him right.   1111
Pan. There's Law and Warrant (Lady) for my curse.   1112
How can the Law forbid my tongue to curse?   1118
Pand. Philip of *France*, on perill of a curse,   1119
Is purchase of a heauy curse from *Rome*,   1134
Bla. That's the curse of *Rome*.   1137
Or let the Church our mother breathe her curse,   1187
A mothers curse, on her reuolting sonne: 1188
Pand. I will denounce a curse vpon his head.   1252
Iohn. It is the curse of Kings, to be attended   1933
CURSES = 2
To my keene curses; for without my wrong   1110
The perill of our curses light on thee   1226
CURST = 2
Thou shalt stand curst, and excommunicate,   1100
If thou stand excommunicate, and curst?   1154
CUSTOMED = 1
No common winde, no customed euent,   1540
CUT = 3
Cut off the sequence of posterity,   393
Or *Hubert*, if you will cut out my tongue,   1679
Pem. Cut him to peeces.   2094
CUTS = 2
Cuts off more circumstance, they are at hand, | *Drum beats.*   371
Cuts off his tale, and talkes of *Arthurs* death.   1927

54

CUTTING = 1
By cutting off your heads: Thus hath he sworne,   2477
CYGNET *see* symet
DAD = 1
Since I first cal'd my brothers father Dad.   783
DAIES = 2
Weare out the daies in Peace; but ere Sun-set,   1035
Dol. All daies of glory, ioy, and happinesse.   1502
DAMME = 1
As raine to water, or deuill to his damme;   425
DAMNATION = 1
Witnesse against vs to damnation.   1943
DAMND = 4
(If thou didst this deed of death) art y damn'd *Hubert.*   2121
Thou'rt damn'd as blacke, nay nothing is so blacke,   2124
Thou art more deepe damn'd then Prince Lucifer: 2125
By some damn'd hand was rob'd, and tane away.   2209
DAMNED = 2
Bast. It is a damned, and a bloody worke,   2056
We will vntread the steps of damned flight,   2513
DANCING = 1
Vpon the dancing banners of the French,   618
DANGER = 4*1
Much danger do I vndergo for thee. *Exeunt*   1715
Apt, liable to be employ'd in danger,   1951
Nor tempt the danger of my true defence;   2084
Euen in the iawes of danger, and of death: 2369
Dol. Strike vp our drummes, to finde this danger out.   2435
DANGEROUS = 2
To breake into this dangerous argument.   1771
Of dangerous Maiesty, when perchance it frownes   1938
DANGEROUSLY = 1
Do prophesie vpon it dangerously: 1911
DANGERS = 1
Among the thornes, and dangers of this world.   2146
DARE = 1
Hub. Not for my life: But yet I dare defend   2088
DARES = 2
Who dares not stirre by day, must walke by night,   181
Who liues and dares but say, thou didst not well   284
DARKELY = 1
When I spake darkely, what I purposed: 1957
DARST = 1*1
Aus. Thou dar'st not say so villaine for thy life.   1058
Big. Out dunghill: dar'st thou braue a Nobleman?   2087
DASHD = 1
And when that we haue dash'd them to the ground,   719
DATE = 1
My date of life out, for his sweete liues losse.   2109
DAUGHTER = 2*1
Hub. That daughter there of Spaine, the Lady *Blanch*   738
Command thy sonne and daughter to ioyne hands.   852
Fran. 'Tis true (faire daughter) and this blessed day,   1000
DAUL = 1
DAULPHIN *see also* Daul., Dol., Dolphin = 1*1
Enter before Angiers, Philip King of France, Lewis, Daul-|phin,
Austria, Constance, Arthur.   292

DAULPHIN cont.
I doe pray to thee, thou vertuous *Daulphin,*   1244
DAUNTLESSE = 2
   In briefe, a brauer choyse of dauntlesse spirits   366
   The dauntlesse spirit of resolution.   2221
DAY = 42*2
   Now blessed be the houre by night or day   174
   Who dares not stirre by day, must walke by night,   181
   Who by the hand of France, this day hath made   612
   Commander of this hot malicious day,   625
   To whom in fauour she shall giue the day,   707
   But they will quake and tremble all this day.   939
   Fran. 'Tis true (faire daughter) and this blessed day,   1000
   To solemnize this day the glorious sunne   1002
   The yearely course that brings this day about,   1006
   Shall neuer see it, but a holy day.   1007
   Const. A wicked day, and not a holy day.   1008
   What hath this day deseru'd? what hath it done,   1009
   Nay, rather turne this day out of the weeke,   1012
   This day of shame, oppression, periury.   1013
   Pray that their burthens may not fall this day,   1015
   But (on this day) let Sea-men feare no wracke,   1017
   No bargaines breake that are not this day made;   1018
   This day all things begun, come to ill end,   1019
   To curse the faire proceedings of this day: 1022
   Let not the howres of this vngodly day   1034
   Daul. Father, to Armes. | *Blanch.* Vpon thy wedding day?   1232
   Bla. The Sun's orecast with bloud: faire day adieu,   1259
   * Bast. Now by my life, this day grows wondrous hot,   1285
   The Sunne is in the heauen, and the proud day,   1333
   Then, in despight of brooded watchfull day,   1351
   What haue you lost by losing of this day?   1501
   No scope of Nature, no distemper'd day,   1539
   I should be as merry as the day is long: 1591
   Ar. Are you sicke Hubert? you looke pale to day,   1601
   That ere the next Ascension day at noone,   1872
   And on that day at noone, whereon he sayes   1877
   * Bast. Once more to day well met, distemper'd Lords,   2019
   On this Ascension day, remember well,   2189
   Iohn. Is this Ascension day? did not the Prophet   2192
   Say, that before Ascension day at noone,   2193
   A bare-rib'd death, whose office is this day   2433
   Iohn. How goes the day with vs? oh tell me *Hubert.*   2440
   In spight of spight, alone vpholds the day.   2464
   For if the French be Lords of this loud day,   2475
   I say againe, if *Lewis* do win the day,   2491
   Behold another day breake in the East: 2493
   If *Lewis,* by your assistance win the day.   2500
   The day shall not be vp so soone as I,   2547
DAYES = 3
   Your tender kinsman, and to choake his dayes   1775
   Three dayes before: but this from Rumors tongue   1842
   Two long dayes iourney (Lords) or ere we meete.   2017
DAYLY = 1
   That dayly breake-vow, he that winnes of all,   890
DAY-WEARIED = 1
   Of the old, feeble, and day-wearied Sunne,   2496

DEAD = 14*4

Whose valour plucks dead Lyons by the beard;	438
Or adde a royall number to the dead:	661
Oh now doth death line his dead chaps with steele,	666
He will awake my mercie, which lies dead:	1599
*Art. No, in good sooth: the fire is dead with griefe,	1685
Your Vnckle must not know but you are dead.	1708
The suite which you demand is gone, and dead.	1802
My discontented Peeres. What? Mother dead?	1846
Iohn. My mother dead?	1904
To wish him dead, but thou hadst none to kill him.	1931
Ile strike thee dead. Put vp thy sword betime,	2100
From forth this morcell of dead Royaltie?	2148
*Bast. They found him dead, and cast into the streets,	2207
Your breath first kindled the dead coale of warres,	2336
I doubt he will be dead, or ere I come. Exeunt	2602
Ioh. Poyson'd, ill fare: dead, forsooke, cast off,	2643
*Sal. You breath these dead newes in as dead an eare	2675

DEADLY = 1

And proue a deadly blood-shed, but a iest,	2054

DEAFE = 1

The sea enraged is not halfe so deafe,	766

DEAFES = *1

*Aust. What cracker is this same that deafes our eares	447

DEALE = 1

We cannot deale but with the very hand	2273

DEALT = 1

I come to learne how you haue dealt for him:	2375

DEARE = 1

My picked man of Countries: my deare sir,	203

DEATH = 33*3

His lands to me, and tooke it on his death	118
Madam, Ile follow you vnto the death.	162
Arth. God shall forgiue you Cordelions death	305
Oh now doth death line his dead chaps with steele,	666
The others peace: till then, blowes, blood, and death.	674
At your industrious Scenes and acts of death.	690
More free from motion, no not death himselfe	768
Bast. Heeres a stay, | That shakes the rotten carkasse of old death	771
*That spits forth death, and mountaines, rockes, and seas,	774
Which onely liues but by the death of faith,	1143
That faith would liue againe by death of need:	1145
Though that my death were adiunct to my Act, | By heauen I would doe it.	1356
Iohn. Death. | Hub. My Lord.	1367
Death, death, O amiable, louely death,	1408
The foule corruption of a sweet childes death.	1799
Pem. Indeed we heard how neere his death he was,	1805
No certaine life atchieu'd by others death:	1823
Yong Arthurs death is common in their mouths,	1912
Cuts off his tale, and talkes of Arthurs death.	1927
Why vrgest thou so oft yong Arthurs death?	1929
I faintly broke with thee of Arthurs death:	1952
Betweene my conscience, and my Cosins death.	1973
*P. Oh death, made proud with pure & princely beuty,	2034
Sal. Oh he is bold, and blushes not at death,	2076
(If thou didst this deed of death) art y damn'd Hubert.	2121

DEATH _cont._
Euen in the iawes of danger, and of death: 2369
A bare-rib'd death, whose office is this day 2433
Pem. It is the Count _Meloone._ | _Sal._ Wounded to death. 2469
Mel. Haue I not hideous death within my view, 2483
For I do see the cruell pangs of death 2520
Death hauing praide vpon the outward parts 2621
*Counfound themselues. 'Tis strange y death shold sing: 2626
Who chaunts a dolefull hymne to his owne death, 2628
The life and death of King Iohn. 2730
DEATH-BED = 1
Vpon his death-bed he by will bequeath'd 117
DECAY = 2
And sullen presage of your owne decay: 33
The iminent decay of wrested pompe. 2159
DECEASD = 1
He tels vs _Arthur_ is deceas'd to night. 1803
DECEASED = 1
Of thy deceased brother, _Geffreyes_ sonne, 13
DECEAST = 1
With them a Bastard of the Kings deceast, 359
DECEIT = 1
Yet to auoid deceit I meane to learne; 225
DECEITE = 1
Since I must loose the vse of all deceite? 2488
DECEIUE = 2
Which though I will not practice to deceiue, 224
What in the world should make me now deceiue, 2487
DEED = 4
Exec. I hope your warrant will beare out the deed. 1576
Pem. This is the man should do the bloody deed: 1787
The deed, which both our tongues held vilde to name. 1966
(If thou didst this deed of death) art y damn'd _Hubert._ 2121
DEEDE = 4
No in deede is't not: and I would to heauen 1596
Exec. I am best pleas'd to be from such a deede. 1662
Quoted, and sign'd to do a deede of shame, 1947
The earth had not a hole to hide this deede. 2035
DEEDS = 3
Your sharpest Deeds of malice on this Towne. 694
How oft the sight of meanes to do ill deeds, 1944
Make deeds ill done? Had'st not thou beene by, 1945
DEEPE = 3*1
*Deepe shame had struck me dumbe, made me break off, 1960
Thou art more deepe damn'd then Prince Lucifer: 2125
Come, come; for thou shalt thrust thy hand as deepe 2311
And mocke the deepe mouth'd Thunder: for at hand 2429
DEEPE-SWORNE = 1
Was deepe-sworne faith, peace, amity, true loue 1162
DEERE = 8
Yet sell your face for fiue pence and 'tis deere: 161
That art the issue of my deere offence 270
And out of my deere loue Ile giue thee more, 457
But thou art faire, and at thy birth (deere boy) 972
As deere be to thee, as thy father was. 1302
Arthur tane prisoner? diuers deere friends slaine? 1389
Of your deere Mother-England: blush for shame: 2407

DEERE *cont.*

Euen on that Altar, where we swore to you | Deere Amity, and
euerlasting loue. 2480

DEERELY = 1

Liues in this bosome, deerely cherished. 1323

DEEREST = 1

The blood and deerest valued bloud of *France.* 1276

DEFENCE = 6

Which was so strongly vrg'd past my defence. 271
We must awake indeuor for defence, 376
Nor tempt the danger of my true defence; 2084
They saw we had a purpose of defence. 2245
Where honourable rescue, and defence 2269
Our selues well sinew'd to our defence. 2698

DEFEND = 1 *1

*That for thine owne gaine shouldst defend mine honor? 255
Hub. Not for my life: But yet I dare defend 2088

DEFIANCE = *1

Chat. Then take my Kings defiance from my mouth, 26

DEFIE = 3

Iohn. My life as soone: I doe defie thee *France,* 455
Why then defie each other, and pell-mell, 720
Con. No, I defie all Counsell, all redresse, 1406

DEGENERATE = 1

And you degenerate, you ingrate Reuolts, 2405

DELIGHT = 1

Neuer to be infected with delight, 2068

DELIUER = 3

But from the inward motion to deliuer 222
Your Highnes should deliuer vp your Crowne. 1873
Deliuer him to safety, and returne, 1879

DELIUERD = 1

How I may be deliuer'd of these woes. 1439

DEMAND = 4

Doe in his name religiously demand 1067
Pope *Innocent,* I doe demand of thee. 1073
The suite which you demand is gone, and dead. 1802
Why may not I demand of thine affaires, | As well as thou of mine? 2557

DEMANDS = 1

England impatient of your iust demands, 350

DEN = 2

Good den Sir *Richard,* Godamercy fellow, 195
At your den sirrah, with your Lionnesse, 598

DENIE = 1

Lady. Hast thou denied thy selfe a *Faulconbridge?* | *Bast.* As faithfully
as I denie the deuill. 264

DENIED = 1

Lady. Hast thou denied thy selfe a *Faulconbridge?* | *Bast.* As faithfully
as I denie the deuill. 264

DENIES = 1

Fra. A greater powre then We denies all this, 682

DENNE = 1

What, shall they seeke the Lion in his denne, 2225

DENOUNCE = 1

Pand. I will denounce a curse vpon his head. 1252

DENOUNCING = 1

Plainly denouncing vengeance vpon *Iohn.* 1544

DENY = 3
Deny their office: onely you do lacke   1698
With barbarous ignorance, and deny his youth   1776
And so ingratefull, you deny me that.   2651
DEPART = 1
K.Iohn. Beare mine to him, and so depart in peace,   28
DEPARTED = 1
Hath willingly departed with a part,   884
DEPARTURE = 1
On their departure, most of all shew euill: 1500
DEPEND = 1
Beene sworne my Souldier, bidding me depend   1051
DEPENDING = 1
Then, whereupon our weale on you depending,   1782
DEPOSD = 1
Be by some certaine king, purg'd and depos'd.   686
DEPUTIE = 1
Iohn. In Vs, that are our owne great Deputie,   679
DEPUTIES = 1
Pan. Haile you annointed deputies of heauen;   1063
DESERUD = 1
What hath this day deseru'd? what hath it done,   1009
DESERUE = 1
Become thy great birth, nor deserue a Crowne.   971
DESIRE = *1
K.Iohn. Goe, *Faulconbridge*, now hast thou thy desire,   185
DESIRES = 2
Desires your Maiestie to leaue the field,   2446
With contemplation, and deuout desires.   2509
DESIRING = 1
Desiring thee to lay aside the sword   17
DESOLATION = 1
Euen till vnfenced desolation | Leaue them as naked as the vulgar ayre: 700
DESPAIRE *see also* dispaire = 1
But in despaire, dye vnder their blacke weight.   1228
DESPERATE = 1
As doth the furie of two desperate men,   953
DESPIGHT = 1
Then, in despight of brooded watchfull day,   1351
DESTINY = 1
Thinke you I beare the Sheeres of destiny?   1809
DESTROY = 1
Made it no conscience to destroy a Prince.   1954
DESTRUCTION = 2
Iohn. We from the West will send destruction | Into this Cities bosome.   723
To push destruction, and perpetuall shame   2687
DETERMIND = 1
Hath drawne him from his owne determin'd ayd,   905
DETERMINE = 1
King *Lewis*, determine what we shall doe strait.   449
DETESTABLE = 1
And I will kisse thy detestable bones,   1412
DEUICE = 1
And not alone in habit and deuice,   220
DEUILL *see also* diuel, diuell = 7
Lady. Hast thou denied thy selfe a *Faulconbridge*? | *Bast.* As faithfully
as I denie the deuill.   264

DEUILL *cont.*
As raine to water, or deuill to his damme;	425
Aust. What the deuill art thou?	434
Bast. One that wil play the deuill sir with you,	435
Con. Looke to that Deuill, lest that *France* repent,	1124
Con. O *Lewis,* stand fast, the deuill tempts thee heere	1138
Some ayery Deuill houers in the skie,	1286

DEUISE = 2
Thou canst not (Cardinall) deuise a name	1076
Out of your grace, deuise, ordaine, impose	1181

DEUOURED = 2
These Lincolne-Washes haue deuoured them,	2599
Deuoured by the vnexpected flood.	2674

DEUOUT = 1
With contemplation, and deuout desires.	2509

DEW = 1
Before the dew of euening fall, shall fleete	592

DEWE = 1
Let me wipe off this honourable dewe,	2296

DIALOGUE = 1
Sauing in Dialogue of Complement,	211

DID *l.*88 104 112 125 126 136 368 441 442 631 855 1168 1240 1337 1465 1528 1529 1616 1620 1633 1703 1751 1907 1919 *1932 1940 1999 2192 2195 2210 2211 *2460 2541 2543 2544 2585 2672 2723 2725 = 38*2

DIDE = 3
Dide in the dying slaughter of their foes,	634
Mes. My Liege, her eare | Is stopt with dust: the first of Aprill di'de	1838
The Lady *Constance* in a frenzie di'de	1841

DIDST = 10
Who liues and dares but say, thou didst not well	284
And though thou now confesse thou didst but iest	937
Iohn. Thou idle Dreamer, wherefore didst thou so?	1874
But, thou didst vnderstand me by my signes,	1962
And didst in signes againe parley with sinne,	1963
Yea, without stop, didst let thy heart consent;	1964
(If thou didst this deed of death) art y damn'd *Hubert.*	2121
As thou shalt be, if thou didst kill this childe.	2127
Bast. If thou didst but consent | To this most cruell Act: do but dispaire,	2129
Bast. Who didst thou leaue to tend his Maiesty?	2589

DIE *see also* dye = 1
Arth. O this will make my mother die with griefe.	1303

DIED = 1
Which died in *Geffrey*: and the hand of time,	399

DIES = 1*2
*Bla. There where my fortune liues, there my life dies.	1271
Euen at that newes he dies: and then the hearts	1549
*Heauen take my soule, and England keep my bones. *Dies*	2006

DIFFERENCE = 2
Dolph. Bethinke you father, for the difference	1133
The fearefull difference of incensed kings:	1169

DIFFERENCES = 1
In vndetermin'd differences of kings.	669

DIFFERENT = 1
The different plague of each calamitie.	1444

DIFFIDENCE = 1
And wound her honor with this diffidence.	73

DIGNITIE = 1
Finde liable to our Crowne and Dignitie,   806
DIM = 1
As dim and meager as an Agues fitte,   1470
DIRECT = 1
Yet indirection thereby growes direct,   1207
DIRECTION = 2
From all direction, purpose, course, intent.   901
To your direction: *Hubert*, what newes with you?   1786
DIRECTLY = 1
Out of the path which shall directly lead   1514
DISALLOW = 1
K.Iohn. What followes if we disallow of this?   21
DISCARDED = 1
And welcome home againe discarded faith,   2473
DISCIPLINE = 3
Call for our cheefest men of discipline,   332
Though all these English, and their discipline   567
Bast. O prudent discipline! From North to South: 728
DISCLAIMD = 1
I haue disclaim'd Sir *Robert* and my land,   260
DISCOLOURED = 1
Coldly embracing the discoloured earth,   616
DISCONTENT = 2
What may be wrought out of their discontent,   1564
Doth moue the murmuring lips of discontent   1770
DISCONTENTED = 2
My discontented Peeres. What? Mother dead?   1846
Our discontented Counties doe reuolt: 2175
DISCONTENTS = 1
Now Powers from home, and discontents at home   2156
DISCORD = 1
Set armed discord 'twixt these periur'd Kings,   1036
DISCREDITE = 1
Discredite more in hiding of the fault,   1750
DISEASE = 1
Pand. Before the curing of a strong disease,   1497
DISFIGURED = 1
Of plaine old forme, is much disfigured,   1739
DISGUISD = 2
Art. O now you looke like *Hubert*. All this while | You were disguis'd.   1705
This Ship-boyes semblance hath disguis'd me quite.   2000
DISHABITED = 1
Had bin dishabited, and wide hauocke made   526
DISIOYND *see* dis-ioynd
DISIOYNE *see* dis-ioyne
DISIOYNING = 1
And by disioyning hands hell lose a soule.   1125
DISMEMBER = 1
They whurle a-sunder, and dismember mee.   1263
DISMISSE = 1
And he hath promis'd to dismisse the Powers | Led by the Dolphin.   2232
DISORDER = 1
When there is such disorder in my witte: 1487
DISPAIRE = 1
Bast. If thou didst but consent | To this most cruell Act: do but
dispaire,   2129

DISPATCH = 1
Therefore I will be sodaine, and dispatch.   1600
DISPATCHD = 2
Rob. And once dispatch'd him in an Embassie   107
For many carriages hee hath dispatch'd   2700
DISPITIOUS = 1
Turning dispitious torture out of doore?   1607
DISPLAY = 1
That did display them when we first marcht forth: 631
DISPLAYED = 1
Who are at hand triumphantly displayed   619
DISPLEASURE = 1
To meet displeasure farther from the dores,   2228
DISPOSD = 1
So hot a speed, with such aduice dispos'd,   1393
DISPOSE = 1
Needs must you lay your heart at his dispose,   276
DISPOSING = 1
To the disposing of the Cardinall,   2702
DISPOSSESSE = 2
To dispossesse that childe which is not his.   139
Phil. Of no more force to dispossesse me sir,   140
DISPOSSEST = 1
Sal. The king hath dispossest himselfe of vs,   2021
DISROBE = 1
That did disrobe the Lion of that robe.   442
DISSEUER = 1
That done, disseuer your vnited strengths,   702
DISTEMPERD = 1*1
No scope of Nature, no distemper'd day,   1539
Bast. Once more to day well met, distemper'd Lords,   2019
DISTRUST = 1
Let not the world see feare and sad distrust   2214
DISTURBD = 1
With course disturb'd euen thy confining shores,   652
DIS-IOYND = 1
Is scattered and dis-ioyn'd from fellowship.   1385
DIS-IOYNE = 1
Fra. I may dis-ioyne my hand, but not my faith.   1193
DIUE = 1
To diue like Buckets in concealed Welles,   2393
DIUEL = 1
With that same purpose-changer, that slye diuel,   888
DIUELL = 3
Bast. Thou wer't better gaul the diuell Salsbury.   2097
That you shall thinke the diuell is come from hell.   2102
Sal. That misbegotten diuell *Falconbridge,*   2463
DIUERS = 1
Arthur tane prisoner? diuers deere friends slaine?   1389
DIUIDED = 1
And she a faire diuided excellence,   754
DIUINELY = 1
Is most diuinely vow'd vpon the right   543
DO *l.*630 675 683 692 757 761 776 812 817 835 841 963 1113 *1123 1454
    1604 1605 1630 1635 1637 1648 1660 1692 1697 1698 1715 *1745 1746
    1781 1785 1787 1791 1792 1793 *1808 1832 1854 1911 1944 1947 1999

DO *cont.*
2002 2042 2043 2050 2091 2099 2103 2122 2130 2138 2423 *2436 2491
2510 2511 2520 2641 2649 2680 2681 2697 2715 2720 2729 = 62*4
DOE *l.*95 182 249 250 274 311 369 384 449 453 455 461 474 846 847 930
1067 1073 1084 1097 1122 1150 1183 1201 1244 1251 1331 1357 1358
1449 1485 2175 2212 2244 2376 = 35
DOES *l.*469 = 1
DOEST *l.*2555 = 1
DOFF = 1
Thou weare a Lyons hide, doff it for shame,   1054
DOGGE = 1
And, like a dogge that is compell'd to fight,   1695
DOGGED = 2
Ile fill these dogged Spies with false reports: 1709
Doth dogged warre bristle his angry crest,   2154
DOGGES = 1
As maids of thirteene do of puppi-dogges.   776
DOING = 2
And being not done, where doing tends to ill,   1203
The truth is then most done not doing it: 1204
DOL = 13*8
DOLEFULL = 1
Who chaunts a dolefull hymne to his owne death,   2628
DOLPH = 4
DOLPHIN *see also Dolph.* = 15*4
Of *Lewes* the Dolphin, and that louely maid.   740
Is the yong Dolphin euery way compleat,   748
Iohn. If that the Dolphin there thy Princely sonne,   800
Iohn. Speake then Prince Dolphin, can you loue this | Ladie?   843
*Enter King Iohn, France, Dolphin, Blanch, Elianor, Philip, | Austria,
Constance.*   998
Enter France, Dolphin, Pandulpho, Attendants.   1382
That thou for truth giu'st out are landed heere? | *Mes.* Vnder the
Dolphin.   1849
Big. Away, toward *Burie*, to the Dolphin there.   2117
Like a kinde Host, the Dolphin and his powers.   2200
And he hath promis'd to dismisse the Powers | Led by the Dolphin.   2232
*Enter (in Armes) Dolphin, Salisbury, Meloone, Pem-| broke, Bigot,
Souldiers.*   2250
And Noble Dolphin, albeit we sweare   2260
Pand. The *Dolphin* is too wilfull opposite   2378
Bast. And thou shalt finde it (Dolphin) do not doubt | *Exeunt.*   2436
That was expected by the Dolphin heere,   2450
Enter Dolphin, and his Traine.   2524
Mes. Where is my Prince, the Dolphin? | *Dol.* Heere: what newes? 2534
Bast. The Dolphin is preparing hither-ward,   2669
Who halfe an houre since came from the Dolphin,   2693
DOLPHINE = 2
Anon becomes a Mountaine. O noble Dolphine,   1562
The Dolphine rages at our verie heeles.   2690
DOLPHINES = 1
Whose priuate with me of the Dolphines loue,   2013
DOMINATIONS = 1
Call not me slanderer, thou and thine vsurpe | The Dominations,
Royalties, and rights   477

DOMINIONS = 1
Shall tythe or toll in our dominions: 1081
DONE *l.*394 485 702 959 960 1009 1202 1203 1204 1734 1792 1945 2036
2568 2699 = 15
DOOMD = 1
Big. Or when he doom'd this Beautie to a graue,   2038
DOOME = 1
Alter not the doome fore-thought by heauen.   1245
DOORE = 2
Turning dispitious torture out of doore?   1607
Out of the weake doore of our fainting Land: 2688
DOORES = 2
Enter the two Kings with their powers, | at seuerall doores.   646
It would not out at windowes, nor at doores,   2636
DORE = 1*1
*And ere since sit's on's horsebacke at mine Hostesse dore   596
That hand which had the strength, euen at your dore,   2391
DORES = 1
To meet displeasure farther from the dores,   2228
DOST *l.**72 415 417 927 940 941 1040 1044 1053 1060 1069 1192 1217
1218 1363 2147 2291 = 16*1
DOTH *l.*80 99 197 218 275 398 405 523 *579 617 624 666 823 953 1101
1210 1250 1362 1395 1696 1748 1756 1770 1794 1818 1915 1985 2037
2075 2154 2158 2164 2293 2297 2370 2383 2388 2608 *2611 2616
= 38*2
DOUBLE = 3
Hub. Why answer not the double Maiesties,   796
Sal. Therefore, to be possess'd with double pompe,   1726
Ioh. Some reasons of this double Corronation   1757
DOUBT = 6*1
Of that I doubt, as all mens children may.   71
Aust. Doe so king *Philip*, hang no more in doubt.   1150
And so I would be heere, but that I doubt   1592
To all our sorrowes, and ere long I doubt. *Exeunt*   1820
Or turn'd an eye of doubt vpon my face;   1958
**Bast.* And thou shalt finde it (Dolphin) do not doubt | *Exeunt.*   2436
I doubt he will be dead, or ere I come. *Exeunt*   2602
DOUBTFULL = 1
The little number of your doubtfull friends.   2204
DOUBTLESSE = 1
And, pretty childe, sleepe doubtlesse, and secure,   1710
DOUBTS = 1
Con. I who doubts that, a Will: a wicked will,   496
DOUER = 1
But Douer Castle: London hath receiu'd   2199
DOWNE = 20
Kneele thou downe *Philip*, but rise more great,   170
That holds in chase mine honour vp and downe.   234
Fran. Excuse it is to beat vsurping downe.   416
Wilt thou resigne them, and lay downe thy Armes?   454
Before we will lay downe our iust-borne Armes,   659
Wee'l put thee downe, 'gainst whom these Armes wee | (beare,   660
Till their soule-fearing clamours haue braul'd downe   697
To tread downe faire respect of Soueraigntie,   979
O then tread downe my need, and faith mounts vp,   1146

65

DOWNE *cont.*

Keepe my need vp, and faith is trodden downe.	1147
And pour's downe mischiefe. *Austrias* head lye there,	1287
Which else runnes tickling vp and downe the veines,	1343
Lies in his bed, walkes vp and downe with me,	1479
Poure downe thy weather: how goes all in France?	1827
Ar. The Wall is high, and yet will I leape downe.	1997
If I get downe, and do not breake my limbes,	2002
Goe I to make the *French* lay downe their Armes. *Exit.*	2191
And wilde amazement hurries vp and downe	2203
That hauing our faire order written downe,	2255
He flatly saies, hee'll not lay downe his Armes.	2380

DOWNE-TRODEN = 1

For this downe-troden equity, we tread	547

DOWRIE = 2

Giue with our Neece a dowrie large enough,	785
Her Dowrie shall weigh equall with a Queene:	802

DOZEN = 1

Offending Charity: If but a dozen French	1558

DRAGON = 1

Bast. Saint *George* that swindg'd the Dragon,	595

DRAGONS = 1

With Ladies faces, and fierce Dragons spleenes,	362

DRAW = 4

Shall draw this breefe into as huge a volume:	400
To draw my answer from thy Articles?	408
Iohn. Cosen, goe draw our puisance together,	1272
That I must draw this mettle from my side	2267

DRAWES = 1*1

It drawes toward supper in conclusion so.	214
*Drawes those heauen-mouing pearles fro(m) his poor eies,	471

DRAWING = 1

Till this aduantage, this vile drawing byas,	898

DRAWNE = 5*1

Drawne in the flattering table of her eie. | *Whispers with Blanch.*	819
Bast. Drawne in the flattering table of her eie,	821
*That hang'd, and drawne, and quarter'd there should be	825
Hath drawne him from his owne determin'd ayd,	905
That such an Army could be drawne in France, | And she not heare of it?	1836
I am a scribled forme drawne with a pen	2639

DREADFULL = 5

In dreadfull triall of our kingdomes King.	593
Like Heralds 'twixt two dreadfull battailes set:	1796
Iohn. With-hold thy speed, dreadfull Occasion:	1844
With dreadfull pompe of stout inuasion.	1895
The dreadfull motion of a murderous thought,	1980

DREADING = 1

Dreading the curse that money may buy out,	1091

DREAMER = 1

Iohn. Thou idle Dreamer, wherefore didst thou so?	1874

DREAMES = 1

Possest with rumors, full of idle dreames,	1866

DREW = 1

Before I drew this gallant head of warre,	2366

DRIFT = 1
   Fran. Our Thunder from the South, | Shall raine their drift of bullets on
this Towne.   726
DRINKE = *1
   *Approaching neere these eyes, would drinke my teares,   1639
DRIUE = 1*1
   Bast. Bell, Booke, & Candle, shall not driue me back,   1310
   Nay heare me *Hubert,* driue these men away,   1655
DROOPE = 1
   But wherefore doe you droope? why looke you sad?   2212
DROP = 5
   And then we shall repent each drop of bloud,   341
   Fra. England thou hast not sau'd one drop of blood   655
   Where but by chance a siluer drop hath falne,   1447
   Euen to that drop ten thousand wiery fiends   1448
   I must be breefe, least resolution drop   1608
DROPS = 1
   But this effusion of such manly drops,   2300
DROSSE = 1
   And by the merit of vilde gold, drosse, dust,   1092
DROWNE = 1
   To hang thee on. Or wouldst thou drowne thy selfe,   2134
DROWSIE = 1
   Vexing the dull eare of a drowsie man;   1494
DROWZIE = 1
   Sound on into the drowzie race of night: 1338
DRUM = 1
   Cuts off more circumstance, they are at hand, | *Drum beats.*   371
DRUMME = 2
   An eccho with the clamor of thy drumme,   2424
   And euen at hand, a drumme is readie brac'd,   2425
DRUMMES = 2*1
   Like *Amazons,* come tripping after drummes: 2409
   Strike vp the drummes, and let the tongue of warre   2420
   Dol. Strike vp our drummes, to finde this danger out.   2435
DRUMS = 2*1
   The interruption of their churlish drums   370
   Shall braying trumpets, and loud churlish drums   1236
   Bast. Indeede your drums being beaten, wil cry out;   2422
DRUNKE = 1
   Ioh. Oh where hath our Intelligence bin drunke?   1834
DUBD = 1
   What, I am dub'd, I haue it on my shoulder: 258
DUETIE = 1
   With al true duetie: On toward *Callice,* hoa. | *Exeunt.*   1379
DUKE = 4
   By this braue Duke came early to his graue: 298
   Welcome before the gates *Angiers* Duke.   310
   And let yong *Arthur* Duke of Britaine in,   611
   For wee'l create yong *Arthur* Duke of Britaine   872
DULL = 1
   Vexing the dull eare of a drowsie man;   1494
DUMBE = *1
   *Deepe shame had struck me dumbe, made me break off,   1960
DUNGHILL = *1
   Big. Out dunghill: dar'st thou braue a Nobleman?   2087

DURST = 1
That in mine eare I durst not sticke a rose,   150
DUST = 6
And by the merit of vilde gold, drosse, dust,   1092
And stop this gap of breath with fulsome dust,   1415
Shall blow each dust, each straw, each little rub   1513
A graine, a dust, a gnat, a wandering haire,   1671
Mes. My Liege, her eare | Is stopt with dust: the first of Aprill di'de   1838
That all my bowels crumble vp to dust: 2638
DUTIE = 1
To pay that dutie which you truly owe,   553
DWARFISH = 1
To whip this dwarfish warre, this Pigmy Armes   2389
DWELLING = 1
(Which some suppose the soules fraile dwelling house)   2607
DYE = 8
Rescue those breathing liues to dye in beds,   734
Teach thou this sorrow, how to make me dye,   951
Which in the very meeting fall, and dye.   954
But in despaire, dye vnder their blacke weight.   1228
And so hee'll dye: and rising so againe,   1471
As good to dye, and go; as dye, and stay.   2004
That I must dye heere, and liue hence, by Truth?   2490
DYING = 1
Dide in the dying slaughter of their foes,   634
EACH = 8
And then we shall repent each drop of bloud,   341
Why then defie each other, and pell-mell,   720
Austria and France shoot in each others mouth.   729
I am with both, each Army hath a hand,   1261
The different plague of each calamitie.   1444
Shall blow each dust, each straw, each little rub   1513
EAGLE = 1
And like an Eagle, o're his ayerie towres,   2403
EARE = 8*1
So much my conscience whispers in your eare,   48
That in mine eare I durst not sticke a rose,   150
As Gods owne souldier, rounded in the eare,   887
Vexing the dull eare of a drowsie man;   1494
Mes. My Liege, her eare | Is stopt with dust: the first of Aprill di'de   1838
And whisper one another in the eare.   1914
(As lowd as thine) rattle the Welkins eare,   2428
Should scape the true acquaintance of mine eare.   2570
Sal. You breath these dead newes in as dead an eare   2675
EARES = 4*1
Aust. What cracker is this same that deafes our eares   447
To make a faithlesse errour in your eares,   536
Our eares are cudgel'd, not a word of his   780
Heare me without thine eares, and make reply   1348
Without eyes, eares, and harmefull sound of words: 1350
EARLE = 1
And Earle of Richmond, and this rich faire Towne   873
EARLY = 1
By this braue Duke came early to his graue: 298
EARTH = 9*1
Some sinnes doe beare their priuiledge on earth,   274
Qu. Thou monstrous slanderer of heauen and earth.   475

EARTH *cont.*

Con. Thou monstrous Iniurer of heauen and earth,	476
Coldly embracing the discoloured earth,	616
That swayes the earth this Climate ouer-lookes,	658
That no supporter but the huge firme earth	994
The meager cloddy earth to glittering gold:	1005
Ioh. Oh, when the last accompt twixt heauen & earth	1941
The earth had not a hole to hide this deede.	2035
As it on earth hath bene thy seruant still.	2683

EARTHIE = 1

Iohn. What earthie name to Interrogatories	1074

EARTH-QUAKE = 1

Doth make an earth-quake of Nobility:	2293

EASE = 2

I can with ease translate it to my will:	830
Nor conuersant with Ease, and Idlenesse,	2069

EASIE = 3

This might haue beene preuented, and made whole | With very easie arguments of loue,	41
How easie dost thou take all *England* vp,	2147
To winne this easie match, plaid for a Crowne?	2359

EASIER = 1

Or the light losse of *England,* for a friend: | Forgoe the easier.	1135

EASILY = 1

May easily winne a womans: aye my mother,	282

EASLIE = 1

I will enforce it easlie to my loue.	832

EAST = 2

By East and West let France and England mount.	695
Behold another day breake in the East:	2493

EAT = 2

Sir *Robert* might haue eat his part in me	247
But now will Canker-sorrow eat my bud,	1467

ECCHO = 1

An eccho with the clamor of thy drumme,	2424

EDMONDSBURY = 2

Sal. Lords, I will meet him at S.(aint) *Edmondsbury,*	2008
Vpon the Altar at S.(aint) *Edmondsbury,*	2479

EDUCATION = 1

In titles, honors, and promotions, | As she in beautie, education, blood,	808

EELE = 1

My armes, such eele skins stuft, my face so thin,	149

EFFECT = 2

Ar. Too fairely *Hubert,* for so foule effect,	1611
Sal. To this effect, before you were new crown'd	1752

EFFUSION = 1

But this effusion of such manly drops,	2300

EHAR = *1

EIE = 4

Dol. I do my Lord, and in her eie I find	812
Drawne in the flattering table of her eie. | *Whispers with Blanch.*	819
Bast. Drawne in the flattering table of her eie,	821
Why holdes thine eie that lamentable rhewme,	943

EIES = 2*1

Be thou as lightning in the eies of *France*;	29
*Drawes those heauen-mouing pearles fro(m) his poor eies,	471
Comfort your Citties eies, your winking gates:	521

EITHER = 1
  This must be answer'd either heere, or hence.   1807
ELBOW = 2
  Thus leaning on mine elbow I begin,   204
  Iohn. I marrie, now my soule hath elbow roome,   2635
ELDER = 3
  K.Iohn. Is that the elder, and art thou the heyre?   65
  That *Geffrey* was thy elder brother borne,   401
  Sonne to the elder brother of this man,   545
ELDEST = 3
  Borne in *Northamptonshire*, and eldest sonne | As I suppose, to *Robert*
  Faulconbridge,   59
  Philip, good old Sir *Roberts* wiues eldest sonne.   167
  Of this oppressed boy; this is thy eldest sonnes sonne,   479
ELE = 5
ELEA = 2*1
ELEANOR = *1
  **Alarums*, excursions, Retreat. Enter Iohn, Eleanor, Arthur | Bastard,*
  Hubert, Lords.   1297
ELEN = 1
ELI = 1*2
ELIANOR = *1
  **Enter King Iohn, France, Dolphin, Blanch, Elianor, Philip, | Austria,*
  Constance.   998
ELINOR see also Ele., Elea., Elen. = *1
  **Enter King Iohn, Queene Elinor, Pembroke, Essex, and Sa-| lisbury,*
  with the Chattylion of France.   2
ELINOR = *2
ELSE = 8
  Or else it must go wrong with you and me,   47
  In at the window, or else ore the hatch: 180
  Twice fifteene thousand hearts of Englands breed. | *Bast.* Bastards and
  else.   582
  Else what a mockerie should it be to sweare?   1216
  Which else runnes tickling vp and downe the veines,   1343
  In vndeserued extreames: See else your selfe,   1687
  Bast. 'Tis true, to hurt his master, no mans else.   2032
  That vnder-goe this charge? Who else but I,   2353
EMBASSIE = 4
  K.Iohn. Silence (good mother) heare the Embassie.   11
  The farthest limit of my Embassie.   27
  Rob. And once dispatch'd him in an Embassie   107
  Con. Stay for an answer to your Embassie,   337
EMBATTAILED = 1
  That were embattailed, and rank'd in Kent.   1925
EMBOUNDED = 1
  Which was embounded in this beauteous clay,   2141
EMBRACE = 2
  Embrace him, loue him, giue him welcome hether.   304
  It is our safetie, and we must embrace   2009
EMBRACING = 1
  Coldly embracing the discoloured earth,   616
EMPEROR = 2
  To *Germany*, there with the Emperor   108
  My innocent life against an Emperor.   2089
EMPLOY *see* imploy

EMPLOYD = 2
Your tale must be how he employ'd my mother.   106
Apt, liable to be employ'd in danger,   1951
EMPLOYMENT = 1
At your employment, at your seruice sir: 208
EMPTY = 1
An empty Casket, where the Iewell of life   2208
ENCOUNTER = 1
And let beleefe, and life encounter so,   952
END = 2*1
This day all things begun, come to ill end,   1019
But on my Liege, for very little paines | Will bring this labor to an
happy end. *Exit.*   1295
Dol. There end thy braue, and turn thy face in peace,   2413
ENDAMAGEMENT = 1
Haue hither march'd to your endamagement.   515
ENDEERED = 1
And thou, to be endeered to a King,   1953
ENDEUOR *see* indeuor
ENDING = 1
Fore-tell the ending of mortality.   2609
ENDLES = *1
Hub. Vnkinde remembrance: thou, & endles night,   2567
ENDS = 2
But that which ends all counsell, true Redresse: 1407
Out of the bloody fingers ends of *Iohn.*   1553
ENEMIES = 5
You came in Armes to spill mine enemies bloud,   1027
That the times enemies may not haue this   1778
O, let me haue no subiect enemies,   1893
Hub. Arme you against your other enemies: 1974
Her Enemies rankes? I must withdraw, and weepe   2280
ENEMY = 3
Being no further enemy to you | Then the constraint of hospitable zeale,   549
Pand. So mak'st thou faith an enemy to faith,   1194
Your Nobles will not heare you, but are gone | To offer seruice to your
enemy: 2201
ENFLAMD = 1
To stop their marches 'fore we are enflam'd: 2174
ENFORCE *see also* inforce = 2
With swifter spleene then powder can enforce   763
I will enforce it easlie to my loue.   832
ENFORCED *see* inforced
ENFRANCHISEMENT *see* infranchisement
ENG = *1
ENGLAND see also Eng. = 38*6
The borrowed Maiesty of *England* heere.   9
Euen till that *England* hedg'd in with the maine,   319
My Lord *Chattilion* may from *England* bring   339
What *England* saies, say breefely gentle Lord,   346
England impatient of your iust demands,   350
*Enter K.(ing) of England, Bastard, Queene, Blanch, Pembroke, | and
others.*   379
Fran. Peace be to *England,* if that warre returne   386
From *France* to *England,* there to liue in peace: 387
England we loue, and for that *Englands* sake,   388
But thou from louing *England* art so farre,   391

ENGLAND cont.

And this his sonne, *England* was *Geffreys* right,	402
England and *Ireland, Angiers, Toraine, Maine,*	452
Cit. Who is it that hath warn'd vs to the walles? | *Fra.* 'Tis France, for	
England.	506
Iohn. England for it selfe: | You men of Angiers, and my louing	
subiects.	508
*Iohn. Doth not the Crowne of England, prooue the | King?	579
Fra. England thou hast not sau'd one drop of blood	655
Fra. Speake Citizens for England, whose your king.	676
* Hub. The king of England, when we know the king.	677
By East and West let France and England mount.	695
Is neere to England, looke vpon the yeeres	739
* Fra. Speake England first, that hath bin forward first	798
Brother of England, how may we content	867
France friend with *England*, what becomes of me?	956
Tell him this tale, and from the mouth of *England,*	1079
Fra. Brother of *England*, you blaspheme in this.	1088
Or the light losse of *England*, for a friend: | Forgoe the easier.	1135
* Fra. Thou shalt not need. *England*, I will fall fro(m) thee.	1253
Iohn. Cosen away for *England*, haste before,	1304
Iohn. For *England* Cosen, goe.	1377
And bloudy *England* into *England* gone,	1390
Fra. Well could I beare that *England* had this praise,	1397
Con. To *England*, if you will.	1452
Is now in England ransacking the Church,	1557
For England go; I will whet on the King.	1566
Mes. From France to England, neuer such a powre | For any forraigne	
preparation,	1828
**Heauen take my soule, and England keep my bones. *Dies*	2006
How easie dost thou take all *England* vp,	2147
Is fled to heauen: and *England* now is left	2150
Of your deere Mother-England: blush for shame:	2407
Mel. Lead me to the Reuolts of England heere.	2467
Bast. A Friend. What art thou? | *Hub.* Of the part of England.	2553
This England neuer did, nor neuer shall	2723
If England to it selfe, do rest but true. *Exeunt.*	2729

ENGLANDS = 5*2

England we loue, and for that *Englands* sake,	388
*Cit. In breefe, we are the King of Englands subiects	573
Twice fifteene thousand hearts of Englands breed. | *Bast.* Bastards and	
else.	582
Arthur of Britaine, Englands King, and yours.	621
King *Iohn,* your king and Englands, doth approach,	624
Saue what is opposite to *Englands* loue.	1185
*Thy foote to Englands Throne. And therefore marke:	1515

ENGLISH see also E.Har. = 12*1

And to rebuke the vsurpation | Of thy vnnaturall Vncle, English *Iohn,*	302
Then now the *English* bottomes haue waft o're,	367
Though all these English, and their discipline	567
Much worke for teares in many an English mother,	613
Enter English Herald with Trumpet.	622
There stucke no plume in any English Crest,	628
Our lustie English, all with purpled hands,	633
Full thirty thousand Markes of English coyne:	850
To traine ten thousand English to their side;	1560
The youth saies well. Now heare our *English* King,	2382

ENGLISH cont.
Mel. Fly Noble English, you are bought and sold,	2471
When English measure backward their owne ground	2527
*Mes. The Count *Meloone* is slaine: The English Lords	2536

ENGLISHMAN = 2
Thinking this voyce an armed Englishman.	2399
(For that my Grandsire was an Englishman)	2503

ENIOY = 1
And like thy brother to enioy thy land:	143

ENIOYES = 1
And King ore him, and all that he enioyes:	546

ENKINDLED = 2
With eyes as red as new enkindled fire,	1884
With that same weake winde, which enkindled it:	2340

ENOUGH = 4
Giue with our Neece a dowrie large enough,	785
Iohn. Enough. | I could be merry now, *Hubert,* I loue thee.	1371
Enough to stifle such a villaine vp.	2137
Let hell want paines enough to torture me:	2142

ENQUIRE *see* inquire

ENRAGD = 1
That neuer saw the giant-world enrag'd,	2308

ENRAGED = 1
The sea enraged is not halfe so deafe,	766

ENSUE = 1
We had a kinde of light, what would ensue:	2060

ENSUES = 1
Or ouerthrow incureable ensues.	2183

ENTER = 39*7
*Enter King Iohn, Queene Elinor, Pembroke, Essex, and Sa-|lisbury, with the Chattylion of France.	2
Enter a Sheriffe.	50
Enter Robert Faulconbridge, and Philip.	57
Enter Lady Faulconbridge and Iames Gurney.	232
*Enter before Angiers, Philip King of France, Lewis, Daul-|phin, Austria, Constance, Arthur.	292
Enter Chattilion.	343
*Enter K.(ing) of England, Bastard, Queene, Blanch, Pembroke, | and others.	379
Trumpet sounds. | Enter a Citizen vpon the walles.	504
Heere after excursions, Enter the Herald of France | with Trumpets to the gates.	608
To enter Conquerors, and to proclaime	620
Enter English Herald with Trumpet.	622
Enter the two Kings with their powers, | at seuerall doores.	646
Enter Constance, Arthur, and Salisbury.	921
*Enter King Iohn, France, Dolphin, Blanch, Elianor, Philip, | Austria, Constance.	998
Enter Pandulph.	1061
*Allarums, Excursions: Enter Bastard with Austria's | head.	1283
Enter Iohn, Arthur, Hubert.	1288
*Alarums, excursions, Retreat. Enter Iohn, Eleanor, Arthur | Bastard, Hubert, Lords.	1297
Enter France, Dolphin, Pandulpho, Attendants.	1382
Enter Constance.	1399
Enter Hubert and Executioners.	1570
Enter Arthur.	1579

ENTER *cont.*
   Enter Iohn, Pembroke, Salisbury, and other Lordes.   1717
   Enter Hubert.   1784
   Io. They burn in indignation: I repent: *Enter Mes.*   1821
   Enter Bastard and Peter of Pomfret.   1851
   Enter Hubert.   1905
   Enter Arthur on the walles.   1996
   Enter Pembroke, Salisbury, & Bigot.   2007
   Enter Bastard.   2018
   Enter Hubert.   2073
   Enter King Iohn and Pandolph, attendants.   2166
   Enter Bastard.   2197
   *Enter (in Armes) Dolphin, Salisbury, Meloone, Pem-| broke, Bigot, Souldiers.   2250
   Enter Pandulpho.   2315
   Enter Bastard.   2371
   Alarums. Enter Iohn and Hubert.   2439
   Enter a Messenger.   2444
   Enter Salisbury, Pembroke, and Bigot.   2459
   Enter Meloon wounded.   2466
   Enter Dolphin, and his Traine.   2524
   Enter a Messenger.   2533
   Enter Bastard and Hubert, seuerally.   2550
   Enter Prince Henry, Salisburie, and Bigot.   2604
   Enter Pembroke.   2610
   Enter Bastard.   2658
ENTERPRIZE = 1
   Yea, thrust this enterprize into my heart,   2343
ENTERTAINE = 1
   The mis-plac'd-*Iohn* should entertaine an houre,   1518
ENTRANCE = 2
   Our iust and lineall entrance to our owne;   382
   And giue you entrance: but without this match,   765
ENTREAT *see* intreat
ENTREATIES *see* intreaties
ENTRED = 1
   Within this bosome, neuer entred yet   1979
ENVENOM – 1
   Envenom him with words, or get thee gone,   984
ENUIE = 1
   But now I enuie at their libertie,   1458
EQUALITY = 1
   Of both your Armies, whose equality   638
EQUALL = 2
   You equall Potents, fierie kindled spirits,   672
   Her Dowrie shall weigh equall with a Queene: 802
EQUITY = 1
   For this downe-troden equity, we tread   547
ERE = 17*1
   For ere thou canst report, I will be there: 30
   That ere I heard: shall I produce the men? | *K.Iohn.* Let them approach: 53
   And I am I, how ere I was begot.   184
   And so ere answer knowes what question would,   210
   Then ere the coward hand of *France* can win; | Submit thee boy.   458
   *And ere since sit's on's horsebacke at mine Hostesse dore   596
   Weare out the daies in Peace; but ere Sun-set,   1035
   To ashes, ere our blood shall quench that fire: 1278

ERE *cont.*

And ere our comming see thou shake the bags	1305
To all our sorrowes, and ere long I doubt. *Exeunt*	1820
That ere the next Ascension day at noone,	1872
Two long dayes iourney (Lords) or ere we meete.	2017
That leaues the print of blood where ere it walkes.	2024
Bast. What ere you thinke, good words I thinke | were best.	2026
Yet I am none. Whose tongue so ere speakes false,	2092
And grapple with him ere he come so nye.	2229
He is forsworne, if ere those eyes of yours	2492
I doubt he will be dead, or ere I come. *Exeunt*	2602

ERRAND = 1

To thee King *Iohn* my holy errand is:	1064

ERROUR = 1

To make a faithlesse errour in your eares,	536

ESCAPD = 1

My selfe, well mounted, hardly haue escap'd.	2600

ESCAPE *see* scape

ESPIE = 1

And quarter'd in her heart, hee doth espie	823

ESSEX = *1

Enter King Iohn, Queene Elinor, Pembroke, Essex, and Sa-|lisbury, with the Chattylion of France.	2

ESSEX = 1

ESTATE = 1

How wildely then walkes my Estate in France?	1847

ETERNALL = 1

Holding th'eternall spirit against her will,	1401

EUEN = 33

Euen till that *England* hedg'd in with the maine,	319
Euen till that vtmost corner of the West	322
One must proue greatest. While they weigh so euen,	644
With course disturb'd euen thy confining shores,	652
Euen till vnfenced desolation | Leaue them as naked as the vulgar ayre:	700
And lay this Angiers euen with the ground,	713
Made to run euen, vpon euen ground;	897
And euen before this truce, but new before,	1164
Is husband in my mouth? euen for that name	1239
Euen to that drop ten thousand wiery fiends	1448
Euen in the instant of repaire and health,	1498
For euen the breath of what I meane to speake,	1512
Euen at that newes he dies: and then the hearts	1549
Euen in the matter of mine innocence:	1641
Euen with the fierce lookes of these bloody men.	1650
Euen at my gates, with rankes of forraigne powres;	1969
My Crowne I should giue off? euen so I haue:	2194
And euen there, methinkes an Angell spake,	2316
Euen in the iawes of danger, and of death:	2369
That hand which had the strength, euen at your dore,	2391
Euen at the crying of your Nations crow,	2398
And euen at hand, a drumme is readie brac'd,	2425
This newes was brought to *Richard* but euen now,	2452
Euen on that Altar, where we swore to you | Deere Amity, and euerlasting loue.	2480
Which bleeds away, euen as a forme of waxe	2485
But euen this night, whose blacke contagious breath	2494
Euen this ill night, your breathing shall expire,	2497

EUEN *cont.*

Euen with a treacherous fine of all your liues:	2499
Euen to our Ocean, to our great King *Iohn.*	2518
Pem. He is more patient | Then when you left him; euen now he sung.	2617
Hen. Euen so must I run on, and euen so stop.	2677

EUENING = 1

Before the dew of euening fall, shall fleete	592

EUENT = 1

No common winde, no customed euent,	1540

EUER *see also* ere = 12

Ele. What now my sonne, haue I not euer said	37
And haue is haue, how euer men doe catch:	182
Con. My bed was euer to thy sonne as true	421
Euer in *France* shall be kept festiuall:	1001
Thou euer strong vpon the stronger side;	1043
Who-euer wins, on that side shall I lose:	1268
(If euer I remember to be holy)	1313
What euer torment you do put me too.	1660
That euer wall-ey'd wrath, or staring rage	2048
That euer Spider twisted from her wombe	2132
Bast. By all the bloud that euer fury breath'd,	2381
Mes. Who euer spoke it, it is true my Lord.	2545

EUERLASTING = 2

That to their euerlasting residence,	591
Euen on that Altar, where we swore to you | Deere Amity, and euerlasting loue.	2480

EUERLASTINGLY = 1

I do bequeath my faithfull seruices | And true subiection euerlastingly.	2715

EUERMORE = 1

To rest without a spot for euermore.	2718

EUERY = 3

I would giue it euery foot to haue this face:	154
Is the yong Dolphin euery way compleat,	748
Since all, and euery part of what we would	1755

EUILL = 2

On their departure, most of all shew euill:	1500
To acquaint you with this euill, that you might	2582

EUILLY = 1

This Act so euilly borne shall coole the hearts	1534

EUILS = 1

The fit is strongest: Euils that take leaue	1499

EX = *1

P. There tel the king, he may inquire vs out. *Ex. Lords.*	2118

EXAMINED = 1

K.Iohn. Mine eye hath well examined his parts,	97

EXAMPLE = 2

Doth want example: who hath read, or heard	1395
Grow great by your example, and put on	2220

EXAMPLED = 1

Exampled by this heynous spectacle.	2055

EXCELLENCE = 2

And she a faire diuided excellence,	754
And breathing to his breathlesse Excellence	2065

EXCEPT = 2

Phil. I know not why, except to get the land:	81
(Except this Cittie now by vs besiedg'd)	805

EXCESSE = 1
Is wastefull, and ridiculous excesse.   1733
EXCLAMATION = 1
That we shall stop her exclamation,   879
EXCOMMUNICATE = 2
Thou shalt stand curst, and excommunicate,   1100
If thou stand excommunicate, and curst?   1154
EXCURSIONS = 1*2
Heere after excursions, Enter the Herald of France | with Trumpets to
the gates.   608
*Allarums, Excursions: Enter Bastard with Austria's | head.   1283
*Alarums, excursions, Retreat. Enter Iohn, Eleanor, Arthur | Bastard,
Hubert, Lords.   1297
EXCUSD = 1
Pem. All murthers past, do stand excus'd in this: 2050
EXCUSE = 2
Fran. Excuse it is to beat vsurping downe.   416
Doth make the fault the worse by th'excuse: 1748
EXCUSING = 1
And oftentimes excusing of a fault,   1747
EXEC = 2
EXECUTIONER see Exec.
EXECUTIONERS = 1
Enter Hubert and Executioners.   1570
EXERCISE = 1
The rich aduantage of good exercise,   1777
EXEUNT = 16*1
For thou wast got i'th way of honesty. | *Exeunt all but bastard.*   190
Who sayes it was, he lyes, I say twas not. | *Exeunt.*   289
*Command the rest to stand, God and our right. *Exeunt*   607
To this vnlook'd for vnprepared pompe. *Exeunt.*   881
Iohn. No more then he that threats. To Arms let's hie. | *Exeunt.*   1280
With al true duetie: On toward *Callice,* hoa. | *Exeunt.*   1379
If you say I, the King will not say no. *Exeunt.*   1568
Much danger do I vndergo for thee. *Exeunt*   1715
To all our sorrowes, and ere long I doubt. *Exeunt*   1820
I coniure thee but slowly: run more fast. *Exeunt.*   1994
Our Partie may well meet a prowder foe. *Exeunt.*   2248
Bast. And thou shalt finde it (Dolphin) do not doubt | *Exeunt.*   2436
Weaknesse possesseth me, and I am faint. *Exeunt.*   2457
And happie newnesse, that intends old right. *Exeunt*   2522
To try the faire aduenture of to morrow. *Exeunt*   2548
I doubt he will be dead, or ere I come. *Exeunt*   2602
If England to it selfe, do rest but true. *Exeunt.*   2729
EXHALATION = 1
No naturall exhalation in the skie,   1538
*EXIT see also Ex. = 7*2*
Pembroke looke too't: farewell *Chattillion.* | *Exit Chat. and Pem.*   35
There's toyes abroad, anon Ile tell thee more. | *Exit Iames.*   244
Gaine be my Lord, for I will worship thee. *Exit.*   919
But on my Liege, for very little paines | Will bring this labor to an
happy end. *Exit.*   1295
My widow-comfort, and my sorrowes cure. *Exit.*   1490
Fra. I feare some out-rage, and Ile follow her. *Exit.*   1491
Bast. The spirit of the time shall teach me speed. *Exit*   1898
And heauen it selfe doth frowne vpon the Land. *Exit.*   2164
Goe I to make the *French* lay downe their Armes. *Exit.*   2191

EXPECTATION = 1
Fresh expectation troubled not the Land	1724

EXPECTED = 1
That was expected by the Dolphin heere,	2450

EXPEDIENT = 3
His marches are expedient to this towne,	354
Who painefully with much expedient march	529
The angry Lords, with all expedient hast,	1993

EXPEDITION = 1
Kin. How much vnlook'd for, is this expedition.	374

EXPEDITIONS = 1
This expeditions charge: what men are you?	56

EXPIRE = 1
Euen this ill night, your breathing shall expire,	2497

EXPRESSE = 2
The summes I haue collected shall expresse:	1863
As bid me tell my tale in expresse words:	1959

EXTENDS = 1
That mercie, which fierce fire, and Iron extends,	1699

EXTERIOR = 1
Exterior forme, outward accoutrement;	221

EXTERIORLY = 1
Which howsoeuer rude exteriorly,	1982

EXTERNALL = 1
Who hauing no externall thing to loose,	892

EXTREAMES = 2
In vndeserued extreames: See else your selfe,	1687
Hen. Oh vanity of sicknesse: fierce extreames	2619

EYD = 1
That euer wall-ey'd wrath, or staring rage	2048

EYE *see also* eie = 17
K.Iohn. Mine eye hath well examined his parts,	97
Before the eye and prospect of your Towne,	514
The shadow of my selfe form'd in her eye,	814
Clap'd on the outward eye of fickle France,	904
Turning with splendor of his precious eye	1004
Good *Hubert, Hubert, Hubert* throw thine eye	1359
Shee lookes vpon them with a threatning eye:	1505
But for containing fire to harme mine eye:	1643
Hub. Well, see to liue: I will not touch thine eye,	1701
To seeke the beauteous eye of heauen to garnish,	1732
Liues in his eye: that close aspect of his,	1790
A fearefull eye thou hast. Where is that blood,	1824
Or turn'd an eye of doubt vpon my face;	1958
Gouerne the motion of a kinglye eye:	2215
Vnthred the rude eye of Rebellion,	2472
Right in thine eye. Away, my friends, new flight,	2521
Iohn. Oh Cozen, thou art come to set mine eye:	2661

EYES *see also* eies = 26*1
These eyes, these browes, were moulded out of his;	397
By our best eyes cannot be censured:	639
Making that idiot laughter keepe mens eyes,	1344
Or if that thou couldst see me without eyes,	1347
Without eyes, eares, and harmefull sound of words:	1350
Out at mine eyes, in tender womanish teares.	1609
Must you with hot Irons, burne out both mine eyes?	1612
Why then you must. Will you put out mine eyes?	1632

EYES *cont.*
These eyes, that neuer did, nor neuer shall | So much as frowne on you.   1633
*Approaching neere these eyes, would drinke my teares,   1639
And told me *Hubert* should put out mine eyes,   1646
Art. O saue me *Hubert*, saue me: my eyes are out   1649
Art. Is there no remedie? | *Hub.* None, but to lose your eyes.   1668
Must needes want pleading for a paire of eyes: 1677
So I may keepe mine eyes. O spare mine eyes,   1680
Nay, it perchance will sparkle in your eyes: 1694
And look'd vpon, I hope, with chearefull eyes.   1719
With eyes as red as new enkindled fire,   1884
With wrinkled browes, with nods, with rolling eyes.   1917
And foule immaginarie eyes of blood   1990
Sal. Trust not those cunning waters of his eyes,   2110
And snarleth in the gentle eyes of peace: 2155
Of bragging horror: So shall inferior eyes   2218
Startles mine eyes, and makes me more amaz'd   2302
Commend these waters to those baby-eyes   2307
He is forsworne, if ere those eyes of yours   2492
EYE-BALLS = 1
And put my eye-balls in thy vaultie browes,   1413
EYE-OFFENDING = 1
Patch'd with foule Moles, and eye-offending markes,   968
FACD = 5
A halfe-fac'd groat, fiue hundred pound a yeere?   102
Together with that pale, that white-fac'd shore,   316
'Tis not the rounder of your old-fac'd walles,   565
And I shall shew you peace, and faire-fac'd league: 732
That smooth-fac'd Gentleman, tickling commoditie,   894
FACE = 15*2
Elen. He hath a tricke of *Cordelions* face,   93
Philip. Because he hath a half-face like my father?   100
With halfe that face would he haue all my land,   101
My armes, such eele skins stuft, my face so thin,   149
I would giue it euery foot to haue this face: 154
Your face hath got fiue hundred pound a yeere,   160
Yet sell your face for fiue pence and 'tis deere: 161
Looke heere vpon thy brother *Geffreyes* face,   396
Fran. Stand in his face to contradict his claime.   587
Turne face to face, and bloody point to point: 704
Fra. What sai'st thou boy? looke in the Ladies face.   811
Sal. In this the Anticke, and well noted face   1738
Or turn'd an eye of doubt vpon my face;   1958
Threaten the threatner, and out-face the brow   2217
You taught me how to know the face of right,   2341
Dol. There end thy braue, and turn thy face in peace,   2413
FACED = 1
Out-faced Infant State, and done a rape   394
FACES = 2
Compare our faces, and be Iudge your selfe   87
With Ladies faces, and fierce Dragons spleenes,   362
FAINT = 3
Weaknesse possesseth me, and I am faint. *Exeunt.*   2457
In faint Retire: Oh brauely came we off,   2528
I am the Symet to this pale faint Swan,   2627
FAINTING = 1
Out of the weake doore of our fainting Land: 2688

FAINTLY = 1
I faintly broke with thee of *Arthurs* death: 1952
FAIRE = 24*1
To this faire Iland, and the Territories: 15
At least from faire fiue hundred pound a yeere: 77
(Faire fall the bones that tooke the paines for me)   86
Salute thee for her King, till then faire boy   323
And she a faire diuided excellence,   754
For *Angiers*, and faire *Toraine Maine, Poyctiers*,   803
And Earle of Richmond, and this rich faire Towne   873
When his faire Angels would salute my palme,   911
But thou art faire, and at thy birth (deere boy)   972
To tread downe faire respect of Soueraigntie,   979
Fran. 'Tis true (faire daughter) and this blessed day,   1000
To curse the faire proceedings of this day: 1022
I *Pandulph*, of faire *Millane* Cardinall,   1065
Const. O faire returne of banish'd Maiestie.   1254
Bla. The Sun's orecast with bloud: faire day adieu,   1259
For your faire safety: so I kisse your hand.   1314
Fra. O faire affliction, peace.   1420
In the faire multitude of those her haires;   1446
O Lord, my boy, my *Arthur*, my faire sonne,   1488
Can you not reade it? Is it not faire writ?   1610
Ba. Here's a good world: knew you of this faire work?   2119
And make faire weather in your blustring land: 2188
That hauing our faire order written downe,   2255
Of this most faire occasion, by the which   2512
To try the faire aduenture of to morrow. *Exeunt*   2548
FAIRELY = 1
Ar. Too fairely *Hubert*, for so foule effect,   1611
FAIRER = 1
Where should he finde it fairer, then in *Blanch*:   742
FAIRE-FACD = 1
And I shall shew you peace, and faire-fac'd league: 732
FAIRE-PLAY = 1
Bast. According to the faire-play of the world,   2372
FAITH = 15*2
Fra. And by my faith, this league that we haue made   865
That Broker, that still breakes the pate of faith,   889
Since Kings breake faith vpon commoditie,   918
Yea, faith it selfe to hollow falshood change.   1020
Bla. The Lady *Constance* speakes not from her faith, | But from her
need.   1140
Which onely liues but by the death of faith,   1143
That faith would liue againe by death of need: 1145
O then tread downe my need, and faith mounts vp,   1146
Keepe my need vp, and faith is trodden downe.   1147
Was deepe-sworne faith, peace, amity, true loue   1162
Play fast and loose with faith? so iest with heauen,   1173
Vn-sweare faith sworne, and on the marriage bed   1176
Fra. I may dis-ioyne my hand, but not my faith.   1193
Pand. So mak'st thou faith an enemy to faith,   1194
A voluntary zeale, and an vn-urg'd Faith   2261
And welcome home againe discarded faith,   2473
FAITHES = 1
And keepe our faithes firme and inuiolable.   2258

FAITHFULL = 3
  Philip. Your faithfull subiect, I a gentleman,   58
  Like true, inseparable, faithfull loues, | Sticking together in calamitie.   1450
  I do bequeath my faithfull seruices | And true subiection euerlastingly.   2715
FAITHFULLY = 1
  Lady. Hast thou denied thy selfe a *Faulconbridge?* | *Bast.* As faithfully
  as I denie the deuill.   264
FAITHLESSE = 1
  To make a faithlesse errour in your eares,   536
FAITHS = 1*1
  The faiths of men, nere stained with reuolt: 1723
  *Where be your powres? Shew now your mended faiths,   2685
FALCONBRIDGE = 3
  Then I haue nam'd. The Bastard *Falconbridge*   1556
  Mes. My Lord: your valiant kinsman *Falconbridge,*   2445
  Sal. That misbegotten diuell *Falconbridge,*   2463
FALL = 10*1
  (Faire fall the bones that tooke the paines for me)   86
  Before the dew of euening fall, shall fleete   592
  Which in the very meeting fall, and dye.   954
  Pray that their burthens may not fall this day,   1015
  And dost thou now fall ouer to my foes?   1053
  * *Fra.* Thou shalt not need. *England,* I will fall fro(m) thee.   1253
  That *Iohn* may stand, then *Arthur* needs must fall, | So be it, for it
  cannot be but so.   1524
  Dol. But what shall I gaine by yong *Arthurs* fall?   1526
  Then let the worst vn-heard, fall on your head.   1857
  Pet. Fore-knowing that the truth will fall out so.   1875
  Seeke out King *Iohn,* and fall before his feete: 2474
FALNE = 3
  Where but by chance a siluer drop hath falne,   1447
  As doth a Rauen on a sicke-falne beast,   2158
  By his perswasion, are againe falne off,   2537
FALSE = 8
  And if she did play false, the fault was hers,   126
  False blood to false blood ioyn'd. Gone to be freinds?   923
  Sal. As true as I beleeue you thinke them false,   948
  Ile fill these dogged Spies with false reports: 1709
  I idely heard: if true, or false I know not.   1843
  Yet I am none. Whose tongue so ere speakes false,   2092
  Why should I then be false, since it is true   2489
FALSELY = 1
  Had falsely thrust vpon contrary feete,   1923
FALSHOOD = 3
  Yea, faith it selfe to hollow falshood change.   1020
  And falshood, falshood cures, as fire cooles fire   1208
FAMILIARLY = 1
  Talkes as familiarly of roaring Lyons,   775
FANGS *see* phangs
FANTASIED = 1
  I finde the people strangely fantasied,   1865
FANTASIES = 1
  With many legions of strange fantasies,   2624
FAR = 1
  We grant thou canst out-scold vs: Far thee well,   2414
FARE *see also* far = 2
  Remember: Madam, Fare you well,   1374

FARE *cont.*
Ioh. Poyson'd, ill fare: dead, forsooke, cast off,   2643
FARES = 2
Hub. Badly I feare; how fares your Maiesty?   2441
Hen. How fares your Maiesty?   2642
FAREWELL = 4
Pembroke looke too't: farewell *Chattillion.* | *Exit Chat. and Pem.*   35
Ele. Farewell gentle Cosen. | *Iohn.* Coz, farewell.   1315
So thriue it in your game, and so farewell.   1813
FAREYOUWELL = 1
Fareyouwell: had you such a·losse as I,   1484
FARRE = 3
Neere or farre off, well wonne is still well shot,   183
But thou from louing *England* art so farre,   391
And now 'tis farre too huge to be blowne out   2339
FARTHER = 1
To meet displeasure farther from the dores,   2228
FARTHEST = 1
The farthest limit of my Embassie.   27
FARTHINGS = 1
Lest men should say, looke where three farthings goes,   151
FASHIOND = 1
For putting on so new a fashion'd robe.   1744
FAST = 6
Vpon good Friday, and nere broke his fast: 248
To our fast closed gates: for at this match,   762
Con. O *Lewis,* stand fast, the deuill tempts thee heere   1138
Play fast and loose with faith? so iest with heauen,   1173
Fast to the chaire: be heedfull: hence, and watch.   1575
I coniure thee but slowly: run more fast. *Exeunt.*   1994
FASTING = 1
A fasting Tyger safer by the tooth,   1191
FAT = 1
Set at libertie: the fat ribs of peace   1307
FATHER = 27*1
That is well knowne, and as I thinke one father: 68
And were our father, and this sonne like him: 89
O old sir *Robert* Father, on my knee   90
Philip. Because he hath a half-face like my father?   100
Rob. My gracious Liege, when that my father liu'd,   103
Your brother did imploy my father much.   104
Betweene my father, and my mother lay,   114
As I haue heard my father speake himselfe   115
Had of your father claim'd this sonne for his,   130
Insooth, good friend, your father might haue kept   131
My brother might not claime him, nor your father   134
My father gaue me honor, yours gaue land: 173
Then good my mother, let me know my father,   262
Lady. King Richard Cordelion was thy father,   266
Madam I would not wish a better father: 273
With all my heart I thanke thee for my father: 283
Liker in feature to his father *Geffrey*   423
My boy a bastard? by my soule I thinke | His father neuer was so true
begot,   426
*Queen. Theres a good mother boy, that blots thy fa-|(ther   429
Since I first cal'd my brothers father Dad.   783
Good Father Cardinall, cry thou Amen   1109

FATHER *cont.*
Dolph. Bethinke you father, for the difference	1133
Fra. Good reuerend father, make my person yours,	1155
My reuerend father, let it not be so;	1180
Daul. Father, to Armes. | *Blanch.* Vpon thy wedding day?	1232
Father, I may not wish the fortune thine:	1266
As deere be to thee, as thy father was.	1302
And Father Cardinall, I haue heard you say	1461

FATHERS = 10
And in the meane time soiourn'd at my fathers;	111
My fathers land, as was my fathers will.	123
Your fathers wife did after wedlocke beare him:	125
My mothers sonne did get your fathers heyre,	136
Your fathers heyre must haue your fathers land.	137
Rob. Shal then my fathers Will be of no force,	138
This in our foresaid holy Fathers name	1072
Shall waite vpon your Fathers Funerall.	2708

FAULCONBRIDGE = 7*2
Enter Robert Faulconbridge, and Philip.	57
Borne in *Northamptonshire*, and eldest sonne | As I suppose, to *Robert Faulconbridge,*	59
K.Iohn. What art thou? | *Robert.* The son and heire to that same *Faulconbridge.*	63
Eli. Whether hadst thou rather be a *Faulconbridge,*	142
K.Iohn. Goe, *Faulconbridge,* now hast thou thy desire,	185
Enter Lady Faulconbridge and Iames Gurney.	232
Lady. Hast thou denied thy selfe a *Faulconbridge?* | *Bast.* As faithfully as I denie the deuill.	264
Sal. Stand by, or I shall gaul you *Faulconbridge.*	2096
Big. What wilt thou do, renowned *Faulconbridge?*	2103

FAULT = 9
And if she did play false, the fault was hers,	126
Which fault lyes on the hazards of all husbands	127
And so doth yours: your fault, was not your follie,	275
Is it my fault, that I was *Geffreyes* sonne?	1595
And oftentimes excusing of a fault,	1747
Doth make the fault the worse by th'excuse:	1748
Discredite more in hiding of the fault,	1750
Then did the fault before it was so patch'd.	1751
The image of a wicked heynous fault	1789

FAUOUR = 3
To whom in fauour she shall giue the day,	707
Iohn. Speake on with fauour, we are bent to heare.	737
But I do loue the fauour, and the forme	2511

FAYRER = 1
Is yet the couer of a fayrer minde,	1983

FAYRE-PLAY-ORDERS = 1
Send fayre-play-orders, and make comprimise, | Insinuation, parley, and base truce	2236

FEARD = 3
What we so fear'd he had a charge to do.	1793
Sal. Indeed we fear'd his sicknesse was past cure.	1804
Bast. But if you be a-feard to heare the worst,	1856

FEARE = 11*2
Kings of our feare, vntill our feares resolu'd	685
But (on this day) let Sea-men feare no wracke,	1017
My Mother is assayled in our Tent, | And tane I feare.	1291

FEARE *cont.*

Her Highnesse is in safety, feare you not:	1294
Fra. I feare some out-rage, and Ile follow her. *Exit.*	1491
Hub. Vncleanly scruples feare not you: looke too't.	1577
And more, more strong, then lesser is my feare	1759
Pem. And when it breakes, I feare will issue thence	1798
Not knowing what they feare, but full of feare.	1867
Let not the world see feare and sad distrust	2214
Hub. Badly I feare; how fares your Maiesty?	2441
Hub. The King I feare is poyson'd by a Monke,	2580

FEAREFULL = 5

With fearefull bloudy issue arbitrate.	44
The fearefull difference of incensed kings:	1169
A fearefull eye thou hast. Where is that blood,	1824
Whilst he that heares, makes fearefull action	1916
Blacke, fearefull, comfortlesse, and horrible.	2577

FEAREFULLY = 1

And I do fearefully beleeue 'tis done,	1792

FEARES = 6*3

Kings of our feare, vntill our feares resolu'd	685
For I am sicke, and capeable of feares,	933
Opprest with wrongs, and therefore full of feares,	934
A widdow, husbandles, subiect to feares,	935
A woman naturally borne to feares;	936
Why then your feares, which (as they say) attend	1773
Io. Why seek'st thou to possesse me with these feares?	1928
*And those thy feares, might haue wrought feares in me.	1961

FEARING = 1

Till their soule-fearing clamours haue braul'd downe	697

FEAST = 2

What, shall our feast be kept with slaughtered men?	1235
To feast vpon whole thousands of the French.	2434

FEASTS = 2

And now he feasts, mousing the flesh of men	668
Nor met with Fortune, other then at feasts,	2309

FEATHERS = 1

Be Mercurie, set feathers to thy heeles,	1896

FEATURE = 2

Liker in feature to his father *Geffrey*	423
Vpon thy feature, for my rage was blinde,	1989

FEAUER = 2

Iohn. This Feauer that hath troubled me so long,	2442
Iohn. Aye me, this tyrant Feauer burnes mee vp,	2454

FED = 1

Must by the hungry now be fed vpon:	1308

FEE = 1

Which heauen shall take in nature of a fee:	472

FEEBLE = 2

Which cannot heare a Ladies feeble voyce,	1425
Of the old, feeble, and day-wearied Sunne,	2496

FEEBLED = 1

Shall that victorious hand be feebled heere,	2400

FEED = 1

And brought in matter that should feed this fire;	2338

FEELE = 2

I am not mad: too well, too well I feele	1443
In their continuance, will not feele themselues.	2620

FEELING = 1
Then feeling what small things are boysterous there,   1673
FEETE = 2
Had falsely thrust vpon contrary feete,   1923
Seeke out King *Iohn*, and fall before his feete: 2474
FELL = 2
And rowze from sleepe that fell Anatomy   1424
Of that fell poison which assayleth him.   2614
FELLOW = 4*1
K.Iohn. A good blunt fellow: why being yonger born   79
Good den Sir *Richard*, Godamercy fellow,   195
Fellow be gone: I cannot brooke thy sight,   957
Tell me thou fellow, is not France forsworne?   983
A fellow by the hand of Nature mark'd,   1946
FELLOWSHIP = 1
Is scattered and dis-ioyn'd from fellowship.   1385
FELT = 1
Before the childe himselfe felt he was sicke: 1806
FESTIUALL = 1
Euer in *France* shall be kept festiuall: 1001
FETCH = 1
It makes the course of thoughts to fetch about,   1741
FEUER = 1
To make a shaking feuer in your walles,   534
FEW = 1
There's few or none do know me, if they did,   1999
FHER = 1
FICKLE = 1
Clap'd on the outward eye of fickle France,   904
FIELD = 9*1
A Souldier by the Honor-giuing-hand | Of *Cordelion*, Knighted in the
field.   61
Bast. Speed then to take aduantage of the field.   605
Cry hauocke kings, backe to the stained field   671
That heere come sacrifices for the field.   735
Whom zeale and charitie brought to the field,   886
When he intendeth to become the field: 2223
Desires your Maiestie to leaue the field,   2446
Pem. They say King *Iohn* sore sick, hath left the field.   2465
From forth the noise and rumour of the Field;   2506
Last in the field, and almost Lords of it.   2532
FIELDS = 1
A cockred-silken wanton braue our fields,   2239
FIEND = 2
There is not yet so vgly a fiend of hell   2126
Is, as a fiend, confin'd to tyrannize,   2656
FIENDS = 1
Euen to that drop ten thousand wiery fiends   1448
FIERCE = 6*1
Chat. The proud controle of fierce and bloudy warre,   22
With Ladies faces, and fierce Dragons spleenes,   362
Such temperate order in so fierce a cause,   1394
Euen with the fierce lookes of these bloody men.   1650
That mercie, which fierce fire, and Iron extends,   1699
Their Needl's to Lances, and their gentle hearts | To fierce and bloody
inclination.   2411
Hen. Oh vanity of sicknesse: fierce extreames   2619

FIERIE = 2
 You equall Potents, fierie kindled spirits,   672
 And quench this fierie indignation,   1640
FIERY = 2
 Rash, inconsiderate, fiery voluntaries,   361
 And cull'd these fiery spirits from the world   2367
FIFT = 1
 Foure fixed, and the fift did whirle about   1907
FIFTEENE = 1
 Twice fifteene thousand hearts of Englands breed. | *Bast.* Bastards and
 else.   582
FIGGE = 1
 Giue yt a plum, a cherry, and a figge,   463
FIGHT = 6
 The awlesse Lion could not wage the fight,   279
 To parlie or to fight, therefore prepare.   373
 Then after fight who shall be king of it?   714
 Thou Fortunes Champion, that do'st neuer fight   1044
 And, like a dogge that is compell'd to fight,   1695
 The French fight coldly, and retyre themselues.   2453
FIGURD = 1
 Figur'd quite ore with burning Meteors.   2304
FIGURE = 1
 Resolueth from his figure 'gainst the fire?   2486
FILL = 3
 (If not fill vp the measure of her will)   877
 Ile fill these dogged Spies with false reports: 1709
 Vpon her gentle bosom, and fill vp   2279
FILS = 1
 Con. Greefe fils the roome vp of my absent childe: 1478
FIND = 1
 Dol. I do my Lord, and in her eie I find   812
FINDE = 12*2
 Where should he finde it fairer, then in *Blanch*:   742
 Where should he finde it purer then in *Blanch*?   744
 Finde liable to our Crowne and Dignitie,   806
 That I can finde, should merit any hate.   838
 So we could finde some patterne of our shame: 1398
 Shall finde but bloodie safety, and vntrue.   1533
 And binde the boy, which you shall finde with me   1574
 And finde th'inheritance of this poore childe,   1815
 I finde the people strangely fantasied,   1865
 Ile finde a thousand shifts to get away;   2003
 And finde no checke? Let vs my Liege to Armes: 2242
 Dol. Strike vp our drummes, to finde this danger out.   2435
 Bast. And thou shalt finde it (Dolphin) do not doubt | *Exeunt.*   2436
 Hub. Why heere walke I in the black brow of night | To finde you out.   2573
FINDES = 1
 And findes them perfect *Richard*: sirra speake,   98
FINDING = 1
 Finding thee fit for bloody villanie: 1950
FINE = 2
 Paying the fine of rated Treachery,   2498
 Euen with a treacherous fine of all your liues: 2499
FINGERS = 3
 And ring these fingers with thy houshold wormes,   1414
 Out of the bloody fingers ends of *Iohn*.   1553

FINGERS *cont.*
To thrust his ycie fingers in my maw;   2645
FINISHED = 1
Left to be finished by such as shee,   753
FIRE = 13*2
And now insteed of bulletts wrapt in fire   533
When the rich blood of kings is set on fire: 665
*He speakes plaine Cannon fire, and smoake, and bounce,   778
And falshood, falshood cures, as fire cooles fire   1208
To ashes, ere our blood shall quench that fire: 1278
But for containing fire to harme mine eye: 1643
Art. No, in good sooth: the fire is dead with griefe,   1685
That mercie, which fierce fire, and Iron extends,   1699
With eyes as red as new enkindled fire,   1884
Be stirring as the time, be fire with fire,   2216
And brought in matter that should feed this fire;   2338
Resolueth from his figure 'gainst the fire?   2486
Vpon a Parchment, and against this fire | Do I shrinke vp.   2640
FIRME = 2
That no supporter but the huge firme earth   994
And keepe our faithes firme and inuiolable.   2258
FIRST = 12*2
Iohn. For our aduantage, therefore heare vs first: 512
That did display them when we first marcht forth: 631
From first to last, the on-set and retyre: 637
Since I first cal'd my brothers father Dad.   783
Fra. Speake England first, that hath bin forward first   798
That I did so when I was first assur'd.   855
First made to heauen, first be to heauen perform'd,   1197
Therefore thy later vowes, against thy first,   1219
For since the birth of *Caine*, the first male-childe   1464
Mes. My Liege, her eare | Is stopt with dust: the first of Aprill di'de 1838
Your breath first kindled the dead coale of warres,   2336
But when it first did helpe to wound it selfe.   2725
FIST = 1
But buffets better then a fist of France: 781
FIT = 3
But I will fit it with some better tune.   1325
The fit is strongest: Euils that take leaue   1499
Finding thee fit for bloody villanie: 1950
FITS = 1
And fits the mounting spirit like my selfe;   216
FITTE = 1
As dim and meager as an Agues fitte,   1470
FITTING = 1
Hub. O my sweet sir, newes fitting to the night,   2576
FIUE = 7
At least from faire fiue hundred pound a yeere: 77
A halfe-fac'd groat, fiue hundred pound a yeere?   102
Your face hath got fiue hundred pound a yeere,   160
Yet sell your face for fiue pence and 'tis deere: 161
Poyctiers and *Aniow*, these fiue Prouinces   848
Hub. My Lord, they say fiue Moones were seene to | (night: 1906
Ioh. Fiue Moones?   1909
FIXED = 2
By this time from their fixed beds of lime   525
Foure fixed, and the fift did whirle about   1907

FLAGGES = 1
  These flagges of France that are aduanced heere   513
FLAT = 1
  Aust. Rebellion, flat rebellion.   1229
FLATLY = 1
  He flatly saies, hee'll not lay downe his Armes.   2380
FLATS = 1
  Passing these Flats, are taken by the Tide,   2598
FLATTER = 1
  Further I will not flatter you, my Lord,   833
FLATTERING = 2
  Drawne in the flattering table of her eie. | *Whispers with Blanch.*   819
  Bast. Drawne in the flattering table of her eie,   821
FLED = 1
  Is fled to heauen: and *England* now is left   2150
FLEETE = 1
  Before the dew of euening fall, shall fleete   592
FLESH = 3
  And now he feasts, mousing the flesh of men   668
  We owe thee much: within this wall of flesh   1319
  And flesh his spirit in a warre-like soyle,   2240
FLESHLY = 1
  Nay, in the body of this fleshly Land,   1970
FLIE = 1
  King *Iohn* did flie an houre or two before   2543
FLIGHT = 2
  We will vntread the steps of damned flight,   2513
  Right in thine eye. Away, my friends, new flight,   2521
FLING = 1
  The mouth of passage shall we fling wide ope,   764
FLINTIE = 1
  The flintie ribbes of this contemptuous Citie,   698
FLOOD = 4
  Fra. So by a roaring Tempest on the flood,   1383
  Aloft the flood, and can giue audience   1860
  And like a bated and retired Flood,   2514
  Deuoured by the vnexpected flood.   2674
FLOTE = 1
  Did neuer flote vpon the swelling tide,   368
FLOUT = *1
  *Bast. By heauen, these scroyles of Angiers flout you | (kings,   687
FLY = 1
  Mel. Fly Noble English, you are bought and sold,   2471
FLYE = 1
  And flye (like thought) from them, to me againe.   1897
FOE = 1
  Our Partie may well meet a prowder foe. *Exeunt.*   2248
FOES = 3
  Dide in the dying slaughter of their foes,   634
  And dost thou now fall ouer to my foes?   1053
  Against the Pope, and count his friends my foes.   1098
FOLDED = 1
  They shoote but calme words, folded vp in smoake,   535
FOLLIE = 1
  And so doth yours: your fault, was not your follie,   275
FOLLOW = 5*1
  Bequeath thy land to him, and follow me?   157

FOLLOW *cont.*
Madam, Ile follow you vnto the death.   162
Will I not thinke of home, but follow Armes.   324
Fra. I feare some out-rage, and Ile follow her. *Exit.*   1491
And follow me with speed: Ile to the King: 2162
And follow vnacquainted colours heere: 2283
FOLLOWES = 1
K.Iohn. What followes if we disallow of this?   21
FOND = 2
Fra. You are as fond of greefe, as of your childe.   1477
Then, haue I reason to be fond of griefe?   1483
FONDLY = 1
But if you fondly passe our proffer'd offer,   564
FOOD = 1
My life, my ioy, my food, my all the world: 1489
FOOLE = 2
And sooth'st vp greatnesse. What a foole art thou,   1047
A ramping foole, to brag, and stamp, and sweare,   1048
FOOLES = *1
Lew. Women & fooles, breake off your conference.   450
FOOLISH = 1*1
Lame, foolish, crooked, swart, prodigious,   967
*Reade heere yong *Arthur.* How now foolish rheume?   1606
FOOT = 9
I would giue it euery foot to haue this face: 154
Bast. A foot of Honor better then I was,   192
But many a many foot of Land the worse.   193
Whose foot spurnes backe the Oceans roaring tides,   317
And wheresoere this foot of mine doth tread,   1362
Me thinkes I see this hurley all on foot;   1554
Within the Arras: when I strike my foot   1572
Three foot of it doth hold; bad world the while: 1818
It may lie gently at the foot of peace,   2329
FOOTE = 4*1
*Thy foote to Englands Throne. And therefore marke: 1515
Iohn. Nay, but make haste: the better foote before.   1892
With our pure Honors: nor attend the foote   2023
If thou but frowne on me, or stirre thy foote,   2098
Lye at the proud foote of a Conqueror,   2724
FOOTING = 1
Shall we vpon the footing of our land,   2235
FOOTSTEPS = 1
For it shall strew the footsteps of my rising: 226
FOR *see also* longed-for *l.*24 25 30 45 69 74 86 130 161 188 190 197 199
217 223 226 252 *255 268 283 299 323 332 337 347 374 376 377 388 467
487 489 493 507 508 512 519 522 527 547 574 589 602 613 645 676 721
735 762 786 803 846 854 858 861 872 881 909 912 919 928 932 933 970
991 993 1054 1058 1110 *1112 1113 1116 1133 1135 1201 1213 1239
1295 1304 1314 1331 1373 1377 1433 1437 1464 1512 1525 1532 1555
1566 1589 1611 1625 1643 1654 1677 1686 1700 1702 1711 1715 1725
1744 1766 1767 1781 1829 1832 1849 1855 1858 1880 1900 1934 1940
1950 1989 2016 2039 2075 2088 2109 2111 2116 2153 2181 2211 2253
2272 2311 2347 2358 2359 2375 2383 2407 2408 2421 2429 2431 2449
2475 2503 2520 *2631 2671 2681 2700 2710 2718 = 150*5
FORBID = 2
How can the Law forbid my tongue to curse?   1118
From whose obedience I forbid my soule,   2063

FORCE = 5
  Rob. Shal then my fathers Will be of no force,   138
  Phil. Of no more force to dispossesse me sir,   140
  Against whose furie and vnmatched force,   278
  So wilfully dost spurne; and force perforce   1069
  Vse our Commission in his vtmost force.   1309
FORCED = 1
  His little kingdome of a forced graue.   1816
FORCES = 2
  Chat. Then turne your forces from this paltry siege,   348
  His forces strong, his Souldiers confident: 355
FORCIBLY = 1
  To inforce these rights, so forcibly with-held,   23
FORE = 1
  To stop their marches 'fore we are enflam'd: 2174
FORESAID = 1
  This in our foresaid holy Fathers name   1072
FORE-HEAD = 1
  Is warlike *Iohn*: and in his fore-head sits   2432
FORE-KNOWING = 1
  Pet. Fore-knowing that the truth will fall out so.   1875
FORE-RUNNER = 1
  Arthur that great fore-runner of thy bloud,   295
FORE-TELL = 1
  Fore-tell the ending of mortality.   2609
FORE-THOUGHT = 1
  Alter not the doome fore-thought by heauen.   1245
FORE-WEARIED = 1
  Fore-wearied in this action of swift speede,   539
FORGET = 7
  For new made honor doth forget mens names: 197
  Iohn. We like not this, thou dost forget thy selfe.   1060
  For then 'tis like I should forget my selfe: 1433
  O, if I could, what griefe should I forget?   1434
  If I were mad, I should forget my sonne,   1441
  I would not haue you (Lord) forget your selfe,   2083
  Least I, by marking of your rage, forget   2085
FORGIUE = 3*1
  Arth. God shall forgiue you *Cordelions* death   305
  **Iohn.* Then God forgiue the sinne of all those soules,   590
  Thrust but these men away, and Ile forgiue you,   1659
  Forgiue the Comment that my passion made   1988
FORGOE = 1
  Or the light losse of *England,* for a friend: | Forgoe the easier.   1135
FORMD = 1
  The shadow of my selfe form'd in her eye,   814
FORME = 12
  K.Iohn. From henceforth beare his name | Whose forme thou bearest: 168
  Exterior forme, outward accoutrement;   221
  Pand. All forme is formelesse, Order orderlesse,   1184
  Stuffes out his vacant garments with his forme;   1482
  I will not keepe this forme vpon my head,   1486
  Of plaine old forme, is much disfigured,   1739
  And you haue slander'd Nature in my forme,   1981
  Forme such another? This is the very top,   2044
  Which bleeds away, euen as a forme of waxe   2485
  But I do loue the fauour, and the forme   2511

FORME *cont.*
  To set a forme vpon that indigest   2632
  I am a scribled forme drawne with a pen   2639
FORMELESSE = 1
  Pand. All forme is formelesse, Order orderlesse,   1184
FORMER = 2
  Our former scruple in our strong barr'd gates: 684
  Then speake againe, not all thy former tale,   946
FORRAGE = 1
  Oh let it not be said: forrage, and runne   2227
FORRAIGNE = 2
  Mes. From France to England, neuer such a powre | For any forraigne
  preparation,   1828
  Euen at my gates, with rankes of forraigne powres;   1969
FORREINE = 1
  And confident from forreine purposes,   321
FORREN = 1
  To stranger-bloud, to forren Royalty;   2178
FORREYNERS = 1
  When aduerse Forreyners affright my Townes   1894
FORSAKE = *1
  Elinor. I like thee well: wilt thou forsake thy fortune,   156
FORSOOKE = 1
  Ioh. Poyson'd, ill fare: dead, forsooke, cast off,   2643
FORSWORNE = 7
  Tell me thou fellow, is not France forsworne?   983
  Proues valuelesse: you are forsworne, forsworne,   1026
  To sweare, sweares only not to be forsworne,   1215
  But thou dost sweare, onely to be forsworne,   1217
  And most forsworne, to keepe what thou dost sweare,   1218
  He is forsworne, if ere those eyes of yours   2492
FORTH = 12*1
  And ready mounted are they to spit forth   517
  Iohn. Vp higher to the plaine, where we'l set forth   603
  That did display them when we first marcht forth: 631
  Then in a moment Fortune shall cull forth   705
  *That spits forth death, and mountaines, rockes, and seas,   774
  Arise forth from the couch of lasting night,   1410
  That none so small aduantage shall step forth   1536
  Vpon the bosome of the ground, rush forth   1573
  Yong Lad come forth; I haue to say with you.   1578
  Hub. Come forth: Do as I bid you do.   1648
  From forth the streets of Pomfret, whom I found   1869
  From forth this morcell of dead Royaltie?   2148
  From forth the noise and rumour of the Field;   2506
FORTIFIED = 1
  Dol. What he hath won, that hath he fortified: 1392
FORTUNE = 11*2
  Elinor. I like thee well: wilt thou forsake thy fortune,   156
  Bast. Brother adieu, good fortune come to thee,   189
  Then in a moment Fortune shall cull forth   705
  Nature and Fortune ioyn'd to make thee great.   973
  And with the halfe-blowne Rose. But Fortune, oh,   975
  France is a Bawd to Fortune, and king *Iohn,*   981
  That strumpet Fortune, that vsurping *Iohn*:   982
  Vpon thy starres, thy fortune, and thy strength,   1052
  Father, I may not wish the fortune thine: 1266

FORTUNE *cont.*
   Dolph. Lady, with me, with me thy fortune lies.   1270
   *Bla. There where my fortune liues, there my life dies.   1271
   No, no: when Fortune meanes to men most good,   1504
   Nor met with Fortune, other then at feasts,   2309
FORTUNES = 3
   Haue sold their fortunes at their natiue homes,   363
   To make a hazard of new fortunes heere: 365
   Thou Fortunes Champion, that do'st neuer fight   1044
FORWARD = 1*1
   *Fra. Speake England first, that hath bin forward first   798
   Sal. Or rather then set forward, for 'twill be   2016
FOSTERED = 1
   That like a Lion fostered vp at hand,   2328
FOUGHT = 2
   And fought the holy Warres in *Palestine,*   297
   Oh, what a noble combat hast fought   2294
FOULE = 6
   Patch'd with foule Moles, and eye-offending markes,   968
   Elea. O foule reuolt of French inconstancy.   1255
   Ar. Too fairely *Hubert,* for so foule effect,   1611
   The foule corruption of a sweet childes death.   1799
   So foule a skie, cleeres not without a storme,   1826
   And foule immaginarie eyes of blood   1990
FOULE-PLAY = 1
   Sal. It is apparant foule-play, and 'tis shame   1811
FOUND = 2*1
   From forth the streets of Pomfret, whom I found   1869
   Found it too precious Princely, for a graue.   2039
   *Bast. They found him dead, and cast into the streets,   2207
FOUNDATION = 1
   There is no sure foundation set on blood: 1822
FOURE = 2
   Foure fixed, and the fift did whirle about   1907
   The other foure, in wondrous motion.   1908
FOURTEENE = 1
   Full fourteene weekes before the course of time: 121
FOWLE = 1
   Dol. Ah fowle, shrew'd newes. Beshrew thy very | (hart: 2540
FRA = 24*8
FRAILE = 1
   (Which some suppose the soules fraile dwelling house)   2607
FRAILETY = 1
   And from the organ-pipe of frailety sings   2629
FRAN = 7
FRANCE see also Fra., Fran. = 53*8
   *Enter King Iohn, Queene Elinor, Pembroke, Essex, and Sa-| lisbury,
   with the Chattylion of France.   2
   King Iohn. | **Now say Chatillion,* what would *France* with vs?   4
   Chat. Thus (after greeting) speakes the King | of France,   6
   Chat. Philip of *France,* in right and true behalfe   12
   Controlement for controlement: so answer *France.*   25
   Be thou as lightning in the eies of *France*;   29
   Till she had kindled *France* and all the world,   39
   I am a Souldier, and now bound to *France.*   158
   For *France,* for *France,* for it is more then need.   188

FRANCE cont.
```
*Enter before Angiers, Philip King of France, Lewis, Daul-|phin,
Austria, Constance, Arthur.                                          292
Till Angiers, and the right thou hast in France,                     315
*K.Iohn. Peace be to France: If France in peace permit               381
If not, bleede France, and peace ascend to heauen.                   383
From France to England, there to liue in peace:                      387
*K.Iohn. From whom hast thou this great commission | (France,        407
Queen. Who is it thou dost call vsurper France?                      417
Iohn. My life as soone: I doe defie thee France,                     455
Then ere the coward hand of France can win; | Submit thee boy.       458
Cit. Who is it that hath warn'd vs to the walles? | Fra. 'Tis France, for
England.                                                             506
These flagges of France that are aduanced heere                      513
France. When I haue saide, make answer to vs both.                   541
Heere after excursions, Enter the Herald of France | with Trumpets to
the gates.                                                           608
Who by the hand of France, this day hath made                        612
That is remoued by a staffe of France.                               629
*Iohn. France, hast thou yet more blood to cast away?                648
In this hot triall more then we of France,                           656
By East and West let France and England mount.                       695
I like it well. France, shall we knit our powres,                    712
Austria and France shoot in each others mouth.                       729
But buffets better then a fist of France:                            781
I see a yeelding in the lookes of France:                            790
Phillip of France, if thou be pleas'd withall,                       851
And France, whose armour Conscience buckled on,                      885
Clap'd on the outward eye of fickle France,                          904
France friend with England, what becomes of me?                      956
And with her golden hand hath pluckt on France                       978
France is a Bawd to Fortune, and king Iohn,                          981
Tell me thou fellow, is not France forsworne?                        983
*Enter King Iohn, France, Dolphin, Blanch, Elianor, Philip, | Austria,
Constance.                                                           998
Euer in France shall be kept festiuall:                             1001
Pand. Philip of France, on perill of a curse,                       1119
And raise the power of France vpon his head,                        1121
*Elea. Look'st thou pale France? do not let go thy hand.            1123
Con. Looke to that Deuill, lest that France repent,                 1124
France, thou maist hold a serpent by the tongue,                    1189
*Eng. France, y shalt rue this houre within this houre.             1256
Is it as he will? well then, France shall rue.                      1258
France, I am burn'd vp with inflaming wrath,                        1273
The blood and deerest valued bloud of France.                       1276
Enter France, Dolphin, Pandulpho, Attendants.                       1382
Ore-bearing interruption spight of France?                          1391
Yet I remember, when I was in France,                               1587
Poure downe thy weather: how goes all in France?                    1827
Mes. From France to England, neuer such a powre | For any forraigne
preparation,                                                        1828
That such an Army could be drawne in France, | And she not heare of
it?                                                                 1836
How wildely then walkes my Estate in France?                        1847
Vnder whose conduct came those powres of France,                    1848
Sal. The Count Meloone, a Noble Lord of France,                     2012
Pand. Haile noble Prince of France:                                 2321
```

FREE = 2
More free from motion, no not death himselfe   768
Can tast the free breath of a sacred King?   1075
FREEZE = 1
Of all his people, and freeze vp their zeale,   1535
FREINDS = 1
False blood to false blood ioyn'd. Gone to be freinds?   923
FRENCH see also F.Her. = 11*2
And merciles proceeding, by these French.   520
Behold the French amaz'd vouchsafe a parle,   532
Vpon the dancing banners of the French,   618
Elea. O foule reuolt of French inconstancy.   1255
Offending Charity: If but a dozen French   1558
*Bast. The French (my Lord) mens mouths are ful of it: 1882
Told of a many thousand warlike French,   1924
*Iohn. Now keep your holy word, go meet the French,   2172
Goe I to make the French lay downe their Armes. Exit.   2191
To feast vpon whole thousands of the French.   2434
The French fight coldly, and retyre themselues.   2453
Pem. Vp once againe: put spirit in the French,   2461
For if the French be Lords of this loud day,   2475
FRENCHMENS = 1
Hither returne all gilt with Frenchmens blood: 627
FRENCH-MENS = 1
Wade to the market-place in French-mens bloud,   335
FRENZIE = 1
The Lady Constance in a frenzie di'de   1841
FRESH = 1*1
*Pan. How green you are, and fresh in this old world?   1530
Fresh expectation troubled not the Land   1724
FRIDAY = 1
Vpon good Friday, and nere broke his fast: 248
FRIEND = 11
Insooth, good friend, your father might haue kept   131
France friend with England, what becomes of me?   956
Or the light losse of England, for a friend: | Forgoe the easier.   1135
And my good friend, thy voluntary oath   1322
Iohn. Good friend, thou hast no cause to say so yet,   1329
On yon young boy: Ile tell thee what my friend,   1360
Art. Alas, I then haue chid away my friend,   1663
He shew'd his warrant to a friend of mine,   1788
Bast. A Friend. What art thou? | Hub. Of the part of England.   2553
Thou art my friend, that know'st my tongue so well: 2562
Thou maist be-friend me so much, as to thinke   2565
FRIENDLY = 1
This friendly treatie of our threatned Towne.   797
FRIENDS = 8*1
Be friends a-while, and both conioyntly bend   693
Against the Pope, and count his friends my foes.   1098
To doe your pleasure, and continue friends.   1183
Arthur tane prisoner? diuers deere friends slaine?   1389
That we shall see and know our friends in heauen: 1462
The little number of your doubtfull friends.   2204
And is't not pitty, (oh my grieued friends)   2275
*Sal. I did not thinke the King so stor'd with friends.   2460
Right in thine eye. Away, my friends, new flight,   2521

FRIGHT = 1
And fright him there? and make him tremble there?   2226
FRIGHTING = 1
Thou shalt be punish'd for thus frighting me,   932
FRIGHTS = 1
Startles, and frights consideration: 1742
FROM *l.*26 52 77 132 153 168 179 222 280 318 321 339 348 387 391 *407
  408 *409 445 *471 484 525 566 589 *636 637 723 725 726 728 768 845
  900 901 905 906 976 1066 1071 1079 1094 1102 1134 *1140 1141 1149
  1175 *1253 1385 1410 1424 1455 1468 1550 1662 1828 1842 1869 1897
  *2011 2063 2102 2132 2148 2156 2170 2173 2219 2228 2267 2286 2318
  2367 2374 2390 2486 2506 2569 2629 2693 2694 = 74*8
FRONTS = 1
Why stand these royall fronts amazed thus: 670
FROWNE = 4
The grapling vigor, and rough frowne of Warre | Is cold in amitie, and
painted peace,   1029
These eyes, that neuer did, nor neuer shall | So much as frowne on you.   1633
If thou but frowne on me, or stirre thy foote,   2098
And heauen it selfe doth frowne vpon the Land. *Exit.*   2164
FROWNES = 1
Of dangerous Maiesty, when perchance it frownes   1938
FROWNING = 1
Hang'd in the frowning wrinkle of her brow,   822
FRUITE = 1
The bloome that promiseth a mightie fruite.   789
FUL = *1
  Bast. The *French* (my Lord) mens mouths are ful of it: 1882
FULL = 11
Full fourteene weekes before the course of time: 121
But with a heart full of vnstained loue,   309
The Canons haue their bowels full of wrath,   516
Full thirty thousand Markes of English coyne: 850
Opprest with wrongs, and therefore full of feares,   934
Full of vnpleasing blots, and sightlesse staines,   966
Is all too wanton, and too full of gawdes   1335
My head with more ill newes: for it is full.   1855
Possest with rumors, full of idle dreames,   1866
Not knowing what they feare, but full of feare.   1867
Full warm of blood, of mirth, of gossipping: 2310
FULNESSE = 1
Whose fulnesse of perfection lyes in him.   755
FULSOME = 1
And stop this gap of breath with fulsome dust,   1415
FUNERALL = 1
Shall waite vpon your Fathers Funerall.   2708
FURIE = 3
Against whose furie and vnmatched force,   278
In mortall furie halfe so peremptorie, | As we to keepe this Citie.   769
As doth the furie of two desperate men,   953
FURTHER = 4
Being no further enemy to you | Then the constraint of hospitable zeale,   549
Further I will not flatter you, my Lord,   833
Which for our goods, we do no further aske,   1781
And be no further harmefull then in shewe.   2330
FURY = 1
  Bast. By all the bloud that euer fury breath'd,   2381

GAIND = 1
Must be as boysterously maintain'd as gain'd. 1521
GAINE = 2*1
*That for thine owne gaine shouldst defend mine honor? 255
Gaine be my Lord, for I will worship thee. *Exit.* 919
Dol. But what shall I gaine by yong *Arthurs* fall? 1526
GAINST = 3
Their Iron indignation 'gainst your walles: 518
Wee'l put thee downe, 'gainst whom these Armes wee | (beare, 660
Resolueth from his figure 'gainst the fire? 2486
GALL *see* gaul
GALLANT = 2
Before I drew this gallant head of warre, 2366
No: know the gallant Monarch is in Armes, 2402
GAME = 2
So thriue it in your game, and so farewell. 1813
Haue I not heere the best Cards for the game 2358
GANTLETS = 1
Their thimbles into armed Gantlets change, 2410
GAP = 1
And stop this gap of breath with fulsome dust, 1415
GAPE = 1
As in a Theater, whence they gape and point 689
GARMENTS = 1
Stuffes out his vacant garments with his forme; 1482
GARNISH = 1
To seeke the beauteous eye of heauen to garnish, 1732
GATES = 11
Welcome before the gates *Angiers* Duke. 310
Comfort your Citties eies, your winking gates: 521
Haue brought a counter-checke before your gates, 530
Haue we ramm'd vp our gates against the world. 578
Heere after excursions, Enter the Herald of France | with Trumpets to the gates. 608
F.Her. You men of Angiers open wide your gates, 610
Open your gates, and giue the Victors way. 635
Our former scruple in our strong barr'd gates: 684
To our fast closed gates: for at this match, 762
Fra. Now Cittizens of Angires ope your gates, 856
Euen at my gates, with rankes of forraigne powres; 1969
GAUE = 4
My father gaue me honor, yours gaue land: 173
The latest breath that gaue the sound of words 1161
That in your Chambers gaue you chasticement? 2401
GAUL = 2
Sal. Stand by, or I shall gaul you *Faulconbridge.* 2096
Bast. Thou wer't better gaul the diuell Salsbury. 2097
GAWDES = 1
Is all too wanton, and too full of gawdes 1335
GEFFREY = 3
Which died in *Geffrey*: and the hand of time, 399
That *Geffrey* was thy elder brother borne, 401
Liker in feature to his father *Geffrey* 423
GEFFREYES = 5
Of thy deceased brother, *Geffreyes* sonne, 13
Looke heere vpon thy brother *Geffreyes* face, 396
And this is *Geffreyes* in the name of God: 403

GEFFREYES *cont.*
My name is *Constance*, I was *Geffreyes* wife,   1430
Is it my fault, that I was *Geffreyes* sonne?   1595
GEFFREYS = 1
And this his sonne, *England* was *Geffreys* right,   402
GENERALL = 1
Is much more generall, then these lines import.   2014
GENERATION = 1
Being but the second generation | Remoued from thy sinne-conceiuing
wombe.   483
GENTLE = 15
What *England* saies, say breefely gentle Lord,   346
Our Trumpet call'd you to this gentle parle.   511
And make a ryot on the gentle brow | Of true sincerity? O holy Sir 1178
Some gentle order, and then we shall be blest   1182
Ele. Farewell gentle Cosen. | *Iohn.* Coz, farewell.   1315
Iohn. Come hether *Hubert*. O my gentle *Hubert*,   1318
Fra. Patience good Lady, comfort gentle *Constance*.   1405
He hath a sterne looke, but a gentle heart: 1664
For I must vse thee. O my gentle Cosen,   1880
Iohn. Gentle kinsman, go | And thrust thy selfe into their Companies, 1887
This gentle offer of the perillous time.   2010
And snarleth in the gentle eyes of peace: 2155
But since you are a gentle conuertite,   2186
Vpon her gentle bosom, and fill vp   2279
Their Needl's to Lances, and their gentle hearts | To fierce and bloody
inclination.   2411
GENTLEMAN = 4
Philip. Your faithfull subiect, I a gentleman,   58
When this same lusty gentleman was got: 116
That smooth-fac'd Gentleman, tickling commoditie,   894
Iohn. Spoke like a sprightfull Noble Gentleman.   1899
GENTLEMEN = 1
Yong Gentlemen would be as sad as night   1588
GENTLY = 1
It may lie gently at the foot of peace,   2329
GENTRY = 1
To grace the Gentry of a Land remote,   2282
GEORGE = 2
And if his name be *George*, Ile call him *Peter*;   196
Bast. Saint *George* that swindg'd the Dragon,   595
GERMANY = 1
To *Germany*, there with the Emperor   108
GET = 11
Phil. I know not why, except to get the land: 81
Phil. Well sir, by this you cannot get my land,   105
Who as you say, tooke paines to get this sonne,   129
My mothers sonne did get your fathers heyre,   136
Then was his will to get me, as I think.   141
Could get me sir *Robert* could not doe it;   250
Bast. Now by this light were I to get againe,   272
Envenom him with words, or get thee gone,   984
If I get downe, and do not breake my limbes,   2002
Ile finde a thousand shifts to get away;   2003
Auant thou hatefull villain, get thee gone.   2077
GHOST = 1
And he will looke as hollow as a Ghost,   1469

GIANT *see* gyant
GIANT-WORLD = 1
  That neuer saw the giant-world enrag'd,   2308
GIDDY = 2
  Against these giddy loose suggestions: 1223
  Ioh. Thou hast made me giddy   1852
GIFTS *see* guifts
GILD = 1
  Shall gild her bridall bed and make her rich   807
GILDE = 1
  To gilde refined Gold, to paint the Lilly;   1728
GILT = 1
  Hither returne all gilt with Frenchmens blood: 627
GIRDLE = 1
  That as a waste doth girdle you about   523
GIUE = 34*1
  I giue heauen thankes I was not like to thee.   91
  I would giue it euery foot to haue this face: 154
  Bast. Our Country manners giue our betters way.   164
  Bast. Brother by th'mothers side, giue me your hand,   172
  Bast. Iames Gournie, wilt thou giue vs leaue a while?   241
  Embrace him, loue him, giue him welcome hether.   304
  The rather, that you giue his off-spring life,   306
  I giue you welcome with a powerlesse hand,   308
  Till your strong hand shall helpe to giue him strength,   326
  And out of my deere loue Ile giue thee more,   457
  Giue grandame kingdome, and it grandame will   462
  Giue yt a plum, a cherry, and a figge,   463
  Or shall we giue the signall to our rage,   571
  Open your gates, and giue the Victors way.   635
  To whom in fauour she shall giue the day,   707
  And giue you entrance: but without this match,   765
  Giue with our Neece a dowrie large enough,   785
  Ioh. Then I doe giue *Volquessen, Toraine, Maine,*   847
  Will giue her sadnesse very little cure: 866
  That giue you cause to proue my saying true.   949
  Law cannot giue my childe his kingdome heere;   1115
  Giue me thy hand, I had a thing to say,   1324
  To giue me audience: If the mid-night bell   1336
  I could giue better comfort then you doe.   1485
  Hub. Giue me the Iron I say, and binde him heere.   1651
  Let him come backe, that his compassion may | Giue life to yours.   1665
  Good Lords, although my will to giue, is liuing,   1801
  Aloft the flood, and can giue audience   1860
  Shall giue a holinesse, a puritie,   2052
  My Crowne I should giue off? euen so I haue: 2194
  To giue vs warrant from the hand of heauen,   2318
  And shall I now giue ore the yeelded Set?   2360
  Pan. Giue me leaue to speake.   2417
  My arme shall giue thee helpe to beare thee hence,   2519
  Hen. I haue a kinde soule, that would giue thanks,   2719
GIUEN = 2
  Whose leisure I haue staid, haue giuen him time   352
  As they haue giuen these hayres their libertie: 1457
GIUES = 1
  He giues the bastinado with his tongue: 779

GIUING = 2
A Souldier by the Honor-giuing-hand | Of *Cordelion*, Knighted in the
  field. 61
By giuing it the worship of Reuenge. 2071
GIUST = 1
That thou for truth giu'st out are landed heere? | *Mes.* Vnder the
  Dolphin. 1849
GLAD = 2
Dol. As heartily as he is glad he hath him. 1509
I am not glad that such a sore of Time 2263
GLEW = 1
Doe glew themselues in sociable griefe, 1449
GLISTER = 1
Away, and glister like the god of warre 2222
GLITTERING = 1
The meager cloddy earth to glittering gold: 1005
GLORIE = 1
The lineall state, and glorie of the Land, 2713
GLORIFIE = 1
Do glorifie the bankes that bound them in: 757
GLORIFIED = 1
Till my attempt so much be glorified, 2364
GLORIOUS = 2
And kisse him with a glorious victory: 708
To solemnize this day the glorious sunne 1002
GLORY = 4
Bast. Ha Maiesty: how high thy glory towres, 664
Dol. All daies of glory, ioy, and happinesse. 1502
Till I haue set a glory to this hand, 2070
K.Iohn. Thus haue I yeelded vp into your hand | The Circle of my glory. 2167
GLOW = 1
And glow with shame of your proceedings, *Hubert*: 1693
GNAT = 1
A graine, a dust, a gnat, a wandering haire, 1671
GO = 16*6
Or else it must go wrong with you and me, 47
*Elinor. Nay, I would haue you go before me thither. 163
If lustie loue should go in quest of beautie, 741
If zealous loue should go in search of vertue, 743
Go we as well as hast will suffer vs, 880
*Con. Thou maist, thou shalt, I will not go with thee, 989
*Elea. Look'st thou pale *France*? do not let go thy hand. 1123
Go with me to the King, 'tis wonderfull, 1563
For England go; I will whet on the King. 1566
*Dol. Strong reasons makes strange actions: let vs go, 1567
Hub. Go stand within: let me alone with him. 1661
*Hub. Is this your promise? Go too, hold your toong. 1675
Hub. Silence, no more; go closely in with mee, 1714
Sal. The colour of the King doth come, and go 1794
Pem. Stay yet (Lord Salisbury) Ile go with thee, 1814
Iohn. Gentle kinsman, go | And thrust thy selfe into their Companies, 1887
Go after him: for he perhaps shall neede 1900
As good to dye, and go; as dye, and stay. 2004
Bast. Go, beare him in thine armes: 2144
*Iohn. Now keep your holy word, go meet the *French*, 2172
And send him word by me, which way you go. 2447
Bast. Whether doest thou go? | *Hub.* What's that to thee? 2555

GOD = 5*2
Arth. God shall forgiue you *Cordelions* death 305
And this is *Geffreyes* in the name of God: 403
But God hath made her sinne and her, the plague 488
**Iohn.* Then God forgiue the sinne of all those soules, 590
*Command the rest to stand, God and our right. *Exeunt* 607
Which we God knowes, haue turn'd another way, | To our owne
vantage. 869
Away, and glister like the god of warre 2222
GODAMERCY = 1
Good den Sir *Richard*, Godamercy fellow, 195
GODS = 2
Whiles we Gods wrathfull agent doe correct 384
As Gods owne souldier, rounded in the eare, 887
GOE = 14*1
**K.Iohn.* Goe, *Faulconbridge*, now hast thou thy desire, 185
Cons. Doe childe, goe to yt grandame childe, 461
Sal. Pardon me Madam, | I may not goe without you to the kings. 987
Let goe the hand of that Arch-heretique, 1120
Vpon my knee I beg, goe not to Armes | Against mine Vncle. 1241
Which is the side that I must goe withall? 1260
Iohn. Cosen, goe draw our puisance together, 1272
I had a thing to say, but let it goe: 1332
Ele. My blessing goe with thee. 1376
Iohn. For *England* Cosen, goe. 1377
Pand. Courage and comfort, all shall yet goe well. 1386
Fra. What can goe well, when we haue runne so ill? 1387
I prethee Lady goe away with me. 1403
Goe I to make the *French* lay downe their Armes. *Exit.* 2191
That vnder-goe this charge? Who else but I, 2353
GOES = 4
Lest men should say, looke where three farthings goes, 151
You are the Hare of whom the Prouerb goes, 437
Poure downe thy weather: how goes all in France? 1827
Iohn. How goes the day with vs? oh tell me *Hubert.* 2440
GOING = 1
And others more, going to seeke the graue 1885
GOLD = 4
The meager cloddy earth to glittering gold: 1005
And by the merit of vilde gold, drosse, dust, 1092
When gold and siluer becks me to come on. 1311
To gilde refined Gold, to paint the Lilly; 1728
GOLDEN = 2
And with her golden hand hath pluckt on France 978
That it in goldèn letters should be set 1010
GONE = 10*2
Legitimation, name, and all is gone; 261
**Con.* Gone to be married? Gone to sweare a peace? 922
False blood to false blood ioyn'd. Gone to be freinds? 923
Fellow be gone: I cannot brooke thy sight, 957
Envenom him with words, or get thee gone, 984
And bloudy *England* into *England* gone, 1390
If that yong *Arthur* be not gone alreadie, 1548
The suite which you demand is gone, and dead. 1802
Auant thou hatefull villain, get thee gone. 2077
Your Nobles will not heare you, but are gone | To offer seruice to your
enemy: 2201

GONE *cont.*
  Bast. Art thou gone so? I do but stay behinde,   2680
GOOD = 38*8
  K.Iohn. Silence (good mother) heare the Embassie.   11
  * *K.Iohn.* A good blunt fellow: why being yonger born   79
  Then good my Liedge let me haue what is mine,   122
  Insooth, good friend, your father might haue kept   131
  Philip, good old Sir *Roberts* wiues eldest sonne.   167
  Bast. Brother adieu, good fortune come to thee,   189
  Good den Sir *Richard*, Godamercy fellow,   195
  O me, 'tis my mother: how now good Lady,   230
  Gour. Good leaue good *Philip.*   242
  Vpon good Friday, and nere broke his fast: 248
  We know his handy-worke, therefore good mother   251
  Bast. Knight, knight good mother, Basilisco-like: 257
  Then good my mother, let me know my father,   262
  * *Fra.* Fro(m) that supernal Iudge that stirs good thoughts   409
  * *Queen.* Theres a good mother boy, that blots thy fa-|(ther   429
  Const. There's a good grandame boy | That would blot thee.   430
  There's a good grandame.   464
  Arthur. Good my mother peace,   465
  Sal. What other harme haue I good Lady done,   959
  Good Father Cardinall, cry thou Amen   1109
  Fra. Good reuerend father, make my person yours,   1155
  And my good friend, thy voluntary oath   1322
  To say what good respect I haue of thee.   1327
  Iohn. Good friend, thou hast no cause to say so yet,   1329
  Yet it shall come, for me to doe thee good.   1331
  Good *Hubert, Hubert, Hubert* throw thine eye   1359
  Fra. Patience good Lady, comfort gentle *Constance.*   1405
  No, no: when Fortune meanes to men most good,   1504
  Ar. Good morrow *Hubert.*   1580
  Hub. Good morrow, little Prince.   1581
  Or what good loue may I performe for you?   1625
  * *Art.* No, in good sooth: the fire is dead with griefe,   1685
  The rich aduantage of good exercise,   1777
  Good Lords, although my will to giue, is liuing,   1801
  Good ground be pittifull, and hurt me not: 1998
  As good to dye, and go; as dye, and stay.   2004
  Bast. What ere you thinke, good words I thinke | were best.   2026
  * *Ba.* Here's a good world: knew you of this faire work?   2119
  Bast. Away then with good courage: yet I know   2247
  Mes. Be of good comfort: for the great supply   2449
  And will not let me welcome this good newes.   2455
  After such bloody toile, we bid good night,   2530
  * *Dol.* Well: keepe good quarter, & good care to night,   2546
  * *Sal.* Be of good comfort (Prince) for you are borne   2631
GOODNIGHT *see* good
GOODS = 1
  Which for our goods, we do no further aske,   1781
GOODWIN = 2
  Are wrack'd three nights ago on *Goodwin* sands.   2451
  Are cast away, and sunke on *Goodwin* sands.   2539
GOSSIPPING = 1
  Full warm of blood, of mirth, of gossipping: 2310
GOT = 5
  When this same lusty gentleman was got: 116

GOT *cont.*
  Your face hath got fiue hundred pound a yeere,   160
  When I was got, Sir *Robert* was away.   175
  For thou wast got i'th way of honesty. | *Exeunt all but bastard.*   190
  When I was got, Ile send his soule to hell.   285
GOUERNE = 1
  Gouerne the motion of a kinglye eye: 2215
GOUR = 1
GOURNIE = 1
  Bast. Iames Gournie, wilt thou giue vs leaue a while?   241
GRACE = 4*1
  Out of your grace, deuise, ordaine, impose   1181
  Iohn. So shall it be: your Grace shall stay behinde   1299
  To grace occasions: let it be our suite,   1779
  To grace the Gentry of a Land remote,   2282
  *Dol. Your Grace shall pardon me, I will not backe: 2331
GRACELESSE = 1
  The gracelesse action of a heauy hand,   2057
GRACING = 1
  Gracing the scroule that tels of this warres losse,   662
GRACIOUS = 3
  Rob. My gracious Liege, when that my father liu'd,   103
  There was not such a gracious creature borne: 1466
  Remembers me of all his gracious parts,   1481
GRAINE = 1
  A graine, a dust, a gnat, a wandering haire,   1671
GRANDAM = 1
  Grandam, I will not wish thy wishes thriue: 1267
GRANDAME = 9
  I am thy grandame *Richard*, call me so.   177
  Const. There's a good grandame boy | That would blot thee.   430
  Queen. Come to thy grandame child.   460
  Cons. Doe childe, goe to yt grandame childe,   461
  Giue grandame kingdome, and it grandame will   462
  There's a good grandame.   464
  Thy Grandame loues thee, and thy Vnkle will   1301
  I leaue your highnesse: Grandame, I will pray   1312
GRANDAMES = 1
  His grandames wrongs, and not his mothers shames   470
GRANDAMS = 1
  A womans will, a cankred Grandams will.   497
GRANDSIRE = 1
  (For that my Grandsire was an Englishman)   2503
GRANT = 3
  Con. Oh, if thou grant my need,   1142
  I will both heare, and grant you your requests.   1763
  We grant thou canst out-scold vs: Far thee well,   2414
GRAPLING = 1
  The grapling vigor, and rough frowne of Warre | Is cold in amitie, and
  painted peace,   1029
GRAPPLE = 1
  And grapple with him ere he come so nye.   2229
GRAUE = 8
  By this braue Duke came early to his graue: 298
  I would that I were low laid in my graue,   466
  Iohn. A Graue. | *Hub.* He shall not liue.   1369
  Looke who comes heere? a graue vnto a soule,   1400

GRAUE *cont.*
  His little kingdome of a forced graue.   1816
  And others more, going to seeke the graue   1885
  Big. Or when he doom'd this Beautie to a graue,   2038
  Found it too precious Princely, for a graue.   2039
GREAT = 19*2
  Kneele thou downe *Philip*, but rise more great,   170
  Arthur that great fore-runner of thy bloud,   295
  *K.Iohn. From whom hast thou this great commission | (*France,*   407
  As great *Alcides* shooes vpon an Asse: 444
  Iohn. In Vs, that are our owne great Deputie,   679
  *Hub. Heare vs great kings, vouchsafe awhile to stay   731
  Become thy great birth, nor deserue a Crowne.   971
  Nature and Fortune ioyn'd to make thee great.   973
  To me and to the state of my great greefe,   992
  Lets kings assemble: for my greefe's so great,   993
  Thou little valiant, great in villanie,   1042
  So vnder him that great supremacy   1083
  Ar. As little Prince, hauing so great a Title   1582
  Be great in act, as you haue beene in thought: 2213
  That borrow their behauiours from the great,   2219
  Grow great by your example, and put on   2220
  And great affections wrastling in thy bosome   2292
  And with a great heart heaue away this storme: 2306
  The great Metropolis and Sea of Rome: 2325
  Mes. Be of good comfort: for the great supply   2449
  Euen to our Ocean, to our great King *Iohn.*   2518
GREATER = 1
  Fra. A greater powre then We denies all this,   682
GREATEST = 1
  One must proue greatest. While they weigh so euen,   644
GREATNESSE = 4
  And sooth'st vp greatnesse. What a foole art thou,   1047
  That Greatnesse should so grossely offer it;   1812
  Your Worth, your Greatnesse, and Nobility.   2086
  Your Soueraigne greatnesse and authoritie.   2171
GREEFE = 8
  For greefe is proud, and makes his owner stoope,   991
  To me and to the state of my great greefe,   992
  For, being not mad, but sensible of greefe,   1437
  Pand. You hold too heynous a respect of greefe.   1475
  Fra. You are as fond of greefe, as of your childe.   1477
  Con. Greefe fils the roome vp of my absent childe: 1478
  Saying, what lacke you? and where lies your greefe? 1624
  Bast. But there is little reason in your greefe.   2029
GREEFES = 3
  Lets kings assemble: for my greefe's so great,   993
  Sal. Our greefes, and not our manners reason now.   2028
  Since it hath beene before hand with our greefes.   2722
GREEN = *1
  *Pan. How green you are, and fresh in this old world? 1530
GREENE = 1
  That yon greene boy shall haue no Sunne to ripe   788
GREENES = 1
  In warlike march, these greenes before your Towne, 548
GREETING = 1
  Chat. Thus (after greeting) speakes the King | of France, 6

GREEUOUSLY = 1
I do suspect thee very greeuously. 2138
GRIEFE = 4*1
Arth. O this will make my mother die with griefe. 1303
O, if I could, what griefe should I forget? 1434
Doe glew themselues in sociable griefe, 1449
Then, haue I reason to be fond of griefe? 1483
**Art.* No, in good sooth: the fire is dead with griefe, 1685
GRIEUD = 1
Are not you grieu'd that *Arthur* is his prisoner? 1508
GRIEUED = 1
And is't not pitty, (oh my grieued friends) 2275
GRIEUES = 1
By making many: Oh it grieues my soule, 2266
GRIM = 1
Con. If thou that bidst me be content, wert grim 964
GRIN = 1
Come, grin on me, and I will thinke thou smil'st, 1417
GRIPE = 1
And he that speakes, doth gripe the hearers wrist, 1915
GROAT = 1
A halfe-fac'd groat, fiue hundred pound a yeere? 102
GROSSELY = 3
Are led so grossely by this medling Priest, 1090
Though you, and al the rest so grossely led, 1095
That Greatnesse should so grossely offer it; 1812
GROUELING = 1
Many a widdowes husband groueling lies, 615
GROUND = 7
Whose sonnes lye scattered on the bleeding ground: 614
And lay this Angiers euen with the ground, 713
And when that we haue dash'd them to the ground, 719
Made to run euen, vpon euen ground; 897
Vpon the bosome of the ground, rush forth 1573
Good ground be pittifull, and hurt me not: 1998
When English measure backward their owne ground 2527
GROW = 1
Grow great by your example, and put on 2220
GROWES = 1
Yet indirection thereby growes direct, 1207
GROWS = *1
**Bast.* Now by my life, this day grows wondrous hot, 1285
GUARD = 2
Heauen guard my mothers honor, and my Land. 78
To guard a Title, that was rich before; 1727
GUARDED = 1
So strongly guarded: Cosen, looke not sad, 1300
GUARDIAN = 1
That Iudge hath made me guardian to this boy, 412
GUIFTS = 1
Of Natures guifts, thou mayst with Lillies boast, 974
GUILTIE = 1
Be guiltie of the stealing that sweete breath 2140
GURNEY see also Gour., Gournie = 1
Enter Lady Faulconbridge and Iames Gurney. 232
GYANT = 1
Colbrand the Gyant, that same mighty man, 236

H = *1
HA *l*.664 2123 = 2
HABIT = 1
   And not alone in habit and deuice,   220
HAD *l*.39 130 146 147 288 526 1324 1332 1342 1397 1476 1484 1503 1619
  1628 1793 1923 1930 1948 *1960 2030 2035 2060 2245 2303 2391 2468
  2584 = 28*1, *1
   H. No had (my Lord?) why, did you not prouoke me?   1932
HADST *l*.142 288 1931 1945 *1956 = 4*1
HAILE = 2
   Pan. Haile you annointed deputies of heauen;   1063
   Pand. Haile noble Prince of *France*:   2321
HAIRE = 3
   I am not mad: this haire I teare is mine,   1429
   A graine, a dust, a gnat, a wandering haire,   1671
   Are turned to one thred, one little haire: 2664
HAIRES = 2
   In the faire multitude of those her haires;   1446
   Fra. Binde vp your haires. | *Con*. Yes that I will: and wherefore will I
   do it?   1453
HALFE = 7
   With halfe that face would he haue all my land,   101
   He is the halfe part of a blessed man,   752
   The sea enraged is not halfe so deafe,   766
   In mortall furie halfe so peremptorie, | As we to keepe this Citie. 769
   And now it is halfe conquer'd, must I backe,   2348
   Ile tell thee *Hubert*, halfe my power this night   2597
   Who halfe an houre since came from the Dolphin,   2693
HALFE-BLOWNE = 1
   And with the halfe-blowne Rose. But Fortune, oh,   975
HALFE-FACD = 1
   A halfe-fac'd groat, fiue hundred pound a yeere?   102
HALF-FACE = 1
   Philip. Because he hath a half-face like my father?   100
HALTING = 1
   (Not trusting to this halting Legate heere,   2430
HAMMER = 1
   I saw a Smith stand with his hammer (thus)   1918
HAMMERD = 1
   Are you more stubborne hard, then hammer'd Iron?   1644
HAND = 56*2
   And put the same into yong *Arthurs* hand,   19
   A Souldier by the Honor-giuing-hand | Of *Cordelion*, Knighted in the
   field.   61
   Bast. Brother by th'mothers side, giue me your hand,   172
   Nor keepe his Princely heart from *Richards* hand: 280
   I giue you welcome with a powerlesse hand,   308
   Till your strong hand shall helpe to giue him strength,   326
   Cuts off more circumstance, they are at hand, | *Drum beats*. 371
   Which died in *Geffrey*: and the hand of time,   399
   Arthur of *Britaine*, yeeld thee to my hand,   456
   Then ere the coward hand of *France* can win; | Submit thee boy. 458
   Loe in this right hand, whose protection   542
   Who by the hand of France, this day hath made   612
   Who are at hand triumphantly displayed   619
   Rather lost more. And by this hand I sweare   657
   Holdes hand with any Princesse of the world.   810

HAND *cont.*

Not that I haue the power to clutch my hand,	910
But for my hand, as vnattempted yet,	912
What meanes that hand vpon that breast of thine?	942
And with her golden hand hath pluckt on France	978
Without th'assistance of a mortall hand:	1085
And meritorious shall that hand be call'd,	1103
Let goe the hand of that Arch-heretique,	1120
Elea. Look'st thou pale *France*? do not let go thy hand.	1123
This royall hand and mine are newly knit,	1157
Then keepe in peace that hand which thou dost hold.	1192
Fra. I may dis-ioyne my hand, but not my faith.	1193
I am with both, each Army hath a hand,	1261
For your faire safety: so I kisse your hand.	1314
Giue me thy hand, I had a thing to say,	1324
A Scepter snatch'd with an vnruly hand,	1520
And with my hand, at midnight held your head;	1621
Iohn. We cannot hold mortalities strong hand.	1800
Who with his Sheeres, and Measure in his hand,	1921
Thy hand hath murdred him: I had a mighty cause	1930
Hub. Heere is your hand and Seale for what I did.	1940
Is to be made, then shall this hand and Seale	1942
A fellow by the hand of Nature mark'd,	1946
And consequently, thy rude hand to acte	1965
Yong *Arthur* is aliue: This hand of mine	1976
Is yet a maiden, and an innocent hand.	1977
The gracelesse action of a heauy hand,	2057
If that it be the worke of any hand.	2058
Sal. If that it be the worke of any hand?	2059
It is the shamefull worke of *Huberts* hand,	2061
Till I haue set a glory to this hand,	2070
A thousand businesses are briefe in hand,	2163
K.Iohn. Thus haue I yeelded vp into your hand | The Circle of my glory.	2167
Pan. Take againe | From this my hand, as holding of the Pope	2169
By some damn'd hand was rob'd, and tane away.	2209
We cannot deale but with the very hand	2273
Come, come; for thou shalt thrust thy hand as deepe	2311
To giue vs warrant from the hand of heauen,	2318
That like a Lion fostered vp at hand,	2328
That hand which had the strength, euen at your dore,	2391
Shall that victorious hand be feebled heere,	2400
And euen at hand, a drumme is readie brac'd,	2425
And mocke the deepe mouth'd Thunder: for at hand	2429
Since it hath beene before hand with our greefes.	2722

HANDS = 7*1

Our colours do returne in those same hands	630
Our lustie English, all with purpled hands,	633
Command thy sonne and daughter to ioyne hands.	852
Fra. It likes vs well young Princes: close your hands	853
And by disioyning hands hell lose a soule.	1125
No longer then we well could wash our hands,	1165
And shall these hands so lately purg'd of bloud?	1170
O, that these hands could so redeeme my sonne,	1456

HANDY-WORKE = 1

We know his handy-worke, therefore good mother	251

HAND-KERCHER = 1

I knit my hand-kercher about your browes	1618

HANG = 5*3

And hang a Calues skin on those recreant limbes.	1055
*Phil. And hang a Calues-skin on those recreant limbs	1057
*Phil. And hang a Calues-skin on those recreant limbs.	1059
Bast. And hang a Calues-skin on his recreant limbs.	1127
Aust. Doe so king Philip, hang no more in doubt.	1150
*Bast. Hang nothing but a Calues skin most sweet lout.	1151
And teaches mee to kill or hang my selfe:	1440
To hang thee on. Or wouldst thou drowne thy selfe,	2134

HANGD = 2*1

Hang'd in the frowning wrinkle of her brow,	822
*That hang'd, and drawne, and quarter'd there should be	825
I shall yeeld vp my Crowne, let him be hang'd	1878

HANGS = 1

Iohn. Now by the sky that hangs aboue our heads,	711

HAPPIE = 2

Sal. When we were happie, we had other names.	2468
And happie newnesse, that intends old right. Exeunt	2522

HAPPILY = 2

To consummate this businesse happily.	2705
And happily may your sweet selfe put on	2712

HAPPINESSE = 1

Dol. All daies of glory, ioy, and happinesse.	1502

HAPPY = 4

Out of one side her happy Minion,	706
But on my Liege, for very little paines | Will bring this labor to an happy end. Exit.	1295
Now happy he, whose cloake and center can	2160
And I haue made a happy peace with him,	2231

HARBOURAGE = 1

Craues harbourage within your Citie walles.	540

HARBOURD = 1

Were harbour'd in their rude circumference:	568

HARD = 2

Const. O, vpon my knee made hard with kneeling,	1243
Are you more stubborne hard, then hammer'd Iron?	1644

HARDLY = 1

My selfe, well mounted, hardly haue escap'd.	2600

HARE = 1

You are the Hare of whom the Prouerb goes	437

HARKE = 1

Ele. Come hether little kinsman, harke, a worde.	1317

HARME = 6

Sal. What other harme haue I good Lady done,	959
But spoke the harme, that is by others done?	960
Con. Which harme within it selfe so heynous is,	961
My Vnckle practises more harme to me:	1593
But for containing fire to harme mine eye:	1643
And would not harme me.	1683

HARMEFULL = 3

As it makes harmefull all that speake of it.	962
Without eyes, eares, and harmefull sound of words:	1350
And be no further harmefull then in shewe.	2330

HARNESSD = 1

This harness'd Maske, and vnaduised Reuell,	2386

HARSH = 1

To whom he sung in rude harsh sounding rimes,	1871

HART = 1
    Dol. Ah fowle, shrew'd newes, Beshrew thy very | (hart: 2540
HAST *l.**185 254 264 315 392 *407 *648 655 715 925 1050 1201 1211 1234
    1329 1824 1852 2294 2560 = 16*3, 3
    Go we as well as hast will suffer vs,   880
    Iohn. Doth *Arthur* liue? O hast thee to the Peeres,   1985
    The angry Lords, with all expedient hast,   1993
HASTE *see also* hast = 6
    But who comes in such haste in riding robes?   227
    That hot rash haste so indirectly shedde.   342
    Iohn. Cosen away for *England,* haste before,   1304
    Iohn. Nay, but make haste: the better foote before.   1892
    Standing on slippers, which his nimble haste   1922
    Hub. Lords, I am hot with haste, in seeking you,   2074
HASTIE = 1
    Or teach thy hastie spleene to do me shame,   2099
HASTILY = 1
    What brings you heere to Court so hastily?   231
HATCH = 2
    In at the window, or else ore the hatch: 180
    To cudgell you, and make you take the hatch,   2392
HATE = 2
    That I can finde, should merit any hate.   838
    Thou hate and terror to prosperitie,   1411
HATEFULL = 3
    That takes away by any secret course | Thy hatefull life.   1105
    A passion hatefull to my purposes: 1346
    Auant thou hatefull villain, get thee gone.   2077
HATH *l.**92 93 97 100 160 228 351 412 488 506 556 612 640 *798 884 905
    909 958 978 1009 1031 1111 1261 1274 1392 1395 1447 1495 1506 1509
    1516 1664 1689 1834 1835 1930 2000 2021 2031 2036 2075 *2198 2199
    2230 2232 2298 2322 2344 2349 2350 2431 2442 *2465 2477 2542 2593
    2633 2635 2665 2683 2700 2722 = 60*4
HATING = 1
    Sal. Murther, as hating what himselfe hath done,   2036
HAUE *see also* Godamercy *l.**24 34 37 41 74 101 115 122 131 137 154
    *163 182 247 258 260 352 363 367 485 486 515 516 530 541 570 578 640
    697 719 788 857 862 *865 869 910 *924 931 959 1021 1023 1024 1099
    1108 1327 1330 1387 1457 1461 1483 1501 1556 1578 1584 1616 1626
    1627 1635 1645 *1647 1663 1758 1761 1772 1778 1780 1783 1810 1825
    1845 1862 1863 1889 1893 *1961 1981 *2040 2041 2070 2083 2167 2194
    2213 2231 2246 2356 2357 2358 2373 2375 2483 2516 2538 2568 2599
    2600 2719 = 91*7, 1
    And haue is haue, how euer men doe catch: 182
HAUING = 6
    Who hauing no externall thing to loose,   892
    And in their rage, I hauing hold of both,   1262
    Con. No, no, I will not, hauing breath to cry: 1421
    Ar. As little Prince, hauing so great a Title   1582
    That hauing our faire order written downe,   2255
    Death hauing praide vpon the outward parts   2621
HAUOCKE = 2
    Had bin dishabited, and wide hauocke made   526
    Cry hauocke kings, backe to the stained field   671
HAYRES = 1
    As they haue giuen these hayres their libertie: 1457

HAZARD = 1
To make a hazard of new fortunes heere: 365
HAZARDS = 2
Which fault lyes on the hazards of all husbands   127
I will vpon all hazards well beleeue   2561
HE *see also* a = 101*4
HEAD = 17*1
That still I lay vpon my mothers head,   84
I would set an Oxe-head to your Lyons hide: | And make a monster of
you.   599
Makes it take head from all indifferency,   900
What dost thou meane by shaking of thy head?   940
But as we, vnder heauen, are supreame head,   1082
And raise the power of *France* vpon his head,   1121
Pand. I will denounce a curse vpon his head.   1252
*Allarums, Excursions: Enter Bastard with Austria's | head.   1283
And pour's downe mischiefe. *Austrias* head lye there,   1287
I will not keepe this forme vpon my head,   1486
Art. Haue you the heart? When your head did but | ake,   1616
And with my hand, at midnight held your head;   1621
And strew'd repentant ashes on his head.   1690
My head with more ill newes: for it is full.   1855
Then let the worst vn-heard, fall on your head.   1857
Hub. My Lord. | **Ioh.* Had'st thou but shooke thy head, or made a
pause   1955
Before I drew this gallant head of warre,   2366
Is warlike *Iohn*: and in his fore-head sits   2432
HEADS = 3
Iohn. Now by the sky that hangs aboue our heads,   711
And when they talke of him, they shake their heads,   1913
By cutting off your heads: Thus hath he sworne,   2477
HEALE = 2
Iohn. We will heale vp all,   871
And heale the inueterate Canker of one wound,   2265
HEALTH = 2
Euen in the instant of repaire and health,   1498
That for the health and Physicke of our right,   2272
HEARD = 12
The thunder of my Cannon shall be heard.   31
That ere I heard: shall I produce the men? | *K.Iohn.* Let them approach: 53
As I haue heard my father speake himselfe   115
Doth want example: who hath read, or heard   1395
And Father Cardinall, I haue heard you say   1461
Pem. Indeed we heard how neere his death he was,   1805
I idely heard: if true, or false I know not.   1843
Then let the worst vn-heard, fall on your head.   1857
Or haue you read, or heard, or could you thinke?   2041
After they heard yong *Arthur* was aliue?   2206
Haue I not heard these Islanders shout out   2356
This vn-heard sawcinesse and boyish Troopes,   2387
HEARE = 23*1
K.Iohn. Silence (good mother) heare the Embassie.   11
Which none but heauen, and you, and I, shall heare.   49
Aust. Peace. | *Bast.* Heare the Cryer.   432
These men of Angiers, let vs heare them speake,   502
Iohn. For our aduantage, therefore heare vs first: 512
Aust. Peace, no more. | *Bast.* O tremble: for you heare the Lyon rore. 601

HEARE *cont.*
* *Hub.* Heare vs great kings, vouchsafe awhile to stay   731
Perseuer not, but heare me mighty kings.   736
Iohn. Speake on with fauour, we are bent to heare.   737
Heare me, Oh, heare me. | *Aust.* Lady *Constance*, peace.   1037
O husband heare me: aye, .alacke, how new   1238
Heare me without thine eares, and make reply   1348
Which cannot heare a Ladies feeble voyce,   1425
Now heare me speake with a propheticke spirit: 1511
Pan. O Sir, when he shall heare of your approach,   1547
Nay heare me *Hubert*, driue these men away,   1655
I will both heare, and grant you your requests.   1763
That such an Army could be drawne in France, | And she not heare of
it?   1836
Your noble mother; and as I heare, my Lord,   1840
Bast. But if you be a-feard to heare the worst,   1856
Hub. Do but heare me sir. | *Bast.* Ha? Ile tell thee what.   2122
Your Nobles will not heare you, but are gone | To offer seruice to your
enemy: 2201
The youth saies well. Now heare our *English* King,   2382
HEARERS = 1
And he that speakes, doth gripe the hearers wrist,   1915
HEARES = 1
Whilst he that heares, makes fearefull action   1916
HEARST = 1
Hear'st thou the newes abroad, who are arriu'd?   1881
HEART *see also* hart = 16
Needs must you lay your heart at his dispose,   276
Nor keepe his Princely heart from *Richards* hand: 280
With all my heart I thanke thee for my father: 283
Richard that rob'd the Lion of his heart,   296
But with a heart full of vnstained loue,   309
And quarter'd in her heart, hee doth espie   823
Art. Haue you the heart? When your head did but | ake,   1616
He hath a sterne looke, but a gentle heart: 1664
And be thou hee. | *Mes.* With all my heart, my Liege.   1902
Yea, without stop, didst let thy heart consent,   1964
My heart hath melted at a Ladies teares,   2298
And with a great heart heaue away this storme: 2306
Yea, thrust this enterprize into my heart,   2343
Lyes heauie on me: oh, my heart is sicke.   2443
The tackle of my heart, is crack'd and burnt,   2662
My heart hath one poore string to stay it by,   2665
HEARTILY = 2
Dol. As heartily as he is glad he hath him.   1509
Bend their best studies, heartily request   1768
HEARTS = 6
He that perforce robs Lions of their hearts,   281
Twice fifteene thousand hearts of Englands breed. | *Bast.* Bastards and
else.   582
This Act so euilly borne shall coole the hearts   1534
Euen at that newes he dies: and then the hearts   1549
To sound the purposes of all their hearts,   1765
Their Needl's to Lances, and their gentle hearts | To fierce and bloody
inclination.   2411
HEAT = 1
A rage, whose heat hath this condition;   1274

HEATE = 2*1
  Hub. Heate me these Irons hot, and looke thou stand   1571
  The Iron of it selfe, though heate red hot,   1638
  Hub. I can heate it, Boy.   1684
HEAUE = 1
  And with a great heart heaue away this storme: 2306
HEAUEN = 42*7
  Which none but heauen, and you, and I, shall heare.   49
  I put you o're to heauen, and to my mother;   70
  Heauen guard my mothers honor, and my Land.   78
  I giue heauen thankes I was not like to thee.   91
  K.Iohn. Why what a mad-cap hath heauen lent vs here? 92
  Heauen lay not my transgression to my charge,   269
  Aust. The peace of heauen is theirs y lift their swords 328
  If not, bleede *France*, and peace ascend to heauen.   383
  Their proud contempt that beats his peace to heauen.   385
  Which heauen shall take in nature of a fee: 472
  I, with these Christall beads heauen shall be brib'd   473
  Qu. Thou monstrous slanderer of heauen and earth.   475
  Con. Thou monstrous Iniurer of heauen and earth,   476
  Against th'involnerable clouds of heauen,   558
  Bast. By heauen, these scroyles of Angiers flout you | (kings, 687
  Make worke vpon our selues, for heauen or hell.   721
  Fra. By heauen Lady, you shall haue no cause   1021
  Pan. Haile you annointed deputies of heauen;   1063
  But as we, vnder heauen, are supreame head,   1082
  Heauen knowes they were besmear'd and ouer-staind 1167
  Play fast and loose with faith? so iest with heauen,   1173
  First made to heauen, first be to heauen perform'd,   1197
  Alter not the doome fore-thought by heauen.   1245
  By heauen *Hubert*, I am almost asham'd   1326
  The Sunne is in the heauen, and the proud day,   1333
  Though that my death were adiunct to my Act, | By heauen I would doe
  it.   1356
  I am not mad, I would to heauen I were,   1432
  That we shall see and know our friends in heauen: 1462
  When I shall meet him in the Court of heauen   1472
  Abbortiues, presages, and tongues of heauen,   1543
  No in deede is't not: and I would to heauen   1596
  If heauen be pleas'd that you must vse me ill,   1631
  For heauen sake *Hubert* let me not be bound: 1654
  Art. O heauen: that there were but a moth in yours,   1670
  The breath of heauen, hath blowne his spirit out,   1689
  Art. O heauen! I thanke you *Hubert*.   1713
  To seeke the beauteous eye of heauen to garnish,   1732
  Ioh. Oh, when the last accompt twixt heauen & earth.   1941
  *Heauen take my soule, and England keep my bones. *Dies* 2006
  By heauen, I thinke my sword's as sharpe as yours.   2082
  Is fled to heauen: and *England* now is left   2150
  And heauen it selfe doth frowne vpon the Land. *Exit.* 2164
  Then had I seene the vaultie top of heauen   2303
  To giue vs warrant from the hand of heauen,   2318
  Dol. The Sun of heauen (me thought) was loth to set; 2525
  Bast. With-hold thine indignation, mighty heauen,   2595
  Where heauen he knowes how we shall answer him.   2670
  And then my soule shall waite on thee to heauen,   2682

HEAUENS = 2
Arme, arme, you heauens, against these periur'd Kings,   1032
A widdow cries, be husband to me (heauens)   1033
HEAUEN-MOUING = *1
*Drawes those heauen-mouing pearles fro(m) his poor eies,   471
HEAUIE = 1
Lyes heauie on me: oh, my heart is sicke.   2443
HEAUN = 1
But (heau'n be thank'd) it is but voluntary.   2196
HEAUY = 5
Is purchase of a heauy curse from *Rome*,   1134
So heauy, as thou shalt not shake them off   1227
Had bak'd thy bloud, and made it heauy, thicke,   1342
Still and anon cheer'd vp the heauy time;   1623
The gracelesse action of a heauy hand,   2057
HEDGD = 1
Euen till that *England* hedg'd in with the maine,   319
HEE *l.*200 *468 751 823 1902 2700 = 5*1
HEEDFULL = 1
Fast to the chaire: be heedfull: hence, and watch.   1575
HEELES = 3
With many hundreds treading on his heeles: 1870
Be Mercurie, set feathers to thy heeles,   1896
The Dolphine rages at our verie heeles.   2690
HEELL = 2
And so hee'll dye: and rising so againe,   1471
He flatly saies, hee'll not lay downe his Armes.   2380
HEERE = 35*4
The borrowed Maiesty of *England* heere.   9
K.Io. Heere haue we war for war, & bloud for bloud,   24
What brings you heere to Court so hastily?   231
That right in peace which heere we vrge in warre,   340
To make a hazard of new fortunes heere: 365
With burden of our armor heere we sweat: 389
Looke heere vpon thy brother *Geffreyes* face,   396
These flagges of France that are aduanced heere   513
Which heere we came to spout against your Towne,   562
*Heere after excursions, Enter the Herald of France | with Trumpets to
the gates.*   608
Fra. Know him in vs, that heere hold vp his right.   678
And beare possession of our Person heere,   680
That heere come sacrifices for the field.   735
Heere is my Throne bid kings come bow to it.   996
Fra. Heere comes the holy Legat of the Pope.   1062
And from Pope *Innocent* the Legate heere,   1066
Law cannot giue my childe his kingdome heere;   1115
Con. O *Lewis*, stand fast, the deuill tempts thee heere   1138
Looke who comes heere? a graue vnto a soule,   1400
And so I would be heere, but that I doubt   1592
*Reade heere yong *Arthur*. How now foolish rheume?   1606
Hub. Giue me the Iron I say, and binde him heere.   1651
Iohn. Heere once againe we sit: once against crown'd   1718
This must be answer'd either heere, or hence.   1807
That thou for truth giu'st out are landed heere? | *Mes.* Vnder the
Dolphin.   1849
Hub. Heere is your hand and Seale for what I did.   1940
Sal. This is the prison: What is he lyes heere?   2033

HEERE *cont.*

And follow vnacquainted colours heere:	2283
What heere? O Nation that thou couldst remoue,	2284
Haue I not heere the best Cards for the game	2358
Shall that victorious hand be feebled heere,	2400
Pleade for our interest, and our being heere.	2421
(Not trusting to this halting Legate heere,	2430
That was expected by the Dolphin heere,	2450
Mel. Lead me to the Reuolts of England heere.	2467
That I must dye heere, and liue hence, by Truth?	2490
Mes. Where is my Prince, the Dolphin? | *Dol.* Heere: what newes?	2534
*Hub. Why heere walke I in the black brow of night | To finde you out.	2573
Hen. Let him be brought into the Orchard heere:	2615

HEERES = 1

Bast. Heeres a stay, | That shakes the rotten carkasse of old death	771

HEIGHTH = 1

The heighth, the Crest: or Crest vnto the Crest	2045

HEIRE = *1

K.Iohn. What art thou? | **Robert.* The son and heire to that same *Faulconbridge.*	63

HELD = 3

To inforce these rights, so forcibly with-held,	23
And with my hand, at midnight held your head;	1621
The deed, which both our tongues held vilde to name.	1966

HELL = 8

When I was got, Ile send his soule to hell.	285
Make worke vpon our selues, for heauen or hell.	721
And by disioyning hands hell lose a soule.	1125
Clamors of hell, be measures to our pomp?	1237
That you shall thinke the diuell is come from hell.	2102
There is not yet so vgly a fiend of hell	2126
Let hell want paines enough to torture me:	2142
Within me is a hell, and there the poyson	2655

HELMETS = 1

With vnhack'd swords, and Helmets all vnbruis'd,	560

HELPE = 4

Till your strong hand shall helpe to giue him strength,	326
And by whose helpe I meane to chastise it.	414
My arme shall giue thee helpe to beare thee hence,	2519
But when it first did helpe to wound it selfe.	2725

HEN = 8

HENCE = 7

So hence: be thou the trumpet of our wrath,	32
Their Armours that march'd hence so siluer bright,	626
Fast to the chaire: be heedfull: hence, and watch.	1575
This must be answer'd either heere, or hence.	1807
That I must dye heere, and liue hence, by Truth?	2490
In lieu whereof, I pray you beare me hence	2505
My arme shall giue thee helpe to beare thee hence,	2519

HENCEFORTH = 1

K.Iohn. From henceforth beare his name | Whose forme thou bearest:	168

HENRY see also *Hen.* = 2

And brought Prince *Henry* in their companie,	2592
Enter Prince Henry, Salisburie, and Bigot.	2604

HER *l.*40 73 229 318 323 358 487 488 489 490 491 493 706 802 807 812 814 819 821 822 823 846 849 862 863 866 868 875 877 878 879 978 1045

HER *cont.*
  *1140 1141 1187 1188 1293 1294 1320 1401 1446 *1491 1838 2132 2279
  2280 2726 = 52*2
HERALD see also E.Har., F.Her. = 2
  *Heere after excursions, Enter the Herald of France | with Trumpets to
  the gates.*   608
  Enter English Herald with Trumpet.   622
HERALDS = 1*1
  Hubert. Heralds, from off our towres we might behold   636
  Like Heralds 'twixt two dreadfull battailes set: 1796
HERE = 2*1
  Essex. My Liege, here is the strangest controuersie   51
  K.Iohn. Why what a mad-cap hath heauen lent vs here?   92
  Can hold it vp: here I and sorrowes sit,   995
HERES = 2*1
  Out of his ragges. Here's a large mouth indeede,   773
  And here's a Prophet that I brought with me   1868
  Ba. Here's a good world: knew you of this faire work?   2119
HERETIQUE = 2
  From his Allegeance to an heretique,   1102
  Let goe the hand of that Arch-heretique,   1120
HERS = 1
  And if she did play false, the fault was hers,   126
HETHER = 4
  At our importance hether is he come,   300
  Embrace him, loue him, giue him welcome hether.   304
  Ele. Come hether little kinsman, harke, a worde.   1317
  Iohn. Come hether *Hubert.* O my gentle *Hubert,*   1318
HEW = 1
  To smooth the yce, or adde another hew   1730
HEYNOUS = 4
  Con. Which harme within it selfe so heynous is,   961
  Pand. You hold too heynous a respect of greefe.   1475
  The image of a wicked heynous fault   1789
  Exampled by this heynous spectacle.   2055
HEYRE = 4
  K.Iohn. Is that the elder, and art thou the heyre?   65
  My mothers sonne did get your fathers heyre,   136
  Your fathers heyre must haue your fathers land.   137
  And to his shape were heyre to all this land,   152
HIDE = 5
  And a may catch your hide and you alone: 436
  Can hide you from our messengers of Warre,   566
  I would set an Oxe-head to your Lyons hide: | And make a monster of
  you.   599
  Thou weare a Lyons hide, doff it for shame,   1054
  The earth had not a hole to hide this deede.   2035
HIDEOUS = 2
  Presented thee more hideous then thou art.   1991
  Mel. Haue I not hideous death within my view,   2483
HIDING = 1
  Discredite more in hiding of the fault,   1750
HIE = *1
  Iohn. No more then he that threats. To Arms let's hie. | *Exeunt.* 1280
HIGH = 5
  To treat of high affaires touching that time: 109
  Bast. Ha Maiesty: how high thy glory towres,   664

HIGH *cont.*
  Among the high tides in the Kalender?   1011
  And that high Royalty was nere pluck'd off: 1722
  Ar. The Wall is high, and yet will I leape downe.   1997
HIGHER = 1
  Iohn. Vp higher to the plaine, where we'l set forth   603
HIGHNES = 1*3
  **Dol.* She is sad and passionate at your highnes Tent.   864
  * *Pem.* This once again (but that your Highnes pleas'd)   1720
  *We breath'd our Councell: but it pleas'd your Highnes   1753
  Your Highnes should deliuer vp your Crowne.   1873
HIGHNESSE = 3*1
  Her Highnesse is in safety, feare you not: 1294
  I leaue your highnesse: Grandame, I will pray   1312
  Doth make a stand, at what your Highnesse will.   1756
  **Pem.* His Highnesse yet doth speak, & holds beleefe,   2611
HIGH-BORNE = 1
  I am too high-borne to be proportied   2332
HILL = 1
  Fra. It shall be so, and at the other hill   606
HIM *l.*28 34 89 94 107 125 134 135 147 157 196 268 288 304 326 352 356
  357 443 *468 474 482 544 546 554 574 577 678 708 755 828 874 905 984
  1079 1083 1087 1111 1149 1248 1365 1465 1472 1473 1509 1523 1550
  1594 1598 *1647 1651 1661 1665 1696 1876 1878 1879 1900 1913 1930
  1931 2008 2015 2025 2094 2107 2108 2143 2144 *2207 2226 2229 2231
  2375 2447 *2448 2478 2502 2581 2585 2614 2615 2618 2670 2694 = 87*4
HIMSELFE = 12
  As I haue heard my father speake himselfe   115
  Hath put himselfe in Armes, the aduerse windes   351
  More free from motion, no not death himselfe   768
  Himselfe loues traytor, this is pittie now;   824
  Who in that sale sels pardon from himselfe: 1094
  Vnlesse he doe submit himselfe to *Rome.*   1122
  But hold himselfe safe in his prisonment.   1546
  Before the childe himselfe felt he was sicke: 1806
  Sal. The king hath dispossest himselfe of vs,   2021
  Sal. Murther, as hating what himselfe hath done,   2036
  As *Lewis* himselfe: so (Nobles) shall you all,   2313
  Himselfe to *Rome,* his spirit is come in,   2323
HIS *see also* on's *l.*94 97 110 117 118 119 130 132 135 139 141 147 152 168
  196 200 247 248 251 276 280 285 296 298 299 301 306 *325 353 354 355
  385 392 397 402 423 425 427 428 *468 470 *471 490 574 587 651 653
  666 667 678 773 779 780 829 905 911 944 980 991 1003 1004 1067 1087
  1098 1102 1115 1116 1121 1127 1249 1252 1309 1337 1364 1468 1479
  1480 1481 1482 1508 1532 1535 1537 1541 1546 1550 1598 1605 1665
  1689 1690 1696 †775 1776 1780 1783 1785 1788 1790 1795 1797 1804
  1805 1816 1870 1918 1919 1921 1922 1927 2022 2031 2032 2065 2109
  2110 2154 2173 2200 2225 2240 2323 2345 2349 2380 2383 2390 2403
  2404 2432 2474 2486 2524 2537 2589 2594 2605 2606 *2611 2622 2628
  2630 2645 2648 2701 2709 = 153*4
HITHER *see also* hether = 4
  Some Trumpet summon hither to the walles   501
  Haue hither march'd to your endamagement.   515
  Hither returne all gilt with Frenchmens blood: 627
  But as I trauail'd hither through the land,   1864
HITHER-WARD = 1
  Bast. The Dolphin is preparing hither-ward,   2669

HOA = 1*1
With al true duetie: On toward *Callice*, hoa. | *Exeunt.*   1379
Hub. Whose there? Speake hoa, speake quickely, or | I shoote.   2551
HOAST = 1
Of smiling peace to march a bloody hoast,   1177
HOLD = 19*2
For him, and in his right, we hold this Towne.   574
We for the worthiest hold the right from both.   589
We hold our Towne for neither: yet for both.   645
Fra. Know him in vs, that heere hold vp his right.   678
Can hold it vp: here I and sorrowes sit,   995
France, thou maist hold a serpent by the tongue,   1189
Then keepe in peace that hand which thou dost hold.   1192
And in their rage, I hauing hold of both,   1262
Pand. You hold too heynous a respect of greefe.   1475
Makes nice of no vilde hold to stay him vp: 1523
But hold himself safe in his prisonment.   1546
Hub. Is this your promise? Go too, hold your toong.   1675
Let me not hold my tongue: let me not *Hubert*,   1678
If what in rest you haue, in right you hold,   1772
Iohn. We cannot hold mortalities strong hand.   1800
Three foot of it doth hold; bad world the while: 1818
Iohn. With-hold thy speed, dreadfull Occasion: 1844
Hold out this tempest. Beare away that childe,   2161
We hold our time too precious to be spent | with such a brabler.   2415
Bast. With-hold thine indignation, mighty heauen,   2595
Which in their throng, and presse to that last hold,   2625
HOLDES = 2
Holdes hand with any Princesse of the world.   810
Why holdes`thine eie that lamentable rhewme,   943
HOLDING = 2
Holding th'eternall spirit against her will,   1401
Pan. Take againe | From this my hand, as holding of the Pope   2169
HOLDS = 5*2
That holds in chase mine honour vp and downe.   234
Of him it holds, stands vp *Plantagenet*,   544
For he that holds his Kingdome, holds the Law: 1116
Bast. All Kent hath yeelded: nothing there holds out   2198
Pem. His Highnesse yet doth speak, & holds beleefe,   2611
Which holds but till thy newes be vttered,   2666
HOLE = 1
The earth had not a hole to hide this deede.   2035
HOLINESSE = 2
Shall giue a holinesse, a puritie,   2052
And from his holinesse vse all your power   2173
HOLLOW = 2
Yea, faith it selfe to hollow falshood change.   1020
And he will looke as hollow as a Ghost,   1469
HOLPE = 1
Sir *Robert* neuer holpe to make this legge.   253
HOLY = 16*1
And fought the holy Warres in *Palestine*,   297
Shall neuer see it, but a holy day.   1007
Const. A wicked day, and not a holy day.   1008
Fra. Heere comes the holy Legat of the Pope.   1062
To thee King *Iohn* my holy errand is: 1064
Why thou against the Church, our holy Mother,   1068

HOLY *cont.*
  Keepe *Stephen Langton* chosen Archbishop | Of *Canterbury* from that
  holy Sea: 1070
  This in our foresaid holy Fathers name   1072
  And make a ryot on the gentle brow | Of true sincerity? O holy Sir   1178
  (If euer I remember to be holy)   1313
  Con. Thou art holy to belye me so,   1428
  The Incense of a Vow, a holy Vow: 2066
  Iohn. Now keep your holy word, go meet the *French,* 2172
  Looke where the holy Legate comes apace,   2317
  And on our actions set the name of right | With holy breath. 2319
  That so stood out against the holy Church,   2324
  My holy Lord of Millane, from the King   2374
HOME = 8
  That to my home I will no more returne   314
  Will I not thinke of home, but follow Armes.   324
  We will beare home that lustie blood againe,   561
  Teach vs some sence. Sirrah, were I at home   597
  Now Powers from home, and discontents at home   2156
  And welcome home againe discarded faith,   2473
  Now, these her Princes are come home againe,   2726
HOMES = 1
  Haue sold their fortunes at their natiue homes,   363
HONESTY = 1
  For thou wast got i'th way of honesty. | *Exeunt all but bastard.* 190
HONOR = 10*1
  And wound her honor with this diffidence.   73
  Heauen guard my mothers honor, and my Land.   78
  My father gaue me honor, yours gaue land: 173
  Bast. A foot of Honor better then I was,   192
  For new made honor doth forget mens names: 197
  *That for thine owne gaine shouldst defend mine honor? 255
  Blan. That she is bound in honor still to do   841
  His Honor, Oh thine Honor, *Lewis* thine Honor.   1249
  As we with honor and respect may take,   2695
HONORS = 2
  In titles, honors, and promotions, | As she in beautie, education, blood, 808
  With our pure Honors: nor attend the foote   2023
HONOR-GIUING-HAND = 1
  A Souldier by the Honor-giuing-hand | Of *Cordelion,* Knighted in the
  field.   61
HONOUR = 2
  That holds in chase mine honour vp and downe.   234
  I (by the honour of my marriage bed)   2346
HONOURABLE = 4
  An honourable conduct let him haue,   34
  From a resolu'd and honourable warre,   906
  Where honourable rescue, and defence   2269
  Let me wipe off this honourable dewe,   2296
HONOURD = 1
  I honour'd him, I lou'd him, and will weepe   2108
HOORDING = 1
  Of hoording Abbots, imprisoned angells   1306
HOPE = 5
  Some proper man I hope, who was it mother?   263
  Exec. I hope your warrant will beare out the deed. 1576
  And look'd vpon, I hope, with chearefull eyes.   1719

HOPE *cont.*
As to my ample hope was promised,   2365
What surety of the world, what hope, what stay,   2678
HOPES = 1
Lest that their hopes prodigiously be crost: 1016
HORNE = 1
That will take paines to blow a horne before her?   229
HORRIBLE = 2
Your vilde intent must needs seeme horrible.   1674
Blacke, fearefull, comfortlesse, and horrible.   2577
HORROR = 1
Of bragging horror: So shall inferior eyes   2218
HORSEBACKE = *1
*And ere since sit's on's horsebacke at mine Hostesse dore   596
HOSPITABLE = 1
Being no further enemy to you | Then the constraint of hospitable zeale,   549
HOST = 1
Like a kinde Host, the Dolphin and his powers.   2200
HOSTESSE = *1
*And ere since sit's on's horsebacke at mine Hostesse dore   596
HOSTILITIE = 1
Hostilitie, and ciuill tumult reignes   1972
HOT = 10*2
That hot rash haste so indirectly shedde.   342
Commander of this hot malicious day,   625
In this hot triall more then we of France,   656
*Bast. Now by my life, this day grows wondrous hot,   1285
So hot a speed, with such aduice dispos'd,   1393
*Hub. Heate me these Irons hot, and looke thou stand   1571
Must you with hot Irons, burne out both mine eyes?   1612
And with hot Irons must I burne them out.   1636
The Iron of it selfe, though heate red hot,   1638
Hub. Lords, I am hot with haste, in seeking you,   2074
There is so hot a summer in my bosome,   2637
Iohn. The salt in them is hot.   2654
HOUERS = 1
Some ayery Deuill houers in the skie,   1286
HOURE = 7*2
Now blessed be the houre by night or day   174
*Eng. France, y shalt rue this houre within this houre.   1256
The mis-plac'd-Iohn should entertaine an houre,   1518
And like the watchfull minutes, to the houre,   1622
Big. Who kill'd this Prince? | Hub. 'Tis not an houre since I left him
well: 2106
Was borne to see so sad an houre as this,   2277
King Iohn did flie an houre or two before   2543
Who halfe an houre since came from the Dolphin,   2693
HOURELY = 1
Sh'adulterates hourely with thine Vnckle Iohn,   977
HOUSE = 3
To breake within the bloody house of life,   1935
Th'vncleanly sauours of a Slaughter-house,   2115
(Which some suppose the soules fraile dwelling house)   2607
HOUSHOLD = 1
And ring these fingers with thy houshold wormes,   1414
HOW = 35*2
How that ambitious *Constance* would not cease   38

HUBERT cont.
I were your sonne, so you would loue me, Hubert:	1597
Ar. Are you sicke Hubert? you looke pale to day,	1601
Ar. Too fairely *Hubert*, for so foule effect,	1611
And told me *Hubert* should put out mine eyes,	1646
Art. O saue me *Hubert*, saue me: my eyes are out	1649
For heauen sake *Hubert* let me not be bound:	1654
Nay heare me *Hubert*, driue these men away,	1655
Art. Hubert, the vtterance of a brace of tongues,	1676
Let me not hold my tongue: let me not *Hubert*,	1678
Or *Hubert*, if you will cut out my tongue,	1679
And glow with shame of your proceedings, *Hubert*:	1693
Art. O now you looke like *Hubert*. All this while | You were disguis'd.	1705
That *Hubert* for the wealth of all the world, | Will not offend thee.	1711
Art. O heauen! I thanke you *Hubert*.	1713
Enter Hubert.	1784
To your direction: *Hubert*, what newes with you?	1786
Iohn. Hubert, away with him: imprison him,	1876
Enter Hubert.	1905
Enter Hubert.	2073
(If thou didst this deed of death) art y damn'd *Hubert*.	2121
Iohn. That villaine *Hubert* told me he did liue.	2210
Alarums. Enter Iohn and Hubert.	2439
Iohn. How goes the day with vs? oh tell me *Hubert*.	2440
Commend me to one *Hubert*, with your King;	2501
Enter Bastard and Hubert, seuerally.	2550
Bast. Hubert, I thinke. | *Hub.* Thou hast a perfect thought:	2559
Ile tell thee *Hubert*, halfe my power this night	2597

HUBERT = *1
HUBERTS = 1*1
*I would not haue beleeu'd him: no tongue but *Huberts*.	1647
It is the shamefull worke of *Huberts* hand,	2061

HUE *see* hew
HUG = 1
To hug with swine, to seeke sweet safety out	2396

HUGE = 3
Shall draw this breefe into as huge a volume:	400
That no supporter but the huge firme earth	994
And now 'tis farre too huge to be blowne out	2339

HUMOR = 2
More vpon humor, then aduis'd respect.	1939
This inundation of mistempred humor,	2179

HUMORS = 2
And all th'vnsetled humors of the Land,	360
By slaues, that take their humors for a warrant,	1934

HUMOUROUS = 1
But when her humourous Ladiship is by	1045

HUNDRED = 3
At least from faire fiue hundred pound a yeere:	77
A halfe-fac'd groat, fiue hundred pound a yeere?	102
Your face hath got fiue hundred pound a yeere,	160

HUNDREDS = 1
With many hundreds treading on his heeles:	1870

HUNGRY = 1
Must by the hungry now be fed vpon:	1308

HUNTSMEN = 1
And like a iolly troope of Huntsmen come	632

HURLEY = 1
Me thinkes I see this hurley all on foot;   1554
HURRIES = 1
And wilde amazement hurries vp and downe   2203
HURT = 2
Good ground be pittifull, and hurt me not: 1998
Bast. 'Tis true, to hurt his master, no mans else.   2032
HUSBAND = 7
What woman post is this? hath she no husband   228
As thine was to thy husband, and this boy   422
Many a widdowes husband groueling lies,   615
A widdow cries, be husband to me (heauens)   1033
O husband heare me: aye, alacke, how new   1238
Is husband in my mouth? euen for that name   1239
Husband, I cannot pray that thou maist winne: 1264
HUSBANDLES = 1
A widdow, husbandles, subiect to feares,   935
HUSBANDS = 2
Which fault lyes on the hazards of all husbands   127
To make roome for him in my husbands bed: 268
HUSH = 1
My tongue shall hush againe this storme of warre,   2187
HYMNE = 1
Who chaunts a dolefull hymne to his owne death,   2628
I = 384*9, 6
No sir, saies question, I sweet sir at yours,   209
Lady. Sir *Roberts* sonne, I thou vnreuerend boy,   238
I, with these Christall beads heauen shall be brib'd   473
Con. I who doubts that, a Will: a wicked will,   496
If you say I, the King will not say no. *Exeunt.*   1568
Iohn. I marrie, now my soule hath elbow roome,   2635
IADES = 1
I'de play incessantly vpon these Iades,   699
IAMES = 4
Enter Lady Faulconbridge and Iames Gurney.   232
Bast. Iames Gournie, wilt thou giue vs leaue a while?   241
Bast. Philip, sparrow, *Iames,*   243
There's toyes abroad, anon Ile tell thee more. | *Exit Iames.*   244
IAWES = 1
Euen in the iawes of danger, and of death: 2369
ICE *see* yce
ICY *see* ycy
IDE = 1
I'de play incessantly vpon these Iades,   699
IDELY = 1
I idely heard: if true, or false I know not.   1843
IDIOT = 1
Making that idiot laughter keepe mens eyes,   1344
IDLE = 4
And straine their cheekes to idle merriment,   1345
Possest with rumors, full of idle dreames,   1866
Iohn. Thou idle Dreamer, wherefore didst thou so?   1874
Doth`by the idle Comments that it makes,   2608
IDLELY = 1
Mocking the ayre with colours idlely spred,   2241
IDLENESSE = 1
Nor conuersant with Ease, and Idlenesse,   2069

IEOPARDIE = 1
   Looke to thy selfe, thou art in ieopardie.   1279
IERUSALEM = 1
   Do like the Mutines of Ierusalem,   692
IEST = 3
   And though thou now confesse thou didst but iest   937
   Play fast and loose with faith? so iest with heauen,   1173
   And proue a deadly blood-shed, but a iest,   2054
IEWELL = 1
   An empty Casket, where the Iewell of life   2208
IF *l.*21 76 88 120 126 128 133 146 148 196 288 *381 383 386 428 564 581
   715 741 743 745 749 751 760 800 828 831 845 851 877 950 964 1014
   1142 1154 1225 1313 1336 1339 1341 1347 1434 1441 1452 1463 1503
   1548 1558 1568 1598 1630 1631 1645 1679 1692 1772 1843 1856 1999
   2002 2058 2059 2098 2121 2127 2129 2131 2139 2244 2462 2475 2491
   2492 2500 2564 2584 2704 2729 = 78*1
IFAITH *see* yfaith
IGNORANCE = 1
   With barbarous ignorance, and deny his youth   1776
ILAND = 1
   To this faire Iland, and the Territories: 15
ILANDERS = 1
   And coopes from other lands her Ilanders,   318
ILE *l.*159 162 196 244 285 439 445 457 730 1360 1365 1373 1375 *1491
   1659 1709 1814 1975 2001 2003 2100 2101 2123 2162 2579 2597 = 25*1,
   1
   That blood which ow'd the bredth of all this Ile,   1817
ILL = 12
   It ill beseemes this presence to cry ayme | To these ill-tuned repetitions: 499
   This day all things begun, come to ill end,   1019
   And being not done, where doing tends to ill,   1203
   Fra. What can goe well, when we haue runne so ill?   1387
   If heauen be pleas'd that you must vse me ill,   1631
   With these ill tydings: Now? What sayes the world   1853
   My head with more ill newes: for it is full.   1855
   How oft the sight of meanes to do ill deeds,   1944
   Make deeds ill done? Had'st not thou beene by,   1945
   Euen this ill night, your breathing shall expire,   2497
   Bast. Shew me the very wound of this ill newes,   2578
   Ioh. Poyson'd, ill fare: dead, forsooke, cast off,   2643
ILL-TUNED = 1
   It ill beseemes this presence to cry ayme | To these ill-tuned repetitions: 499
IMAGE = 1
   The image of a wicked heynous fault   1789
IMINENT = 1
   The iminent decay of wrested pompe.   2159
IMMAGINARIE = 1
   And foule immaginarie eyes of blood   1990
IMPATIENCE = 1
   Pem. Sir, sir, impatience hath his priuiledge.   2031
IMPATIENT = 1
   England impatient of your iust demands,   350
IMPEACH = 1
   Vnder whose warrant I impeach thy wrong,   413
IMPEDIMENT = 1
   Whose passage vext with thy impediment,   650

IMPLOY = 1
Your brother did imploy my father much.   104
IMPORT = 1
Is much more generall, then these lines import.   2014
IMPORTANCE = 1
At our importance hether is he come,   300
IMPOSE = 1
Out of your grace, deuise, ordaine, impose   1181
IMPRISON = 1
Iohn. Hubert, away with him: imprison him,   1876
IMPRISONED = 1
Of hoording Abbots, imprisoned angells   1306
IN = 261*12
INCENSE = 1
The Incense of a Vow, a holy Vow: 2066
INCENSED = 2
The fearefull difference of incensed kings: 1169
Throw this report on their incensed rage,   1986
INCESSANTLY = 1
I'de play incessantly vpon these Iades,   699
INCLINATION = 1
Their Needl's to Lances, and their gentle hearts | To fierce and bloody
inclination.   2411
INCONSIDERATE = 1
Rash, inconsiderate, fiery voluntaries,   361
INCONSTANCY = 1
Elea. O foule reuolt of French inconstancy.   1255
INCUREABLE = 1
Or ouerthrow incureable ensues.   2183
INDEED = 3
Hub. Indeed I haue beene merrier.   1584
Sal. Indeed we fear'd his sicknesse was past cure.   1804
Pem. Indeed we heard how neere his death he was,   1805
INDEEDE *see also* deede = 1*1
Out of his ragges. Here's a large mouth indeede,   773
Bast. Indeede your drums being beaten, wil cry out;   2422
INDENTURE = 1
As seale to this indenture of my loue: 313
INDEUOR = 1
We must awake indeuor for defence,   376
INDIFFERENCY = 1
Makes it take head from all indifferency,   900
INDIGEST = 1
To set a forme vpon that indigest   2632
INDIGNATION = 3*1
Their Iron indignation 'gainst your walles: 518
And quench this fierie indignation,   1640
Io. They burn in indignation: I repent: *Enter Mes.*   1821
Bast. With-hold thine indignation, mighty heauen,   2595
INDIRECT = 1
Is to mistake again, though indirect,   1206
INDIRECTION = 1
Yet indirection thereby growes direct,   1207
INDIRECTLY = 1
That hot rash haste so indirectly shedde.   342
INDUE = 1
I shall indue you with: Meane time, but aske   1760

INDUSTRIOUS = 1
At your industrious Scenes and acts of death.   690
INFAITH *see* yfaith
INFANT = 1
Out-faced Infant State, and done a rape   394
INFANTS = 1
That whiles warme life playes in that infants veines,   1517
INFECTED = 1
Neuer to be infected with delight,   2068
INFECTION = 1
But such is the infection of the time,   2271
INFERIOR = 1
Of bragging horror: So shall inferior eyes   2218
INFERRE = 1
That need, must needs inferre this principle,   1144
INFINITE = 1
Beyond the infinite and boundlesse reach of mercie,   2120
INFIXED = 1
Till now, infixed I beheld my selfe,   818
INFLAMING = 1
France, I am burn'd vp with inflaming wrath,   1273
INFORCE = 1
To inforce these rights, so forcibly with-held,   23
INFORCED = 1
Vpon the spot of this inforced cause,   2281
INFORTUNATE = 1
Infortunate in nothing but in thee: 480
INFRANCHISEMENT = 1
Th'infranchisement of *Arthur*, whose restraint   1769
INGLORIOUS = 1
Bast. Oh inglorious league: 2234
INGRATE = 1
And you degenerate, you ingrate Reuolts,   2405
INGRATEFULL = 1
And so ingratefull, you deny me that.   2651
INHABITE = 1
That I haue seene inhabite in those cheekes?   1825
INHERITANCE = 2
Doth he lay claime to thine inheritance?   80
And finde th'inheritance of this poore childe,   1815
INIURER = 1
Con. Thou monstrous Iniurer of heauen and earth,   476
INIURIE = 1
Her iniurie the Beadle to her sinne,   491
INIURY = 1
And with her plague her sinne: his iniury   490
INIUSTICE = 1
Of sterne Iniustice, and confused wrong: 2274
INNOCENCE = 1
Euen in the matter of mine innocence: 1641
INNOCENCIE = 1
Like Riuers of remorse and innocencie.   2113
INNOCENT = 6
And from Pope *Innocent* the Legate heere,   1066
Pope *Innocent*, I doe demand of thee.   1073
Hub. If I talke to him, with his innocent prate   1598
Is yet a maiden, and an innocent hand.   1977

INNOCENT *cont.*

Then to be butcher of an innocent childe.	1984
My innocent life against an Emperor.	2089

INQUIRE = *1

*P. There tel the king, he may inquire vs out. *Ex. Lords.*	2118

INSEPARABLE = 1

Like true, inseparable, faithfull loues, | Sticking together in calamitie.	1450

INSIDE *see* in-side

INSINUATION = 1

Send fayre-play-orders, and make comprimise, | Insinuation, parley, and	
base truce	2236

INSOLENT = 1

Queen. Out insolent, thy bastard shall be King,	419

INSOOTH = 3

Insooth, good friend, your father might haue kept	131
Insooth he might: then if he were my brothers,	133
Insooth I would you were a little sicke,	1602

INSTANT = 1

Euen in the instant of repaire and health,	1498

INSTANTLY = 1

And instantly returne with me againe.	2686

INSTEED = 1

And now insteed of bulletts wrapt in fire	533

INSTRUCT = 1

I will instruct my sorrowes to bee proud,	990

INSTRUMENT = 2

Loe, by my troth, the Instrument is cold,	1682
Or vsefull seruing-man, and Instrument	2334

INTELLIGENCE = 1

Ioh. Oh where hath our Intelligence bin drunke?	1834

INTEND = 1

Well, Ile not say what I intend for thee:	1373

INTENDETH = 1

When he intendeth to become the field:	2223

INTENDS = 1

And happie newnesse, that intends old right. *Exeunt*	2522

INTENT = 2

From all direction, purpose, course, intent.	901
Your vilde intent must needs seeme horrible.	1674

INTEREST = 3

The vn-owed interest of proud swelling State:	2152
Acquainted me with interest to this Land,	2342
Pleade for our interest, and our being heere.	2421

INTERRD = 1

Hen. At Worster must his bodie be interr'd, | For so he will'd it.	2709

INTERROGATORIES = 1

Iohn. What earthie name to Interrogatories	1074

INTERRUPTED = 1

Her presence would haue interrupted much.	862

INTERRUPTION = 2

The interruption of their churlish drums	370
Ore-bearing interruption spight of *France*?	1391

INTO *l.*19 120 400 411 724 1338 1352 1390 1771 1888 1948 2167 *2207 2312 2343 2410 2612 2615 = 17*1

INTREAT = 1

Through my burn'd bosome: nor intreat the North	2647

INTREATIES = 1
And will not temporize with my intreaties: 2379
INUASION = 1
With dreadfull pompe of stout inuasion. 1895
INUASIUE = 1
To Armes Inuasiue? Shall a beardlesse boy, 2238
INUETERATE = 1
And heale the inueterate Canker of one wound, 2265
INUIOLABLE = 1
And keepe our faithes firme and inuiolable. 2258
INUISIBLE = 1
Leaues them inuisible, and his seige is now 2622
INUNDATION = 2
This inundation of mistempred humor, 2179
Being an ordinary Inundation: 2299
INUOCATION = 1
Which scornes a moderne Inuocation. 1426
INVOLNERABLE = 1
Against th'involnerable clouds of heauen, 558
INWARD = 2
But from the inward motion to deliuer 222
And the coniunction of our inward soules 1158
IN-SIDE = 1
Dol. Out-side or in-side, I will not returne 2363
IO = 1*1
IOANE = 1
Well, now can I make any *Ioane* a Lady, 194
IOH = 5*3
IOHN see also Io., Ioh., K.Io., K.Iohn. = 29*4
*Enter King Iohn, Queene Elinor, Pembroke, Essex, and Sa-|lisbury,
with the Chattylion of France.* 2
And to rebuke the vsurpation | Of thy vnnaturall Vncle, English *Iohn*, 302
Then thou and *Iohn*, in manners being as like, 424
King *Iohn*, this is the very summe of all: 451
King *Iohn*, your king and Englands, doth approach, 624
Iohn to stop *Arthurs* Title in the whole, 883
Sh'adulterates hourely with thine Vnckle *Iohn*, 977
France is a Bawd to Fortune, and king *Iohn*, 981
That strumpet Fortune, that vsurping *Iohn*: 982
*Enter King Iohn, France, Dolphin, Blanch, Elianor, Philip, | Austria,
Constance.* 998
To thee King *Iohn* my holy errand is: 1064
Enter Iohn, Arthur, Hubert. 1288
*Alarums, excursions, Retreat. Enter Iohn, Eleanor, Arthur | Bastard,
Hubert, Lords.* 1297
'Tis strange to thinke how much King *Iohn* hath lost 1506
Iohn hath seiz'd *Arthur*, and it cannot be, 1516
The mis-plac'd-*Iohn* should entertaine an houre, 1518
That *Iohn* may stand, then *Arthur* needs must fall, | So be it, for it
cannot be but so. 1524
Iohn layes you plots: the times conspire with you, 1531
Plainly denouncing vengeance vpon *Iohn*. 1544
Out of the bloody fingers ends of *Iohn*. 1553
Enter Iohn, Pembroke, Salisbury, and other Lordes. 1717
Enter King Iohn and Pandolph, attendants. 2166
The next is this: King *Iohn* hath reconcil'd 2322
And come ye now to tell me *Iohn* hath made 2344

ISSUE = 5
With fearefull bloudy issue arbitrate.   44
That art the issue of my deere offence   270
On this remoued issue, plagued for her,   489
Con. Lo; now: now see the issue of your peace.   1404
Pem. And when it breakes, I feare will issue thence   1798
IST = 3
No in deede is't not: and I would to heauen   1596
And is't not pitty, (oh my grieued friends)   2275
To vnder-prop this Action? Is't not I   2352
IT *see also* is't, 't, too't, wil't, yt = 166*4, 1
Giue grandame kingdome, and it grandame will   462
ITALIAN = 1
Adde thus much more, that no *Italian* Priest   1080
ITH = 1
For thou wast got i'th way of honesty. | *Exeunt all but bastard.*   190
ITSELFE *see* selfe
IUDGD = 1
Come from the Country to be iudg'd by you   52
IUDGE = 3*1
Compare our faces, and be Iudge your selfe   87
**Fra.* Fro(m) that supernal Iudge that stirs good thoughts   409
That Iudge hath made me guardian to this boy,   412
*Though churlish thoughts themselues should bee your | Iudge,   836
IUGLING = 1
This iugling witchcraft with reuennue cherish,   1096
IUST = 3
In such a iust and charitable warre.   329
England impatient of your iust demands,   350
Our iust and lineall entrance to our owne;   382
IUSTICE = 1
To doe him Iustice, and reuenge on you.   474
IUST-BORNE = 1
Before we will lay downe our iust-borne Armes,   659
KALENDER = 1
Among the high tides in the Kalender?   1011
KEENE = 1
To my keene curses; for without my wrong   1110
KEEP = *2
*Heauen take my soule, and England keep my bones. *Dies*   2006
**Iohn.* Now keep your holy word, go meet the *French*,   2172
KEEPE = 15*1
Nor keepe his Princely heart from *Richards* hand: 280
Vnlesse thou let his siluer Water, keepe | A peacefull progresse to the Ocean.   653
In mortall furie halfe so peremptorie, | As we to keepe this Citie.   769
Keepe *Stephen Langton* chosen Archbishop | Of *Canterbury* from that holy Sea: 1070
Keepe my need vp, and faith is trodden downe.   1147
Then keepe in peace that hand which thou dost hold.   1192
And most forsworne, to keepe what thou dost sweare,   1218
Iohn. Hubert, keepe this boy: *Philip* make vp,   1290
Making that idiot laughter keepe mens eyes,   1344
Hub. And Ile keepe him so, | That he shall not offend your Maiesty.   1365
I will not keepe this forme vpon my head,   1486
So I may keepe mine eyes. O spare mine eyes,   1680
Bast. Keepe the peace, I say.   2095

KEEPE *cont.*
And keepe it safe for our remembrance:	2253
And keepe our faithes firme and inuiolable.	2258
Dol. Well: keepe good quarter, & good care to night,	2546

KEEPER = 1
Thou art his keeper.	1364

KENT = 1*1
That were embattailed, and rank'd in Kent.	1925
Bast. All Kent hath yeelded: nothing there holds out	2198

KEPT = 5
Insooth, good friend, your father might haue kept	131
Euer in *France* shall be kept festiuall:	1001
It is religion that doth make vowes kept,	1210
What, shall our feast be kept with slaughtered men?	1235
So I were out of prison, and kept Sheepe	1590

KERCHER = 1
I knit my hand-kercher about your browes	1618

KILL = 3
And teaches mee to kill or hang my selfe:	1440
To wish him dead, but thou hadst none to kill him.	1931
As thou shalt be, if thou didst kill this childe.	2127

KILLD = 2
Of *Arthur*, whom they say is kill'd to night, on your | (suggestion.	1886
Big. Who kill'd this Prince? | *Hub.* 'Tis not an houre since I left him well:	2106

KIN = 1

KINDE = 5
Which trust accordingly kinde Cittizens,	537
Vnyoke this seysure, and this kinde regreete?	1172
We had a kinde of light, what would ensue:	2060
Like a kinde Host, the Dolphin and his powers.	2200
Hen. I haue a kinde soule, that would giue thankes,	2719

KINDLED = 3
Till she had kindled *France* and all the world,	39
You equall Potents, fierie kindled spirits,	672
Your breath first kindled the dead coale of warres,	2336

KINDRED-ACTION = 1
Of any kindred-action like to this?	1396

KING see also *K.Io.*, *K.Iohn*, *Kin.* = 57*10
Enter King Iohn, Queene Elinor, Pembroke, Essex, and Sa-| lisbury, with the Chattylion of France.	2
Chat. Thus (after greeting) speakes the King | of France,	6
Philip. Most certain of one mother, mighty King,	67
Th'aduantage of his absence tooke the King,	110
Lady. King *Richard Cordelion* was thy father,	266
Enter before Angiers, Philip King of France, Lewis, Daul-| phin, Austria, Constance, Arthur.	292
Salute thee for her King, till then faire boy	323
Enter K.(ing) of England, Bastard, Queene, Blanch, Pembroke, | and others.	379
That thou hast vnder-wrought his lawfull King,	392
How comes it then that thou art call'd a King,	404
Queen. Out insolent, thy bastard shall be King,	419
King *Lewis*, determine what we shall doe strait.	449
King *Iohn*, this is the very summe of all:	451
But on the sight of vs your lawfull King,	528
And let vs in. Your King, whose labour'd spirits	538

KING cont.

And King ore him, and all that he enioyes:	546
Cit. In breefe, we are the King of Englands subiects	573
Iohn. Acknowledge then the King, and let me in.	575
Cit. That can we not: but he that proues the King	576
Iohn. Doth not the Crowne of England, prooue the | King?	579
In dreadfull triall of our kingdomes King.	593
Arthur of Britaine, Englands King, and yours.	621
King *Iohn*, your king and Englands, doth approach,	624
Fra. Speake Citizens for England, whose your king.	676
Hub. The king of England, when we know the king.	677
Be by some certaine king, purg'd and depos'd.	686
Then after fight who shall be king of it?	714
Bast. And if thou hast the mettle of a king,	715
France is a Bawd to Fortune, and king *Iohn*,	981
Enter King Iohn, France, Dolphin, Blanch, Elianor, Philip, | Austria,	
Constance.	998
To thee King *Iohn* my holy errand is:	1064
Can tast the free breath of a sacred King?	1075
Aust. King *Philip*, listen to the Cardinall.	1126
Iohn. The king is moud, and answers not to this.	1148
Aust. Doe so king *Philip*, hang no more in doubt.	1150
'Tis strange to thinke how much King *Iohn* hath lost	1506
Go with me to the King, 'tis wonderfull,	1563
For England go; I will whet on the King.	1566
If you say I, the King will not say no. *Exeunt.*	1568
Sal. The colour of the King doth come, and go	1794
And thou, to be endeered to a King,	1953
The King by me requests your presence straight.	2020
Sal. The king hath dispossest himselfe of vs,	2021
The practice, and the purpose of the king:	2062
Arthur doth liue, the king hath sent for you.	2075
P. There tel the king, he may inquire vs out. *Ex. Lords.*	2118
And follow me with speed: Ile to the King:	2162
Enter King Iohn and Pandolph, attendants.	2166
The next is this: King *Iohn* hath reconcil'd	2322
My holy Lord of Millane, from the King	2374
The youth saies well. Now heare our *English* King,	2382
The King doth smile at, and is well prepar'd	2388
Sal. I did not thinke the King so stor'd with friends.	2460
Pem. They say King *Iohn* sore sick, hath left the field.	2465
Seeke out King *Iohn*, and fall before his feete:	2474
Commend me to one *Hubert*, with your King;	2501
Euen to our Ocean, to our great King *Iohn*.	2518
King *Iohn* did flie an houre or two before	2543
Hub. The King I feare is poyson'd by a Monke,	2580
Whose Bowels sodainly burst out: The King	2587
At whose request the king hath pardon'd them,	2593
Away before: Conduct me to the king,	2601
My Liege, my Lord: but now a King, now thus.	2676
When this was now a King, and now is clay?	2679
The life and death of King Iohn.	2730

KING = 2*1

KINGDOME = 6

Giue grandame kingdome, and it grandame will	462
Law cannot giue my childe his kingdome heere;	1115
For he that holds his Kingdome, holds the Law:	1116

KINGDOME *cont.*
His little kingdome of a forced graue.   1816
This kingdome, this Confine of blood, and breathe   1971
Betweene this chastiz'd kingdome and my selfe,   2337
KINGDOMES = 4
Which now the mannage of two kingdomes must   43
In dreadfull triall of our kingdomes King.   593
Betweene our kingdomes and our royall selues,   1163
Nor let my kingdomes Riuers take their course   2646
KINGLYE = 1
Gouerne the motion of a kinglye eye: 2215
KINGS = 21*3
Chat. Then take my Kings defiance from my mouth,   26
With them a Bastard of the Kings deceast,   359
Enter the two Kings with their powers, | *at seuerall doores.*   646
With slaughter coupled to the name of kings.   663
When the rich blood of kings is set on fire: 665
In vndetermin'd differences of kings.   669
Cry hauocke kings, backe to the stained field   671
Kings of our feare, vntill our feares resolu'd   685
Bast. By heauen, these scroyles of Angiers flout you | (kings,   687
Hub. Heare vs great kings, vouchsafe awhile to stay   731
Perseuer not, but heare me mighty kings.   736
Two such controlling bounds shall you be, kings,   759
Bast. Mad world, mad kings, mad composition: 882
Of kings, of beggers, old men, yong men, maids,   891
Since Kings breake faith vpon commoditie,   918
I haue a Kings oath to the contrarie.   931
Sal. Pardon me Madam, | I may not goe without you to the kings.   987
Lets kings assemble: for my greefe's so great,   993
Heere is my Throne bid kings come bow to it.   996
Arme, arme, you heauens, against these periur'd Kings,   1032
Set armed discord 'twixt these periur'd Kings,   1036
Iohn. Though you, and all the Kings of Christendom   1089
The fearefull difference of incensed kings: 1169
Iohn. It is the curse of Kings, to be attended   1933
KINNE = 1
Come Lady I will shew thee to my kinne,   286
KINSMAN = 4
Ele. Come hether little kinsman, harke, a worde.   1317
Your tender kinsman, and to choake his dayes   1775
Iohn. Gentle kinsman, go | And thrust thy selfe into their Companies,   1887
Mes. My Lord: your valiant kinsman *Falconbridge*,   2445
KIO = *1
KIOHN = 13*5
KISSE = 6
Aust. Vpon thy cheeke lay I this zelous kisse,   312
And kisse him with a glorious victory: 708
For your faire safety: so I kisse your hand.   1314
And I will kisse thy detestable bones,   1412
And kisse the lippes of vnacquainted change,   1551
To make his bleake windes kisse my parched lips,   2648
KNAUE = 1
What meanes this scorne, thou most vntoward knaue?   256
KNEE = 4
O old sir *Robert* Father, on my knee   90
Vpon my knee I beg, goe not to Armes | Against mine Vncle.   1241

KNEE *cont.*

Const. O, vpon my knee made hard with kneeling,	1243
To whom with all submission on my knee,	2714

KNEELE = 1

Kneele thou downe *Philip*, but rise more great,	170

KNEELING = 2

Const. O, vpon my knee made hard with kneeling,	1243
Kneeling before this ruine of sweete life,	2064

KNEW = 1*1

Ba. Here's a good world: knew you of this faire work?	2119
Bast. So on my soule he did, for ought he knew:	2211

KNIGHT = 3

A landlesse Knight, makes thee a landed Squire:	186
Bast. Knight, knight good mother, Basilisco-like:	257

KNIGHTED = 1

A Souldier by the Honor-giuing-hand | Of *Cordelion*, Knighted in the field.	61

KNIGHTLY = 1

And when my knightly stomacke is suffis'd,	201

KNIT = 4

I like it well. France, shall we knit our powres,	712
This royall hand and mine are newly knit,	1157
I knit my hand-kercher about your browes	1618
That knit your sinewes to the strength of mine.	2314

KNOT = 1

For by this knot, thou shalt so surely tye	786

KNOW = 22*1

Phil. I know not why, except to get the land:	81
We know his handy-worke, therefore good mother	251
Then good my mother, let me know my father,	262
Hub. The king of England, when we know the king.	677
Fra. Know him in vs, that heere hold vp his right.	678
I know she is not for this match made vp,	861
Fra. I am perplext, and know not what to say.	1152
If thou vouchsafe them. But if not, then know	1225
Iohn. Doe not I know thou wouldst?	1358
That we shall see and know our friends in heauen:	1462
I shall not know him: therefore neuer, neuer	1473
Your Vnckle must not know but you are dead.	1708
I idely heard: if true, or false I know not.	1843
And on the winking of Authoritie | To vnderstand a Law; to know the meaning	1936
There's few or none do know me, if they did,	1999
Returne, and tell him so: we know the worst.	2025
Bast. Away then with good courage: yet I know	2247
May know wherefore we tooke the Sacrament,	2257
You taught me how to know the face of right,	2341
And, as you answer, I doe know the scope	2376
No: know the gallant Monarch is in Armes,	2402
Hub. Why know you not? The Lords are all come | backe,	2590
Sal. It seemes you know not then so much as we,	2691

KNOWES = 6

And so ere answer knowes what question would,	210
Where is she and her sonne, tell me, who knowes?	863
Which we God knowes, haue turn'd another way, | To our owne vantage.	869
Heauen knowes they were besmear'd and ouer-staind	1167

KNOWES *cont.*
Where heauen he knowes how we shall answer him. 2670
And knowes not how to do it, but with teares. 2720
KNOWING = 2
Not knowing what they feare, but full of feare. 1867
Pet. Fore-knowing that the truth will fall out so. 1875
KNOWLEDGE = 2
But for the certaine knowledge of that truth, 69
Would beare thee from the knowledge of thy selfe, 2286
KNOWNE = 2
That is well knowne, and as I thinke one father: 68
Then if you had at leisure knowne of this. 2584
KNOWST = 1
Thou art my friend, that know'st my tongue so well: 2562
LABOR = 1
But on my Liege, for very little paines | Will bring this labor to an
happy end. *Exit.* 1295
LABOURD = 1
And let vs in. Your King, whose labour'd spirits 538
LACKE = 2
Saying, what lacke you? and where lies your greefe? 1624
Deny their office: onely you do lacke 1698
LACKING = 1
Creatures of note for mercy, lacking vses. 1700
LAD = 1
Yong Lad come forth; I haue to say with you. 1578
LADIE = 2
*Iohn. Speake then Prince Dolphin, can you loue this | Ladie? 843
Is not the Ladie *Constance* in this troope? 860
LADIES = 4*1
With Ladies faces, and fierce Dragons spleenes, 362
*Fra. What sai'st thou boy? looke in the Ladies face. 811
Which cannot heare a Ladies feeble voyce, 1425
My heart hath melted at a Ladies teares, 2298
For your owne Ladies, and pale-visag'd Maides, 2408
LADISHIP = 1
But when her humourous Ladiship is by 1045
LADY = 19*3
Well, now can I make any *Ioane* a Lady, 194
O me, 'tis my mother: how now good Lady, 230
Enter Lady Faulconbridge and Iames Gurney. 232
Come Lady I will shew thee to my kinne, 286
King. A wonder Lady: lo vpon thy wish | Our Messenger *Chattilion* is
arriu'd, 344
With her her Neece, the Lady *Blanch of Spaine,* 358
Fra. Peace Lady, pause, or be more temperate, 498
*Hub. That daughter there of Spaine, the Lady *Blanch* 738
Whose veines bound richer blood then Lady *Blanch?* 746
This widdow Lady? In her right we came, 868
We make him Lord of. Call the Lady *Constance,* 874
Sal. What other harme haue I good Lady done, 959
Fra. By heauen Lady, you shall haue no cause 1021
Heare me, Oh, heare me. | *Aust.* Lady *Constance,* peace. 1037
*Pan. There's Law and Warrant (Lady) for my curse. 1112
*Bla. The Lady *Constance* speakes not from her faith, | But from her
need. 1140
Dolph. Lady, with me, with me thy fortune lies. 1270

LADY *cont.*

I prethee Lady goe away with me.	1403
Fra. Patience good Lady, comfort gentle *Constance.*	1405
Pand. Lady, you vtter madnesse, and not sorrow.	1427
Pan. You, in the right of Lady *Blanch* your wife,	1527
The Lady *Constance* in a frenzie di'de	1841

LADY = 4*1

LAID = 1

I would that I were low laid in my graue,	466

LAIDE = 1

The Canon of the Law is laide on him,	482

LAIES = 1

Arthur Plantaginet, laies most lawfull claime	14

LAMBE = 1

And I will sit as quiet as a Lambe.	1656

LAME = 1

Lame, foolish, crooked, swart, prodigious,	967

LAMENTABLE = 1

Why holdes thine eie that lamentable rhewme,	943

LANCES = 1

Their Needl's to Lances, and their gentle hearts | To fierce and bloody inclination.	2411

LAND = 29

Heauen guard my mothers honor, and my Land.	78
Phil. I know not why, except to get the land:	81
What doth moue you to claime your brothers land.	99
With halfe that face would he haue all my land,	101
Phil. Well sir, by this you cannot get my land,	105
My fathers land, as was my fathers will.	123
Your fathers heyre must haue your fathers land.	137
And like thy brother to enioy thy land:	143
Lord of thy presence, and no land beside.	145
And to his shape were heyre to all this land,	152
Bequeath thy land to him, and follow me?	157
Bast. Brother, take you my land, Ile take my chance;	159
My father gaue me honor, yours gaue land:	173
But many a many foot of Land the worse.	193
I haue disclaim'd Sir *Robert* and my land,	260
To land his Legions all as soone as I:	353
And all th'vnsetled humors of the Land,	360
Fresh expectation troubled not the Land	1724
Was leuied in the body of a land.	1830
But as I trauail'd hither through the land,	1864
Nay, in the body of this fleshly Land,	1970
And heauen it selfe doth frowne vpon the Land. *Exit.*	2164
And make faire weather in your blustring land:	2188
Shall we vpon the footing of our land,	2235
To grace the Gentry of a Land remote,	2282
Acquainted me with interest to this Land,	2342
After yong *Arthur*, claime this Land for mine,	2347
Out of the weake doore of our fainting Land:	2688
The lineall state, and glorie of the Land,	2713

LANDED = 2

A landlesse Knight, makes thee a landed Squire:	186
That thou for truth giu'st out are landed heere? | *Mes.* Vnder the Dolphin.	1849

LANDLESSE = 1
A landlesse Knight, makes thee a landed Squire: 186
LANDS = 2
His lands to me, and tooke it on his death 118
And coopes from other lands her Ilanders, 318
LANGTON = 1
Keepe *Stephen Langton* chosen Archbishop | Of *Canterbury* from that
holy Sea: 1070
LARGE = 5
In the large composition of this man? 96
But truth is truth, large lengths of seas and shores 113
This little abstract doth containe that large, 398
Out of his ragges. Here's a large mouth indeede, 773
Giue with our Neece a dowrie large enough, 785
LAST = 4*1
From first to last, the on-set and retyre: 637
And, in the last repeating, troublesome, 1736
Ioh. Oh, when the last accompt twixt heauen & earth 1941
Last in the field, and almost Lords of it. 2532
Which in their throng, and presse to that last hold, 2625
LASTING = 2
Arise forth from the couch of lasting night, 1410
His soule and body to their lasting rest. 2630
LATE = 1
Hen. It is too late, the life of all his blood 2605
LATELY = 1
And shall these hands so lately purg'd of bloud? 1170
LATER = 1
Therefore thy later vowes, against thy first, 1219
LATEST = 1
The latest breath that gaue the sound of words 1161
LAUGHTER = 1
Making that idiot laughter keepe mens eyes, 1344
LAW = 9*1
The Canon of the Law is laide on him, 482
Pan. There's Law and Warrant (Lady) for my curse. 1112
Cons. And for mine too, when Law can do no right. 1113
Let it be lawfull, that Law barre no wrong: 1114
Law cannot giue my childe his kingdome heere; 1115
For he that holds his Kingdome, holds the Law: 1116
Therefore since Law it selfe is perfect wrong, 1117
How can the Law forbid my tongue to curse? 1118
And on the winking of Authoritie | To vnderstand a Law; to know the
meaning 1936
Hu. I am no villaine. *Sal.* Must I rob | (the Law? 2078
LAWFULL = 6
Arthur Plantaginet, laies most lawfull claime 14
That thou hast vnder-wrought his lawfull King, 392
But on the sight of vs your lawfull King, 528
Pand. Then by the lawfull power that I haue, 1099
Con. O lawfull let it be | That I haue roome with *Rome* to curse a
while, 1107
Let it be lawfull, that Law barre no wrong: 1114
LAY = 15
Desiring thee to lay aside the sword 17
Doth he lay claime to thine inheritance? 80
That still I lay vpon my mothers head, 84

LAY *cont.*

Betweene my father, and my mother lay,	114
Heauen lay not my transgression to my charge,	269
Needs must you lay your heart at his dispose,	276
Aust. Vpon thy cheeke lay I this zelous kisse,	312
Wee'll lay before this towne our Royal bones,	334
Or lay on that shall make your shoulders cracke.	446
Wilt thou resigne them, and lay downe thy Armes?	454
Before we will lay downe our iust-borne Armes,	659
And lay this Angiers euen with the ground,	713
Doth lay it open to vrge on reuenge.	2037
Goe I to make the *French* lay downe their Armes. *Exit.*	2191
He flatly saies, hee'll not lay downe his Armes.	2380

LAYES = 1

Iohn layes you plots: the times conspire with you,	1531

LE *l.*2357 = 1

LEAD = 2

Out of the path which shall directly lead	1514
Mel. Lead me to the Reuolts of England heere.	2467

LEAGUE = 6*1

And I shall shew you peace, and faire-fac'd league:	732
Fra. And by my faith, this league that we haue made	865
And our oppression hath made vp this league:	1031
Married in league, coupled, and link'd together	1159
O make a league with me, 'till I haue pleas'd	1845
Bast. Oh inglorious league:	2234
The bloud of malice, in a vaine of league,	2289

LEANE = 1

Another leane, vnwash'd Artificer,	1926

LEANING = 1

Thus leaning on mine elbow I begin,	204

LEAPE = 1

Ar. The Wall is high, and yet will I leape downe.	1997

LEARND = 1

The Copie of your speede is learn'd by them:	1831

LEARNE = 2

Yet to auoid deceit I meane to learne;	225
I come to learne how you haue dealt for him:	2375

LEAST = 5

At least from faire fiue hundred pound a yeere:	77
Least zeale now melted by the windie breath	793
I must be breefe, least resolution drop	1608
Least I, by marking of your rage, forget	2085
Or if he doe, let it at least be said	2244

LEAUE = 13

Bast. Iames Gournie, wilt thou giue vs leaue a while?	241
Gour. Good leaue good *Philip.*	242
And leaue your children, wiues, and you in peace.	563
Shall leaue his natiue channell, and ore-swell	651
Euen till vnfenced desolation | Leaue them as naked as the vulgar ayre:	700
And leaue those woes alone, which I alone | Am bound to vnder-beare.	985
I leaue your highnesse: Grandame, I will pray	1312
The fit is strongest: Euils that take leaue	1499
My Nobles leaue me, and my State is braued,	1968
Pan. Giue me leaue to speake.	2417
Desires your Maiestie to leaue the field,	2446
Bast. Who didst thou leaue to tend his Maiesty?	2589

LEAUE *cont.*
With purpose presently to leaue this warre. 2696
LEAUES = 2
That leaues the print of blood where ere it walkes. 2024
Leaues them inuisible, and his seige is now 2622
LEAUING = 1
Leauing our ranknesse and irregular course, 2515
LED = 3
Are led so grossely by this medling Priest, 1090
Though you, and al the rest so grossely led, 1095
And he hath promis'd to dismisse the Powers | Led by the Dolphin. 2232
LEFT = 7*1
Left to be finished by such as shee, 753
Big. Who kill'd this Prince? | *Hub.* 'Tis not an houre since I left him
well: 2106
I left him well. 2143
Is fled to heauen: and *England* now is left 2150
*Pem. They say King *Iohn* sore sick, hath left the field. 2465
I left him almost speechlesse, and broke out 2581
Pem. He is more patient | Then when you left him; euen now he sung. 2617
Which he hath left so shapelesse, and so rude. 2633
LEGAT = 2
Fra. Heere comes the holy Legat of the Pope. 1062
Iohn. The Legat of the Pope hath beene with mee, 2230
LEGATE = 3
And from Pope *Innocent* the Legate heere, 1066
Looke where the holy Legate comes apace, 2317
(Not trusting to this halting Legate heere, 2430
LEGGE = 1
Sir *Robert* neuer holpe to make this legge. 253
LEGIONS = 2
To land his Legions all as soone as I: 353
With many legions of strange fantasies, 2624
LEGITIMATION = 1
Legitimation, name, and all is gone; 261
LEGITTIMATE = 1
K.Iohn. Sirra, your brother is Legittimate, 124
LEGS = 1
And if my legs were two such riding rods, 148
LEISURE = 2
Whose leisure I haue staid, haue giuen him time 352
Then if you had at leisure knowne of this. 2584
LENGTHS = 1
But truth is truth, large lengths of seas and shores 113
LENT = *1
*K.Iohn. Why what a mad-cap hath heauen lent vs here? 92
LESSER = 1
And more, more strong, then lesser is my feare 1759
LEST *see also* least = 4
Lest men should say, looke where three farthings goes, 151
Lest vnaduis'd you staine your swords with bloud, 338
Lest that their hopes prodigiously be crost: 1016
Con. Looke to that Deuill, lest that *France* repent, 1124
LET = 53*2
An honourable conduct let him haue, 34
That ere I heard: shall I produce the men? | *K.Iohn.* Let them approach: 53
Then good my Liedge let me haue what is mine, 122

LET *cont.*

Then good my mother, let me know my father,	262
Let them be welcome then, we are prepar'd.	378
Const. Let me make answer: thy vsurping sonne.	418
These men of Angiers, let vs heare them speake,	502
And let vs in. Your King, whose labour'd spirits	538
Iohn. Acknowledge then the King, and let me in.	575
And let yong *Arthur* Duke of Britaine in,	611
Vnlesse thou let his siluer Water, keepe | A peacefull progresse to the Ocean.	653
Then let confusion of one part confirm	673
By East and West let France and England mount.	695
Fra. Let it be so: say, where will you assault?	722
Let in that amitie which you haue made,	857
And let beleefe, and life encounter so,	952
Or if it must stand still, let wiues with childe	1014
But (on this day) let Sea-men feare no wracke,	1017
Let not the howres of this vngodly day	1034
Con. O lawfull let it be | That I haue roome with *Rome* to curse a while,	1107
Let it be lawfull, that Law barre no wrong:	1114
Let goe the hand of that Arch-heretique,	1120
Elea. Look'st thou pale *France*? do not let go thy hand.	1123
My reuerend father, let it not be so;	1180
Or let the Church our mother breathe her curse,	1187
Thy tongue against thy tongue. O let thy vow	1196
I had a thing to say, but let it goe:	1332
Dol. Strong reasons makes strange actions: let vs go,	1567
For heauen sake *Hubert* let me not be bound:	1654
Hub. Go stand within: let me alone with him.	1661
Let him come backe, that his compassion may | Giue life to yours.	1665
Let me not hold my tongue: let me not *Hubert*,	1678
To grace occasions: let it be our suite,	1779
Iohn. Let it be so: I do commit his youth	1785
Then let the worst vn-heard, fall on your head.	1857
I shall yeeld vp my Crowne, let him be hang'd	1878
O, let me haue no subiect enemies,	1893
Yea, without stop, didst let thy heart consent,	1964
Big. To morrow morning let vs meete him then.	2015
Let hell want paines enough to torture me:	2142
Let not the world see feare and sad distrust	2214
Oh let it not be said: forrage, and runne	2227
And finde no checke? Let vs my Liege to Armes:	2242
Or if he doe, let it at least be said	2244
Dol. My Lord *Melloone*, let this be coppied out,	2252
Let me wipe off this honourable dewe,	2296
Let me haue audience: I am sent to speake:	2373
Strike vp the drummes, and let the tongue of warre	2420
And will not let me welcome this good newes.	2455
Hen. Let him be brought into the Orchard heere:	2615
Nor let my kingdomes Riuers take their course	2646
Straight let vs seeke, or straight we shall be sought,	2689
Bast. Let it be so, and you my noble Prince,	2706
Bast. Oh let vs pay the time: but needfull woe,	2721

LETS = 1*1

Lets kings assemble: for my greefe's so great,	993
Iohn. No more then he that threats. To Arms let's hie. | *Exeunt.*	1280

LETTER = *1
*Pem. Who brought that Letter from the Cardinall?   2011
LETTERS = 1
That it in golden letters should be set   1010
LEUIED = 1
Was leuied in the body of a land.   1830
LEW = *1
LEWES = 2
Of *Lewes* the Dolphin, and that louely maid.   740
Lewes marry *Blaunch*? O boy, then where art thou?   955
LEWIS see also Lew. = 6*2
*Enter before Angiers, Philip King of France, Lewis, Daul-|phin,
Austria, Constance, Arthur.*   292
King *Lewis*, determine what we shall doe strait.   449
*Shall *Lewis* haue *Blaunch*, and *Blaunch* those Prouinces?   924
Con. O *Lewis*, stand fast, the deuill tempts thee heere   1138
His Honor, Oh thine Honor, *Lewis* thine Honor.   1249
As *Lewis* himselfe: so (Nobles) shall you all,   2313
I say againe, if *Lewis* do win the day,   2491
If *Lewis*, by your assistance win the day.   2500
LEWIS = 2
LIABLE = 3
Finde liable to our Crowne and Dignitie,   806
Apt, liable to be employ'd in danger,   1951
And such as to my claime are liable,   2354
LIBERTIE = 4
Set at libertie: the fat ribs of peace   1307
As they haue giuen these hayres their libertie: 1457
But now I enuie at their libertie,   1458
That you haue bid vs aske his libertie,   1780
LIBERTY = 1
Counts it your weale: he haue his liberty.   1783
LIE *see also* lye = 1
It may lie gently at the foot of peace,   2329
LIEDGE = 1
Then good my Liedge let me haue what is mine,   122
LIEGE = 9
Essex. My Liege, here is the strangest controuersie   51
But that I am as well begot my Liege   85
Rob. My gracious Liege, when that my father liu'd,   103
K.Iohn. What is thy name?| *Bast. Philip* my Liege, so is my name
begun,   165
But on my Liege, for very little paines | Will bring this labor to an
happy end. *Exit.*   1295
Mes. My Liege, her eare | Is stopt with dust: the first of Aprill di'de   1838
And be thou hee. | *Mes.* With all my heart, my Liege.   1902
And finde no checke? Let vs my Liège to Armes: 2242
My Liege, my Lord: but now a King, now thus.   2676
LIEN *see* lyen
LIES *see also* lyes = 8
Bast. It lies as sightly on the backe of him   443
Many a widdowes husband groueling lies,   615
Dolph. Lady, with me, with me thy fortune lies.   1270
He lies before me: dost thou vnderstand me?   1363
Lies in his bed, walkes vp and downe with me,   1479
He will awake my mercie, which lies dead: 1599
Saying, what lacke you? and where lies your greefe?   1624

LIES *cont.*

Not truely speakes: who speakes not truly, Lies. 2093

LIEU = 1

In lieu whereof, I pray you beare me hence 2505

LIFE = 24*2

The rather, that you giue his off-spring life, 306

Iohn. My life as soone: I doe defie thee *France,* 455

And let beleefe, and life encounter so, 952

Aus. Thou dar'st not say so villaine for thy life. 1058

That takes away by any secret course | Thy hatefull life. 1105

Bla. There where my fortune liues, there my life dies. 1271

Bast. Now by my life, this day grows wondrous hot, 1285

My life, my ioy, my food, my all the world: 1489

Life is as tedious as a twice-told tale, 1493

That whiles warme life playes in that infants veines, 1517

Dol. And loose it, life and all, as *Arthur* did. 1529

Dol. May be he will not touch yong *Arthurs* life, 1545

Let him come backe, that his compassion may | Giue life to yours. 1665

Haue I commandement on the pulse of life? 1810

No certaine life atchieu'd by others death: 1823

To breake within the bloody house of life, 1935

Kneeling before this ruine of sweete life, 2064

Hub. Not for my life: But yet I dare defend 2088

My innocent life against an Emperor. 2089

My date of life out, for his sweete liues losse. 2109

The life, the right, and truth of all this Realme 2149

An empty Casket, where the Iewell of life 2208

Retaining but a quantity of life, 2484

Hen. It is too late, the life of all his blood 2605

And all the shrowds wherewith my life should saile, 2663

The life and death of King Iohn. 2730

LIFT = 1*1

Aust. The peace of heauen is theirs y lift their swords 328

Lift vp thy brow (renowned *Salisburie*) 2305

LIGHT = 5

Bast. Now by this light were I to get againe, 272

Or the light losse of *England,* for a friend: | Forgoe the easier. 1135

The perill of our curses light on thee 1226

Vnto the Raine-bow; or with Taper-light 1731

We had a kinde of light, what would ensue: 2060

LIGHTNING = 1

Be thou as lightning in the eies of *France*; 29

LIKE = 43*1

And were our father, and this sonne like him: 89

I giue heauen thankes I was not like to thee. 91

Philip. Because he hath a half-face like my father? 100

And like thy brother to enioy thy land: 143

And I had his, sir *Roberts* his like him, 147

Elinor. I like thee well: wilt thou forsake thy fortune, 156

And then comes answer like an Absey booke: 206

And fits the mounting spirit like my selfe; 216

Bast. Knight, knight good mother, Basilisco-like: 257

Then thou and *Iohn,* in manners being as like, 424

And then our Armes, like to a muzled Beare, 555

And like a iolly troope of Huntsmen come 632

Both are alike, and both alike we like: 643

Do like the Mutines of Ierusalem, 692

LIKE *cont.*

How like you this wilde counsell mighty States,	709
I like it well. France, shall we knit our powres,	712
If he see ought in you that makes him like,	828
Like a poore begger, raileth on the rich.	913
Like a proud riuer peering ore his bounds?	944
Hast thou not spoke like thunder on my side?	1050
Iohn. We like not this, thou dost forget thy selfe.	1060
And like a ciuill warre setst oath to oath,	1195
Of any kindred-action like to this?	1396
And be a Carrion Monster like thy selfe;	1416
For then 'tis like I should forget my selfe:	1433
Like true, inseparable, faithfull loues, | Sticking together in calamitie.	1450
And like the watchfull minutes, to the houre,	1622
And, like a dogge that is compell'd to fight,	1695
Art. O now you looke like *Hubert.* All this while | You were disguis'd.	1705
And like a shifted winde vnto a saile,	1740
Like Heralds 'twixt two dreadfull battailes set:	1796
And flye (like thought) from them, to me againe.	1897
Iohn. Spoke like a sprightfull Noble Gentleman.	1899
Like Riuers of remorse and innocencie.	2113
Like a kinde Host, the Dolphin and his powers.	2200
Away, and glister like the god of warre	2222
And flesh his spirit in a warre-like soyle,	2240
That like a Lion fostered vp at hand,	2328
To diue like Buckets in concealed Welles,	2393
To lye like pawnes, lock'd vp in chests and truncks,	2395
And like an Eagle, o're his ayerie towres,	2403
Like *Amazons,* come tripping after drummes:	2409
And like a bated and retired Flood,	2514
Sal. And the like tender of our loue wee make	2717

LIKENESSE = 1

In likenesse of a new vntrimmed Bride.	1139

LIKER = 1

Liker in feature to his father *Geffrey*	423

LIKES = *1

Fra. It likes vs well young Princes: close your hands	853

LIKING = 1

That any thing he see's which moues his liking,	829

LILLIES = 1

Of Natures guifts, thou mayst with Lillies boast,	974

LILLY = 1

To gilde refined Gold, to paint the Lilly;	1728

LIMBES = 2

And hang a Calues skin on those recreant limbes.	1055
If I get downe, and do not breake my limbes,	2002

LIMBS = 1*2

Phil. And hang a Calues-skin on those recreant limbs	1057
Phil. And hang a Calues-skin on those recreant limbs.	1059
Bast. And hang a Calues-skin on his recreant limbs.	1127

LIME = 1

By this time from their fixed beds of lime	525

LIMIT = 1

The farthest limit of my Embassie.	27

LIMITED = 1

And warrant limited vnto my tongue.	2377

LIMMES = 1
To whom am I beholding for these limmes?   252
LINCOLNE-WASHES = 1
These Lincolne-Washes haue deuoured them,   2599
LINE *see also* lyne = 2
Oh now doth death line his dead chaps with steele,   666
Meet in one line: and vast confusion waites   2157
LINEALL = 2
Our iust and lineall entrance to our owne;   382
The lineall state, and glorie of the Land,   2713
LINES = 1
Is much more generall, then these lines import.   2014
LINKD = 1
Married in league, coupled, and link'd together   1159
LION *see also* lyon = 6
The awlesse Lion could not wage the fight,   279
Richard that rob'd the Lion of his heart,   296
That did disrobe the Lion of that robe.   442
A cased Lion by the mortall paw,   1190
What, shall they seeke the Lion in his denne,   2225
That like a Lion fostered vp at hand,   2328
LIONNESSE = 1
At your den sirrah, with your Lionnesse,   598
LIONS *see also* lyons = 1
He that perforce robs Lions of their hearts,   281
LIPPES = 2
Aust. And your lippes too, for I am well assur'd,   854
And kisse the lippes of vnacquainted change,   1551
LIPS = 2
Doth moue the murmuring lips of discontent   1770
To make his bleake windes kisse my parched lips,   2648
LIST = *1
Old Qu. Son, list to this coniunction, make this match   784
LISTEN = 1
Aust. King *Philip*, listen to the Cardinall.   1126
LITTER = 2
To crowch in litter of your stable plankes,   2394
Set on toward *Swinsted*: to my Litter straight,   2456
LITTLE = 18
Something about a little from the right,   179
This little abstract doth containe that large,   398
And victorie with little losse doth play   617
Will giue her sadnesse very little cure: 866
Thou little valiant, great in villanie,   1042
But on my Liege, for very little paines | Will bring this labor to an
happy end. *Exit.*   1295
Ele. Come hether little kinsman, harke, a worde.   1317
Shall blow each dust, each straw, each little rub   1513
Or, as a little snow, tumbled about,   1561
Hub. Good morrow, little Prince.   1581
Ar. As little Prince, hauing so great a Title   1582
Insooth I would you were a little sicke,   1602
As patches set vpon a little breach,   1749
His little kingdome of a forced graue.   1816
Bast. But there is little reason in your greefe.   2029
Put but a little water in a spoone,   2135
The little number of your doubtfull friends.   2204

LITTLE *cont.*
  Are turned to one thred, one little haire: 2664
LIUD = 1
  Rob. My gracious Liege, when that my father liu'd,   103
LIUE = 8
  From *France* to *England*, there to liue in peace: 387
  That faith would liue againe by death of need: 1145
  Iohn. A Graue. | *Hub.* He shall not liue.   1369
  Hub. Well, see to liue: I will not touch thine eye,   1701
  Iohn. Doth *Arthur* liue? O hast thee to the Peeres,   1985
  Arthur doth liue, the king hath sent for you.   2075
  Iohn. That villaine *Hubert* told me he did liue.   2210
  That I must dye heere, and liue hence, by Truth?   2490
LIUES = 8*1
  Who liues and dares but say, thou didst not well   284
  Iohn. To verifie our title with their liues.   584
  Rescue those breathing liues to dye in beds,   734
  Which onely liues but by the death of faith,   1143
  * *Bla.* There where my fortune liues, there my life dies.   1271
  Liues in this bosome, deerely cherished.   1323
  Liues in his eye: that close aspect of his,   1790
  My date of life out, for his sweete liues losse.   2109
  Euen with a treacherous fine of all your liues: 2499
LIUING = 2
  When liuing blood doth in these temples beat   405
  Good Lords, although my will to giue, is liuing,   1801
LO = 2
  King. A wonder Lady: lo vpon thy wish | Our Messenger *Chattilion* is
  arriu'd,   344
  Con. Lo; now: now see the issue of your peace.   1404
LOCKD = 1
  To lye like pawnes, lock'd vp in chests and truncks,   2395
LOCKE = 1
  And till it be vndoubted, we do locke   683
LOE = 2
  Loe in this right hand, whose protection   542
  Loe, by my troth, the Instrument is cold,   1682
LONDON = 1
  But Douer Castle: London hath receiu'd   2199
LONG = 7
  By long and vehement suit I was seduc'd   267
  I should be as merry as the day is long: 1591
  To all our sorrowes, and ere long I doubt. *Exeunt*   1820
  Two long dayes iourney (Lords) or ere we meete.   2017
  And he, long traded in it, makes it seeme   2112
  Iohn. This Feauer that hath troubled me so long,   2442
  And your supply, which you haue wish'd so long,   2538
LONGD-FOR-CHANGE = 1
  With any long'd-for-change, or better State.   1725
LONGER = 1
  No longer then we well could wash our hands,   1165
LOOKD = 2
  And look'd vpon, I hope, with chearefull eyes.   1719
  Stoope lowe within those bounds we haue ore-look'd,   2516
LOOKE = 21*3
  Pembroke looke too't: farewell *Chattillion.* | *Exit Chat. and Pem.*   35
  Lest men should say, looke where three farthings goes,   151

LOOKE *cont.*

Looke heere vpon thy brother *Geffreyes* face,	· 396
To looke into the blots and staines of right,	411
Sirra looke too't, yfaith I will, yfaith.	440
Is neere to England, looke vpon the yeeres	739
Fra. What sai'st thou boy? looke in the Ladies face.	811
Why dost thou looke so sadly on my sonne?	941
Con. Looke to that Deuill, lest that *France* repent,	1124
Looke to thy selfe, thou art in ieopardie.	1279
So strongly guarded: Cosen, looke not sad,	1300
Looke who comes heere? a graue vnto a soule,	1400
And he will looke as hollow as a Ghost,	1469
Hub. Heate me these Irons hot, and looke thou stand	1571
Hub. Vncleanly scruples feare not you: looke too't.	1577
Ar. Are you sicke Hubert? you looke pale to day,	1601
Nor looke vpon the Iron angerly:	1658
He hath a sterne looke, but a gentle heart:	1664
Though to no vse, but still to looke on you.	1681
Art. O now you looke like *Hubert.* All this while | You were disguis'd.	1705
But wherefore doe you droope? why looke you sad?	2212
Looke where the holy Legate comes apace,	2317
Pand. You looke but on the out-side of this worke.	2362
To out-looke Conquest, and to winne renowne	2368

LOOKES = 5

That swayes the earth this Climate ouer-lookes,	658
I see a yeelding in the lookes of France:	790
Puts on his pretty lookes, repeats his words,	1480
Shee lookes vpon them with a threatning eye:	1505
Euen with the fierce lookes of these bloody men.	1650

LOOKST = *1

Elea. Look'st thou pale *France*? do not let go thy hand.	1123

LOOSE = 6

Who hauing no externall thing to loose,	892
Play fast and loose with faith? so iest with heauen,	1173
Against these giddy loose suggestions:	1223
Dol. And loose it, life and all, as *Arthur* did.	1529
I am amaz'd me thinkes, and loose my way	2145
Since I must loose the vse of all deceite?	2488

LORD = 27*2

Lord of thy presence, and no land beside.	145
My Lord *Chattilion* may from *England* bring	339
What *England* saies, say breefely gentle Lord,	346
Then tell vs, Shall your Citie call vs Lord,	569
Lord of our presence Angiers, and of you.	681
Dol. I do my Lord, and in her eie I find	812
Further I will not flatter you, my Lord,	833
We make him Lord of. Call the Lady *Constance*,	874
Gaine be my Lord, for I will worship thee. *Exit.*	919
Bast. My Lord I rescued her,	1293
Iohn. Death. | *Hub.* My Lord.	1367
O Lord, my boy, my *Arthur*, my faire sonne,	1488
Pem. Stay yet (Lord Salisbury) Ile go with thee,	1814
Your noble mother; and as I heare, my Lord,	1840
Bast. The *French* (my Lord) mens mouths are ful of it:	1882
Besides I met Lord *Bigot*, and Lord *Salisburie*	1883
Hub. My Lord, they say fiue Moones were seene to | (night:	1906
H. No had (my Lord?) why, did you not prouoke me?	1932

LORD *cont.*
  Hub. My Lord. | **Ioh.* Had'st thou' but shooke thy head, or made a
pause   1955
  Sal. The Count *Meloone*, a Noble Lord of France,   2012
  Hub. Stand backe Lord Salsbury, stand backe I say   2081
  I would not haue you (Lord) forget your selfe,   2083
  Second a Villaine, and a Murtherer? | *Hub.* Lord *Bigot*, I am none.   2104
  Dol. My Lord *Melloone*, let this be coppied out,   2252
  My holy Lord of Millane, from the King   * 2374
  Mes. My Lord: your valiant kinsman *Falconbridge*,   2445
  Mes. Who euer spoke it, it is true my Lord.   2545
  My Liege, my Lord: but now a King, now thus.   2676
LORDES = 1
  Enter Iohn, Pembroke, Salisbury, and other Lordes.   1717
LORDS = 12*3
  **Alarums, excursions, Retreat. Enter Iohn, Eleanor, Arthur | Bastard,
Hubert, Lords.*   1297
  Good Lords, although my will to giue, is liuing,   1801
  The angry Lords, with all expedient hast,   1993
  Sal. Lords, I will meet him at S.(aint) *Edmondsbury*,   2008
  Two long dayes iourney (Lords) or ere we meete.   2017
  *Bast. Once more to day well met, distemper'd Lords,   2019
  Hub. Lords, I am hot with haste, in seeking you,   2074
  *P. There tel the king, he may inquire vs out. *Ex. Lords.*   2118
  Iohn. Would not my Lords returne to me againe   2205
  Returne the president to these Lords againe,   2254
  For if the French be Lords of this loud day,   2475
  Last in the field, and almost Lords of it.   2532
  *Mes. The Count *Meloone* is slaine: The English Lords   2536
  Hub. Why know you not? The Lords are all come | backe,   2590
  With whom your selfe, my selfe, and other Lords,   2703
LOSE *see also* loose = 4
  And by disioyning hands hell lose a soule.   1125
  Vncle, I needs must pray that thou maist lose: 1265
  Who-euer wins, on that side shall I lose: 1268
  Art. Is there no remedie? | *Hub.* None, but to lose your eyes.   1668
LOSING = 1
  What haue you lost by losing of this day?   1501
LOSSE = 6
  And victorie with little losse doth play   617
  Gracing the scroule that tels of this warres losse,   662
  Or the light losse of *England*, for a friend: | Forgoe the easier. 1135
  Assured losse, before the match be plaid.   1269
  Fareyouwell: had you such a losse as I,   1484
  My date of life out, for his sweete liues losse.   2109
LOST = 5
  Rather lost more. And by this hand I sweare   657
  Are we not beaten? Is not *Angiers* lost?   1388
  Yong *Arthur* is my sonne, and he is lost: 1431
  What haue you lost by losing of this day?   1501
  'Tis strange to thinke how much King *Iohn* hath lost   1506
LOTH = *1
  *Dol. The Sun of heauen (me thought) was loth to set;   2525
LOUD = 4
  I do protest I neuer lou'd my selfe   817
  Shall braying trumpets, and loud churlish drums   1236
  I honour'd him, I lou'd him, and will weepe   2108

LOUD *cont.*
For if the French be Lords of this loud day,   2475
LOVE = 38*1
This might haue beene preuented, and made whole | With very easie
arguments of loue,   41
Subiected tribute to commanding loue,   277
Embrace him, loue him, giue him welcome hether.   304
But with a heart full of vnstained loue,   .   309
As seale to this indenture of my loue: 313
To make a more requitall to your loue.   327
England we loue, and for that *Englands* sake,   388
And out of my deere loue Ile giue thee more,   457
If lustie loue should go in quest of beautie,   741
If zealous loue should go in search of vertue,   743
If loue ambitious, sought a match of birth,   745
Can in this booke of beautie read, I loue: 801
In such a loue, so vile a Lout as he.   826
I will enforce it easlie to my loue.   832
That all I see in you is worthie loue,   834
Iohn. Speake then Prince Dolphin, can you loue this | Ladie?   843
Dol. Nay aske me if I can refraine from loue,   845
For I doe loue her most vnfainedly.   846
For then I should not loue thee: no, nor thou   970
Was deepe-sworne faith, peace, amity, true loue   1162
So newly ioyn'd in loue? so strong in both,   1171
Saue what is opposite to *Englands* loue.   1185
Blan. Now shall I see thy loue, what motiue may   1246
And with aduantage meanes to pay thy loue: 1321
But (ah) I will not, yet I loue thee well,   1353
Iohn. Enough. | I could be merry now, *Hubert*, I loue thee.   1371
And busse thee as thy wife: Miseries Loue, | O come to me.   1418
Fra. Binde vp those tresses: O what loue I note   1445
I were your sonne, so you would loue me, Hubert: 1597
I warrant I loue you more then you do me.   1604
Or what good loue may I performe for you?   1625
Nay, you may thinke my loue was craftie loue,   1629
Whose priuate with me of the Dolphines loue,   2013
Swearing Allegiance, and the loue of soule   2177
Euen on that Altar, where we swore to you | Deere Amity, and
euerlasting loue.   2480
The loue of him, and this respect besides   2502
But I do loue the fauour, and the forme   ,   2511
Sal. And the like tender of our loue wee make   2717
LOUELY = 2
Of *Lewes* the Dolphin, and that louely maid.   740
Death, death, O amiable, louely death,   1408
LOUES = 4
Himselfe loues traytor, this is pittie now;   824
Thy Grandame loues thee, and thy Vnkle will   1301
Like true, inseparable, faithfull loues, | Sticking together in calamitie.   1450
I haue a way to winne their loues againe: 1889
LOUING = 4
But thou from louing *England* art so farre,   391
Iohn. England for it selfe: | You men of Angiers, and my louing
subiects.   508
Fra. You louing men of Angiers, *Arthurs* subiects,   510
And nere haue spoke a louing word to you: 1627

LOUST = 1
And by my troth I thinke thou lou'st me well.   1354
LOUT = 1*1
    In such a loue, so vile a Lout as he.   826
    *Bast. Hang nothing but a Calues skin most sweet lout.   1151
LOW = 1
    I would that I were low laid in my graue,   466
LOWD = 2
    That shall reuerberate all, as lowd as thine.   2426
    (As lowd as thine) rattle the Welkins eare,   2428
LOWE = 1
    Stoope lowe within those bounds we haue ore-look'd,   2516
LOYALL = 1
    To him will we proue loyall, till that time   577
LUCIFER = 1
    Thou art more deepe damn'd then Prince Lucifer: 2125
LUSTIE = 4
    We will beare home that lustie blood againe,   561
    Our lustie English, all with purpled hands,   633
    If lustie loue should go in quest of beautie,   741
    What Cannoneere begot this lustie blood,   777
LUSTY = 2
    When this same lusty gentleman was got: 116
    What lusty Trumpet thus doth summon vs?   2370
LYE = 4
    Whose sonnes lye scattered on the bleeding ground: 614
    And pour's downe mischiefe. *Austrias* head lye there,   1287
    To lye like pawnes, lock'd vp in chests and truncks,   2395
    Lye at the proud foote of a Conqueror,   2724
LYEN = 1
    Many a poore mans sonne would haue lyen still,   1626
LYES = 5
    Which fault lyes on the hazards of all husbands   127
    Who sayes it was, he lyes, I say twas not. | *Exeunt.*   289
    Whose fulnesse of perfection lyes in him.   755
    Sal. This is the prison: What is he lyes heere?   2033
    Lyes heauie on me: oh, my heart is sicke.   2443
LYMOGES = 1
    O *Lymoges*, O *Austria*, thou dost shame   1040
LYNE = 1
    We will not lyne his thin-bestained cloake   2022
LYON = 1
    Aust. Peace, no more. | *Bast.* O tremble: for you heare the Lyon rore.   601
LYONS = 6
    Whose valour plucks dead Lyons by the beard;   438
    Blan. O well did he become that Lyons robe,   441
    I would set an Oxe-head to your Lyons hide: | And make a monster of
    you.   599
    Lyons more confident, Mountaines and rockes   767
    Talkes as familiarly of roaring Lyons,   775
    Thou weare a Lyons hide, doff it for shame,   1054
MAD = 9
    Bast. Mad world, mad kings, mad composition: 882
    I am not mad: this haire I teare is mine,   1429
    I am not mad, I would to heauen I were,   1432
    Preach some Philosophy to make me mad,   1435
    For, being not mad, but sensible of greefe,   1437

MAD *cont.*
If I were mad, I should forget my sonne,   1441
I am not mad: too well, too well I feele   1443
MADAM = 8*1
Bast. Madam, and if my brother had my shape   146
Madam, Ile follow you vnto the death.   162
**Bast.* Madam by chance, but not by truth, what tho;   178
Come Madam, and come *Richard*, we must speed   187
Madam, I was not old Sir *Roberts* sonne,   246
Madam I would not wish a better father: 273
Ar. I do beseech you Madam be content.   963
Sal. Pardon me Madam, | I may not goe without you to the kings.   987
Remember: Madam, Fare you well,   1374
MADAME = 1
Phil. I Madame? No, I haue no reason for it,   74
MADE = 27*4
This might haue beene preuented, and made whole | With very easie
arguments of loue,   41
For new made honor doth forget mens names: 197
That Iudge hath made me guardian to this boy,   412
I am not worth this coyle that's made for me.   467
But God hath made her sinne and her, the plague   488
Had bin dishabited, and wide hauocke made   526
Who by the hand of France, this day hath made   612
And two such shores, to two such streames made one,   758
Let in that amitie which you haue made,   857
I know she is not for this match made vp,   861
**Fra.* And by my faith, this league that we haue made   865
Made to run euen, vpon euen ground;   897
This newes hath made thee a most vgly man.   958
And made his Maiestie the bawd to theirs.   980
No bargaines breake that are not this day made;   1018
And our oppression hath made vp this league: 1031
First made to heauen, first be to heauen perform'd,   1197
Const. O, vpon my knee made hard with kneeling,   1243
Had bak'd thy bloud, and made it heauy, thicke,   1342
Ioh. Thou hast made me giddy   1852
Is to be made, then shall this hand and Seale   1942
Made it no conscience to destroy a Prince.   1954
Hub. My Lord. | **Ioh.* Had'st thou but shooke thy head, or made a
pause   1955
*Deepe shame had struck me dumbe, made me break off,   1960
Forgiue the Comment that my passion made   1988
**P.* Oh death, made proud with pure & princely beuty,   2034
And I haue made a happy peace with him,   2231
And come ye now to tell me *Iohn* hath made   2344
Because that *Iohn* hath made his peace with *Rome?*   2349
But staid, and made the Westerne Welkin blush,   2526
As this hath made me. Who was he that said   2542
MADLY = 1
Or madly thinke a babe of clowts were he;   1442
MADNESSE = 1
Pand. Lady, you vtter madnesse, and not sorrow.   1427
MAD-CAP = *1
**K.Iohn.* Why what a mad-cap hath heauen lent vs here?   92
MAID = 2
Of *Lewes* the Dolphin, and that louely maid.   740

MAID *cont.*
But the word Maid, cheats the poore Maide of that.   893
MAIDE = 1
But the word Maid, cheats the poore Maide of that.   893
MAIDEN = 2
Vpon the maiden vertue of the Crowne: 395
Is yet a maiden, and an innocent hand.   1977
MAIDES = 1
For your owne Ladies, and pale-visag'd Maides,   2408
MAIDS = 2
As maids of thirteene do of puppi-dogges.   776
Of kings, of beggers, old men, yong men, maids,   891
MAIESTIE = 4
And made his Maiestie the bawd to theirs.   980
Const. O faire returne of banish'd Maiestie.   1254
Desires your Maiestie to leaue the field,   2446
And they are all about his Maiestie.   2594
MAIESTIES = 1
Hub. Why answer not the double Maiesties,   796
MAIESTY = 16
In my behauiour to the Maiesty,   8
The borrowed Maiesty of *England* heere.   9
Elea. A strange beginning: borrowed Maiesty?   10
Bast. Ha Maiesty: how high thy glory towres,   664
Haue I not pawn'd to you my Maiesty?   1023
Resembling Maiesty, which being touch'd and tride,   1025
Dolph. I muse your Maiesty doth seeme so cold,   1250
Hub. I am much bounden to your Maiesty.   1328
Hub. And Ile keepe him so, | That he shall not offend your Maiesty. 1365
Ile send those powers o're to your Maiesty.   1375
Of dangerous Maiesty, when perchance it frownes,   1938
Now for the bare-pickt bone of Maiesty,   2153
Hub. Badly I feare; how fares your Maiesty?   2441
Bast. Who didst thou leaue to tend his Maiesty?   2589
Hen. How fares your Maiesty?   2642
And spleene of speede, to see your Maiesty.   2660
MAINE = 5
To *Ireland, Poyctiers, Aniowe, Torayne, Maine,*   16
Euen till that *England* hedg'd in with the maine,   319
England and *Ireland, Angiers, Toraine, Maine,*   452
For *Angiers*, and faire *Toraine Maine, Poyctiers,*   803
Iohn. Then I doe giue *Volquessen, Toraine, Maine,*   847
MAINTAIND = 1
Must be as boysterously maintain'd as gain'd.   1521
MAINTAINE = 1
Sweat in this businesse, and maintaine this warre?   2355
MAIST *l.*420 *989 1189 1264 1265 2565 = 5*1
MAKE = 46*2
Well, now can I make any *Ioane* a Lady,   194
Sir *Robert* neuer holpe to make this legge.   253
To make roome for him in my husbands bed: 268
To make a more requitall to your loue.   327
But we will make it subiect to this boy.   336
To make a hazard of new fortunes heere: 365
Const. Let me make answer: thy vsurping sonne.   418
Or lay on that shall make your shoulders cracke.   446
To make a shaking feuer in your walles,   534

149

MAKE *cont.*
To make a faithlesse errour in your eares,	536
France. When I haue saide, make answer to vs both.	541
I would set an Oxe-head to your Lyons hide: | And make a monster of you.	599
Make worke vpon our selues, for heauen or hell.	721
*Old Qu. Son, list to this coniunction, make this match	784
Shall gild her bridall bed and make her rich	807
We make him Lord of. Call the Lady *Constance,*	874
Teach thou this sorrow, how to make me dye,	951
Nature and Fortune ioyn'd to make thee great.	973
Fra. Good reuerend father, make my person yours,	1155
Make such vnconstant children of our selues	1174
And make a ryot on the gentle brow | Of true sincerity? O holy Sir	1178
It is religion that doth make vowes kept,	1210
And better conquest neuer canst thou make,	1221
Iohn. Hubert, keepe this boy: *Philip* make vp,	1290
Arth. O this will make my mother die with griefe.	1303
Heare me without thine eares, and make reply	1348
Preach some Philosophy to make me mad,	1435
*Dol. There's nothing in this world can make me ioy,	1492
May then make all the claime that *Arthur* did.	1528
Art. And if you do, you will but make it blush,	1692
Doth make the fault the worse by th'excuse:	1748
Doth make a stand, at what your Highnesse will.	1756
O make a league with me, 'till I haue pleas'd	1845
Iohn. Nay, but make haste: the better foote before.	1892
Make deeds ill done? Had'st not thou beene by,	1945
Ile make a peace betweene your soule, and you.	1975
And make them tame to their obedience.	1987
And make faire weather in your blustring land:	2188
Goe I to make the *French* lay downe their Armes. *Exit.*	2191
And fright him there? and make him tremble there?	2226
Send fayre-play-orders, and make comprimise, | Insinuation, parley, and base truce	2236
Perchance the Cardinall cannot make your peace;	2243
Doth make an earth-quake of Nobility:	2293
To cudgell you, and make you take the hatch,	2392
What in the world should make me now deceiue,	2487
To make his bleake windes kisse my parched lips,	2648
Sal. And the like tender of our loue wee make	2717
And we shall shocke them: Naught shall make vs rue,	2728

MAKER = 1
To be a widdow-maker: oh, and there	2268

MAKES = 13*1
A landlesse Knight, makes thee a landed Squire:	186
Becomes a sonne and makes your sonne a shadow:	816
If he see ought in you that makes him like,	828
Makes it take head from all indifferency,	900
As it makes harmefull all that speake of it.	962
For greefe is proud, and makes his owner stoope,	991
Makes nice of no vilde hold to stay him vp:	1523
*Dol. Strong reasons makes strange actions: let vs go,	1567
It makes the course of thoughts to fetch about,	1741
Makes sound opinion sicke, and truth suspected,	1743
Whilst he that heares, makes fearefull action	1916
And he, long traded in it, makes it seeme	2112

MAKES *cont.*

Startles mine eyes, and makes me more amaz'd	2302
Doth by the idle Comments that it makes,	2608

MAKING = 2

Making that idiot laughter keepe mens eyes,	1344
By making many: Oh it grieues my soule,	2266

MAKST = 2

Pand. So mak'st thou faith an enemy to faith,	1194
And mak'st an oath the suretie for thy truth,	1213

MALE-CHILDE = 1

For since the birth of *Caine*, the first male-childe	1464

MALICE = 4

Our Cannons malice vainly shall be spent	557
Your sharpest Deeds of malice on this Towne.	694
There is no malice in this burning cole,	1688
The bloud of malice, in a vaine of league,	2289

MALICIOUS = 1

Commander of this hot malicious day,	625

MAN = 14*2

Eli. Out on thee rude man, y dost shame thy mother,	72
In the large composition of this man?	96
My picked man of Countries: my deare sir,	203
Colbrand the Gyant, that same mighty man,	236
Some proper man I hope, who was it mother?	263
Sonne to the elder brother of this man,	545
He is the halfe part of a blessed man,	752
Is but the vaine breath of a common man:	929
Beleeue me, I doe not beleeue thee man,	930
This newes hath made thee a most vgly man.	958
Aus. O that a man should speake those words to me.	1056
Purchase corrupted pardon of a man,	1093
Hubert shall be your man, attend on you	1378
Vexing the dull eare of a drowsie man;	1494
Pem. This is the man should do the bloody deed:	1787
Or vsefull seruing-man, and Instrument	2334

MANLY = 1

But this effusion of such manly drops,	2300

MANNAGE = 1

Which now the mannage of two kingdomes must	43

MANNER = 1

Sal. Nay, 'tis in a manner done already,	2699

MANNERS = 4

Bast. Our Country manners giue our betters way.	164
Then thou and *Iohn*, in manners being as like,	424
Sal. Our greefes, and not our manners reason now.	2028
Therefore 'twere reason you had manners now.	2030

MANS = 2

Many a poore mans sonne would haue lyen still,	1626
Bast. 'Tis true, to hurt his master, no mans else.	2032

MANY = 12

But many a many foot of Land the worse.	193
Fran. As many and as well-borne bloods as those. | *Bast.* Some Bastards too.	585
Much worke for teares in many an English mother,	613
Many a widdowes husband groueling lies,	615
Many a poore mans sonne would haue lyen still,	1626
With many hundreds treading on his heeles:	1870

MANY *cont.*
Told of a many thousand warlike French,	1924
By making many: Oh it grieues my soule,	2266
And I with him, and many moe with mee,	2478
With many legions of strange fantasies,	2624
For many carriages hee hath dispatch'd	2700

MARCH = 4
Who painefully with much expedient march	529
In warlike march, these greenes before your Towne,	548
Of smiling peace to march a bloody hoast,	1177
Wherein we step after a stranger, march	2278

MARCHD = 2
Haue hither march'd to your endamagement.	515
Their Armours that march'd hence so siluer bright,	626

MARCHES = 2
His marches are expedient to this towne,	354
To stop their marches 'fore we are enflam'd:	2174

MARCHT = 1
That did display them when we first marcht forth:	631

MARIES = 1
For at Saint Maries Chappell presently,	858

MARKD = 1
A fellow by the hand of Nature mark'd,	1946

MARKE = 1*1
Marke how they whisper, vrge them while their soules | Are capeable of	
this ambition,	791
*Thy foote to Englands Throne. And therefore marke:	1515

MARKES = 2
Full thirty thousand Markes of English coyne:	850
Patch'd with foule Moles, and eye-offending markes,	968

MARKET-PLACE = 1
Wade to the market-place in *French*-mens bloud,	335

MARKING = 1
Least I, by marking of your rage, forget	2085

MARRIAGE = 3
The rights of marriage shallbe solemniz'd.	859
Vn-sweare faith sworne, and on the marriage bed	1176
I (by the honour of my marriage bed)	2346

MARRIE = 3
Sir *Robert* could doe well, marrie to confesse	249
To these two Princes, if you marrie them:	760
Iohn. I marrie, now my soule hath elbow roome,	2635

MARRIED = 2*1
Con. Gone to be married? Gone to sweare a peace?	922
Married in league, coupled, and link'd together	1159
Against the blood that thou hast married?	1234

MARRY = 2
That marry wiues: tell me, how if my brother	128
Lewes marry *Blaunch*? O boy, then where art thou?	955

MASKE = 1
This harness'd Maske, and vnaduised Reuell,	2386

MASTER = 2
Snatch at his Master that doth tarre him on.	1696
Bast. 'Tis true, to hurt his master, no mans else.	2032

MASTEREST = 1
Which owe the crowne, that thou ore-masterest?	406

MATCH = 6*1
If loue ambitious, sought a match of birth,	745
To our fast closed gates: for at this match,	762
And giue you entrance: but without this match,	765
*Old Qu. Son, list to this coniunction, make this match	784
I know she is not for this match made vp,	861
Assured losse, before the match be plaid.	1269
To winne this easie match, plaid for a Crowne?	2359

MATCHT = *1
| *Strength matcht with strength, and power confronted \| power, | 641 |

MATTER = 4
And picke strong matter of reuolt, and wrath	1552
And O, what better matter breeds for you,	1555
Euen in the matter of mine innocence:	1641
And brought in matter that should feed this fire;	2338

MAULE = 1
| Or Ile so maule you, and your tosting-Iron, | 2101 |

MAW = 1
| To thrust his ycie fingers in my maw; | 2645 |

MAY l.71 282 339 436 867 928 988 1015 1091 1130 1193 1200 1246 1266
1439 1524 1528 1545 1564 1583 1625 1629 1665 1680 1778 *2118 2248
2257 2329 2482 2507 2557 2588 2695 2707 2712 = 36*1

MAYST = 1
| Of Natures guifts, thou mayst with Lillies boast, | 974 |

ME l.47 76 82 86 118 122 128 140 141 157 *163 *172 173 177 230 247 250
262 287 412 418 467 477 575 736 845 863 909 930 932 950 951 956 964
983 987 992 1024 1033 1037 1039 1051 *1056 1078 1097 1156 1238 1270
*1310 1311 1324 1331 1336 1347 1348 1354 1355 1363 1403 1417 1419
1428 1435 1476 1479 1481 *1492 1511 1554 1563 *1571 1574 1585 1586
1593 1594 1597 1604 1619 1631 1645 1646 1649 1651 1654 1655 1660
1661 1678 1683 1697 *1808 1845 1852 1858 1868 1891 1893 1897 *1898
1901 *1928 *1932 1959 *1960 *1961 1962 1967 1968 1998 1999 2000
2005 2013 2020 2091 2098 2099 2114 2122 2142 2145 2162 2205 2210
2262 2296 2302 *2331 2341 2342 2344 2345 2373 2383 2417 2440 2442
2443 2447 2454 2455 2457 2467 2487 2501 2505 *2525 2542 2565 2568
2578 2601 2649 2651 2655 2686 = 149*15

MEAGER = 2
| The meager cloddy earth to glittering gold: | 1005 |
| As dim and meager as an Agues fitte, | 1470 |

MEANE = 6
And in the meane time soiourn'd at my fathers;	111
Yet to auoid deceit I meane to learne;	225
And by whose helpe I meane to chastise it.	414
What dost thou meane by shaking of thy head?	940
For euen the breath of what I meane to speake,	1512
I shall indue you with: Meane time, but aske	1760

MEANES = 6
What meanes this scorne, thou most vntoward knaue?	256
What meanes that hand vpon that breast of thine?	942
And with aduantage meanes to pay thy loue:	1321
No, no: when Fortune meanes to men most good,	1504
How oft the sight of meanes to do ill deeds,	1944
He meanes to recompence the paines you take,	2476

MEANETIME see meane

MEANING = 1
| And on the winking of Authoritie \| To vnderstand a Law; to know the meaning | 1936 |

MEASURE = 4
  (If not fill vp the measure of her will)   877
  Yet in some measure satisfie her so,   878
  Who with his Sheeres, and Measure in his hand,   1921
  When English measure backward their owne ground   2527
MEASURES = 1
  Clamors of hell, be measures to our pomp?   1237
MEDCINE = 1
  That present medcine must be ministred,   2182
MEDLING = 1
  Are led so grossely by this medling Priest,   1090
MEE *l.*691 1263 1440 1714 2230 2454 2478 = 7
MEET = 5*1
  When I shall meet him in the Court of heauen   1472
  Sal. Lords, I will meet him at S.(aint) *Edmondsbury,*   2008
  Meet in one line: and vast confusion waites   2157
  Iohn. Now keep your holy word, go meet the *French,*   2172
  To meet displeasure farther from the dores,   2228
  Our Partie may well meet a prowder foe. *Exeunt.*   2248
MEETE = 3
  Big. To morrow morning let vs meete him then.   2015
  Two long dayes iourney (Lords) or ere we meete.   2017
  If you thinke meete, this afternoone will poast   2704
MEETING = 1
  Which in the very meeting fall, and dye.   954
MEL = 3
MELANCHOLY = 1
  Or if that surly spirit melancholy   1341
MELL = 1
  Why then defie each other, and pell-mell,   720
MELLOONE = 1
  Dol. My Lord *Melloone,* let this be coppied out,   2252
MELOON see also Mel. = 1
  Enter Meloon wounded.   2466
MELOONE = 2*2
  Sal. The Count *Meloone,* a Noble Lord of France,   2012
  *Enter (in Armes) Dolphin, Salisbury, Meloone, Pem-|broke, Bigot,
  Souldiers.*   2250
  Pem. It is the Count *Meloone.* | *Sal.* Wounded to death.   2469
  Mes. The Count *Meloone* is slaine: The English Lords   2536
MELTED = 2
  Least zeale now melted by the windie breath   793
  My heart hath melted at a Ladies teares,   2298
MEN = 23*1
  That ere I heard: shall I produce the men? | *K.Iohn.* Let them approach: 53
  This expeditions charge: what men are you?   56
  Lest men should say, looke where three farthings goes,   151
  And haue is haue, how euer men doe catch: 182
  Call for our cheefest men of discipline,   332
  These men of Angiers, let vs heare them speake,   502
  Iohn. England for it selfe: | You men of Angiers, and my louing
  subiects.   508
  Fra. You louing men of Angiers, *Arthurs* subiects,   510
  F.Her. You men of Angiers open wide your gates,   610
  E.Har. Reioyce you men of Angiers, ring your bels,   623
  And now he feasts, mousing the flesh of men   668
  Of kings, of beggers, old men, yong men, maids,   891

MEN *cont.*

As doth the furie of two desperate men,	953
But (on this day) let Sea-men feare no wracke,	1017
What, shall our feast be kept with slaughtered men?	1235
No, no: when Fortune meanes to men most good,	1504
Euen with the fierce lookes of these bloody men.	1650
Nay heare me *Hubert*, driue these men away,	1655
Thrust but these men away, and Ile forgiue you,	1659
The faiths of men, nere stained with reuolt:	1723
Bast. How I haue sped among the Clergy men,	1862
Hub. Old men, and Beldames, in the streets	1910
What men prouided? What munition sent	2351

MENDED = *1

*Where be your powres? Shew now your mended faiths,	2685

MENS = 4*1

Of that I doubt, as all mens children may.	71
For new made honor doth forget mens names:	197
Wade to the market-place in *French*-mens bloud,	335
Making that idiot laughter keepe mens eyes,	1344
Bast. The *French* (my Lord) mens mouths are ful of it:	1882

MERCIE = 4

Art. 'Mercie on me: | Me thinkes no body should be sad but I:	1585
He will awake my mercie, which lies dead:	1599
That mercie, which fierce fire, and Iron extends,	1699
Beyond the infinite and boundlesse reach of mercie,	2120

MERCILES = 1

And merciles proceeding, by these French.	520

MERCURIE = 1

Be Mercurie, set feathers to thy heeles,	1896

MERCY *see also* Godamercy = 1

Creatures of note for mercy, lacking vses.	1700

MERIT = 2

That I can finde, should merit any hate.	838
And by the merit of vilde gold, drosse, dust,	1092

MERITORIOUS = 1

And meritorious shall that hand be call'd,	1103

MERRIER = 1

Hub. Indeed I haue beene merrier.	1584

MERRIMENT = 1

And straine their cheekes to idle merriment,	1345

MERRY = 2

Iohn. Enough. | I could be merry now, *Hubert*, I loue thee.	1371
I should be as merry as the day is long:	1591

MES = 1

Io. They burn in indignation: I repent: *Enter Mes.*	1821

MES = 8*1

MESSE = 1

Hee and his tooth-picke at my worships messe,	200

MESSENGER *see also* Mes. = 5

King. A wonder Lady: lo vpon thy wish | Our Messenger *Chattilion* is arriu'd,	344
Some speedy Messenger bid her repaire	875
Some Messenger betwixt me, and the Peeres,	1901
Enter a Messenger.	2444
Enter a Messenger.	2533

MESSENGERS = 1

Can hide you from our messengers of Warre,	566

MET = 3*1

Lewis. Before *Angiers* well met braue *Austria*,   294
Besides I met Lord *Bigot*, and Lord *Salisburie*   1883
**Bast.* Once more to day well met, distemper'd Lords,   2019
Nor met with Fortune, other then at feasts,   2309
METEORS = 2
And call them Meteors, prodigies, and signes,   1542
Figur'd quite ore with burning Meteors.   2304
METHINKES *see also* thinkes = 1
And euen there, methinkes an Angell spake,   2316
METHOUGHT *see* thought
METROPOLIS = 1
The great Metropolis and Sea of Rome: 2325
METTLE = 2
Bast. And if thou hast the mettle of a king,   715
That I must draw this mettle from my side   2267
MEW = 1
The steppes of wrong, should moue you to mew vp   1774
MIDNIGHT = 1
And with my hand, át midnight held your head;   1621
MID-NIGHT = 1
To giue me audience: If the mid-night bell ·   1336
MIGHT *l.*41 131 133 134 153 247 *636 1603 *1961 2288 2582 2653 = 10*2
MIGHTIE = 1
The bloome that promiseth a mightie fruite.   789
MIGHTIER = 1
And stirre them vp against a mightier taske: 349
MIGHTY = 5*1
Philip. Most certain of one mother, mighty King,   67
Colbrand the Gyant, that same mighty man,   236
How like you this wilde counsell mighty States,   709
Perseuer not, but heare me mighty kings.   736
Thy hand hath murdred him: I had a mighty cause   1930
**Bast.* With-hold thine indignation, mighty heauen,   2595
MILLANE = 2
I *Pandulph*, of faire *Millane* Cardinall,   1065
My holy Lord of Millane, from the King   2374
MINDE = 3
Pan. Your minde is all as youthfull as your blood.   1510
This murther had not come into my minde.   1948
Is yet the couer of a fayrer minde,   1983
MINE *l.*28 75 97 122 150 204 234 *255 *596 827 1027 1113 1157 1242
1362 1429 1609 1612 1632 1641 1643 1646 1680 1788 1976 2302 2314
2347 2558 2570 2661 = 30*2
MINGLED = 1
And part your mingled colours once againe,   703
MINION = 1
Out of one side her happy Minion,   706
MINISTRED = 1
That present medcine must be ministred,   2182
MINUTE = 1
One minute, nay one quiet breath of rest.   1519
MINUTES = 1
And like the watchfull minutes, to the houre,   1622
MIRACLE = 1
A wonder, or a wondrous miracle,   813

MIRTH = 1
Full warm of blood, of mirth, of gossipping: 2310
MISBEGOTTEN = 1
Sal. That misbegotten diuell *Falconbridge*,   2463
MISCARRY = 2
If they miscarry: we miscarry too.   2462
MISCHIEFE = 1
And pour's downe mischiefe. *Austrias* head lye there,   1287
MISERIES = 1
And busse thee as thy wife: Miseries Loue, | O come to me.   1418
MISHEARD = 1
It is not so, thou hast mispoke, misheard,   925
MISPOKE = 1
It is not so, thou hast mispoke, misheard,   925
MISTAKE = 1
Is to mistake again, though indirect,   1206
MISTEMPRED = 1
This inundation of mistempred humor,   2179
MISTOOKE = 1
The better Act of purposes mistooke,   1205
MIS-PLACD-IOHN = 1
The mis-plac'd-*Iohn* should entertaine an houre,   1518
MOCKE = 1
And mocke the deepe mouth'd Thunder: for at hand   2429
MOCKERIE = 1
Else what a mockerie should it be to sweare?   1216
MOCKING = 1
Mocking the ayre with colours idlely spred,   2241
MODERNE = 1
Which scornes a moderne Inuocation.   1426
MODULE = 1
And then all this thou seest, is but a clod, | And module of confounded
royalty.   2667
MOE = 1
And I with him, and many moe with mee,   2478
MOLES = 1
Patch'd with foule Moles, and eye-offending markes,   968
MOMENT = 1
Then in a moment Fortune shall cull forth   705
MONARCH = 1
No: know the gallant Monarch is in Armes,   2402
MONEY = 1
Dreading the curse that money may buy out,   1091
MONKE = 2
Hub. The King I feare is poyson'd by a Monke,   2580
Hub. A Monke I tell you, a resolued villaine   2586
MONSTER = 2
I would set an Oxe-head to your Lyons hide: | And make a monster of
you.   599
And be a Carrion Monster like thy selfe;   1416
MONSTROUS = 2
Qu. Thou monstrous slanderer of heauen and earth.   475
Con. Thou monstrous Iniurer of heauen and earth,   476
MOOD = 1
Do shew the mood of a much troubled brest,   1791
MOONES = 2
Hub. My Lord, they say fiue Moones were seene to | (night: 1906

MOONES *cont.*
  Ioh. Fiue Moones?   1909
MORCELL = 1
  From forth this morcell of dead Royaltie?   2148
MORE *see also* moe = 39*5
  Eli. Your strong possessio(n) much more then your right,   46
  Phil. Of no more force to dispossesse me sir,   140
  Kneele thou downe *Philip*, but rise more great,   170
  For *France*, for *France*, for it is more then need.   188
  There's toyes abroad, anon Ile tell thee more. | *Exit Iames.* 244
  That to my home I will no more returne   314
  To make a more requitall to your loue.   327
  Cuts off more circumstance, they are at hand, | *Drum beats.* 371
  And out of my deere loue Ile giue thee more,   457
  Fra. Peace Lady, pause, or be more temperate,   498
  Aust. Peace, no more. | *Bast.* O tremble: for you heare the Lyon rore. 601
  Iohn. France, hast thou yet more blood to cast away? 648
  In this hot triall more then we of France,   656
  Rather lost more. And by this hand I sweare   657
  This Vnion shall do more then batterie can   761
  Lyons more confident, Mountaines and rockes   767
  More free from motion, no not death himselfe   768
  Or if you will, to speake more properly,   831
  With her to thee, and this addition more,   849
  Adde thus much more, that no *Italian* Priest   1080
  Aust. Doe so king *Philip*, hang no more in doubt.   1150
  Pan. What canst thou say, but wil perplex thee more? 1153
  Iohn. No more then he that threats. To Arms let's hie. | *Exeunt.* 1280
  Must I behold my pretty *Arthur* more.   1474
  To be more Prince, as may be: you are sad.   1583
  My Vnckle practises more harme to me: 1593
  I warrant I loue you more then you do me.   1604
  Are you more stubborne hard, then hammer'd Iron? 1644
  Hub. Peace: no more. Adieu,   1707
  Hub. Silence, no more; go closely in with mee,   1714
  Discredite more in hiding of the fault,   1750
  And more, more strong, then lesser is my feare   1759
  My head with more ill newes: for it is full.   1855
  And others more, going to seeke the graue   1885
  More vpon humor, then aduis'd respect.   1939
  Out of my sight, and neuer see me more: 1967
  Presented thee more hideous then thou art.   1991
  I coniure thee but slowly: run more fast. *Exeunt.*   1994
  Is much more generall, then these lines import.   2014
  Bast. Once more to day well met, distemper'd Lords, 2019
  Thou art more deepe damn'd then Prince Lucifer: 2125
  Startles mine eyes, and makes me more amaz'd   2302
  Pem. He is more patient | Then when you left him; euen now he sung. 2617
MORNING = 1
  Big. To morrow morning let vs meete him then.   2015
MORROW = 4
  Ar. Good morrow *Hubert.*   1580
  Hub. Good morrow, little Prince.   1581
  Big. To morrow morning let vs meete him then.   2015
  To try the faire aduenture of to morrow. *Exeunt*   2548
MORTALITIES = 1
  Iohn. We cannot hold mortalities strong hand.   1800

MORTALITY = 1
Fore-tell the ending of mortality.   2609
MORTALL = 3
In mortall furie halfe so peremptorie, | As we to keepe this Citie.   769
Without th'assistance of a mortall hand: 1085
A cased Lion by the mortall paw,   1190
MOST = 13*1
Arthur Plantaginet, laies most lawfull claime   14
Philip. Most certain of one mother, mighty King,   67
What meanes this scorne, thou most vntoward knaue?   256
Is most diuinely vow'd vpon the right   543
For I doe loue her most vnfainedly.   846
To a most base and vile-concluded peace.   907
This newes hath made thee a most vgly man.   958
Bast. Hang nothing but a Calues skin most sweet lout.   1151
The truth is then most done not doing it: 1204
And most forsworne, to keepe what thou dost sweare,   1218
On their departure, most of all shew euill: 1500
No, no: when Fortune meanes to men most good,   1504
Bast. If thou didst but consent | To this most cruell Act: do but
dispaire,   2129
Of this most faire occasion, by the which   2512
MOTH = 1
Art. O heauen: that there were but a moth in yours,   1670
MOTHER = 24*3
K.Iohn. Silence (good mother) heare the Embassie.   11
You came not of one mother then it seemes.   66
Philip. Most certain of one mother, mighty King,   67
I put you o're to heauen, and to my mother;   70
Eli. Out on thee rude man, y dost shame thy mother,   72
Your tale must be how he employ'd my mother.   106
Betweene my father, and my mother lay,   114
O me, 'tis my mother: how now good Lady,   230
We know his handy-worke, therefore good mother   251
Bast. Knight, knight good mother, Basilisco-like: 257
But mother, I am not Sir *Roberts* sonne,   259
Then good my mother, let me know my father,   262
Some proper man I hope, who was it mother?   263
May easily winne a womans: aye my mother,   282
With him along is come the Mother Queene,   356
It cannot be, and if thou wert his mother.   428
Queen. Theres a good mother boy, that blots thy fa- | (ther   429
Arthur. Good my mother peace,   465
Qu.Mo. His mother shames him so, poore boy hee | (weepes.   468
Much worke for teares in many an English mother,   613
Why thou against the Church, our holy Mother,   1068
Or let the Church our mother breathe her curse,   1187
My Mother is assayled in our Tent, | And tane I feare.   1291
Arth. O this will make my mother die with griefe.   1303
Your noble mother; and as I heare, my Lord,   1840
My discontented Peeres. What? Mother dead?   1846
Iohn. My mother dead?   1904
MOTHERS = 8*2
Heauen guard my mothers honor, and my Land.   78
That still I lay vpon my mothers head,   84
That this my mothers sonne was none of his;   119
My mothers sonne did get your fathers heyre,   136

KING JOHN

MOTHERS   cont.
*Bast. Brother by th'mothers side, giue me your hand,   172
*Const. O take his mothers thanks, a widdows thanks,   325
His grandames wrongs, and not his mothers shames   470
Vgly, and slandrous to thy Mothers wombe,   965
A mothers curse, on her reuolting sonne: 1188
Where hath it slept? Where is my Mothers care?   1835
MOTHER-ENGLAND = 1
Of your deere Mother-England: blush for shame: 2407
MOTION = 7
But from the inward motion to deliuer   222
More free from motion, no not death himselfe   768
This sway of motion, this commoditie,   899
The other foure, in wondrous motion.   1908
The dreadfull motion of a murderous thought,   1980
Gouerne the motion of a kinglye eye: 2215
Bast. Oh, I am scalded with my violent motion   2659
MOTIUE = 1
Blan. Now shall I see thy loue, what motiue may   1246
MOUD = 1
Iohn. The king is moud, and answers not to this.   1148
MOUE = 3*1
What doth moue you to claime your brothers land.   99
Doth moue the murmuring lips of discontent   1770
The steppes of wrong, should moue you to mew vp   1774
*Now, now you Starres, that moue in your right spheres,   2684
MOUES = 1
That any thing he see's which moues his liking,   829
MOUING = *1
*Drawes those heauen-mouing pearles fro(m) his poor eies,   471
MOULDED = 1
These eyes, these browes, were moulded out of his;   397
MOUNT = 2
Fran. Amen, Amen, mount Cheualiers to Armes.   594
By East and West let France and England mount.   695
MOUNTAINE = 1
Anon becomes a Mountaine. O noble Dolphine,   1562
MOUNTAINES = 1*1
Lyons more confident, Mountaines and rockes   767
*That spits forth death, and mountaines, rockes, and seas,   774
MOUNTED = 2
And ready mounted are they to spit forth   517
My selfe, well mounted, hardly haue escap'd.   2600
MOUNTETH = 1
For courage mounteth with occasion,   377
MOUNTING = 1
And fits the mounting spirit like my selfe;   216
MOUNTS = 1
O then tread downe my need, and faith mounts vp,   1146
MOUSING = 1
And now he feasts, mousing the flesh of men   668
MOUTH = 10*1
*Chat. Then take my Kings defiance from my mouth,   26
Turne thou the mouth of thy Artillerie,   717
Austria and France shoot in each others mouth.   729
The mouth of passage shall we fling wide ope,   764
Out of his ragges. Here's a large mouth indeede,   773

MOUTH · *cont.*
Tell him this tale, and from the mouth of *England*,	1079
Bast. Wil't not be? | Will not a Calues-skin stop that mouth of thine?	1230
Is husband in my mouth? euen for that name	1239
Did with his yron tongue, and brazen mouth	1337
O that my tongue were in the thunders mouth,	1422
With open mouth swallowing a Taylors newes,	1920

MOUTHD = 1
And mocke the deepe mouth'd Thunder: for at hand	2429

MOUTHES = 1
Their battering Canon charged to the mouthes,	696

MOUTHS = 1*1
Bast. The *French* (my Lord) mens mouths are ful of it:	1882
Yong *Arthurs* death is common in their mouths,	1912

MUCH = 21*1
Eli. Your strong possessio(n) much more then your right,	46
So much my conscience whispers in your eare,	48
Your brother did imploy my father much.	104
Kin. How much vnlook'd for, is this expedition.	374
Aust. By how much vnexpected, by so much	375
Who painefully with much expedient march	529
Much worke for teares in many an English mother,	613
Her presence would haue interrupted much.	862
Adde thus much more, that no *Italian* Priest	1080
We owe thee much: within this wall of flesh	1319
Hub. I am much bounden to your Maiesty.	1328
'Tis strange to thinke how much King *Iohn* hath lost	1506
These eyes, that neuer did, nor neuer shall | So much as frowne on you.	1633
Much danger do I vndergo for thee. *Exeunt*	1715
Of plaine old forme, is much disfigured,	1739
Do shew the mood of a much troubled brest,	1791
Is much more generall, then these lines import.	2014
Till my attempt so much be glorified,	2364
Thou maist be-friend me so much, as to thinke	2565
And comfort me with cold. I do not aske you much,	2649
Sal. It seemes you know not then so much as we,	2691

MULTITUDE = 1
In the faire multitude of those her haires;	1446

MUNITION = 1
What men prouided? What munition sent	2351

MURDEROUS = 1
The dreadfull motion of a murderous thought,	1980

MURDRED = 1
Thy hand hath murdred him: I had a mighty cause	1930

MURMURING = 1
Doth moue the murmuring lips of discontent	1770

MURTHER = 2
This murther had not come into my minde.	1948
Sal. Murther, as hating what himselfe hath done,	2036

MURTHERER = 2
Sal. Thou art a Murtherer.	2090
Second a Villaine, and a Murtherer? | *Hub.* Lord *Bigot*, I am none.	2104

MURTHERERS = 1
Sal. Not till I sheath it in a murtherers skin.	2080

MURTHERS = 2
Of murthers Armes: This is the bloodiest shame,	2046
Pem. All murthers past, do stand excus'd in this:	2050

MUSE = 1
Dolph. I muse your Maiesty doth seeme so cold,   1250
MUST = 42
Which now the mannage of two kingdomes must   43
Or else it must go wrong with you and me,   47
Your tale must be how he employ'd my mother.   106
Your fathers heyre must haue your fathers land.   137
Who dares not stirre by day, must walke by night,   181
Come Madam, and come *Richard,* we must speed   187
Needs must you lay your heart at his dispose,   276
We must awake indeuor for defence,   376
One must proue greatest. While they weigh so euen,   644
Or if it must stand still, let wiues with childe   1014
Aust. Well ruffian, I must pocket vp these wrongs,   1128
That need, must needs inferre this principle,   1144
Which is the side that I must goe withall?   1260
Vncle, I needs must pray that thou maist lose: 1265
Must by the hungry now be fed vpon: 1308
Must I behold my pretty *Arthur* more.   1474
Must be as boysterously maintain'd as gain'd.   1521
That *Iohn* may stand, then *Arthur* needs must fall, | So be it, for it
cannot be but so.   1524
I must be breefe, least resolution drop   1608
Must you with hot Irons, burne out both mine eyes?   1612
Hub. Yong Boy, I must. | *Art.* And will you? | *Hub.* And I will.   1613
If heauen be pleas'd that you must vse me ill,   1631
Why then you must. Will you put out mine eyes?   1632
And with hot Irons must I burne them out.   1636
Your vilde intent must needs seeme horrible.   1674
Must needes want pleading for a paire of eyes: 1677
Your Vnckle must not know but you are dead.   1708
Pem. But that your Royall pleasure must be done,   1734
His passion is so ripe, it needs must breake.   1797
This must be answer'd either heere, or hence.   1807
This must not be thus borne, this will breake out   1819
For I must vse thee. O my gentle Cosen,   1880
It is our safetie, and we must embrace   2009
Hu. I am no villaine. *Sal.* Must I rob | (the Law?   2078
That present medcine must be ministred,   2182
That I must draw this mettle from my side   2267
Her Enemies rankes? I must withdraw, and weepe   2280
And now it is halfe conquer'd, must I backe,   2348
Since I must loose the vse of all deceite?   2488
That I must dye heere, and liue hence, by Truth?   2490
Hen. Euen so must I run on, and euen so stop.   2677
Hen. At Worster must his bodie be interr'd, | For so he will'd it.   2709
MUTINES = 1
Do like the Mutines of Ierusalem,   692
MUZLED = 1
And then our Armes, like to a muzled Beare,   555
MY *l.*8 *26 27 31 37 48 51 70 75 78 84 85 90 95 100 101 103 104 105 106
111 114 115 119 122 123 128 133 134 136 138 146 148 149 159 166 173
200 201 202 203 216 226 230 235 258 260 262 268 269 270 271 282 283
286 313 314 339 408 421 426 455 456 457 465 466 509 783 812 814 817
818 827 830 832 833 *839 *865 910 911 912 916 919 938 941 949 990
992 993 996 1023 1049 1050 1051 1053 1064 1098 1110 *1112 1115 1118
1142 1146 1147 1155 1180 1193 1239 1240 1241 1243 *1271 *1285 1291

MY *cont.*
  1293 1295 1303 1318 1322 1346 1352 1354 1356 1360 1361 1368 1376
  1413 1422 1430 1431 1433 1438 1440 1441 1456 1460 1463 1467 1474
  1478 1486 1487 1488 1489 1490 1572 1589 1593 1595 1599 1605 1618
  1621 1629 *1639 1649 1663 1678 1679 1682 1691 1759 1766 1767 1801
  1835 1838 1840 1846 1847 1855 1878 1880 *1882 1894 1903 1904 1906
  *1932 1948 1955 1958 1959 1962 1967 1968 1969 1973 1981 1988 1989
  1992 2002 2005 *2006 2063 2082 2084 2088 2089 2109 2128 2145 2168
  2170 2184 2187 2194 2205 2211 2242 2252 2266 2267 2275 2298 2337
  2343 2346 2354 2361 2364 2365 2374 2377 2379 2443 2445 2456 2483
  2503 2504 2507 2508 2510 2519 2521 2534 2545 2562 2576 2597 2600
  2635 2637 2638 2645 2646 2647 2648 2652 2659 2662 2663 2665 2671
  2676 2682 2703 2706 2714 2715 = 280*13
MYSELFE *see* selfe
NAKED = 1

Euen till vnfenced desolation | Leaue them as naked as the vulgar ayre:	700

NAMD = 1

Then I haue nam'd. The Bastard *Falconbridge*	1556

NAME = 18

K.Iohn. What is thy name? | *Bast.* Philip my Liege, so is my name begun,	165
K.Iohn. From henceforth beare his name | Whose forme thou bearest:	168
And if his name be *George*, Ile call him *Peter*;	196
Legitimation, name, and all is gone;	261
And this is *Geffreyes* in the name of God:	403
With slaughter coupled to the name of kings.	663
And she againe wants nothing, to name want,	750
Doe in his name religiously, demand	1067
This in our foresaid holy Fathers name	1072
Iohn. What earthie name to Interrogatories	1074
Thou canst not (Cardinall) deuise a name	1076
Is husband in my mouth? euen for that name	1239
Be stronger with thee, then the name of wife?	1247
My name is *Constance*, I was *Geffreyes* wife,	1430
The deed, which both our tongues held vilde to name.	1966
Cries out vpon the name of *Salisbury*.	2270
And on our actions set the name of right | With holy breath.	2319

NAMELY = 1

To him that owes it, namely, this yong Prince,	554

NAMES = 2

For new made honor doth forget mens names:	197
Sal. When we were happie, we had other names.	2468

NATION = 1

What heere? O Nation that thou couldst remoue,	2284

NATIONS = 1

Euen at the crying of your Nations crow,	2398

NATIUE = 3

Haue sold their fortunes at their natiue homes,	363
Shall leaue his natiue channell, and ore-swell	651
And chase the natiue beauty from his cheeke,	1468

NATURALL = 2

No naturall exhalation in the skie,	1538
But they will plucke away his naturall cause,	1541

NATURALLY = 1

A woman naturally borne to feares;	936

NATURE = 5

Which heauen shall take in nature of a fee:	472

NATURE *cont.*

Nature and Fortune ioyn'd to make thee great.	973
No scope of Nature, no distemper'd day,	1539
A fellow by the hand of Nature mark'd,	1946
And you haue slander'd Nature in my forme,	1981

NATURES = 1

Of Natures guifts, thou mayst with Lillies boast,	974

NAUGHT *see also* nought = 1

And we shall shocke them: Naught shall make vs rue,	2728

NAY = 12*1

Elinor. Nay, I would haue you go before me thither.	163
If thou hadst sayd him nay, it had beene sinne;	288
Dol. Nay aske me if I can refraine from loue,	845
Nay, rather turne this day out of the weeke,	1012
One minute, nay one quiet breath of rest.	1519
Nay, you may thinke my loue was craftie loue,	1629
Nay, after that, consume away in rust,	1642
Nay heare me *Hubert,* driue these men away,	1655
Nay, it perchance will sparkle in your eyes:	1694
Iohn. Nay, but make haste: the better foote before.	1892
Nay, in the body of this fleshly Land,	1970
Thou'rt damn'd as blacke, nay nothing is so blacke,	2124
Sal. Nay, 'tis in a manner done already,	2699

NEECE = 3

With her her Neece, the Lady *Blanch of Spaine,*	358
Giue with our Neece a dowrie large enough,	785
Iohn. What saie these yong-ones? What say you my | Neece?	839

NEED = 7*1

For *France,* for *France,* for it is more then need.	188
Bla. The Lady *Constance* speakes not from her faith, | But from her need.	1140
Con. Oh, if thou grant my need,	1142
That need, must needs inferre this principle,	1144
That faith would liue againe by death of need:	1145
O then tread downe my need, and faith mounts vp,	1146
Keepe my need vp, and faith is trodden downe.	1147
Fra. Thou shalt not need. *England,* I will fall fro(m) thee.	1253

NEEDE = 3

Art. Alas, what neede you be so boistrous rough?	1652
Go after him: for he perhaps shall neede	1900
Whom he hath vs'd rather for sport, then neede)	2431

NEEDES = 1

Must needes want pleading for a paire of eyes:	1677

NEEDFULL = 1

Bast. Oh let vs pay the time: but needfull woe,	2721

NEEDLESSE = 1

When with a volley of our needlesse shot,	2529

NEEDLS = 1

Their Needl's to Lances, and their gentle hearts | To fierce and bloody inclination.	2411

NEEDS = 6

Needs must you lay your heart at his dispose,	276
That need, must needs inferre this principle,	1144
Vncle, I needs must pray that thou maist lose:	1265
That *Iohn* may stand, then *Arthur* needs must fall, | So be it, for it cannot be but so.	1524
Your vilde intent must needs seeme horrible.	1674

NEEDS *cont.*

His passion is so ripe, it needs must breake.   1797

NEERE = 4*1

Neere or farre off, well wonne is still well shot,   183
Is neere to England, looke vpon the yeeres   739
*Approaching neere these eyes, would drinke my teares,   1639
Pem. Indeed we heard how neere his death he was,   1805
To sowsse annoyance that comes neere his Nest;   2404

NEIGHBOURLY = 1

And not to spend it so vn-neighbourly.   2290

NEITHER = 1

We hold our Towne for neither: yet for both.   645

NEPHEW = 1

Thy Nephew, and right royall Soueraigne.   20

NEPTUNES = 1

That *Neptunes* Armes who clippeth thee about,   2285

NERE = 6

Vpon good Friday, and nere broke his fast: 248
Which till this time my tongue did nere pronounce;   1240
But thou shalt haue: and creepe time nere so slow,   1330
And nere haue spoke a louing word to you: 1627
And that high Royalty was nere pluck'd off: 1722
The faiths of men, nere stained with reuolt: 1723

NEROS = 1

You bloudy Nero's, ripping vp the wombe   2406

NEST = 1

To sowsse annoyance that comes neere his Nest;   2404

NEUER *see also* nere = 25

Would I might neuer stirre from off this place,   153
Sir *Robert* neuer holpe to make this legge.   253
Did neuer flote vpon the swelling tide,   368
My boy a bastard? by my soule I thinke | His father neuer was so true
begot,   426
Zounds, I was neuer so bethumpt with words,   782
I do protest I neuer lou'd my selfe   817
Shall neuer see it, but a holy day.   1007
Thou Fortunes Champion, that do'st neuer fight   1044
And better conquest neuer canst thou make,   1221
I shall not know him: therefore neuer, neuer   1473
Const. He talkes to me, that neuer had a sonne.   1476
And I did neuer aske it you againe: 1620
These eyes, that neuer did, nor neuer shall | So much as frowne on you. 1633
Mes. From France to England, neuer such a powre | For any forraigne
preparation,   1828
Out of my sight, and neuer see me more: 1967
Within this bosome, neuer entred yet   1979
Neuer to taste the pleasures of the world,   2067
Neuer to be infected with delight,   2068
Sal. Vpon our sides it neuer shall be broken.   2259
That neuer saw the giant-world enrag'd,   2308
No, no, on my soule it neuer shall be said.   2361
This England neuer did, nor neuer shall   2723

NEW = 11

For new made honor doth forget mens names: 197
To make a hazard of new fortunes heere: 365
In likenesse of a new vntrimmed Bride.   1139
And euen before this truce, but new before,   1164

NEW *cont.*

Within the scorched veines of one new burn'd:	1209
O husband heare me: aye, alacke, how new	1238
This acte, is as an ancient tale new told,	1735
For putting on so new a fashion'd robe.	1744
Sal. To this effect, before you were new crown'd	1752
With eyes as red as new enkindled fire,	1884
Right in thine eye. Away, my friends, new flight,	2521

NEWES = 14*2

This newes hath made thee a most vgly man.	958
Euen at that newes he dies: and then the hearts	1549
To your direction: *Hubert*, what newes with you?	1786
My head with more ill newes: for it is full.	1855
Hear'st thou the newes abroad, who are arriu'd?	1881
With open mouth swallowing a Taylors newes,	1920
This newes was brought to *Richard* but euen now,	2452
And will not let me welcome this good newes.	2455
Mes. Where is my Prince, the Dolphin? | *Dol.* Heere: what newes?	2534
Dol. Ah fowle, shrew'd newes. Beshrew thy very | (hart:	2540
Bast. Come, come: sans complement, What newes | abroad?	2571
Bast. Breefe then: and what's the newes?	2575
Hub. O my sweet sir, newes fitting to the night,	2576
Bast. Shew me the very wound of this ill newes,	2578
Which holds but till thy newes be vttered,	2666
Sal. You breath these dead newes in as dead an eare	2675

NEWLY = 2

This royall hand and mine are newly knit,	1157
So newly ioyn'd in loue? so strong in both,	1171

NEWNESSE = 1

And happie newnesse, that intends old right. *Exeunt*	2522

NEXT = 2

That ere the next Ascension day at noone,	1872
The next is this: King *Iohn* hath reconcil'd	2322

NEYTHER = 1

Dol. We will attend to neyther:	2419

NICE = 1

Makes nice of no vilde hold to stay him vp:	1523

NIECE *see* neece
NIGH *see* nye
NIGHT = 18*3

Now blessed be the houre by night or day	174
Who dares not stirre by day, must walke by night,	181
To giue me audience: If the mid-night bell	1336
Sound on into the drowzie race of night:	1338
Arise forth from the couch of lasting night,	1410
Yong Gentlemen would be as sad as night	1588
That I might sit all night, and watch with you.	1603
He tels vs *Arthur* is deceas'd to night.	1803
Of *Arthur*, whom they say is kill'd to night, on your | (suggestion.	1886
Hub. My Lord, they say fiue Moones were seene to | (night:	1906
But euen this night, whose blacke contagious breath	2494
Euen this ill night, your breathing shall expire,	2497
After such bloody toile, we bid good night,	2530
I did not thinke to be so sad to night	2541
The stumbling night did part our wearie powres?	2544
Dol. Well: keepe good quarter, & good care to night,	2546
Hub. Vnkinde remembrance: thou, & endles night,	2567

NIGHT *cont.*
    *Hub. Why heere walke I in the black brow of night | To finde you out.   2573
    Hub. O my sweet sir, newes fitting to the night,   2576
    Ile tell thee *Hubert,* halfe my power this night   2597
    For in a night the best part of my powre,   2671
NIGHTS = 1
    Are wrack'd three nights ago on *Goodwin* sands.   2451
NIMBLE = 1
    Standing on slippers, which his nimble haste   1922
NO *l.*74 83 138 140 145 209 219 228 314 469 549 601 628 768 788 892 915
    917 970 994 1017 1018 1021 1039 1080 1111 1113 1114 1150 1165 *1280
    1329 1406 1421 1504 1523 1538 1539 1540 1568 1586 1596 *1647 1668
    1681 *1685 1688 1707 1714 1781 1822 1823 1893 *1932 1954 2032 2078
    2242 2330 2361 2402 2418 2579 = 65*4
NOBBE = 1
    It would not be sir nobbe in any case.   155
NOBILITY = 2
    Your Worth, your Greatnesse, and Nobility.   2086
    Doth make an earth-quake of Nobility: 2293
NOBLE = 11
    Lewis. A noble boy, who would not doe thee right?   311
    Anon becomes a Mountaine. O noble Dolphine,   1562
    Your noble mother; and as I heare, my Lord,   1840
    Iohn. Spoke like a sprightfull Noble Gentleman.   1899
    Sal. The Count *Meloone,* a Noble Lord of France,   2012
    And Noble Dolphin, albeit we sweare   2260
    Dolph. A noble temper dost thou shew in this,   2291
    Oh, what a noble combat hast fought   2294
    Pand. Haile noble Prince of *France*:   2321
    Mel. Fly Noble English, you are bought and sold,   2471
    Bast. Let it be so, and you my noble Prince,   2706
NOBLEMAN = *1
    *Big. Out dunghill: dar'st thou braue a Nobleman?   2087
NOBLER = 1
    Then arme thy constant and thy nobler parts   1222
NOBLES = 3
    My Nobles leaue me, and my State is braued,   1968
    Your Nobles will not heare you, but are gone | To offer seruice to your
    enemy: 2201
    As *Lewis* himselfe: so (Nobles) shall you all,   2313
NOBODY *see* body
NODS = 1
    With wrinkled browes, with nods, with rolling eyes.   1917
NOISE = 1
    From forth the noise and rumour of the Field;   2506
NONE = 12
    Which none but heauen, and you, and I, shall heare.   49
    That is my brothers plea, and none of mine,   75
    That this my mothers sonne was none of his;   119
    Being none of his, refuse him: this concludes,   135
    That none so small aduantage shall step forth   1536
    Ar. Ah, none but in this Iron Age, would do it: 1637
    Art. Is there no remedie? | *Hub.* None, but to lose your eyes.   1668
    To wish him dead, but thou hadst none to kill him.   1931
    There's few or none do know me, if they did,   1999
    Yet I am none. Whose tongue so ere speakes false,   2092
    Second a Villaine, and a Murtherer? | *Hub.* Lord *Bigot,* I am none.   2104

NONE *cont.*
And none of you will bid the winter come   2644
NOONE = 3
That ere the next Ascension day at noone,   1872
And on that day at noone, whereon he sayes   1877
Say, that before Ascension day at noone,   2193
NOR *l.*134 280 970 971 1633 1657 1658 2023 2069 2084 2309 2636 2646
2647 2723 = 16
NORTH = 3
Aust. I from the North.   725
Bast. O prudent discipline! From North to South: 728
Through my burn'd bosome: nor intreat the North 2647
NORTHAMPTONSHIRE = 1
Borne in *Northamptonshire*, and eldest sonne | As I suppose, to *Robert*
Faulconbridge,   59
NOT *l.*37 38 66 81 91 95 134 139 150 155 *178 181 218 220 224 246 250
259 269 273 275 279 284 289 311 324 383 467 470 477 487 565 576 *579
581 655 710 736 749 751 766 768 780 796 833 860 861 877 909 910 925
928 930 946 969 970 983 988 *989 1008 1015 1018 1023 1034 1050 1058
1060 1076 *1123 *1140 1148 1152 1180 1193 1200 1202 1203 1204 1215
1225 1227 1230 1231 1241 1245 *1253 1266 1267 1294 1300 *1310 1353
1358 1366 1370 1373 1388 1421 1427 1429 1432 1437 1443 1466 1473
1486 1508 1545 1548 1568 *1577 1596 1610 *1647 1653 1654 1657 1678
1683 1701 1708 1712 1724 1761 1778 1819 1826 1837 1843 1854 1867
*1932 1945 1948 1978 1992 1998 2002 2022 2028 2035 2076 2080 2083
2088 2091 2093 2107 2110 2111 2126 2181 2192 2201 2205 2214 2227
2263 2275 2290 *2331 2352 2356 2358 2363 2379 2380 2430 *2436 2455
*2460 2483 2541 2547 2557 2579 2590 2596 2620 2636 2649 2691
2720 = 176*13
NOTE = 3
Fra. Binde vp those tresses: O what loue I note 1445
Creatures of note for mercy, lacking vses.   1700
But taking note of thy abhorr'd Aspect,   1949
NOTED = 1
Sal. In this the Anticke, and well noted face 1738
NOTES = 1
Both they and we, perusing ore these notes 2256
NOTHING = 6*3
Infortunate in nothing but in thee: 480
And she againe wants nothing, to name want, 750
Then this, that nothing do I see in you,   835
Bast. Hang nothing but a Calues skin most sweet lout. 1151
That nothing can allay, nothing but blood,   1275
Dol. There's nothing in this world can make me ioy, 1492
Thou'rt damn'd as blacke, nay nothing is so blacke, 2124
Bast. All Kent hath yeelded: nothing there holds out 2198
NOUGHT = 1
That it yeelds nought but shame and bitternesse. 1496
NOW = 60*8
King Iohn. | *Now say *Chatillion*, what would *France* with vs? 4
Ele. What now my sonne, haue I not euer said 37
Which now the mannage of two kingdomes must 43
I am a Souldier, and now bound to *France*. 158
Now blessed be the houre by night or day   174
K.Iohn. Goe, *Faulconbridge*, now hast thou thy desire, 185
Well, now can I make any *Ioane* a Lady,   194
For your conuersion, now your traueller,   199

NOW *cont.*

I shall beseech you; that is question now,	205
O me, 'tis my mother: how now good Lady,	230
Bast. Now by this light were I to get againe,	272
Then now the *English* bottomes haue waft o're,	367
Con. Now shame vpon you where she does or no,	469
And now insteed of bulletts wrapt in fire	533
Oh now doth death line his dead chaps with steele,	666
And now he feasts, mousing the flesh of men	668
Iohn. Now by the sky that hangs aboue our heads,	711
Thy now vnsur'd assurance to the Crowne,	787
Least zeale now melted by the windie breath	793
(Except this Cittie now by vs besiedg'd)	805
Till now, infixed I beheld my selfe,	818
Himselfe loues traytor, this is pittie now;	824
Fra. Now Cittizens of Angires ope your gates,	856
And though thou now confesse thou didst but iest	937
But now in Armes, you strengthen it with yours.	1028
And dost thou now fall ouer to my foes?	1053
As now againe to snatch our palme from palme:	1175
Blan. Now shall I see thy loue, what motiue may	1246
Bast. Now by my life, this day grows wondrous hot,	1285
Must by the hungry now be fed vpon:	1308
Iohn. Enough. | I could be merry now, *Hubert*, I loue thee.	1371
Con. Lo; now: now see the issue of your peace.	1404
But now I enuie at their libertie,	1458
But now will Canker-sorrow eat my bud,	1467
Now heare me speake with a propheticke spirit:	1511
Is now in England ransacking the Church,	1557
Now that their soules are topfull of offence,	1565
*Reade heere yong *Arthur.* How now foolish rheume?	1606
Art. O now you looke like *Hubert.* All this while | You were disguis'd.	1705
With these ill tydings: Now? What sayes the world	1853
Vnder the tide; but now I breath againe	1859
Sal. Our greefes, and not our manners reason now.	2028
Therefore 'twere reason you had manners now.	2030
Is fled to heauen: and *England* now is left	2150
Now for the bare-pickt bone of Maiesty,	2153
Now Powers from home, and discontents at home	2156
Now happy he, whose cloake and center can	2160
Iohn. Now keep your holy word, go meet the *French*,	2172
Therefore thy threatning Colours now winde vp,	2326
And now 'tis farre too huge to be blowne out	2339
And come ye now to tell me *Iohn* hath made	2344
And now it is halfe conquer'd, must I backe,	2348
And shall I now giue ore the yeelded Set?	2360
The youth saies well. Now heare our *English* King,	2382
This newes was brought to *Richard* but euen now,	2452
What in the world should make me now deceiue,	2487
Pem. He is more patient | Then when you left him; euen now he sung.	2617
Leaues them inuisible, and his seige is now	2622
Iohn. I marrie, now my soule hath elbow roome,	2635
My Liege, my Lord: but now a King, now thus.	2676
When this was now a King, and now is clay?	2679
*Now, now you Starres, that moue in your right spheres,	2684
*Where be your powres? Shew now your mended faiths,	2685
Now, these her Princes are come home againe,	2726

NUMBER = 2
 Or adde a royall number to the dead: 661
 The little number of your doubtfull friends.   2204
NYE = 1
 And grapple with him ere he come so nye.   2229
O *l.*90 207 230 *325 441 602 728 756 955 1040 *1056 1107 1138 1146 1149
 1179 1196 1238 1243 1254 1255 1303 1318 1408 1419 1420 1422 1434
 1445 1456 1488 1547 1555 1562 1649 1670 1680 1705 1713 1845 1880
 1893 1985 2284 2576 = 44*2
OATH = 7
 I haue a Kings oath to the contrarie.   931
 And like a ciuill warre setst oath to oath,   1195
 And mak'st an oath the suretie for thy truth,   1213
 Against an oath the truth, thou art vnsure   1214
 And my good friend, thy voluntary oath   1322
 Vpon your oath of seruice to the Pope,   2190
OBEDIENCE = 4
 And make them tame to their obedience.   1987
 From whose obedience I forbid my soule,   2063
 Our people quarrell with obedience,   2176
 And calmely run on in obedience   2517
OBIECT = 1
 That you do see? Could thought, without this obiect 2043
OBSERUATION = 1
 That doth not smoake of obseruation,   218
OCCASION = 3
 For courage mounteth with occasion,   377
 Iohn. With-hold thy speed, dreadfull Occasion: 1844
 Of this most faire occasion, by the which   2512
OCCASIONS = 1
 To grace occasions: let it be our suite,   1779
OCEAN = 3
 Vnlesse thou let his siluer Water, keepe | A peacefull progresse to the
 Ocean.   653
 And it shall be as all the Ocean,   2136
 Euen to our Ocean, to our great King *Iohn.*   2518
OCEANS = 1
 Whose foot spurnes backe the Oceans roaring tides, 317
ODORIFEROUS = 1
 Thou odoriferous stench: sound rottennesse,   1409
OF = 536*18
OFF *l.*153 183 371 393 *450 *636 1227 1722 1927 *1960 2194 2296 2477
 2528 2537 2643 = 13*3
OFFENCE = 4
 That art the issue of my deere offence   270
 To doe offence and scathe in Christendome: 369
 Saue in aspect, hath all offence seal'd vp: 556
 Now that their soules are topfull of offence,   1565
OFFEND = 2
 Hub. And Ile keepe him so, | That he shall not offend your Maiesty. 1365
 That *Hubert* for the wealth of all the world, | Will not offend thee. 1711
OFFENDING = 2
 Patch'd with foule Moles, and eye-offending markes, 968
 Offending Charity: If but a dozen French   1558
OFFER = 4
 But if you fondly passe our proffer'd offer,   564
 That Greatnesse should so grossely offer it;   1812

OFFER *cont.*
This gentle offer of the perillous time. 2010
Your Nobles will not heare you, but are gone | To offer seruice to your enemy: 2201
OFFERS = 1
And brings from him such offers of our peace, 2694
OFFICE = 3
Deny their office: onely you do lacke 1698
A bare-rib'd death, whose office is this day 2433
To do the office for thee, of reuenge, 2681
OFF-SPRING = 1
The rather, that you giue his off-spring life, 306
OFT = 2
Why vrgest thou so oft yong *Arthurs* death? 1929
How oft the sight of meanes to do ill deeds, 1944
OFTENTIMES = 1
And oftentimes excusing of a fault, 1747
OH *see also* O *l.*666 950 975 1037 1142 1249 1834 *1941 1992 2005 *2034 2076 2227 2234 2266 2268 2275 2294 2440 2443 2528 2619 2652 2659 2661 2721 = 24*2
OLD = 11*2
If old Sir *Robert* did beget vs both, 88
O old sir *Robert* Father, on my knee 90
Philip, good old Sir *Roberts* wiues eldest sonne. 167
Bast. My brother *Robert*, old Sir *Roberts* sonne: 235
Madam, I was not old Sir *Roberts* sonne, 246
Bast. Heeres a stay, | That shakes the rotten carkasse of old death 771
Of kings, of beggers, old men, yong men, maids, 891
* *Bast.* Old Time the clocke setter, y bald sexton Time: 1257
* *Pan.* How green you are, and fresh in this old world? 1530
Of plaine old forme, is much disfigured, 1739
Hub. Old men, and Beldames, in the streets 1910
Of the old, feeble, and day-wearied Sunne, 2496
And happie newnesse, that intends old right. *Exeunt* 2522
OLD = *1
OLD-FACD = 1
'Tis not the rounder of your old-fac'd walles, 565
ON = 92*4
ONCE = 5*4
But once he slanderd me with bastardy: 82
Rob. And once dispatch'd him in an Embassie 107
And part your mingled colours once againe, 703
* *Iohn.* Heere once againe we sit: once against crown'd 1718
* *Pem.* This once again (but that your Highnes pleas'd) 1720
Was once superfluous: you were Crown'd before, 1721
* *Bast.* Once more to day well met, distemper'd Lords, 2019
Pem. Vp once againe: put spirit in the French, 2461
ONE = 22
You came not of one mother then it seemes. 66
Philip. Most certain of one mother, mighty King, 67
That is well knowne, and as I thinke one father: 68
Bast. One that wil play the deuill sir with you, 435
One must proue greatest. While they weigh so euen, 644
Fra. England thou hast not sau'd one drop of blood 655
Then let confusion of one part confirm 673
Out of one side her happy Minion, 706
And two such shores, to two such streames made one, 758

ONE *cont.*

But this one word, whether thy tale be true.	947
Within the scorched veines of one new burn'd:	1209
One minute, nay one quiet breath of rest.	1519
Pem. Then I, as one that am the tongue of these	1764
And whisper one another in the eare.	1914
Meet in one line: and vast confusion waites	2157
And heale the inueterate Canker of one wound,	2265
Commend me to one *Hubert,* with your King;	2501
I come one way of the *Plantagenets.*	2566
Are turned to one thred, one little haire:	2664
My heart hath one poore string to stay it .by,	2665

ONELY = 7

That he is not onely plagued for her sin,	487
Which onely liues but by the death of faith,	1143
To sweare, sweares onely not to be forsworne,	1215
But thou dost sweare, onely to be forsworne,	1217
Onely for wantonnesse: by my Christendome,	1589
Deny their office: onely you do lacke	1698
Rests by you onely to be qualified.	2180

ONES = *1

Iohn. What saie these yong-ones? What say you my | Neece?	839

ONS = *1

*And ere since sit's on's horsebacke at mine Hostesse dore	596

ON-SET = 1

From first to last, the on-set and retyre:	637

OPE = 2

The mouth of passage shall we fling wide ope,	764
Fra. Now Cittizens of Angires ope your gates,	856

OPEN = 5

F.Her. You men of Angiers open wide your gates,	610
Open your gates, and giue the Victors way.	635
With open mouth swallowing a Taylors newes,	1920
Doth lay it open to vrge on reuenge.	2037
That being brought into the open ayre,	2612

OPINION = 1

Makes sound opinion sicke, and truth suspected,	1743

OPPOSE = 1

Yet I alone, alone doe me oppose	1097

OPPOSITE = 2

Saue what is opposite to *Englands* loue.	1185
Pand. The *Dolphin* is too wilfull opposite	2378

OPPRESSED = 2

Of this oppressed boy; this is thy eldest sonnes sonne,	479
In the releefe of this oppressed childe,	551

OPPRESSION = 2

This day of shame, oppression, periury.	1013
And our oppression hath made vp this league:	1031

OPPREST = 1

Opprest with wrongs, and therefore full of feares,	934

OR *l.*47 83 144 174 180 183 219 373 425 446 469 498 503 571 661 721 733
813 831 984 1014 1081 1135 1187 1341 1347 1395 1440 1442 1561 1625
1679 1725 1730 1731 1807 1843 *1956 1958 1999 2016 2017 2038 2041
2042 2045 2048 2096 2098 2099 2101 2134 2139 2183 2244 2334 2363
2543 *2551 2602 2689 = 61*2

ORCHARD = 1

Hen. Let him be brought into the Orchard heere:	2615

ORDAINE = 1
Out of your grace, deuise, ordaine, impose 1181
ORDER = 4
Some gentle order, and then we shall be blest 1182
Pand. All forme is formelesse, Order orderlesse, 1184
Such temperate order in so fierce a cause, 1394
That hauing our faire order written downe, 2255
ORDERING = 1
Iohn. Haue thou the ordering of this present time. 2246
ORDERLESSE = 1
Pand. All forme is formelesse, Order orderlesse, 1184
ORDERS = 1
Send fayre-play-orders, and make comprimise, | Insinuation, parley, and
base truce 2236
ORDINANCE = 1
By the compulsion of their Ordinance, 524
ORDINARY = 1
Being an ordinary Inundation: 2299
ORE = 11
I put you o're to heauen, and to my mother; 70
In at the window, or else ore the hatch: 180
Then now the *English* bottomes haue waft o're, 367
And King ore him, and all that he enioyes: 546
Be well aduis'd, tell ore thy tale againe. 926
Like a proud riuer peering ore his bounds? 944
Ile send those powers o're to your Maiesty. 1375
Both they and we, perusing ore these notes 2256
Figur'd quite ore with burning Meteors. 2304
And shall I now giue ore the yeelded Set? 2360
And like an Eagle, o're his ayerie towres, 2403
ORECAST = 1
Bla. The Sun's orecast with bloud: faire day adieu, 1259
ORE-BEARING = 1
Ore-bearing interruption spight of *France*? 1391
ORE-LOOKD = 1
Stoope lowe within those bounds we haue ore-look'd, 2516
ORE-MASTEREST = 1
Which owe the crowne, that thou ore-masterest? 406
ORE-SWELL = 1
Shall leaue his natiue channell, and ore-swell 651
ORGAN-PIPE = 1
And from the organ-pipe of frailety sings 2629
OTHER = 11
And coopes from other lands her Ilanders, 318
Fra. It shall be so, and at the other hill 606
Why then defie each other, and pell-mell, 720
Sal. What other harme haue I good Lady done, 959
Enter Iohn, Pembroke, Salisbury, and other Lordes. 1717
The other foure, in wondrous motion. 1908
Hub. Arme you against your other enemies: 1974
Nor met with Fortune, other then at feasts, 2309
Sal. When we were happie, we had other names. 2468
With whom your selfe, my selfe, and other Lords, 2703
With other Princes that may best be spar'd, . 2707
OTHERS = 6
*Enter K.(ing) of England, Bastard, Queene, Blanch, Pembroke, | and
others.* 379

OTHERS *cont.*

The others peace: till then, blowes, blood, and death.	674
Austria and France shoot in each others mouth.	729
But spoke the harme, that is by others done?	960
No certaine life atchieu'd by others death:	1823
And others more, going to seeke the graue	1885

OUER *see also* o're = 1

And dost thou now fall ouer to my foes?	1053

OUERTHROW = 1

Or ouerthrow incureable ensues.	2183

OUER-BEARE = 1

To ouer-beare it, and we are all well pleas'd,	1754

OUER-LOOKES = 1

That swayes the earth this Climate ouer-lookes,	658

OUER-STAIND = 1

Heauen knowes they were besmear'd and ouer-staind	1167

OUGHT = 2

If he see ought in you that makes him like,	828
Bast. So on my soule he did, for ought he knew:	2211

OUR *l.*32 45 55 87 89 164 300 *330 332 334 345 382 389 *447 511 512 522
555 557 564 566 571 572 578 584 593 604 *607 630 633 *636 639 645
649 659 679 680 681 684 685 711 712 721 726 762 780 785 797 806 870
876 1031 1068 1072 1081 1158 1163 1165 1174 1175 1186 1187 1198
1224 1226 1235 1237 1272 1278 1291 1305 1309 1398 1462 *1753 1779
1781 1782 1820 1834 1966 2009 2023 2028 *2072 2175 2176 2235 2239
2248 2253 2255 2258 2259 2272 2319 2382 2415 2421 *2435 2515 2518
2529 2531 2544 2596 2688 2690 2694 2698 2717 2722 = 116*7

OURS = 2

This toyle of ours should be a worke of thine;	390
As we will ours, against these sawcie walles,	718

OURSELUES *see* selues

OUT *l.*72 76 397 419 457 706 773 1012 1035 1091 1181 1482 1514 1553
1564 1576 1590 1607 1609 1612 1632 1636 1646 1649 1679 1689 1704
1819 1849 1875 1892 1967 *2087 2109 *2118 2161 *2198 2252 2270 2324
2339 2356 2390 2396 *2422 *2435 2474 2574 2581 2587 2636
2688 = 46*6

OUTWARD = 3

Exterior forme, outward accoutrement;	221
Clap'd on the outward eye of fickle France,	904
Death hauing praide vpon the outward parts	2621

OUT-FACE = 1

Threaten the threatner, and out-face the brow	2217

OUT-FACED = 1

Out-faced Infant State, and done a rape	394

OUT-LOOKE = 1

To out-looke Conquest, and to winne renowne	2368

OUT-RAGE = *1

Fra. I feare some out-rage, and Ile follow her. *Exit.*	1491

OUT-SCOLD = 1

We grant thou canst out-scold vs: Far thee well,	2414

OUT-SIDE = 2

Pand. You looke but on the out-side of this worke.	2362
Dol. Out-side or in-side, I will not returne	2363

OWD = 1

That blood which ow'd the bredth of all this Ile,	1817

OWE = 3

Which owe the crowne, that thou ore-masterest?	406

OWE *cont.*
   To pay that dutie which you truly owe,   553
   We owe thee much: within this wall of flesh   1319
OWED = 1
   The vn-owed interest of proud swelling State: 2152
OWES = 2
   To him that owes it, namely, this yong Prince,   554
   For all the Treasure that thine Vnckle owes,   1702
OWNE = 9*1
   And sullen presage of your owne decay: 33
   *That for thine owne gaine shouldst defend mine honor?   255
   Our iust and lineall entrance to our owne;   382
   Iohn. In Vs, that are our owne great Deputie,   679
   Which we God knowes, haue turn'd another way, | To our owne
   vantage.   869
   As Gods owne souldier, rounded in the eare,   887
   Hath drawne him from his owne determin'd ayd,   905
   For your owne Ladies, and pale-visag'd Maides,   2408
   When English measure backward their owne ground   2527
   Who chaunts a dolefull hymne to his owne death,   2628
OWNER = 1
   For greefe is proud, and makes his owner stoope,   991
OXE-HEAD = 1
   I would set an Oxe-head to your Lyons hide: | And make a monster of
   you.   599
P = *2
PAGAN = 1
   And cripple thee vnto a Pagan shore,   2287
PAINEFULLY = 1
   Who painefully with much expedient march   529
PAINES = 6
   (Faire fall the bones that tooke the paines for me)   86
   Who as you say, tooke paines to get this sonne,   129
   That will take paines to blow a horne before her?   229
   But on my Liege, for very little paines | Will bring this labor to an
   happy end. *Exit.*   1295
   Let hell want paines enough to torture me: 2142
   He meanes to recompence the paines you take,   2476
PAINT = 2
   With slaughters pencill; where reuenge did paint   1168
   To gilde refined Gold, to paint the Lilly;   1728
PAINTED = 2
   The grapling vigor, and rough frowne of Warre | Is cold in amitie, and
   painted peace,   1029
   Not painted with the Crimson spots of blood,   1978
PAIRE = 1
   Must needes want pleading for a paire of eyes: 1677
PALE = 3*1
   Together with that pale, that white-fac'd shore,   316
   Elea. Look'st thou pale *France*? do not let go thy hand. 1123
   Ar. Are you sicke Hubert? you looke pale to day,   1601
   I am the Symet to this pale faint Swan,   2627
PALESTINE = 1
   And fought the holy Warres in *Palestine,*   297
PALE-VISAGD = 1
   For your owne Ladies, and pale-visag'd Maides,   2408

PALME = 3
When his faire Angels would salute my palme,   911
As now againe to snatch our palme from palme: 1175
PALTRY = 1
Chat. Then turne your forces from this paltry siege,   348
PAN = 7*3
PAND = 13
PANDOLPH = 1
Enter King Iohn and Pandolph, attendants.   2166
PANDULPH see also Pan., Pand. = 3
Enter Pandulph.   1061
I *Pandulph,* of faire *Millane* Cardinall,   1065
The Cardinall *Pandulph* is within at rest,   2692
PANDULPHO = 2
Enter France, Dolphin, Pandulpho, Attendants.   1382
Enter Pandulpho.   2315
PANGS = 1
For I do see the cruell pangs of death   2520
PARCHED = 1
To make his bleake windes kisse my parched lips,   2648
PARCHMENT = 1
Vpon a Parchment, and against this fire | Do I shrinke vp.   2640
PARDON = 4*1
Sal. Pardon me Madam, | I may not goe without you to the kings.   987
Purchase corrupted pardon of a man,   1093
Who in that sale sels pardon from himselfe: 1094
**Dol.* Your Grace shall pardon me, I will not backe: 2331
Haue done me shame: Braue Soldier, pardon me,   2568
PARDOND = 1
At whose request the king hath pardon'd them,   2593
PARLE = 2
Our Trumpet call'd you to this gentle parle.   511
Behold the French amaz'd vouchsafe a parle,   532
PARLEY = 2
And didst in signes againe parley with sinne,   1963
Send fayre-play-orders, and make comprimise, | Insinuation, parley, and
base truce   2236
PARLIE = 1
To parlie or to fight, therefore prepare.   373
PART = 13
Sir *Robert* might haue eat his part in me   247
Then let confusion of one part confirm   673
And part your mingled colours once againe,   703
He is the halfe part of a blessed man,   752
Hath willingly departed with a part,   884
Vpon which better part, our prayrs come in,   1224
My reasonable part produces reason   1438
Since all, and euery part of what we would   1755
To tug and scamble, and to part by th'teeth   2151
In peace: and part this bodie and my soule   2508
The stumbling night did part our wearie powres?   2544
Bast. A Friend. What art thou? | *Hub.* Of the part of England.   2553
For in a night the best part of my powre,   2671
PARTIE = 2
Vpon my partie: thou cold blooded slaue,   1049
Our Partie may well meet a prowder foe. *Exeunt.*   2248

PARTS = 4
    K.Iohn. Mine eye hath well examined his parts,   97
    Then arme thy constant and thy nobler parts   1222
    Remembers me of all his gracious parts,   1481
    Death hauing praide vpon the outward parts   2621
PARTY = 2
    Vpon the right and party of her sonne.   40
    Iohn. Whose party do the Townesmen yet admit?   675
PASSAGE = 2
    Whose passage vext with thy impediment,   650
    The mouth of passage shall we fling wide ope,   764
PASSE = 1
    But if you fondly passe our proffer'd offer,   564
PASSING = 1
    Passing these Flats, are taken by the Tide,   2598
PASSION = 4
    A passion hatefull to my purposes: 1346
    Then with a passion would I shake the world,   1423
    His passion is so ripe, it needs must breake.   1797
    Forgiue the Comment that my passion made   1988
PASSIONATE = *1
    **Dol.* She is sad and passionate at your highnes Tent.   864
PAST = 3
    Which was so strongly vrg'd past my defence.   271
    Sal. Indeed we fear'd his sicknesse was past cure.   1804
    Pem. All murthers past, do stand excus'd in this: 2050
PATCHD = 2
    Patch'd with foule Moles, and eye-offending markes,   968
    Then did the fault before it was so patch'd.   1751
PATCHES = 1
    As patches set vpon a little breach,   1749
PATE = 1
    That Broker, that still breakes the pate of faith,   889
PATH = 1
    Out of the path which shall directly lead   1514
PATIENCE = 1
    Fra. Patience good Lady, comfort gentle *Constance.*   1405
PATIENT = 1
    Pem. He is more patient | Then when you left him; euen now he sung.   2617
PATTERNE = 1
    So we could finde some patterne of our shame: 1398
PAUSE = 3*1
    We coldly pause for thee, *Chatilion* speake,   347
    Fra. Peace Lady, pause, or be more temperate,   498
    Hub. My Lord. | **Ioh.* Had'st thou but shooke thy head, or made a
    pause   1955
    Then pause not: for the present time's so sicke,   2181
PAW = 1
    A cased Lion by the mortall paw,   1190
PAWND = 1
    Haue I not pawn'd to you my Maiesty?   1023
PAWNES = 1
    To lye like pawnes, lock'd vp in chests and truncks,   2395
PAY = 4
    Our Abbies and our Priories shall pay   55
    To pay that dutie which you truly owe,   553
    And with aduantage meanes to pay thy loue: 1321

PAY *cont.*
Bast. Oh let vs pay the time: but needfull woe,   2721
PAYING = 1
Paying the fine of rated Treachery,   2498
PEACE = 39*5
   K.Iohn. Beare mine to him, and so depart in peace,   28
   *Aust. The peace of heauen is theirs y lift their swords   328
That right in peace which heere we vrge in warre,   340
   *K.Iohn. Peace be to *France*: If France in peace permit   381
If not, bleede *France*, and peace ascend to heauen.   383
Their proud contempt that beats his peace to heauen.   385
   Fran. Peace be to *England*, if that warre returne   386
From *France* to *England*, there to liue in peace: 387
   Aust. Peace. | *Bast.* Heare the Cryer.   432
   Arthur. Good my mother peace,   465
   Fra. Peace Lady, pause, or be more temperate,   498
For bloody power to rush vppon your peace.   527
And leaue your children, wiues, and you in peace.   563
   Aust. Peace, no more. | *Bast.* O tremble: for you heare the Lyon rore.   601
The others peace: till then, blowes, blood, and death.   674
And I shall shew you peace, and faire-fac'd league: 732
To a most base and vile-concluded peace.   907
   *Con. Gone to be married? Gone to sweare a peace?   922
The grapling vigor, and rough frowne of Warre | Is cold in amitie, and
painted peace,   1029
Weare out the daies in Peace; but ere Sun-set,   1035
Heare me, Oh, heare me. | *Aust.* Lady *Constance*, peace.   1037
   Const. War, war, no peace, peace is to me a warre: 1039
Was deepe-sworne faith, peace, amity, true loue   1162
To clap this royall bargaine vp of peace,   1166
Of smiling peace to march a bloody hoast,   1177
Then keepe in peace that hand which thou dost hold.   1192
Set at libertie: the fat ribs of peace   1307
   Con. Lo; now: now see the issue of your peace.   1404
   Fra. O faire affliction, peace.   1420
   Hub. Peace: no more. Adieu,   1707
Ile make a peace betweene your soule, and you.   1975
   Bast. Keepe the peace, I say.   2095
And snarleth in the gentle eyes of peace: 2155
And I haue made a happy peace with him,   2231
Perchance the Cardinall cannot make your peace;   2243
It may lie gently at the foot of peace,   2329
His peace with *Rome*? what is that peace to me?   2345
Because that *Iohn* hath made his peace with *Rome*?   2349
   *Dol. There end thy braue, and turn thy face in peace,   2413
In peace: and part this bodie and my soule   2508
And brings from him such offers of our peace,   2694
PEACEFULL = 1
Vnlesse thou let his siluer Water, keepe | A peacefull progresse to the
Ocean.   653
PEARLES = *1
   *Drawes those heauen-mouing pearles fro(m) his poor eies,   471
PEECES = 1
   Pem. Cut him to peeces.   2094
PEERES = 3
My discontented Peeres. What? Mother dead?   1846
Some Messenger betwixt me, and the Peeres,   1901

PEERES *cont.*
Iohn. Doth *Arthur* liue? O hast thee to the Peeres,   1985
PEERING = 1
Like a proud riuer peering ore his bounds?   944
PEEUISH = 1
Being wrong'd as we are by this peeuish Towne: 716
PELL-MELL = 1
Why then defie each other, and pell-mell,   720
PEM = 1
Pembroke looke too't: farewell *Chattillion.* | *Exit Chat. and Pem.*   35
PEM = 12*6
PEMBROKE see also *P.*, *Pem.* = 5*3
  *Enter King Iohn, Queene Elinor, Pembroke, Essex, and Sa-| lisbury,
  with the Chattylion of France.   2
  Pembroke looke too't: farewell *Chattillion.* | *Exit Chat. and Pem.*   35
  *Enter K.(ing) of England, Bastard, Queene, Blanch, Pembroke, | *and*
  others.   379
  Enter Iohn, Pembroke, Salisbury, and other Lordes.   1717
  Enter Pembroke, Salisbury, & Bigot.   2007
  *Enter (in Armes) Dolphin, Salisbury, Meloone, Pem-| broke, Bigot,
  Souldiers.   2250
  Enter Salisbury, Pembroke, and Bigot.   2459
  Enter Pembroke.   2610
PEN = 1
I am a scribled forme drawne with a pen   2639
PENCE = 1
Yet sell your face for fiue pence and 'tis deere: 161
PENCILL = 1
With slaughters pencill; where reuenge did paint   1168
PENNY = 1
Am I *Romes* slaue? What penny hath *Rome* borne?   2350
PEOPLE = 4
Of all his people, and freeze vp their zeale,   1535
Of all his people shall reuolt from him,   1550
I finde the people strangely fantasied,   1865
Our people quarrell with obedience,   2176
PERADUENTURE = 1
Yet speakes, and peraduenture may recouer.   2588
PERCEIUE = 1
And well shall you perceiue, how willingly   1762
PERCHANCE = 3
Nay, it perchance will sparkle in your eyes: 1694
Of dangerous Maiesty, when perchance it frownes   1938
Perchance the Cardinall cannot make your peace;   2243
PEREMPTORIE = 1
In mortall furie halfe so peremptorie, | As we to keepe this Citie.   769
PERENNEAN = 1
And talking of the Alpes and Appenines, | The Perennean and the riuer
Poe,   212
PERFECT = 3
And findes them perfect *Richard*: sirra speake,   98
Therefore since Law it selfe is perfect wrong,   1117
Bast. Hubert, I thinke. | *Hub.* Thou hast a perfect thought: 2559
PERFECTION = 1
Whose fulnesse of perfection lyes in him.   755
PERFORCE = 2
He that perforce robs Lions of their hearts,   281

PERFORCE *cont.*
So wilfully dost spurne; and force perforce   1069
PERFORMD = 1
First made to heauen, first be to heauen perform'd,   1197
PERFORME = 1
Or what good loue may I performe for you?   1625
PERFORMED = 1
And may not be performed by thy selfe,   1200
PERFUME = 1
To throw a perfume on the Violet, '   1729
PERHAPS = 1
Go after him: for he perhaps shall neede   1900
PERILL = 2
Pand. Philip of *France*, on perill of a curse,   1119
The perill of our curses light on thee   1226
PERILLOUS = 1
This gentle offer of the perillous time.   2010
PERIURD = 3
Arme, arme, you heauens, against these periur'd Kings,   1032
Set armed discord 'twixt these periur'd Kings,   1036
To teach thee safety: thou art periur'd too,   1046
PERIURY = 1
This day of shame, oppression, periury.   1013
PERMIT = *1
K.Iohn. Peace be to *France*: If France in peace permit   381
PERPETUALL = 1
To push destruction, and perpetuall shame   2687
PERPLEX = *1
Pan. What canst thou say, but wil perplex thee more?   1153
PERPLEXT = 1
Fra. I am perplext, and know not what to say.   1152
PERSEUER = 1
Perseuer not, but heare me mighty kings.   736
PERSON = 3
All punish'd in the person of this childe,   492
And beare possession of our Person heere,   680
Fra. Good reuerend father, make my person yours,   1155
PERSWASION = 1
By his perswasion, are againe falne off,   2537
PERUSING = 1
Both they and we, perusing ore these notes   2256
PET = 1
PETER see also Pet. = 2
And if his name be *George*, Ile call him *Peter*;   196
Enter Bastard and Peter of Pomfret.   1851
PETITIONS = 1
Of soft petitions, pittie and remorse,   794
PEYSED = 1
The world, who of it selfe is peysed well,   896
PHANGS = 1
The swords of souldiers are his teeth, his phangs,   667
PHIL = 4*2
PHILIP see also Phil. = 13*2
Chat. Philip of *France*, in right and true behalfe   12
Enter Robert Faulconbridge, and Philip.   57
K.Iohn. What is thy name? | *Bast. Philip* my Liege, so is my name
begun,   165

PHILIP cont.
Philip, good old Sir *Roberts* wiues eldest sonne.	167
Kneele thou downe *Philip*, but rise more great,	170
Gour. Good leaue good *Philip*.	242
Bast. Philip, sparrow, *Iames*,	243
Enter before Angiers, Philip King of France, Lewis, Daul-|phin, Austria, Constance, Arthur.	292
Enter King Iohn, France, Dolphin, Blanch, Elianor, Philip,| Austria, Constance.	998
Pand. Philip of *France*, on perill of a curse,	1119
Aust. King *Philip*, listen to the Cardinall.	1126
Iohn. Philip, what saist thou to the Cardinall?	1131
Aust. Doe so king *Philip*, hang no more in doubt.	1150
While *Philip* breathes.	1289
Iohn. Hubert, keepe this boy: *Philip* make vp,	1290

PHILIP = 3
PHILLIP = 1
Phillip of France, if thou be pleas'd withall,	851

PHILOSOPHY = 1
Preach some Philosophy to make me mad,	1435

PHYSICKE = 1
That for the health and Physicke of our right,	2272

PICKE = 2
Hee and his tooth-picke at my worships messe,	200
And picke strong matter of reuolt, and wrath	1552

PICKED = 1
My picked man of Countries: my deare sir,	203

PICKT = 1
Now for the bare-pickt bone of Maiesty,	2153

PIECES *see* peeces
PIGMY = 1
To whip this dwarfish warre, this Pigmy Armes	2389

PIPE = 1
And from the organ-pipe of frailety sings	2629

PITTIE = 2
Of soft petitions, pittie and remorse,	794
Himselfe loues traytor, this is pittie now;	824

PITTIFULL = 1
Good ground be pittifull, and hurt me not:	1998

PITTY = 1
And is't not pitty, (oh my grieued friends)	2275

PLACD = 1
The mis-plac'd-*Iohn* should entertaine an houre,	1518

PLACE = 3
Would I might neuer stirre from off this place,	153
Wade to the market-place in *French*-mens bloud,	335
And he that stands vpon a slipp'ry place,	1522

PLAGUE = 4
But God hath made her sinne and her, the plague	488
And with her plague her sinne: his iniury	490
And all for her, a plague vpon her.	493
The different plague of each calamitie.	1444

PLAGUED = 2
That he is not onely plagued for her sin,	487
On this remoued issue, plagued for her,	489

PLAID = 2
Assured losse, before the match be plaid.	1269

PLAID *cont.*
To winne this easie match, plaid for a Crowne?   2359
PLAINE = 2*1
    Iohn. Vp higher to the plaine, where we'l set forth   603
    *He speakes plaine Cannon fire, and smoake, and bounce,   778
    Of plaine old forme, is much disfigured,   1739
PLAINLY = 1
    Plainly denouncing vengeance vpon *Iohn.*   1544
PLANKES = 1
    To crowch in litter of your stable plankes,   2394
PLANTAGENET = 2
    Arise Sir *Richard,* and *Plantagenet.*   171
    Of him it holds, stands yong *Plantagenet,*   544
PLANTAGENETS = 1
    I come one way of the *Plantagenets.*   2566
PLANTAGINET = 2
    Arthur Plantaginet, laies most lawfull claime   14
    Ele. The very spirit of *Plantaginet*:   176
PLASTER = 1
    Should seeke a plaster by contemn'd reuolt,   2264
PLAY = 8
    And if she did play false, the fault was hers,   126
    Bast. One that wil play the deuill sir with you,   435
    And victorie with little losse doth play   617
    I'de play incessantly vpon these Iades,   699
    Play fast and loose with faith? so iest with heauen,   1173
    Sal. It is apparant foule-play, and 'tis shame   1811
    Send fayre-play-orders, and make comprimise, | Insinuation, parley, and
    base truce   2236
    Bast. According to the faire-play of the world,   2372
PLAYES = 2
    Stayes in his course, and playes the Alchymist,   1003
    That whiles warme life playes in that infants veines,   1517
PLEA = 1
    That is my brothers plea, and none of mine,   75
PLEADE = 1
    Pleade for our interest, and our being heere.   2421
PLEADING = 1
    Must needes want pleading for a paire of eyes: 1677
PLEASD = 5*2
    Phillip of France, if thou be pleas'd withall,   851
    If heauen be pleas'd that you must vse me ill,   1631
    Exec. I am best pleas'd to be from such a deede.   1662
    * *Pem.* This once again (but that your Highnes pleas'd)   1720
    *We breath'd our Councell: but it pleas'd your Highnes   1753
    To ouer-beare it, and we are all well pleas'd,   1754
    O make a league with me, 'till I haue pleas'd   1845
PLEASE = 1
    Who art thou? | *Bast.* Who thou wilt: and if thou please   2563
PLEASED = 1
    Religiously prouokes. Be pleased then   552
PLEASURE = 2
    To doe your pleasure, and continue friends.   1183
    Pem. But that your Royall pleasure must be done,   1734
PLEASURES = 2
    Attended with the pleasures of the world,   1334
    Neuer to taste the pleasures of the world,   2067

PLOTS = 2
  To cull the plots of best aduantages: 333
  Iohn layes you plots: the times conspire with you, 1531
PLUCKD = 1
  And that high Royalty was nere pluck'd off: 1722
PLUCKE = 1
  But they will plucke away his naturall cause, 1541
PLUCKS = 1
  Whose valour plucks dead Lyons by the beard; 438
PLUCKT = 1
  And with her golden hand hath pluckt on France 978
PLUM = 1
  Giue yt a plum, a cherry, and a figge, 463
PLUME = 1
  There stucke no plume in any English Crest, 628
POAST = 1
  If you thinke meete, this afternoone will poast 2704
POCKET = 1
  Aust. Well ruffian, I must pocket vp these wrongs, 1128
POE = 1
  And talking of the Alpes and Appenines, | The Perennean and the riuer
  Poe, 212
POINT = 3
  As in a Theater, whence they gape and point 689
  Turne face to face, and bloody point to point: 704
POISON = 1
  Of that fell poison which assayleth him. 2614
POLICIE = 1
  Smackes it not something of the policie. 710
POMFRET = 2
  Enter Bastard and Peter of Pomfret. 1851
  From forth the streets of Pomfret, whom I found 1869
POMP = 1
  Clamors of hell, be measures to our pomp? 1237
POMPE = 4
  To this vnlook'd for vnprepared pompe. *Exeunt.* 881
  Sal. Therefore, to be possess'd with double pompe, 1726
  With dreadfull pompe of stout inuasion. 1895
  The iminent decay of wrested pompe. 2159
POOR = *1
  *Drawes those heauen-mouing pearles fro(m) his poor eies, 471
POORE = 7*1
  * *Qu.Mo.* His mother shames him so, poore boy hee | (weepes. 468
  Thy sinnes are visited in this poore childe, 481
  But the word Maid, cheats the poore Maide of that. 893
  Like a poore begger, raileth on the rich. 913
  Because my poore childe is a prisoner. 1460
  Many a poore mans sonne would haue lyen still, 1626
  And finde th'inheritance of this poore childe, 1815
  My heart hath one poore string to stay it by, 2665
POPE = 10
  Fra. Heere comes the holy Legat of the Pope. 1062
  And from Pope *Innocent* the Legate heere, 1066
  Pope *Innocent,* I doe demand of thee. 1073
  To charge me to an answere, as the Pope: 1078
  So tell the Pope, all reuerence set apart | To him and his vsurp'd
  authoritie. 1086

POPE *cont.*

Against the Pope, and count his friends my foes.	1098
Pan. Take againe | From this my hand, as holding of the Pope	2169
Vpon your stubborne vsage of the Pope:	2185
Vpon your oath of seruice to the Pope,	2190
Iohn. The Legat of the Pope hath beene with mee,	2230

POPS = 1

The which if he can proue, a pops me out,	76

POSSESSD = 1

Sal. Therefore, to be possess'd with double pompe,	1726

POSSESSE = *1

*Io. Why seek'st thou to possesse me with these feares?	1928

POSSESSED = 1

And thou possessed with a thousand wrongs:	1340

POSSESSETH = 1

Weaknesse possesseth me, and I am faint. *Exeunt.*	2457

POSSESSION = 4*1

K.Iohn. Our strong possession, and our right for vs.	45
*Eli. Your strong possessio(n) much more then your right,	46
And stalke in blood to our possession?	572
And beare possession of our Person heere,	680
Hub. His words do take possession of my bosome.	1605

POSSEST = 2

I haue possest you with, and thinke them strong.	1758
Possest with rumors, full of idle dreames,	1866

POSSIBLE = 1

Sal. May this be possible? May this be true?	2482

POST = 1

What woman post is this? hath she no husband	228

POSTERITIE = 1

And for amends to his posteritie,	299

POSTERITY = 1

Cut off the sequence of posterity,	393

POTENTS = 1

You equall Potents, fierie kindled spirits,	672

POUND = 3

At least from faire fiue hundred pound a yeere:	77
A halfe-fac'd groat, fiue hundred pound a yeere?	102
Your face hath got fiue hundred pound a yeere,	160

POURE = 2

I would into thy bosome poure my thoughts:	1352
Poure downe thy weather: how goes all in France?	1827

POURS = 1

And pour's downe mischiefe. *Austrias* head lye there,	1287

POWDER = 1

With swifter spleene then powder can enforce	763

POWER = 9*1

For bloody power to rush vppon your peace.	527
*Strength matcht with strength, and power confronted | power,	641
Not that I haue the power to clutch my hand,	910
Pand. Then by the lawfull power that I haue,	1099
There is no tongue hath power to curse him right.	1111
And raise the power of *France* vpon his head,	1121
And from his holinesse vse all your power	2173
And tempt vs not to beare aboue our power.	2596
Ile tell thee *Hubert*, halfe my power this night	2597

POWERLESSE = 1
I giue you welcome with a powerlesse hand,   308
POWERS = 5
Enter the two Kings with their powers, | at seuerall doores.   646
Ile send those powers o're to your Maiesty.   1375
Now Powers from home, and discontents at home   2156
Like a kinde Host, the Dolphin and his powers.   2200
And he hath promis'd to dismisse the Powers | Led by the Dolphin.   2232
POWRE = 3
Fra. A greater powre then We denies all this,   682
Mes. From France to England, neuer such a powre | For any forraigne
preparation,   1828
For in a night the best part of my powre,   2671
POWRES = 4*1
I like it well. France, shall we knit our powres,   712
Vnder whose conduct came those powres of France,   1848
Euen at my gates, with rankes of forraigne powres;   1969
The stumbling night did part our wearie powres?   2544
*Where be your powres? Shew now your mended faiths,   2685
POYCTIERS = 3
To *Ireland, Poyctiers, Aniowe, Torayne, Maine,*   16
For *Angiers,* and faire *Toraine Maine, Poyctiers,*   803
Poyctiers and *Aniow,* these fiue Prouinces   848
POYSON = 2
Sweet, sweet, sweet poyson for the ages tooth,   223
Within me is a hell, and there the poyson   2655
POYSOND = 2
Hub. The King I feare is poyson'd by a Monke,   2580
Ioh. Poyson'd, ill fare: dead, forsooke, cast off,   2643
PRACTICE = 2
Which though I will not practice to deceiue,   224
The practice, and the purpose of the king: 2062
PRACTISES = 1
My Vnckle practises more harme to me: 1593
PRAIDE = 1
Death hauing praide vpon the outward parts   2621
PRAISE = 1
Fra. Well could I beare that *England* had this praise,   1397
PRATE = 1
Hub. If I talke to him, with his innocent prate   1598
PRAY = 6
Pray that their burthens may not fall this day,   1015
I doe pray to thee, thou vertuous *Daulphin,*   1244
Husband, I cannot pray that thou maist winne: 1264
Vncle, I needs must pray that thou maist lose: 1265
I leaue your highnesse: Grandame, I will pray   1312
In lieu whereof, I pray you beare me hence   2505
PRAYRS = 1
Vpon which better part, our prayrs come in,   1224
PREACH = 1
Preach some Philosophy to make me mad,   1435
PRECIOUS = 4
Turning with splendor of his precious eye   1004
Any annoyance in that precious sense: 1672
Found it too precious Princely, for a graue.   2039
We hold our time too precious to be spent | with such a brabler.   2415

PREPARATION = 2
All preparation for a bloody siedge   519
Mes. From France to England, neuer such a powre | For any forraigne
preparation,   1828
PREPARD = 3
Let them be welcome then, we are prepar'd.   378
He is prepar'd, and reason to he should,   2384
The King doth smile at, and is well prepar'd   2388
PREPARE = 3
To parlie or to fight, therefore prepare.   373
Hub. Come (Boy) prepare your selfe.   1667
For when you should be told they do prepare,   1832
PREPARING = 1
Bast. The Dolphin is preparing hither-ward,   2669
PRESAGE = 1
And sullen presage of your owne decay: 33
PRESAGES = 1
Abbortiues, presages, and tongues of heauen,   1543
PRESENCE = 5
Lord of thy presence, and no land beside.   145
It ill beseemes this presence to cry ayme | To these ill-tuned repetitions: 499
Lord of our presence Angiers, and of you.   681
Her presence would haue interrupted much.   862
The King by me requests your presence straight.   2020
PRESENCES = 1
Your Royall presences be rul'd by mee,   691
PRESENT = 3
Then pause not: for the present time's so sicke,   2181
That present medcine must be ministred,   2182
Iohn. Haue thou the ordering of this present time.   2246
PRESENTED = 2
Presented thee more hideous then thou art.   1991
Presented to the teares of soft remorse.   2049
PRESENTLY = 2
For at Saint Maries Chappell presently,   858
With purpose presently to leaue this warre.   2696
PRESIDENT = 1
Returne the president to these Lords againe,   2254
PRESSE = 1
Which in their throng, and presse to that last hold,   2625
PRETHEE = 1
I prethee Lady goe away with me.   1403
PRETTY = 3
Must I behold my pretty *Arthur* more.   1474
Puts on his pretty lookes, repeats his words,   1480
And, pretty childe, sleepe doubtlesse, and secure,   1710
PREUAILE = 1
Where how he did preuaile, I shame to speake: 112
PREUENTED = 1
This might haue beene preuented, and made whole | With very easie
arguments of loue,   41
PREYDE *see* praide
PRICKES = 1
Against the winde, the which he prickes and wounds   2623
PRIEST = 2
Adde thus much more, that no *Italian* Priest   1080
Are led so grossely by this medling Priest,   1090

PRIMA *l*.1 997 1569 2165 = 4
PRIMUS *l*.1 = 1
PRINCE = 14*2
   To him that owes it, namely, this yong Prince,   554
   Iohn. Speake then Prince Dolphin, can you loue this | Ladie?   843
   Hub. Good morrow, little Prince.   1581
   Ar. As little Prince, hauing so great a Title   1582
   To be more Prince, as may be: you are sad.   1583
   But you, at your sicke seruice had a Prince: 1628
   Made it no conscience to destroy a Prince.   1954
   Big. Who kill'd this Prince? | *Hub.* 'Tis not an houre since I left him
   well: 2106
   Thou art more deepe damn'd then Prince Lucifer: 2125
   To your proceedings: yet beleeue me Prince,   2262
   Pand. Haile noble Prince of *France*:   2321
   Mes. Where is my Prince, the Dolphin? | *Dol.* Heere: what newes?   2534
   And brought Prince *Henry* in their companie,   2592
   Enter Prince Henry, Salisburie, and Bigot.   2604
   Sal. Be of good comfort (Prince) for you are borne   2631
   Bast. Let it be so, and you my noble Prince,   2706
PRINCELY = 3*1
   Nor keepe his Princely heart from *Richards* hand: 280
   Iohn. If that the Dolphin there thy Princely sonne,   800
   P. Oh death, made proud with pure & princely beuty,   2034
   Found it too precious Princely, for a graue.   2039
PRINCES = 3*1
   To these two Princes, if you marrie them: 760
   Fra. It likes vs well young Princes: close your hands   853
   With other Princes that may best be spar'd,   2707
   Now, these her Princes are come home againe,   2726
PRINCESSE = 2
   Holdes hand with any Princesse of the world.   810
   (The best I had, a Princesse wrought it me)   1619
PRINCIPLE = 1
   That need, must needs inferre this principle,   1144
PRINT = 1
   That leaues the print of blood where ere it walkes.   2024
PRIORIES = 1
   Our Abbies and our Priories shall pay   55
PRISON = 3
   In the vilde prison of afflicted breath: 1402
   So I were out of prison, and kept Sheepe   1590
   Sal. This is the prison: What is he lyes heere?   2033
PRISONER = 3
   Arthur tane prisoner? diuers deere friends slaine?   1389
   Because my poore childe is a prisoner.   1460
   Are not you grieu'd that *Arthur* is his prisoner?   1508
PRISONMENT = 1
   But hold himselfe safe in his prisonment.   1546
PRISONS = 1
   In vaults and prisons, and to thrill and shake,   2397
PRIUATE = 1
   Whose priuate with me of the Dolphines loue,   2013
PRIUILEDGE = 2
   Some sinnes doe beare their priuiledge on earth,   274
   Pem. Sir, sir, impatience hath his priuiledge.   2031

PROCEEDING = 1
And merciles proceeding, by these French.   520
PROCEEDINGS = 4
To curse the faire proceedings of this day: 1022
And glow with shame of your proceedings, *Hubert*:   1693
To your proceedings? Do not seeke to stuffe   1854
To your proceedings: yet beleeue me Prince,   2262
PROCLAIME = 1
To enter Conquerors, and to proclaime   620
PRODIGIES = 1
And call them Meteors, prodigies, and signes,   1542
PRODIGIOUS = 1
Lame, foolish, crooked, swart, prodigious,   967
PRODIGIOUSLY = 1
Lest that their hopes prodigiously be crost: 1016
PRODUCE = 2
That ere I heard: shall I produce the men? | *K.Iohn.* Let them approach: 53
Que. Thou vnaduised scold, I can produce   494
PRODUCES = 1
My reasonable part produces reason   1438
PROFFERD = 1
But if you fondly passe our proffer'd offer,   564
PROFOUND = 1
When such profound respects doe pull you on?   1251
PROGRESSE = 2
Vnlesse thou let his siluer Water, keepe | A peacefull progresse to the
Ocean.   653
That siluerly doth progresse on thy cheekes: 2297
PROMISD = 1
And he hath promis'd to dismisse the Powers | Led by the Dolphin.   2232
PROMISE = *1
Hub. Is this your promise? Go too, hold your toong.   1675
PROMISED = 1
As to my ample hope was promised,   2365
PROMISETH = 1
The bloome that promiseth a mightie fruite.   789
PROMOTIONS = 1
In titles, honors, and promotions, | As she in beautie, education, blood,   808
PRONOUNCE = 1
Which till this time my tongue did nere pronounce;   1240
PROOOUE = *1
Iohn. Doth not the Crowne of England, prooue the | King?   579
PROP = 1
To vnder-prop this Action? Is't not I   2352
PROPER = 1
Some proper man I hope, who was it mother?   263
PROPERLY = 1
Or if you will, to speake more properly,   831
PROPHESIE = 1
Do prophesie vpon it dangerously: 1911
PROPHET = 2
And here's a Prophet that I brought with me   1868
Iohn. Is this Ascension day? did not the Prophet   2192
PROPHETICKE = 1
Now heare me speake with a propheticke spirit: 1511
PROPORTIED = 1
I am too high-borne to be proportied   2332

PROSPECT = 1
Before the eye and prospect of your Towne,   514
PROSPERITIE = 1
Thou hate and terror to prosperitie,   1411
PROSPERITY = 1
Into the purse of rich prosperity   2312
PROTECTION = 1
Loe in this right hand, whose protection   542
PROTEST = 1
I do protest I neuer lou'd my selfe   817
PROUD = 7*2
*Chat. The proud controle of fierce and bloudy warre,   22
Their proud contempt that beats his peace to heauen.   385
Like a proud riuer peering ore his bounds?   944
I will instruct my sorrowes to bee proud,   990
For greefe is proud, and makes his owner stoope,   991
The Sunne is in the heauen, and the proud day,   1333
*P. Oh death, made proud with pure & princely beuty,   2034
The vn-owed interest of proud swelling State: 2152
Lye at the proud foote of a Conqueror,   2724
PROUDLY = 1
Bearing their birth-rights proudly on their backs,   364
PROUE = 6
The which if he can proue, a pops me out,   76
To him will we proue loyall, till that time   577
One must proue greatest. While they weigh so euen,   644
That giue you cause to proue my saying true.   949
And proue a deadly blood-shed, but a iest,   2054
Hub. Do not proue me so: 2091
PROUERB = 1
You are the Hare of whom the Prouerb goes   437
PROUES = 2
Cit. That can we not: but he that proues the King   576
Proues valuelesse: you are forsworne, forsworne,   1026
PROUIDED = 1
What men prouided? What munition sent   2351
PROUINCES = 1*1
Poyctiers and Aniow, these fiue Prouinces   848
*Shall Lewis haue Blaunch, and Blaunch those Prouinces?   924
PROUOKE = *1
*H. No had (my Lord?) why, did you not prouoke me?   1932
PROUOKES = 1
Religiously prouokes. Be pleased then   552
PROWDER = 1
Our Partie may well meet a prowder foe. Exeunt.   2248
PRUDENT = 1
Bast. O prudent discipline! From North to South: 728
PUISANCE = 1
Iohn. Cosen, goe draw our puisance together,   1272
PULL = 1
When such profound respects doe pull you on?   1251
PULSE = 1
Haue I commandement on the pulse of life?   1810
PUNISHD = 2
All punish'd in the person of this childe,   492
Thou shalt be punish'd for thus frighting me,   932

PUPPI-DOGGES = 1
As maids of thirteene do of puppi-dogges.   776
PURCHASE = 2
Purchase corrupted pardon of a man,   1093
Is purchase of a heauy curse from *Rome*,   1134
PURE = 2*1
With our pure Honors: nor attend the foote   2023
P. Oh death, made proud with pure & princely beuty,   2034
Is touch'd, corruptibly: and his pure braine   2606
PURER = 1
Where should he finde it purer then in *Blanch*?   744
PURGD = 2
Be by some certaine king, purg'd and depos'd.   686
And shall these hands so lately purg'd of bloud?   1170
PURITIE = 1
Shall giue a holinesse, a puritie,   2052
PURPLED = 1
Our lustie English, all with purpled hands,   633
PURPOSE = 6
From all direction, purpose, course, intent.   901
Yet am I sworne, and I did purpose, Boy,   1703
Betweene his purpose and his conscience,   1795
The practice, and the purpose of the king: 2062
They saw we had a purpose of defence.   2245
With purpose presently to leaue this warre.   2696
PURPOSED = 1
When I spake darkely, what I purposed: 1957
PURPOSES = 4
And confident from forreine purposes,   321
The better Act of purposes mistooke,   1205
A passion hatefull to my purposes: 1346
To sound the purposes of all their hearts,   1765
PURPOSE-CHANGER = 1
With that same purpose-changer, that slye diuel,   888
PURSE = 1
Into the purse of rich prosperity   2312
PUSH = 1
To push destruction, and perpetuall shame   2687
PUT = 15
And put the same into yong *Arthurs* hand,   19
I put you o're to heauen, and to my mother;   70
Hath put himselfe in Armes, the aduerse windes   351
Wee'l put thee downe, 'gainst whom these Armes wee | (beare,   660
And put my eye-balls in thy vaultie browes,   1413
Why then you must. Will you put out mine eyes?   1632
And told me *Hubert* should put out mine eyes,   1646
What euer torment you do put me too.   1660
Bast. Your sword is bright sir, put it vp againe.   2079
Ile strike thee dead. Put vp thy sword betime,   2100
Put but a little water in a spoone,   2135
Grow great by your example, and put on   2220
Pem. Vp once againe: put spirit in the French,   2461
To the sea side, and put his cause and quarrell   2701
And happily may your sweet selfe put on   2712
PUTS = 1
Puts on his pretty lookes, repeats his words,   1480

PUTTING = 1
  For putting on so new a fashion'd robe.   1744
PYRENEAN *see* Perennean
QU = 1*1
QUAKE = 2
  But they will quake and tremble all this day.   939
  Doth make an earth-quake of Nobility: 2293
QUALIFIED = 1
  Rests by you onely to be qualified.   2180
QUALITIE = 1
  It would allay the burning qualitie   2613
QUANTITY = 1
  Retaining but a quantity of life,   2484
QUARRELL = 2
  Our people quarrell with obedience,   2176
  To the sea side, and put his cause and quarrell   2701
QUARTA *l.*2458 = 1
QUARTER = *1
  Dol. Well: keepe good quarter, & good care to night,   2546
QUARTERD = 1*1
  And quarter'd in her heart, hee doth espie   823
  *That hang'd, and drawne, and quarter'd there should be   825
QUARTUS *l.*1569 2165 = 2
QUE = 1
QUEEN see also Qu., Qu.Mo., Que. = 1
  That thou maist be a Queen, and checke the world.   420
QUEEN = 3*1
QUEENE = 2*2
  Enter King Iohn, Queene Elinor, Pembroke, Essex, and Sa-| lisbury,
  with the Chattylion of France.   2
  With him along is come the Mother Queene,   356
  Enter K.(ing) of England, Bastard, Queene, Blanch, Pembroke, | and
  others.   379
  Her Dowrie shall weigh equall with a Queene: 802
QUENCH = 2
  To ashes, ere our blood shall quench that fire: 1278
  And quench this fierie indignation,   1640
QUEST = 1
  If lustie loue should go in quest of beautie,   741
QUESTION = 3
  I shall beseech you; that is question now,   205
  No sir, saies question, I sweet sir at yours,   209
  And so ere answer knowes what question would,   210
QUICKELY = *1
  Hub. Whose there? Speake hoa, speake quickely, or | I shoote.   2551
QUIET = 2
  One minute, nay one quiet breath of rest.   1519
  And I will sit as quiet as a Lambe.   1656
QUINTA *l.*2523 = 1
QUITE = 2
  This Ship-boyes semblance hath disguis'd me quite.   2000
  Figur'd quite ore with burning Meteors.   2304
QUMO = *1
QUOTED = 1
  Quoted, and sign'd to do a deede of shame,   1947
RACE = 1
  Sound on into the drowzie race of night: 1338

RAGE = 8*2
  Or shall we giue the signall to our rage,   571
  And in their rage, I hauing hold of both,   1262
  A rage, whose heat hath this condition;   1274
  *Fra. Thy rage shall burne thee vp, & thou shalt turne   1277
  *Fra. I feare some out-rage, and Ile follow her. Exit.   1491
  Throw this report on their incensed rage,   1986
  Vpon thy feature, for my rage was blinde,   1989
  That euer wall-ey'd wrath, or staring rage   2048
  Least I, by marking of your rage, forget   2085
  Doth he still rage?   2616
RAGES = 1
  The Dolphine rages at our verie heeles.   2690
RAGGES = 1
  Out of his ragges. Here's a large mouth indeede,   773
RAILE = 1
  Well, whiles I am a begger, I will raile,   914
RAILETH = 1
  Like a poore begger, raileth on the rich.   913
RAINE = 2
  As raine to water, or deuill to his damme;   425
  Fran. Our Thunder from the South, | Shall raine their drift of bullets on
  this Towne.   726
RAINE-BOW = 1
  Vnto the Raine-bow; or with Taper-light   1731
RAISE = 1
  And raise the power of France vpon his head,   1121
RAMMD = 1
  Haue we ramm'd vp our gates against the world.   578
RAMPING = 1
  A ramping foole, to brag, and stamp, and sweare,   1048
RANKD = 1
  That were embattailed, and rank'd in Kent.   1925
RANKES = 2
  Euen at my gates, with rankes of forraigne powres;   1969
  Her Enemies rankes? I must withdraw, and weepe   2280
RANKNESSE = 1
  Leauing our ranknesse and irregular course,   2515
RANSACKING = 1
  Is now in England ransacking the Church,   1557
RAPE = 1
  Out-faced Infant State, and done a rape   394
RASH = 2
  That hot rash haste so indirectly shedde.   342
  Rash, inconsiderate, fiery voluntaries,   361
RATED = 1
  Paying the fine of rated Treachery,   2498
RATHER = 7
  Eli. Whether hadst thou rather be a Faulconbridge,   142
  The rather, that you giue his off-spring life,   306
  Rather lost more. And by this hand I sweare   657
  Nay, rather turne this day out of the weeke,   1012
  Sal. Or rather then set forward, for 'twill be   2016
  Whom he hath vs'd rather for sport, then neede)   2431
  Bast. He will the rather do it, when he sees   2697
RATTLE = 1
  (As lowd as thine) rattle the Welkins eare,   2428

RAUEN = 1	
As doth a Rauen on a sicke-falne beast,	2158
RAYLE = 1	
And why rayle I on this Commoditie?	908
REACH = 1	
Beyond the infinite and boundlesse reach of mercie,	2120
READ = 4	
Doe you not read some tokens of my sonne	95
Can in this booke of beautie read, I loue:	801
Doth want example: who hath read, or heard	1395
Or haue you read, or heard, or could you thinke?	2041
READE = 1*1	
*Reade heere yong *Arthur*. How now foolish rheume?	1606
Can you not reade it? Is it not faire writ?	1610
READIE = 1	
And euen at hand, a drumme is readie brac'd,	2425
READY = 1	
And ready mounted are they to spit forth	517
REALME = 1	
The life, the right, and truth of all this Realme	2149
REASON = 7	
Phil. I Madame? No, I haue no reason for it,	74
My reasonable part produces reason	1438
Then, haue I reason to be fond of griefe?	1483
Sal. Our greefes, and not our manners reason now.	2028
Bast. But there is little reason in your greefe.	2029
Therefore 'twere reason you had manners now.	2030
He is prepar'd, and reason to he should,	2384
REASONABLE = 1	
My reasonable part produces reason	1438
REASONS = 1*1	
Dol. Strong reasons makes strange actions: let vs go,	1567
Ioh. Some reasons of this double Corronation	1757
REBELLION = 4	
Is in thy selfe rebellion to thy selfe:	1220
Aust. Rebellion, flat rebellion.	1229
Vnthred the rude eye of Rebellion,	2472
REBUKE = 1	
And to rebuke the vsurpation | Of thy vnnaturall Vncle, English *Iohn*,	302
RECEIUD = 1	
But Douer Castle: London hath receiu'd	2199
RECOMPENCE = 1	
He meanes to recompence the paines you take,	2476
RECONCILD = 1	
The next is this: King *Iohn* hath reconcil'd	2322
RECOUER = 1	
Yet speakes, and peraduenture may recouer.	2588
RECREANT = 2*2	
And hang a Calues skin on those recreant limbes.	1055
Phil. And hang a Calues-skin on those recreant limbs	1057
Phil. And hang a Calues-skin on those recreant limbes.	1059
Bast. And hang a Calues-skin on his recreant limbs.	1127
RED = 2	
The Iron of it selfe, though heate red hot,	1638
With eyes as red as new enkindled fire,	1884
REDEEME = 1	
O, that these hands could so redeeme my sonne,	1456

REDRESSE = 2
Con. No, I defie all Counsell, all redresse, 1406
But that which ends all counsell, true Redresse: 1407
REFINED = 1
To gilde refined Gold, to paint the Lilly; 1728
REFORMD = 1
What you would haue reform'd, that is not well, 1761
REFRAINE = 1
Dol. Nay aske me if I can refraine from loue, 845
REFUSE = 1
Being none of his, refuse him: this concludes, 135
REGIMENTS = 1
In best appointment all our Regiments. 604
REGREETE = 1
Vnyoke this seysure, and this kinde regreete? 1172
REIGNE = 2
Where we doe reigne, we will alone vphold 1084
To checke his reigne, but they will cherish it. 1537
REIGNES = 1
Hostilitie, and ciuill tumult reignes 1972
REIOYCE = *1
*E.Har. Reioyce you men of Angiers, ring your bels, 623
RELEEFE = 1
In the releefe of this oppressed childe, 551
RELEEUE = 1
Hen. Oh that there were some vertue in my teares, | That might releeue
you. 2652
RELIGION = 2
It is religion that doth make vowes kept, 1210
But thou hast sworne against religion: 1211
RELIGIOUSLY = 2*1
Religiously prouokes. Be pleased then 552
Doe in his name religiously demand 1067
* Pem. Big. Our soules religiously confirme thy words. 2072
RELIGOUS = 1
With all religous strength of sacred vowes, 1160
REMEDIE = 1
Art. Is there no remedie? | *Hub.* None, but to lose your eyes. 1668
REMEMBER = 4
(If euer I remember to be holy) 1313
Remember: Madam, Fare you well, 1374
Yet I remember, when I was in France, 1587
On this Ascension day, remember well, 2189
REMEMBERS = 1
Remembers me of all his gracious parts, 1481
REMEMBRANCE = 1*1
And keepe it safe for our remembrance: 2253
*Hub. Vnkinde remembrance: thou, & endles night, 2567
REMNANT = 1
Where I may thinke the remnant of my thoughts 2507
REMORSE = 3
Of soft petitions, pittie and remorse, 794
Presented to the teares of soft remorse. 2049
Like Riuers of remorse and innocencie. 2113
REMOTE = 1
To grace the Gentry of a Land remote, 2282

REMOUD = 1
   Con. O be remou'd from him, and answere well.   1149
REMOUE = 2
   What heere? O Nation that thou couldst remoue,   2284
   As I vpon aduantage did remoue,   2672
REMOUED = 3
   Being but the second generation | Remoued from thy sinne-conceiuing
   wombe.   483
   On this remoued issue, plagued for her,   489
   That is remoued by a staffe of France.   629
RENOWNE = 1
   To out-looke Conquest, and to winne renowne   2368
RENOWNED = 2
   Big. What wilt thou do, renowned *Faulconbridge?*   2103
   Lift vp thy brow (renowned *Salisburie*)   2305
REPAIRE = 2
   Some speedy Messenger bid her repaire   875
   Euen in the instant of repaire and health,   1498
REPEATING = 1
   And, in the last repeating, troublesome,   1736
REPEATS = 1
   Puts on his pretty lookes, repeats his words,   1480
REPENT = 3
   And then we shall repent each drop of bloud,   341
   Con. Looke to that Deuill, lest that *France* repent,   1124
   Io. They burn in indignation: I repent: *Enter Mes.*   1821
REPENTANT = 1
   And strew'd repentant ashes on his head.   1690
REPETITIONS = 1
   It ill beseemes this presence to cry ayme | To these ill-tuned repetitions: 499
REPLY = 1
   Heare me without thine eares, and make reply   1348
REPORT = 2
   For ere thou canst report, I will be there: 30
   Throw this report on their incensed rage,   1986
REPORTS = 1
   Ile fill these dogged Spies with false reports: 1709
REPUTED = 1
   Or the reputed sonne of *Cordelion*,   144
REQUEST = 2
   Bend their best studies, heartily request   1768
   At whose request the king hath pardon'd them,   2593
REQUESTS = 2
   I will both heare, and grant you your requests.   1763
   The King by me requests your presence straight.   2020
REQUITALL = 1
   To make a more requitall to your loue.   327
RESCUE = 2
   Rescue those breathing liues to dye in beds,   734
   Where honourable rescue, and defence   2269
RESCUED = 1
   Bast. My Lord I rescued her,   1293
RESEMBLING = 1
   Resembling Maiesty, which being touch'd and tride,   1025
RESIDENCE = 1
   That to their euerlasting residence,   591

RESIGNE = 1
Wilt thou resigne them, and lay downe thy Armes? 454
RESISTING = 1
Against the browes of this resisting towne, 331
RESOLUD = 2
Kings of our feare, vntill our feares resolu'd 685
From a resolu'd and honourable warre, 906
RESOLUED = 1
Hub. A Monke I tell you, a resolued villaine 2586
RESOLUETH = 1
Resolueth from his figure 'gainst the fire? 2486
RESOLUTION = 2
I must be breefe, least resolution drop 1608
The dauntlesse spirit of resolution. 2221
RESPECT = 8
Blan. My vnckles will in this respect is mine, 827
To tread downe faire respect of Soueraigntie, 979
To say what good respect I haue of thee. 1327
Pand. You hold too heynous a respect of greefe. 1475
More vpon humor, then aduis'd respect. 1939
Between compulsion, and a braue respect: 2295
The loue of him, and this respect besides 2502
As we with honor and respect may take, 2695
RESPECTIUE = 1
'Tis two respectiue, and too sociable 198
RESPECTS = 1
When such profound respects doe pull you on? 1251
REST = 7*1
*Command the rest to stand, God and our right. *Exeunt* 607
Though you, and al the rest so grossely led, 1095
One minute, nay one quiet breath of rest. 1519
If what in rest you haue, in right you hold, 1772
His soule and body to their lasting rest. 2630
The Cardinall *Pandulph* is within at rest, 2692
To rest without a spot for euermore. 2718
If England to it selfe, do rest but true. *Exeunt.* 2729
RESTRAINT = 1
Th'infranchisement of *Arthur*, whose restraint 1769
RESTS = 1
Rests by you onely to be qualified. 2180
RETAINING = 1
Retaining but a quantity of life, 2484
RETIRE = 1
In faint Retire: Oh brauely came we off, 2528
RETIRED = 1
And like a bated and retired Flood, 2514
RETREAT = *1
**Alarums, excursions, Retreat. Enter Iohn, Eleanor, Arthur | Bastard,*
Hubert, Lords. 1297
RETURNE = 11
That to my home I will no more returne 314
Fran. Peace be to *England*, if that warre returne 386
Hither returne all gilt with Frenchmens blood: 627
Our colours do returne in those same hands 630
Const. O faire returne of banish'd Maiestie. 1254
Deliuer him to safety, and returne, 1879
Returne, and tell him so: we know the worst. 2025

RETURNE *cont.*

Iohn. Would not my Lords returne to me againe	2205
Returne the president to these Lords againe,	2254
Dol. Out-side or in-side, I will not returne	2363
And instantly returne with me againe.	2686

RETYRE = 3

And with a blessed and vn-vext retyre,	559
From first to last, the on-set and retyre:	637
The French fight coldly, and retyre themselues.	2453

REUELL = 1

This harness'd Maske, and vnaduised Reuell,	2386

REUENGE = 5

To doe him Iustice, and reuenge on you.	474
With slaughters pencill; where reuenge did paint	1168
Doth lay it open to vrge on reuenge.	2037
By giuing it the worship of Reuenge.	2071
To do the office for thee, of reuenge,	2681

REUENNUE = 1

This iugling witchcraft with reuennue cherish,	1096

REUERBERATE = 1

That shall reuerberate all, as lowd as thine.	2426

REUERENCE = 1

So tell the Pope, all reuerence set apart | To him and his vsurp'd authoritie.	1086

REUEREND = 2

Fra. Good reuerend father, make my person yours,	1155
My reuerend father, let it not be so;	1180

REUIUE = 1

Hub. But with my breath I can reuiue it Boy.	1691

REUOLT = 7

And blessed shall he be that doth reuolt	1101
Elea. O foule reuolt of French inconstancy.	1255
Of all his people shall reuolt from him,	1550
And picke strong matter of reuolt, and wrath	1552
The faiths of men, nere stained with reuolt:	1723
Our discontented Counties doe reuolt:	2175
Should seeke a plaster by contemn'd reuolt,	2264

REUOLTING = 1

A mothers curse, on her reuolting sonne:	1188

REUOLTS = 2

And you degenerate, you ingrate Reuolts,	2405
Mel. Lead me to the Reuolts of England heere.	2467

RHEUME = 1*1

*Reade heere yong *Arthur.* How now foolish rheume?	1606
For villanie is not without such rheume,	2111

RHEWME = 1

Why holdes thine eie that lamentable rhewme,	943

RHYMES *see* rimes

RIBBES = 1

The flintie ribbes of this contemptuous Citie,	698

RIBD = 1

A bare-rib'd death, whose office is this day	2433

RIBS = 1

Set at libertie: the fat ribs of peace	1307

RICH = 9

When the rich blood of kings is set on fire:	665
Shall gild her bridall bed and make her rich	807

RICH *cont.*
And Earle of Richmond, and this rich faire Towne ` ` 873
Like a poore begger, raileth on the rich. ` ` 913
And say there is no sin but to be rich: ` ` 915
And being rich, my vertue then shall be, ` ` 916
To guard a Title, that was rich before; ` ` 1727
The rich aduantage of good exercise, ` ` 1777
Into the purse of rich prosperity ` ` 2312
RICHARD = 9*1
And findes them perfect *Richard*: sirra speake, ` ` 98
Arise Sir *Richard*, and *Plantagenet*. ` ` 171
I am thy grandame *Richard*, call me so. ` ` 177
Come Madam, and come *Richard*, we must speed ` ` 187
Good den Sir *Richard*, Godamercy fellow, ` ` 195
Lady. King Richard Cordelion was thy father, ` ` 266
And they shall say, when *Richard* me begot, ` ` 287
Richard that rob'd the Lion of his heart, ` ` 296
*Sal. Sir *Richard*, what thinke you? you haue beheld, ` ` 2040
This newes was brought to *Richard* but euen now, ` ` 2452
RICHARDS = 1
Nor keepe his Princely heart from *Richards* hand: ` ` 280
RICHER = 1
Whose veines bound richer blood then Lady *Blanch*? ` ` 746
RICHMOND = 1
And Earle of Richmond, and this rich faire Towne ` ` 873
RIDICULOUS = 2
So slight, vnworthy, and ridiculous ` ` 1077
Is wastefull, and ridiculous excesse. ` ` 1733
RIDING = 2
And if my legs were two such riding rods, ` ` 148
But who comes in such haste in riding robes? ` ` 227
RIGHT = 31*3
Chat. Philip of *France*, in right and true behalfe ` ` 12
Thy Nephew, and right royall Soueraigne. ` ` 20
Vpon the right and party of her sonne. ` ` 40
K.Iohn. Our strong possession, and our right for vs. ` ` 45
Eli. Your strong possessio(n) much more then your right, ` ` 46
Something about a little from the right, ` ` 179
Shadowing their right vnder your wings of warre: ` ` 307
Lewis. A noble boy, who would not doe thee right? ` ` 311
Till *Angiers*, and the right thou hast in *France*, ` ` 315
That right in peace which heere we vrge in warre, ` ` 340
And this his sonne, *England* was *Geffreys* right, ` ` 402
To looke into the blots and staines of right, ` ` 411
Ile smoake your skin-coat and I catch you right, ` ` 439
In right of *Arthur* doe I claime of thee: ` ` 453
Loe in this right hand, whose protection ` ` 542
Is most diuinely vow'd vpon the right ` ` 543
For him, and in his right, we hold this Towne. ` ` 574
Cit. Till you compound whose right is worthiest, ` ` 588
We for the worthiest hold the right from both. ` ` 589
*Command the rest to stand, God and our right. *Exeunt* ` ` 607
Say, shall the currant of our right rome on, ` ` 649
Fra. Know him in vs, that heere hold vp his right. ` ` 678
This widdow Lady? In her right we came, ` ` 868
There is no tongue hath power to curse him right. ` ` 1111
Cons. And for mine too, when Law can do no right. ` ` 1113

ROSE = 2
    That in mine eare I durst not sticke a rose,   150
    And with the halfe-blowne Rose. But Fortune, oh,   975
ROTTEN = 1
    Bast. Heeres a stay, | That shakes the rotten carkasse of old death   771
ROTTENNESSE = 1
    Thou odoriferous stench: sound rottennesse,   1409
ROUGH = 2
    The grapling vigor, and rough frowne of Warre | Is cold in amitie, and
    painted peace,   1029
    Art. Alas, what neede you be so boistrous rough?   1652
ROUNDED = 1
    As Gods owne souldier, rounded in the eare,   887
ROUNDER = 1
    'Tis not the rounder of your old-fac'd walles,   565
ROWZE = 1
    And rowze from sleepe that fell Anatomy   1424
ROY = 1
    Viue le Roy, as I haue bank'd their Townes?   2357
ROYAL = 1
    Wee'll lay before this towne our Royal bones,   334
ROYALL = 8
    Thy Nephew, and right royall Soueraigne.   20
    Or adde a royall number to the dead: 661
    Why stand these royall fronts amazed thus: 670
    Your Royall presences be rul'd by mee,   691
    This royall hand and mine are newly knit,   1157
    Betweene our kingdomes and our royall selues,   1163
    To clap this royall bargaine vp of peace,   1166
    Pem. But that your Royall pleasure must be done,   1734
ROYALTIE = 2
    From forth this morcell of dead Royaltie?   2148
    For thus his Royaltie doth speake in me: 2383
ROYALTIES = 1
    Call not me slanderer, thou and thine vsurpe | The Dominations,
    Royalties, and rights   477
ROYALTY = 3
    And that high Royalty was nere pluck'd off: 1722
    To stranger-bloud, to forren Royalty;   2178
    And then all this thou seest, is but a clod, | And module of confounded
    royalty.   2667
RUB = 1
    Shall blow each dust, each straw, each little rub   1513
RUDE = 6*1
    Eli. Out on thee rude man, y dost shame thy mother,   72
    Were harbour'd in their rude circumference: 568
    To whom he sung in rude harsh sounding rimes,   1871
    And consequently, thy rude hand to acte   1965
    Which howsoeuer rude exteriorly,   1982
    Vnthred the rude eye of Rebellion,   2472
    Which he hath left so shapelesse, and so rude.   2633
RUE = 2*1
    Eng. France, y shalt rue this houre within this houre.   1256
    Is it as he will? well then, *France* shall rue.   1258
    And we shall shocke them: Naught shall make vs rue,   2728
RUFFIAN = 1
    Aust. Well ruffian, I must pocket vp these wrongs,   1128

RUINE = 1
Kneeling before this ruine of sweete life,   2064
RULD = 1
Your Royall presences be rul'd by mee,   691
RUMORS = 2
Three dayes before: but this from Rumors tongue   1842
Possest with rumors, full of idle dreames,   1866
RUMOUR = 1
From forth the noise and rumour of the Field;   2506
RUN = 4
Made to run euen, vpon euen ground;   897
I coniure thee but slowly: run more fast. *Exeunt.*   1994
And calmely run on in obedience   2517
Hen. Euen so must I run on, and euen so stop.   2677
RUNNE = 2
Fra. What can goe well, when we haue runne so ill?   1387
Oh let it not be said: forrage, and runne   2227
RUNNER = 1
Arthur that great fore-runner of thy bloud,   295
RUNNES = 1
Which else runnes tickling vp and downe the veines,   1343
RUSH = 3
For bloody power to rush vppon your peace.   527
Vpon the bosome of the ground, rush forth   1573
Will serue to strangle thee: A rush will be a beame   2133
RUST = 1
Nay, after that, consume away in rust,   1642
RYOT = 1
And make a ryot on the gentle brow | Of true sincerity? O holy Sir   1178
SACRAMENT = 1
May know wherefore we tooke the Sacrament,   2257
SACRED = 2
Can tast the free breath of a sacred King?   1075
With all religous strength of sacred vowes,   1160
SACRIFICES = 1
That heere come sacrifices for the field.   735
SAD = 9*1
Dol. She is sad and passionate at your highnes Tent.   864
Be these sad signes confirmers of thy words?   945
So strongly guarded: Cosen, looke not sad,   1300
To be more Prince, as may be: you are sad.   1583
Art. 'Mercie on me: | Me thinkes no body should be sad but I: 1585
Yong Gentlemen would be as sad as night   1588
But wherefore doe you droope? why looke you sad?   2212
Let not the world see feare and sad distrust   2214
Was borne to see so sad an houre as this,   2277
I did not thinke to be so sad to night   2541
SADLY = 1
Why dost thou looke so sadly on my sonne?   941
SADNESSE = 1
Will giue her sadnesse very little cure: 866
SAFE = 2
But hold himselfe safe in his prisonment.   1546
And keepe it safe for our remembrance: 2253
SAFER = 1
A fasting Tyger safer by the tooth,   1191

SAFETIE = 2
For he that steepes his safetie in true blood, 1532
It is our safetie, and we must embrace 2009
SAFETY = 7
To teach thee safety: thou art periur'd too, 1046
Her Highnesse is in safety, feare you not: 1294
For your faire safety: so I kisse your hand. 1314
Shall finde but bloodie safety, and vntrue. 1533
Your safety: for the which, my selfe and them 1767
Deliuer him to safety, and returne, 1879
To hug with swine, to seeke sweet safety out 2396
SAID = 5
Ele. What now my sonne, haue I not euer said 37
Oh let it not be said: forrage, and runne 2227
Or if he doe, let it at least be said 2244
No, no, on my soule it neuer shall be said. 2361
As this hath made me. Who was he that said 2542
SAIDE = 1
France. When I haue saide, make answer to vs both. 541
SAIE = *1
Iohn. What saie these yong-ones? What say you my | Neece? 839
SAIES = 4
No sir, saies question, I sweet sir at yours, 209
What *England* saies, say breefely gentle Lord, 346
He flatly saies, hee'll not lay downe his Armes. 2380
The youth saies well. Now heare our *English* King, 2382
SAILE = 3
A whole Armado of conuicted saile 1384
And like a shifted winde vnto a saile, 1740
And all the shrowds wherewith my life should saile, 2663
SAINT = 5
Bast. Saint *George* that swindg'd the Dragon, 595
For at Saint Maries Chappell presently, 858
Canonized and worship'd as a Saint, 1104
Sal. Lords, I will meet him at S.(aint) *Edmondsbury,* 2008
Vpon the Altar at S.(aint) *Edmondsbury,* 2479
SAIST = 1*1
Fra. What sai'st thou boy? looke in the Ladies face. 811
Iohn. Philip, what saist thou to the Cardinall? 1131
SAKE = 2
England we loue, and for that *Englands* sake, 388
For heauen sake *Hubert* let me not be bound: 1654
SAL = 32*4
SALE = 1
Who in that sale sels pardon from himselfe: 1094
SALISBURIE = 3
Besides I met Lord *Bigot,* and Lord *Salisburie* 1883
Lift vp thy brow (renowned *Salisburie*) 2305
Enter Prince Henry, Salisburie, and Bigot. 2604
SALISBURY see also Sal. = 6*2
Enter King Iohn, Queene Elinor, Pembroke, Essex, and Sa-| lisbury, with the Chattylion of France. 2
Enter Constance, Arthur, and Salisbury. 921
Enter Iohn, Pembroke, Salisbury, and other Lordes. 1717
Pem. Stay yet (Lord Salisbury) Ile go with thee, 1814
Enter Pembroke, Salisbury, & Bigot. 2007

SALISBURY cont.

*Enter (in Armes) Dolphin, Salisbury, Meloone, Pem-|broke, Bigot,
Souldiers.   2250
Cries out vpon the name of Salisbury.   2270
Enter Salisbury, Pembroke, and Bigot.   2459
SALSBURY = 2

Hub. Stand backe Lord Salsbury, stand backe I say   2081
Bast. Thou wer't better gaul the diuell Salsbury.   2097
SALT = 1

Iohn. The salt in them is hot.   2654
SALUTE = 2

Salute thee for her King, till then faire boy   323
When his faire Angels would salute my palme,   911
SAME = 9*2

And put the same into yong Arthurs hand,   19
K.Iohn. What art thou?| *Robert. The son and heire to that same
Faulconbridge.   63
When this same lusty gentleman was got: 116
Colbrand the Gyant, that same mighty man,   236
*Aust. What cracker is this same that deafes our eares   447
Our colours do returne in those same hands   630
With that same purpose-changer, that slye diuel,   888
And this same byas, this Commoditie,   902
If this same were a Church-yard where we stand,   1339
With this same very Iron, to burne them out.   1704
With that same weake winde, which enkindled it: 2340
SANDS = 2

Are wrack'd three nights ago on Goodwin sands.   2451
Are cast away, and sunke on Goodwin sands.   2539
SANS = *1

*Bast. Come, come: sans complement, What newes | abroad?   2571
SATISFIE = 1

Yet in some measure satisfie her so,   878
SAUAGE = 1

And tame the sauage spirit of wilde warre,   2327
SAUAGERY = 1

The wildest Sauagery, the vildest stroke   2047
SAUD = 1

Fra. England thou hast not sau'd one drop of blood   655
SAUE = 5

To saue vnscratch'd your Citties threatned cheekes: 531
Saue in aspect, hath all offence seal'd vp: 556
Saue what is opposite to Englands loue.   1185
Art. O saue me Hubert, saue me: my eyes are out   1649
SAUING = 1

Sauing in Dialogue of Complement,   211
SAUOURS = 1

Th'vncleanly sauours of a Slaughter-house,   2115
SAW = 3

I saw a Smith stand with his hammer (thus)   1918
They saw we had a purpose of defence.   2245
That neuer saw the giant-world enrag'd,   2308
SAWCIE = 1

As we will ours, against these sawcie walles,   718
SAWCINESSE = 1

This vn-heard sawcinesse and boyish Troopes,   2387

SAY = 35*4

King Iohn.	*Now say *Chatillion*, what would *France* with vs?	4
Who as you say, tooke paines to get this sonne,	129
Lest men should say, looke where three farthings goes,	151
Who liues and dares but say, thou didst not well	284
And they shall say, when *Richard* me begot,	287
Who sayes it was, he lyes, I say twas not.	*Exeunt.*	289
What *England* saies, say breefely gentle Lord,	346
Iohn. Bedlam haue done.	*Con.* I haue but this to say,	485
Say, shall the currant of our right rome on,	649
Fra. Let it be so: say, where will you assault?	722
If not compleat of, say he is not shee,	749
To speake vnto this Cittie: what say you?	799
Iohn. What saie these yong-ones? What say you my	Neece?	839
What you in wisedome still vouchsafe to say.	842
And say there is no sin but to be rich:	915
To say there is no vice, but beggerie:	917
It cannot be, thou do'st but say 'tis so.	927
Aus. Thou dar'st not say so villaine for thy life.	1058
Con. What should he say, but as the Cardinall?	1132
Fra. I am perplext, and know not what to say.	1152
Pan. What canst thou say, but wil perplex thee more?	1153
Giue me thy hand, I had a thing to say,	1324
To say what good respect I haue of thee.	1327
Iohn. Good friend, thou hast no cause to say so yet,	1329
I had a thing to say, but let it goe:	1332
Well, Ile not say what I intend for thee:	1373
And Father Cardinall, I haue heard you say	1461
If you say I, the King will not say no. *Exeunt.*	1568
Yong Lad come forth; I haue to say with you.	1578
Hub. Giue me the Iron I say, and binde him heere.	1651
Why then your feares, which (as they say) attend	1773
Of *Arthur*, whom they say is kill'd to night, on your	(suggestion.	1886
Hub. My Lord, they say fiue Moones were seene to	(night:	1906
Hub. Stand backe Lord Salsbury, stand backe I say	2081
Bast. Keepe the peace, I say.	2095
Say, that before Ascension day at noone,	2193
Pem. They say King *Iohn* sore sick, hath left the field.	2465
I say againe, if *Lewis* do win the day,	2491

SAYD = 1

If thou hadst sayd him nay, it had beene sinne;	288

SAYES = 4

O sir, sayes answer, at your best command,	207
Who sayes it was, he lyes, I say twas not.	*Exeunt.*	289
With these ill tydings: Now? What sayes the world	1853
And on that day at noone, whereon he sayes	1877

SAYING = 2

That giue you cause to proue my saying true.	949
Saying, what lacke you? and where lies your greefe?	1624

SCAENA *l.*1 291 997 1381 1569 2165 2438 = 7

SCALDED = 1

Bast. Oh, I am scalded with my violent motion	2659

SCAMBLE = 1

To tug and scamble, and to part by th'teeth	2151

SCAPE = 1

Should scape the true acquaintance of mine eare.	2570

SCATHE = 1
   To doe offence and scathe in Christendome: 369
SCATTERED = 2
   Whose sonnes lye scattered on the bleeding ground: 614
   Is scattered and dis-ioyn'd from fellowship.   1385
SCENA *l*.1716 2458 2523 2549 2603 = 5
SCENES = 1
   At your industrious Scenes and acts of death.   690
SCEPTER = 1
   A Scepter snatch'd with an vnruly hand,   1520
SCOENA *l*.1282 1995 2249 = 3
SCOLD = 2
   Que. Thou vnaduised scold, I can produce   494
   We grant thou canst out-scold vs: Far thee well,   2414
SCOPE = 2
   No scope of Nature, no distemper'd day,   1539
   And, as you answer, I doe know the scope   2376
SCORCHED = 1
   Within the scorched veines of one new burn'd: 1209
SCORNE = 1
   What meanes this scorne, thou most vntoward knaue?   256
SCORNES = 1
   Which scornes a moderne Inuocation.   1426
SCORNST = 1
   Sir *Roberts* sonne? why scorn'st thou at sir *Robert*?   239
SCRIBLED = 1
   I am a scribled forme drawne with a pen   2639
SCROULE = 1
   Gracing the scroule that tels of this warres losse,   662
SCROYLES = *1
   *Bast. By heauen, these scroyles of Angiers flout you | (kings,   687
SCRUPLE = 1
   Our former scruple in our strong barr'd gates: 684
SCRUPLES = *1
   *Hub. Vncleanly scruples feare not you: looke too't.   1577
SEA = 5
   The sea enragèd is not halfe so deafe,   766
   And all that we vpon this side the Sea,   804
   Keepe *Stephen Langton* chosen Archbishop | Of *Canterbury* from that
   holy Sea: 1070
   The great Metropolis and Sea of Rome: 2325
   To the sea side, and put his cause and quarrell   2701
SEALD = 1
   Saue in aspect, hath all offence seal'd vp: 556
SEALE = 3
   As seale to this indenture of my loue: 313
   Hub. Heere is your hand and Seale for what I did.   1940
   Is to be made, then shall this hand and Seale   1942
SEARCH = 1
   If zealous loue should go in search of vertue,   743
SEAS = 1*1
   But truth is truth, large lengths of seas and shores   113
   *That spits forth death, and mountaines, rockes, and seas,   774
SEA-MEN = 1
   But (on this day) let Sea-men feare no wracke,   1017

SECOND = 2
    Being but the second generation | Remoued from thy sinne-conceiuing
    wombe. 483
    Second a Villaine, and a Murtherer? | *Hub.* Lord *Bigot*, I am none. 2104
SECONDARY = 1
    To be a secondary at controll, 2333
SECRET = 1
    That takes away by any secret course | Thy hatefull life. 1105
SECUNDA *l.*291 1282 1716 2249 = 4
SECUNDUS *l.*920 = 1
SECURE = 2
    That Water-walled Bulwarke, still secure 320
    And, pretty childe, sleepe doubtlesse, and secure, 1710
SECURELY = 1
    And stand securely on their battelments, 688
SEDUCD = 1
    By long and vehement suit I was seduc'd 267
SEE *see also* sea = 21
    I see a yeelding in the lookes of France: 790
    If he see ought in you that makes him like, 828
    That all I see in you is worthie loue, 834
    Then this, that nothing do I see in you, 835
    Shall neuer see it, but a holy day. 1007
    Blan. Now shall I see thy loue, what motiue may 1246
    And ere our comming see thou shake the bags 1305
    Or if that thou couldst see me without eyes, 1347
    Con. Lo; now: now see the issue of your peace. 1404
    That we shall see and know our friends in heauen: 1462
    If that be true, I shall see my boy againe; 1463
    Me thinkes I see this hurley all on foot; 1554
    In vndeserued extreames: See else your selfe, 1687
    Hub. Well, see to liue: I will not touch thine eye, 1701
    Out of my sight, and neuer see me more: 1967
    Or do you almost thinke, although you see, 2042
    That you do see? Could thought, without this obiect 2043
    Let not the world see feare and sad distrust 2214
    Was borne to see so sad an houre as this, 2277
    For I do see the cruell pangs of death 2520
    And spleene of speede, to see your Maiesty. 2660
SEEKE = 10
    Is it Sir *Roberts* sonne that you seeke so? 237
    To seeke the beauteous eye of heauen to garnish, 1732
    To your proceedings? Do not seeke to stuffe 1854
    And others more, going to seeke the graue 1885
    Bring them before me. | *Bast.* I will seeke them out. 1891
    What, shall they seeke the Lion in his denne, 2225
    Should seeke a plaster by contemn'd reuolt, 2264
    To hug with swine, to seeke sweet safety out 2396
    Seeke out King *Iohn*, and fall before his feete: 2474
    Straight let vs seeke, or straight we shall be sought, 2689
SEEKING = 1
    Hub. Lords, I am hot with haste, in seeking you, 2074
SEEKST = *1
    Io. Why seek'st thou to possesse me with these feares? 1928
SEEME = 3
    Dolph. I muse your Maiesty doth seeme so cold, 1250
    Your vilde intent must needs seeme horrible. 1674

SEEME *cont.*
And he, long traded in it, makes it seeme   2112
SEEMES = 2
You came not of one mother then it seemes.   66
Sal. It seemes you know not then so much as we,   2691
SEENE = 3
That I haue seene inhabite in those cheekes?   1825
Hub. My Lord, they say fiue Moones were seene to | (night: 1906
Then had I seene the vaultie top of heauen   2303
SEES = 2
That any thing he see's which moues his liking,   829
Bast. He will the rather do it, when he sees   2697
SEEST = 1
And then all this thou seest, is but a clod, | And module of confounded
royalty.   2667
SEIGE = 1
Leaues them inuisible, and his seige is now   2622
SEIZD = 1
Iohn hath seiz'd *Arthur*, and it cannot be,   1516
SELFE = 38
Compare our faces, and be Iudge your selfe   87
And fits the mounting spirit like my selfe;   216
Lady. Hast thou denied thy selfe a *Faulconbridge*? | *Bast.* As faithfully
as I denie the deuill.   264
Iohn. England for it selfe: | You men of Angiers, and my louing
subiects.   508
The shadow of my selfe form'd in her eye,   814
I do protest I neuer lou'd my selfe   817
Till now, infixed I beheld my selfe,   818
The world, who of it selfe is peysed well,   896
Con. Which harme within it selfe so heynous is,   961
Yea, faith it selfe to hollow falshood change.   1020
Iohn. We like not this, thou dost forget thy selfe.   1060
Therefore since Law it selfe is perfect wrong,   1117
And tell me how you would bestow your selfe?   1156
What since thou sworst, is sworne against thy selfe,   1199
And may not be performed by thy selfe,   1200
Is in thy selfe rebellion to thy selfe: 1220
Looke to thy selfe, thou art in ieopardie.   1279
And be a Carrion Monster like thy selfe;   1416
For then 'tis like I should forget my selfe: 1433
And teaches mee to kill or hang my selfe: 1440
The Iron of it selfe, though heate red hot,   1638
Hub. Come (Boy) prepare your selfe.   1667
In vndeserued extreames: See else your selfe,   1687
Both for my selfe, and them: but chiefe of all   1766
Your safety: for the which, my selfe and them   1767
Iohn. Gentle kinsman, go | And thrust thy selfe into their Companies,   1887
I would not haue you (Lord) forget your selfe,   2083
To hang thee on. Or wouldst thou drowne thy selfe,   2134
And heauen it selfe doth frowne vpon the Land. *Exit.*   2164
Would beare thee from the knowledge of thy selfe,   2286
Betweene this chastiz'd kingdome and my selfe,   2337
My selfe, well mounted, hardly haue escap'd.   2600
With whom your selfe, my selfe, and other Lords,   2703
And happily may your sweet selfe put on   2712
But when it first did helpe to wound it selfe.   2725

SELFE *cont.*
    If England to it selfe, do rest but true. *Exeunt.*   2729
SELL = 1
    Yet sell your face for fiue pence and 'tis deere: 161
SELS = 1
    Who in that sale sels pardon from himselfe: 1094
SELUES = 4
    Make worke vpon our selues, for heauen or hell.   721
    Betweene our kingdomes and our royall selues,   1163
    Make such vnconstant children of our selues   1174
    Our selues well sinew'd to our defence.   2698
SEMBLANCE = 1
    This Ship-boyes semblance hath disguis'd me quite.   2000
SENCE = 1
    Teach vs some sence. Sirrah, were I at home   597
SEND = 5
    When I was got, Ile send his soule to hell.   285
    Iohn. We from the West will send destruction | Into this Cities bosome.   723
    Ile send those powers o're to your Maiesty.   1375
    Send fayre-play-orders, and make comprimise, | Insinuation, parley, and
    base truce   2236
    And send him word by me, which way you go.   2447
SENSE = 1
    Any annoyance in that precious sense: 1672
SENSIBLE = 1
    For, being not mad, but sensible of greefe,   1437
SENT = 3
    Arthur doth liue, the king hath sent for you.   2075
    What men prouided? What munition sent   2351
    Let me haue audience: I am sent to speake: 2373
SEPTIMA *l.*2603 = 1
SEQUENCE = 1
    Cut off the sequence of posterity,   393
SERPENT = 2
    France, thou maist hold a serpent by the tongue,   1189
    He is a very serpent in my way,   1361
SERUANT = 1
    As it on earth hath bene thy seruant still.   2683
SERUE = 1
    Will serue to strangle thee: A rush will be a beame   2133
SERUICE = 4
    At your employment, at your seruice sir: 208
    But you, at your sicke seruice had a Prince: 1628
    Vpon your oath of seruice to the Pope,   2190
    Your Nobles will not heare you, but are gone | To offer seruice to your
    enemy: 2201
SERUICES = 1
    I do bequeath my faithfull seruices | And true subiection euerlastingly.   2715
SERUING-MAN = 1
    Or vsefull seruing-man, and Instrument   2334
SET = 20*1
    I would set an Oxe-head to your Lyons hide: | And make a monster of
    you.   599
    Iohn. Vp higher to the plaine, where we'l set forth   603
    From first to last, the on-set and retyre: 637
    When the rich blood of kings is set on fire: 665
    That it in golden letters should be set   1010

SET *cont.*

Weare out the daies in Peace; but ere Sun-set,	1035
Set armed discord 'twixt these periur'd Kings,	1036
So tell the Pope, all reuerence ˙set apart⌐ To him and his vsurp'd authoritie.	1086
Set at libertie: the fat ribs of peace	1307
As patches set vpon a little breach,	1749
Like Heralds 'twixt two dreadfull battailes set:	1796
There is no sure foundation set on blood:	1822
Be Mercurie, set feathers to thy heeles,	1896
Sal. Or rather then set forward, for 'twill be	2016
Till I haue set a glory to this hand,	2070
And on our actions set the name of right ǀ With holy breath.	2319
And shall I now giue ore the yeelded Set?	2360
Set on toward *Swinsted*: to my Litter straight,	2456
Dol. The Sun of heauen (me thought) was loth to set;	2525
To set a forme vpon that indigest	2632
Iohn. Oh Cozen, thou art come to set mine eye:	2661

SETST = 1

And like a ciuill warre setst oath to oath,	1195

SETTER = *1

Bast. Old Time the clocke setter, y bald sexton Time:	1257

SEUERALL = 2

Which swaies vsurpingly these seuerall titles,	18
Enter the two Kings with their powers, ǀ at seuerall doores.	646

SEUERALLY = 1

Enter Bastard and Hubert, seuerally.	2550

SEXTA *l.*2549 = 1

SEXTON = *1

Bast. Old Time the clocke setter, y bald sexton Time:	1257

SEYSURE = 1

Vnyoke this seysure, and this kinde regreete?	1172

SH = 1

Sh'adulterates hourely with thine Vnckle *Iohn,*	977

SHADOW = 3

The shadow of my selfe form'd in her eye,	814
Which being but the shadow of your sonne,	815
Becomes a sonne and makes your sonne a shadow:	816

SHADOWING = 1

Shadowing their right vnder your wings of warre:	307

SHAKE = 5

So heauy, as thou shalt not shake them off	1227
And ere our comming see thou shake the bags	1305
Then with a passion would I shake the world,	1423
And when they talke of him, they shake their heads,	1913
In vaults and prisons, and to thrill and shake,	2397

SHAKES = 1

Bast. Heeres a stay, ǀ That shakes the rotten carkasse of old death	771

SHAKING = 2

To make a shaking feuer in your walles,	534
What dost thou meane by shaking of thy head?	940

SHAL *l.*138 = 1

SHALL *l.*31 49 53 55 205 226 287 305 326 *330 341 400 419 446 449 472 473 557 569 571 592 606 649 651 705 707 712 714 727 732 759 761 764 788 802 807 876 879 916 *924 1001 1007 1021 1081 1101 1103 1170 1182 1235 1236 1246 1258 1268 *1277 1278 1299 *1310 1331 1366 1370 1378 1386 1462 1463 1472 1473 1513 1514 1526 1533 1534 1536 1547 1550

SHALL *cont.*
1574 1633 1760 1762 1863 1878 *1898 1900 1942 2052 2096 2102 2136
2187 2218 2225 2235 2238 2259 2313 *2331 2360 2361 2400 2423 2426
2427 2497 2519 2547 2670 2682 2689 2708 2711 2723 2728 = 107*6
SHALLBE = 1
   The rights of marriage shallbe solemniz'd.   859
SHALT *l.*786 932 *989 1100 1227 *1253 *1256 *1277 1330 1436 2127 2311
   *2436 = 8*5
SHAME = 16*2
   Eli. Out on thee rude man, y dost shame thy mother,   72
   Where how he did preuaile, I shame to speake: 112
   Con. Now shame vpon you where she does or no,   469
   This day of shame, oppression, periury.   1013
   O *Lymoges*, O *Austria*, thou dost shame   1040
   Thou weare a Lyons hide, doff it for shame,   1054
   So we could finde some patterne of our shame: 1398
   And bitter shame hath spoyl'd the sweet words taste,   1495
   That it yeelds nought but shame and bitternesse.   1496
   And glow with shame of your proceedings, *Hubert*:   1693
   Sal. It is apparant foule-play, and 'tis shame   1811
   Quoted, and sign'd to do a deede of shame,   1947
   *Deepe shame had struck me dumbe, made me break off,   1960
   Of murthers Armes: This is the bloodiest shame,   2046
   Or teach thy hastie spleene to do me shame,   2099
   Of your deere Mother-England: blush for shame: 2407
   Haue done me shame: Braue Soldier, pardon me,   2568
   To push destruction, and perpetuall shame   2687
SHAMEFULL = 1
   It is the shamefull worke of *Huberts* hand,   2061
SHAMES = 1*1
   Qu.Mo. His mother shames him so, poore boy hee | (weepes.   468
   His grandames wrongs, and not his mothers shames   470
SHAPE = 2
   Bast. Madam, and if my brother had my shape   146
   And to his shape were heyre to all this land,   152
SHAPELESSE = 1
   Which he hath left so shapelesse, and so rude.   2633
SHARPE = 1
   By heauen, I thinke my sword's as sharpe as yours.   2082
SHARPEST = 1
   Your sharpest Deeds of malice on this Towne.   694
SHE *see also* sh' = 15*1
SHEATH = 1
   Sal. Not till I sheath it in a murtherers skin.   2080
SHEDDE = 1
   That hot rash haste so indirectly shedde.   342
SHEE *l.*749 753 1505 = 3
SHEEPE = 1
   So I were out of prison, and kept Sheepe   1590
SHEERES = 2
   Thinke you I beare the Sheeres of destiny?   1809
   Who with his Sheeres, and Measure in his hand,   1921
SHERIFFE = 1
   Enter a Sheriffe.   50
SHEW = 7*1
   Come Lady I will shew thee to my kinne,   286
   And I shall shew you peace, and faire-fac'd league: 732

SHEW *cont.*

On their departure, most of all shew euill:	1500
Do shew the mood of a much troubled brest,	1791
Shew boldnesse and aspiring confidence:	2224
Dolph. A noble temper dost thou shew in this,	2291
Bast. Shew me the very wound of this ill newes,	2578
*Where be your powres? Shew now your mended faiths,	2685

SHEWD = 1

He shew'd his warrant to a friend of mine,	1788

SHEWE = 1

And be no further harmefull then in shewe.	2330

SHIFTED = 1

And like a shifted winde vnto a saile,	1740

SHIFTS = 1

Ile finde a thousand shifts to get away;	2003

SHIP-BOYES = 1

This Ship-bóyes semblance hath disguis'd me quite.	2000

SHOCKE = 1

And we shall shocke them: Naught shall make vs rue,	2728

SHOLD *l.**2626 = *1

SHOOES = 1

As great *Alcides* shooes vpon an Asse:	444

SHOOKE = *1

Hub. My Lord. | **Ioh.* Had'st thou but shooke thy head, or made a pause	1955

SHOOT = 1

Austria and France shoot in each others mouth.	729

SHOOTE = 2

They shoote but calme words, folded vp in smoake,	535
*Hub. Whose there? Speake hoa, speake quickely, or | I shoote.	2551

SHORE = 2

Together with that pale, that white-fac'd shore,	316
And cripple thee vnto a Pagan shore,	2287

SHORES = 3

But truth is truth, large lengths of seas and shores	113
With course disturb'd euen thy confining shores,	652
And two such shores, to two such streames made one,	758

SHOT = 2

Neere or farre off, well wonne is still well shot,	183
When with a volley of our needlesse shot,	2529

SHOULD *l.*151 390 741 742 743 744 *825 *836 838 970 1010 *1056 1132 1216 1433 1434 1441 1518 1586 1591 1645 1646 1697 1774 1787 1812 1832 1873 2194 2195 2264 2338 2384 2487 2489 2570 2663 = 34*3

SHOULDER = 1

What, I am dub'd, I haue it on my shoulder:	258

SHOULDERS = 1

Or lay on that shall make your shoulders cracke.	446

SHOULDST *l.**255 = *1

SHOUT = 1

Haue I not heard these Islanders shout out	2356

SHOW *see* shew, shewe

SHOWD *see* shew'd

SHOWRE = 1

This showre, blowne vp by tempest of the soule,	2301

SHREWD = 1

Dol. Ah fowle, shrew'd newes. Beshrew thy very | (hart:	2540

SHRINKE = 1
Vpon a Parchment, and against this fire | Do I shrinke vp.   2640
SHROWDS = 1
And all the shrowds wherewith my life should saile,   2663
SICK = *1
*Pem. They say King *Iohn* sore sick, hath left the field.   2465
SICKE = 8
For I am sicke, and capeable of feares,   933
Ar. Are you sicke Hubert? you looke pale to day,   1601
Insooth I would you were a little sicke,   1602
But you, at your sicke seruice had a Prince: 1628
Makes sound opinion sicke, and truth suspected,   1743
Before the childe himselfe felt he was sicke: 1806
Then pause not: for the present time's so sicke,   2181
Lyes heauie on me: oh, my heart is sicke.   2443
SICKE-FALNE = 1
As doth a Rauen on a sicke-falne beast,   2158
SICKNESSE = 2
Sal. Indeed we fear'd his sicknesse was past cure.   1804
Hen. Oh vanity of sicknesse: fierce extreames   2619
SIDE = 12*1
Bast. Brother by th'mothers side, giue me your hand,   172
Out of one side her happy Minion,   706
And all that we vpon this side the Sea,   804
Thou euer strong vpon the stronger side;   1043
Hast thou not spoke like thunder on my side?   1050
Which is the side that I must goe withall?   1260
Who-euer wins, on that side shall I lose: 1268
To traine ten thousand English to their side;   1560
That I must draw this mettle from my side   2267
Pand. You looke but on the out-side of this worke.   2362
Dol. Out-side or in-side, I will not returne   2363
To the sea side, and put his cause and quarrell   2701
SIDES = 1
Sal. Vpon our sides it neuer shall be broken.   2259
SIEDGE = 1
All preparation for a bloody siedge   519
SIEGE = 1
Chat. Then turne your forces from this paltry siege,   348
SIGHT = 4
But on the sight of vs your lawfull King,   528
Fellow be gone: I cannot brooke thy sight,   957
How oft the sight of meanes to do ill deeds,   1944
Out of my sight, and neuer see me more: 1967
SIGHTLESSE = 1
Full of vnpleasing blots, and sightlesse staines,   966
SIGHTLY = 1
Bast. It lies as sightly on the backe of him   443
SIGNALL = 1
Or shall we giue the signall to our rage,   571
SIGND = 1
Quoted, and sign'd to do a deede of shame,   1947
SIGNES = 4
Be these sad signes confirmers of thy words?   945
And call them Meteors, prodigies, and signes,   1542
But, thou didst vnderstand me by my signes,   1962
And didst in signes againe parley with sinne,   1963

SILENCE = 2
    K.Iohn. Silence (good mother) heare the Embassie.   11
    Hub. Silence, no more; go closely in with mee,   1714
SILKEN = 1
    A cockred-silken wanton braue our fields,   2239
SILUER = 5
    Their Armours that march'd hence so siluer bright,   626
    Vnlesse thou let his siluer Water, keepe | A peacefull progresse to the
    Ocean.   653
    O two such siluer currents when they ioyne   756
    When gold and siluer becks me to come on.   1311
    Where but by chance a siluer drop hath falne,   1447
SILUERLY = 1
    That siluerly doth progresse on thy cheekes: 2297
SIN = 2
    That he is not onely plagued for her sin,   487
    And say there is no sin but to be rich: 915
SINCE = 12*1
    *And ere since sit's on's horsebacke at mine Hostesse dore   596
    Since I first cal'd my brothers father Dad.   783
    Since Kings breake faith vpon commoditie,   918
    Therefore since Law it selfe is perfect wrong,   1117
    What since thou sworst, is sworne against thy selfe,   1199
    For since the birth of *Caine*, the first male-childe   1464
    Since all, and euery part of what we would   1755
    Big. Who kill'd this Prince? | *Hub.* 'Tis not an houre since I left him
    well: 2106
    But since you are a gentle conuertite,   2186
    Since I must loose the vse of all deceite?   2488
    Why should I then be false, since it is true   2489
    Who halfe an houre since came from the Dolphin,   2693
    Since it hath beene before hand with our greefes.   2722
SINCERITY = 1
    And make a ryot on the gentle brow | Of true sincerity? O holy Sir   1178
SINEWD = 1
    Our selues well sinew'd to our defence.   2698
SINEWES = 1
    That knit your sinewes to the strength of mine.   2314
SING = *1
    *Counfound themselues. 'Tis strange y death shold sing: 2626
SINGS = 1
    And from the organ-pipe of frailety sings   2629
SINNE = 8*1
    If thou hadst sayd him nay, it had beene sinne;   288
    But God hath made her sinne and her, the plague   488
    And with her plague her sinne: his iniury   490
    Her iniurie the Beadle to her sinne,   491
    Iohn. Then God forgiue the sinne of all those soules,   590
    And didst in signes againe parley with sinne,   1963
    To the yet vnbegotten sinne of times;   2053
    For I am stifled with this smell of sinne.   2116
    Hub. If I in act, consent, or sinne of thought,   2139
SINNES = 2
    Some sinnes doe beare their priuiledge on earth,   274
    Thy sinnes are visited in this poore childe,   481

SINNE-CONCEIUING = 1
Being but the second generation | Remoued from thy sinne-conceiuing
wombe.   483
SIR *l*.88 90 105 140 147 155 167 171 175 195 203 207 208 209 235 237 238
239 240 246 247 249 250 253 259 260 435 1179 1547 2031 *2040 2079
2122 2576 = 36*1
SIRRA = 3
And findes them perfect *Richard*: sirra speake,   98
K.Iohn. Sirra, your brother is Legittimate,   124
Sirra looke too't, yfaith I will, yfaith.   440
SIRRAH = 2
Teach vs some sence. Sirrah, were I at home   597
At your den sirrah, with your Lionnesse,   598
SIT = 3*1
Can hold it vp: here I and sorrowes sit,   995
That I might sit all night, and watch with you.   1603
And I will sit as quiet as a Lambe.   1656
Iohn. Heere once againe we sit: once against crown'd   1718
SITS = 1*1
*And ere since sit's on's horsebacke at mine Hostesse dore   596
Is warlike *Iohn*: and in his fore-head sits   2432
SKIE = 3
Some ayery Deuill houers in the skie,   1286
No naturall exhalation in the skie,   1538
So foule a skie, cleeres not without a storme,   1826
SKILL = 1
They do confound their skill in couetousnesse,   1746
SKIN = 4*3
And hang a Calues skin on those recreant limbes.   1055
Phil. And hang a Calues-skin on those recreant limbs   1057
Phil. And hang a Calues-skin on those recreant limbs.   1059
Bast. And hang a Calues-skin on his recreant limbs.   1127
Bast. Hang nothing but a Calues skin most sweet lout.   1151
Bast. Wil't not be?| Will not a Calues-skin stop that mouth of thine?   1230
Sal. Not till I sheath it in a murtherers skin.   2080
SKINS = 1
My armes, such eele skins stuft, my face so thin,   149
SKIN-COAT = 1
Ile smoake your skin-coat and I catch you right,   439
SKY = 1
Iohn. Now by the sky that hangs aboue our heads,   711
SLAINE = 1*1
Arthur tane prisoner? diuers deere friends slaine?   1389
Mes. The Count *Meloone* is slaine: The English Lords   2536
SLANDERD = 2
But once he slanderd me with bastardy: 82
And you haue slander'd Nature in my forme,   1981
SLANDERER = 2
Qu. Thou monstrous slanderer of heauen and earth.   475
Call not me slanderer, thou and thine vsurpe | The Dominations,
Royalties, and rights   477
SLANDROUS = 1
Vgly, and slandrous to thy Mothers wombe,   965
SLAUE = 2*2
Lady. Where is that slaue thy brother? where is he?   233
*That bloudy spoyle: thou slaue, thou wretch, y coward,   1041
Vpon my partie: thou cold blooded slaue,   1049

SLAUE *cont.*

Am I *Romes* slaue? What penny hath *Rome* borne?   2350
SLAUES = 1
By slaues, that take their humors for a warrant,   1934
SLAUGHTER = 2
Dide in the dying slaughter of their foes,   634
With slaughter coupled to the name of kings.   663
SLAUGHTERED = 1
What, shall our feast be kept with slaughtered men?   1235
SLAUGHTERS = 1
With slaughters pencill; where reuenge did paint   1168
SLAUGHTER-HOUSE = 1
Th'vncleanly sauours of a Slaughter-house,   2115
SLEEPE = 2
And rowze from sleepe that fell Anatomy   1424
And, pretty childe, sleepe doubtlesse, and secure,   1710
SLEEPING = 1
And but for our approch, those sleeping stones,   522
SLEPT = 1
Where hath it slept? Where is my Mothers care?   1835
SLIGHT = 1
So slight, vnworthy, and ridiculous   1077
SLIPPERS = 1
Standing on slippers, which his nimble haste   1922
SLIPPRY = 1
And he that stands vpon a slipp'ry place,   1522
SLOW = 1
But thou shalt haue: and creepe time nere so slow,   1330
SLOWLY = 1
I coniure thee but slowly: run more fast. *Exeunt.*   1994
SLYE = 1
With that same purpose-changer, that slye diuel,   888
SMACKE = 1
And so am I whether I smacke or no: 219
SMACKES = 1
Smackes it not something of the policie.   710
SMALL = 2
That none so small aduantage shall step forth   1536
Then feeling what small things are boysterous there,   1673
SMALLEST = 1
And if thou want'st a Cord, the smallest thred   2131
SMELL = 1
For I am stifled with this smell of sinne.   2116
SMILE = 1
The King doth smile at, and is well prepar'd   2388
SMILING = 1
Of smiling peace to march a bloody hoast,   1177
SMILST = 1
Come, grin on me, and I will thinke thou smil'st,   1417
SMITH = 1
I saw a Smith stand with his hammer (thus)   1918
SMOAKE = 3*1
That doth not smoake of obseruation,   218
Ile smoake your skin-coat and I catch you right,   439
They shoote but calme words, folded vp in smoake,   535
*He speakes plaine Cannon fire, and smoake, and bounce,   778

SMOAKES = 1
Already smoakes about the burning Crest   2495
SMOOTH = 1
To smooth the yce, or adde another hew   1730
SMOOTH-FACD = 1
That smooth-fac'd Gentleman, tickling commoditie,   894
SNARLETH = 1
And snarleth in the gentle eyes of peace: 2155
SNATCH = 2
As now againe to snatch our palme from palme: 1175
Snatch at his Master that doth tarre him on.   1696
SNATCHD = 1
A Scepter snatch'd with an vnruly hand,   1520
SNOW = 1
Or, as a little snow, tumbled about,   1561
SO *l*.23 25 28 32 48 149 166 177 210 214 219 231 237 240 271 275 342 375
   391 427 *468 606 626 644 722 766 769 782 786 826 855 878 925 927 941
   952 961 993 1058 1069 1077 1083 1086 1090 1095 1150 1170 1171 1173
   1180 1194 1227 1250 1299 1300 1314 1329 1330 1355 1365 1383 1387
   1393 1394 1398 1428 1456 1471 1507 1525 1534 1536 1582 1590 1592
   1597 1611 1634 1652 1680 1744 1751 1785 1793 1797 1812 1813 1826
   1874 1875 1929 2025 2051 2091 2092 2101 2124 2126 2181 2194 2211
   2218 2229 2277 2290 2313 2324 2364 2423 2442 *2460 2538 2541 2547
   2562 2565 2633 2637 2650 2651 2677 2680 2691 2706 2710 = 130*2
SOCIABLE = 2
'Tis two respectiue, and too sociable   198
Doe glew themselues in sociable griefe,   1449
SOCIETY = 1
But this is worshipfull society,   215
SODAINE = 2
Therefore I will be sodaine, and dispatch.   1600
The better arme you to the sodaine time,   2583
SODAINLY = 1
Whose Bowels sodainly burst out: The King   2587
SOFT = 2
Of soft petitions, pittie and remorse,   794
Presented to the teares of soft remorse.   2049
SOIOURND = 1
And in the meane time soiourn'd at my fathers;   111
SOLD = 2
Haue sold their fortunes at their natiue homes,   363
Mel. Fly Noble English, you are bought and sold,   2471
SOLDIER = 1
Haue done me shame: Braue Soldier, pardon me,   2568
SOLE = 1
And this so sole, and so vnmatcheable,   2051
SOLEMNE = *1
Ioh. Why do you bend such solemne browes on me?   1808
SOLEMNITY = 1
To our solemnity: I trust we shall,   876
SOLEMNIZD = 1
The rights of marriage shallbe solemniz'd.   859
SOLEMNIZE = 1
To solemnize this day the glorious sunne   1002
SOME = 19*1
Doe you not read some tokens of my sonne   95
Some proper man I hope, who was it mother?   263

SOME *cont.*

Some sinnes doe beare their priuiledge on earth,	274
Some Trumpet summon hither to the walles	501
Fran. As many and as well-borne bloods as those. | *Bast.* Some Bastards too.	585
Teach vs some sence. Sirrah, were I at home	597
Be by some certaine king, purg'd and depos'd.	686
Some speedy Messenger bid her repaire	875
Yet in some measure satisfie her so,	878
Some gentle order, and then we shall be blest	1182
Some ayery Deuill houers in the skie,	1286
But I will fit it with some better tune.	1325
So we could finde some patterne of our shame:	1398
Preach some Philosophy to make me mad,	1435
*Fra. I feare some out-rage, and Ile follow her. *Exit.*	1491
Ioh. Some reasons of this double Corronation	1757
Some Messenger betwixt me, and the Peeres,	1901
By some damn'd hand was rob'd, and tane away.	2209
(Which some suppose the soules fraile dwelling house)	2607
Hen. Oh that there were some vertue in my teares, | That might releeue you.	2652

SOMETHING = 2

Something about a little from the right,	179
Smackes it not something of the policie.	710

SON = *2

K.Iohn. What art thou? | **Robert.* The son and heire to that same *Faulconbridge.*	63
*Old Qu. Son, list to this coniunction, make this match	784

SONNE = 41

Of thy deceased brother, *Geffreyes* sonne,	13
Ele. What now my sonne, haue I not euer said	37
Vpon the right and party of her sonne.	40
Borne in *Northamptonshire*, and eldest sonne | As I suppose, to *Robert Faulconbridge,*	59
And were our father, and this sonne like him:	89
Doe you not read some tokens of my sonne	95
That this my mothers sonne was none of his;	119
Who as you say, tooke paines to get this sonne,	129
Had of your father claim'd this sonne for his,	130
My mothers sonne did get your fathers heyre,	136
Or the reputed sonne of *Cordelion,*	144
Philip, good old Sir *Roberts* wiues eldest sonne.	167
Bast. My brother *Robert*, old Sir *Roberts* sonne:	235
Is it Sir *Roberts* sonne that you seeke so?	237
Lady. Sir *Roberts* sonne, I thou vnreuerend boy,	238
Sir *Roberts* sonne? why scorn'st thou at sir *Robert*?	239
He is Sir *Roberts* sonne, and so art thou.	240
Madam, I was not old Sir *Roberts* sonne,	246
But mother, I am not Sir *Roberts* sonne,	259
And this his sonne, *England* was *Geffreys* right,	402
Const. Let me make answer: thy vsurping sonne.	418
Con. My bed was euer to thy sonne as true	421
Of this oppressed boy; this is thy eldest sonnes sonne,	479
A Will, that barres the title of thy sonne.	495
Sonne to the elder brother of this man,	545
Iohn. If that the Dolphin there thy Princely sonne,	800
Which being but the shadow of your sonne,	815

SOULDIERS *cont.*
  *Enter (in Armes) Dolphin, Salisbury, Meloone, Pem-|broke, Bigot,
  Souldiers. 2250
SOULE = 19*1
  When I was got, Ile send his soule to hell. 285
  My boy a bastard? by my soule I thinke | His father neuer was so true
  begot, 426
  And by disioyning hands hell lose a soule. 1125
  There is a soule counts thee her Creditor, 1320
  Looke who comes heere? a graue vnto a soule, 1400
  Ile make a peace betweene your soule, and you. 1975
  *Heauen take my soule, and England keep my bones. *Dies* 2006
  From whose obedience I forbid my soule, 2063
  Hub. Vpon my soule. 2128
  Swearing Allegiance, and the loue of soule 2177
  Bast. So on my soule he did, for ought he knew: 2211
  By making many: Oh it grieues my soule, 2266
  This showre, blowne vp by tempest of the soule, 2301
  No, no, on my soule it neuer shall be said. 2361
  In peace: and part this bodie and my soule 2508
  Sal. We do beleeue thee, and beshrew my soule, 2510
  His soule and body to their lasting rest. 2630
  Iohn. I marrie, now my soule hath elbow roome, 2635
  And then my soule shall waite on thee to heauen, 2682
  Hen. I haue a kinde soule, that would giue thankes, 2719
SOULES = 5*2
  *Iohn. Then God forgiue the sinne of all those soules, 590
  Marke how they whisper, vrge them while their soules | Are capeable of
  this ambition, 791
  And the coniunction of our inward soules 1158
  Now that their soules are topfull of offence, 1565
  * Pem. Big. Our soules religiously confirme thy words. 2072
  Away with me, all you whose soules abhorre 2114
  (Which some suppose the soules fraile dwelling house) 2607
SOULE-FEARING = 1
  Till their soule-fearing clamours haue braul'd downe 697
SOUND = 7
  The latest breath that gaue the sound of words 1161
  Sound on into the drowzie race of night: 1338
  Without eyes, eares, and harmefull sound of words: 1350
  Thou odoriferous stench: sound rottennesse, 1409
  Makes sound opinion sicke, and truth suspected, 1743
  To sound the purposes of all their hearts, 1765
  Sound but another, and another shall 2427
SOUNDING = 1
  To whom he sung in rude harsh sounding rimes, 1871
SOUNDS = 1
  Trumpet sounds. | Enter a Citizen vpon the walles. 504
SOUTH = 2
  Fran. Our Thunder from the South, | Shall raine their drift of bullets on
  this Towne. 726
  Bast. O prudent discipline! From North to South: 728
SOWSSE = 1
  To sowsse annoyance that comes neere his Nest; 2404
SOYLE = 1
  And flesh his spirit in a warre-like soyle, 2240

SPAINE = 1*1
With her her Neece, the Lady *Blanch of Spaine*, 358
Hub. That daughter there of Spaine, the Lady *Blanch* 738
SPAKE = 2
When I spake darkely, what I purposed: 1957
And euen there, methinkes an Angell spake, 2316
SPARD = 1
With other Princes that may best be spar'd, 2707
SPARE = 1
So I may keepe mine eyes. O spare mine eyes, 1680
SPARKLE = 1
Nay, it perchance will sparkle in your eyes: 1694
SPARROW = 1
Bast. Philip, sparrow, *Iames*, 243
SPEAK = *1
Pem. His Highnesse yet doth speak, & holds beleefe, 2611
SPEAKE = 19*5
And findes them perfect *Richard*: sirra speake, 98
Where how he did preuaile, I shame to speake: 112
As I haue heard my father speake himselfe 115
We coldly pause for thee, *Chatilion* speake, 347
These men of Angiers, let vs heare them speake, 502
Fra. Speake Citizens for England, whose your king. 676
Iohn. Speake on with fauour, we are bent to heare. 737
Fra. Speake England first, that hath bin forward first 798
To speake vnto this Cittie: what say you? 799
Or if you will, to speake more properly, 831
Iohn. Speake then Prince Dolphin, can you loue this | Ladie? 843
Then speake againe, not all thy former tale, 946
As it makes harmefull all that speake of it. 962
Aus. O that a man should speake those words to me. 1056
Now heare me speake with a propheticke spirit: 1511
For euen the breath of what I meane to speake, 1512
I will not stirre, nor winch, nor speake a word, 1657
To any tongue, speake it of what it will. 1861
Let me haue audience: I am sent to speake: 2373
For thus his Royaltie doth speake in me: 2383
Pan. Giue me leaue to speake. 2417
Bast. No, I will speake. 2418
Hub. Whose there? Speake hoa, speake quickely, or | I shoote. 2551
SPEAKES = 6*2
Chat. Thus (after greeting) speakes the King | of France, 6
*He speakes plaine Cannon fire, and smoake, and bounce, 778
Bla. The Lady *Constance* speakes not from her faith, | But from her
need. 1140
And he that speakes, doth gripe the hearers wrist, 1915
Yet I am none. Whose tongue so ere speakes false, 2092
Not truely speakes: who speakes not truly, Lies. 2093
Yet speakes, and peraduenture may recouer. 2588
SPECTACLE = 1
Exampled by this heynous spectacle. 2055
SPED = 1
Bast. How I haue sped among the Clergy men, 1862
SPEECHLESSE = 1
I left him almost speechlesse, and broke out 2581
SPEED = 5*1
Come Madam, and come *Richard*, we must speed 187

SPEED *cont.*
   Bast. Speed then to take aduantage of the field.   605
   So hot a speed, with such aduice dispos'd,   1393
   Iohn. With-hold thy speed, dreadfull Occasion: 1844
   *Bast. The spirit of the time shall teach me speed. *Exit*   1898
   And follow me with speed: Ile to the King: 2162
SPEEDE = 3
   Fore-wearied in this action of swift speede,   539
   The Copie of your speede is learn'd by them: 1831
   And spleene of speede, to see your Maiesty.   2660
SPEEDY = 1
   Some speedy Messenger bid her repaire   875
SPEND = 1
   And not to spend it so vn-neighbourly.   2290
SPENT = 2
   Our Cannons malice vainly shall be spent   557
   We hold our time too precious to be spent | with such a brabler.   2415
SPHERES = *1
   *Now, now you Starres, that moue in your right spheres,   2684
SPIDER = 1
   That euer Spider twisted from her wombe   2132
SPIES = 1
   Ile fill these dogged Spies with false reports: 1709
SPIGHT = 3
   Ore-bearing interruption spight of *France*?   1391
   In spight of spight, alone vpholds the day.   2464
SPILL = 1
   You came in Armes to spill mine enemies bloud,   1027
SPIRIT = 12*1
   Ele. The very spirit of *Plantaginet*:   176
   And fits the mounting spirit like my selfe;   216
   Or if that surly spirit melancholy   1341
   Holding th'eternall spirit against her will,   1401
   Now heare me speake with a propheticke spirit: 1511
   The breath of heauen, hath blowne his spirit out,   1689
   *Bast. The spirit of the time shall teach me speed. *Exit*   1898
   Oh me, my Vnckles spirit is in these stones,   2005
   The dauntlesse spirit of resolution.   2221
   And flesh his spirit in a warre-like soyle,   2240
   Himselfe to *Rome*, his spirit is come in,   2323
   And tame the sauage spirit of wilde warre,   2327
   Pem. Vp once againe: put spirit in the French,   2461
SPIRITS = 5
   In briefe, a brauer choyse of dauntlesse spirits   366
   And let vs in. Your King, whose labour'd spirits   538
   You equall Potents, fierie kindled spirits,   672
   With my vext spirits, I cannot take a Truce,   938
   And cull'd these fiery spirits from the world   2367
SPIT = 1
   And ready mounted are they to spit forth   517
SPITS = *1
   *That spits forth death, and mountaines, rockes, and seas,   774
SPLEENE = 3
   With swifter spleene then powder can enforce   763
   Or teach thy hastie spleene to do me shame,   2099
   And spleene of speede, to see your Maiesty.   2660

SPLEENES = 1
With Ladies faces, and fierce Dragons spleenes,   362
SPLENDOR = 1
Turning with splendor of his precious eye   1004
SPOKE = 5
But spoke the harme, that is by others done?   960
Hast thou not spoke like thunder on my side?   1050
And nere haue spoke a louing word to you: 1627
Iohn. Spoke like a sprightfull Noble Gentleman.   1899
Mes. Who euer spoke it, it is true my Lord.   2545
SPOONE = 1
Put but a little water in a spoone,   2135
SPORT = 1
Whom he hath vs'd rather for sport, then neede)   2431
SPOT = 2
Vpon the spot of this inforced cause,   2281
To rest without a spot for euermore.   2718
SPOTS = 1
Not painted with the Crimson spots of blood,   1978
SPOUT = 1
Which heere we came to spout against your Towne,   562
SPOYLD = 1
And bitter shame hath spoyl'd the sweet words taste,   1495
SPOYLE = *1
*That bloudy spoyle: thou slaue, thou wretch, y coward,   1041
SPREAD = 1
To spread his colours boy, in thy behalfe,   301
SPRED = 1
Mocking the ayre with colours idlely spred,   2241
SPRIGHTFULL = 1
Iohn. Spoke like a sprightfull Noble Gentleman.   1899
SPRING = 1
The rather, that you giue his off-spring life,   306
SPURNE = 1
So wilfully dost spurne; and force perforce   1069
SPURNES = 1
Whose foot spurnes backe the Oceans roaring tides,   317
SQUIRE = 1
A landlesse Knight, makes thee a landed Squire: 186
STABLE = 1
To crowch in litter of your stable plankes,   2394
STAFFE = 1
That is remoued by a staffe of France.   629
STAID = 2
Whose leisure I haue staid, haue giuen him time   352
But staid, and made the Westerne Welkin blush,   2526
STAIND = 1
Heauen knowes they were besmear'd and ouer-staind   1167
STAINE = 1
Lest vnaduis'd you staine your swords with bloud,   338
STAINED = 2
Cry hauocke kings, backe to the stained field   671
The faiths of men, nere stained with reuolt: 1723
STAINES = 2
To looke into the blots and staines of right,   411
Full of vnpleasing blots, and sightlesse staines,   966

STALKE = 1
And stalke in blood to our possession?   572
STAMP = 1
A ramping foole, to brag, and stamp, and sweare,   1048
STAND = 17*2
Fran. Stand in his face to contradict his claime.   587
*Command the rest to stand, God and our right. *Exeunt*   607
Why stand these royall fronts amazed thus: 670
And stand securely on their battelments,   688
Or if it must stand still, let wiues with childe   1014
Thou shalt stand curst, and excommunicate,   1100
Con. O *Lewis*, stand fast, the deuill tempts thee heere   1138
If thou stand excommunicate, and curst?   1154
If this same were a Church-yard where we stand,   1339
That *Iohn* may stand, then *Arthur* needs must fall, | So be it, for it
cannot be but so.   1524
Hub. Heate me these Irons hot, and looke thou stand   1571
I will not struggle, I will stand stone still: 1653
Hub. Go stand within: let me alone with him.   1661
Doth make a stand, at what your Highnesse will.   1756
I saw a Smith stand with his hammer (thus)   1918
Pem. All murthers past, do stand excus'd in this: 2050
Hub. Stand backe Lord Salsbury, stand backe I say   2081
Sal. Stand by, or I shall gaul you *Faulconbridge.*   2096
STANDING = 1
Standing on slippers, which his nimble haste   1922
STANDS = 2
Of him it holds, stands yong *Plantagenet,*   544
And he that stands vpon a slipp'ry place,   1522
STARING = 1
That euer wall-ey'd wrath, or staring rage   2048
STARRES = 1*1
Vpon thy starres, thy fortune, and thy strength,   1052
*Now, now you Starres, that moue in your right spheres,   2684
START = 1
And so shall you, being beaten: Do but start   2423
STARTLES = 2
Startles, and frights consideration: 1742
Startles mine eyes, and makes me more amaz'd   2302
STATE = 7
Out-faced Infant State, and done a rape   394
To me and to the state of my great greefe,   992
With any long'd-for-change, or better State.   1725
My Nobles leaue me, and my State is braued,   1968
The vn-owed interest of proud swelling State: 2152
To any Soueraigne State throughout the world.   2335
The lineall state, and glorie of the Land,   2713
STATES = 1
How like you this wilde counsell mighty States,   709
STAY = 9*1
Con. Stay for an answer to your Embassie,   337
Hub. Heare vs great kings, vouchsafe awhile to stay   731
Bast. Heeres a stay, | That shakes the rotten carkasse of old death   771
Iohn. So shall it be: your Grace shall stay behinde   1299
Makes nice of no vilde hold to stay him vp: 1523
Pem. Stay yet (Lord Salisbury) Ile go with thee,   1814
As good to dye, and go; as dye, and stay.   2004

224

STAY *cont.*

My heart hath one poore string to stay it by,	2665
What surety of the world, what hope, what stay,	2678
Bast. Art thou gone so? I do but stay behinde,	2680

STAYES = 1

Stayes in his course, and playes the Alchymist,	1003

STEALING = 1

Be guiltie of the stealing that sweete breath	2140

STEELE = 1

Oh now doth death line his dead chaps with steele,	666

STEEPES = 1

For he that steepes his safetie in true blood,	1532

STENCH = 1

Thou odoriferous stench: sound rottennesse,	1409

STEP = 2

That none so small aduantage shall step forth	1536
Wherein we step after a stranger, march	2278

STEPHEN = 1

Keepe *Stephen Langton* chosen Archbishop | Of *Canterbury* from that holy Sea:	1070

STEPPES = 1

The steppes of wrong, should moue you to mew vp	1774

STEPS = 1

We will vntread the steps of damned flight,	2513

STERNE = 2

He hath a sterne looke, but a gentle heart:	1664
Of sterne Iniustice, and confused wrong:	2274

STICKE = 1

That in mine eare I durst not sticke a rose,	150

STICKING = 1

Like true, inseparable, faithfull loues, | Sticking together in calamitie.	1450

STIFLE = 1

Enough to stifle such a villaine vp.	2137

STIFLED = 1

For I am stifled with this smell of sinne.	2116

STILL = 13

That still I lay vpon my mothers head,	84
Neere or farre off, well wonne is still well shot,	183
That Water-walled Bulwarke, still secure	320
Blan. That she is bound in honor still to do	841
What you in wisedome still vouchsafe to say.	842
That Broker, that still breakes the pate of faith,	889
Or if it must stand still, let wiues with childe	1014
Still and anon cheer'd vp the heauy time;	1623
Many a poore mans sonne would haue lyen still,	1626
I will not struggle, I will stand stone still:	1653
Though to no vse, but still to looke on you.	1681
Doth he still rage?	2616
As it on earth hath bene thy seruant still.	2683

STIRRE = 6

Would I might neuer stirre from off this place,	153
Who dares not stirre by day, must walke by night,	181
And stirre them vp against a mightier taske:	349
Ile stirre them to it: Come, away, away.	730
I will not stirre, nor winch, nor speake a word,	1657
If thou but frowne on me, or stirre thy foote,	2098

STIRRING = 2
An Ace stirring him to bloud and strife,	357
Be stirring as the time, be fire with fire,	2216

STIRS = *1
*Fra. Fro(m) that supernal Iudge that stirs good thoughts	409

STOMACKE = 1
And when my knightly stomacke is suffis'd,	201

STONE = 1
I will not struggle, I will stand stone still:	1653

STONES = 2
And but for our approch, those sleeping stones,	522
Oh me, my Vnckles spirit is in these stones,	2005

STOOD = 1
That so stood out against the holy Church,	2324

STOOPE = 2
For greefe is proud, and makes his owner stoope,	991
Stoope lowe within those bounds we haue ore-look'd,	2516

STOP = 7
That we shall stop her exclamation,	879
Iohn to stop Arthurs Title in the whole,	883
Bast. Wil't not be? | Will not a Calues-skin stop that mouth of thine?	1230
And stop this gap of breath with fulsome dust,	1415
Yea, without stop, didst let thy heart consent,	1964
To stop their marches 'fore we are enflam'd:	2174
Hen. Euen so must I run on, and euen so stop.	2677

STOPT = 1
Mes. My Liege, her eare | Is stopt with dust: the first of Aprill di'de	1838

STORD = *1
*Sal. I did not thinke the King so stor'd with friends.	2460

STORME = 3
So foule a skie, cleeres not without a storme,	1826
My tongue shall hush againe this storme of warre,	2187
And with a great heart heaue away this storme:	2306

STOUT = 1
With dreadfull pompe of stout inuasion.	1895

STRAIGHT = 5
The King by me requests your presence straight.	2020
Set on toward Swinsted: to my Litter straight,	2456
I begge cold comfort: and you are so straight	2650
Straight let vs seeke, or straight we shall be sought,	2689

STRAINE = 1
And straine their cheekes to idle merriment,	1345

STRAIT = 1
King Lewis, determine what we shall doe strait.	449

STRANGE = 3*2
Elea. A strange beginning: borrowed Maiesty?	10
'Tis strange to thinke how much King Iohn hath lost	1506
*Dol. Strong reasons makes strange actions: let vs go,	1567
With many legions of strange fantasies,	2624
*Counfound themselues. 'Tis strange y death shold sing:	2626

STRANGELY = 1
I finde the people strangely fantasied,	1865

STRANGER = 1
Wherein we step after a stranger, march	2278

STRANGER-BLOUD = 1
To stranger-bloud, to forren Royalty;	2178

STRANGEST = 1
Essex. My Liege, here is the strangest controuersie   51
STRANGLE = 1
Will serue to strangle thee: A rush will be a beame   2133
STRAW = 1
Shall blow each dust, each straw, each little rub   1513
STREAMES = 1
And two such shores, to two such streames made one,   758
STREETS = 2*1
From forth the streets of Pomfret, whom I found   1869
Hub. Old men, and Beldames, in the streets   1910
Bast. They found him dead, and cast into the streets,   2207
STRENGTH = 5*2
Till your strong hand shall helpe to giue him strength,   326
*Strength matcht with strength, and power confronted | power,   641
Vpon thy starres, thy fortune, and thy strength,   1052
With all religous strength of sacred vowes,   1160
That knit your sinewes to the strength of mine.   2314
That hand which had the strength, euen at your dore,   2391
STRENGTHEN = 1
But now in Armes, you strengthen it with yours.   1028
STRENGTHS = 1
That done, disseuer your vnited strengths,   702
STREW = 1
For it shall strew the footsteps of my rising: 226
STREWD = 1
And strew'd repentant ashes on his head.   1690
STRIFE = 1
An Ace stirring him to bloud and strife,   357
STRIKE = 3*1
Within the Arras: when I strike my foot   1572
Ile strike thee dead. Put vp thy sword betime,   2100
Strike vp the drummes, and let the tongue of warre   2420
Dol. Strike vp our drummes, to finde this danger out.   2435
STRING = 1
My heart hath one poore string to stay it by,   2665
STRIUE = *1
Pem. When Workemen striue to do better then wel,   1745
STROKE = 2
Win you this Citie without stroke, or wound,   733
The wildest Sauagery, the vildest stroke   2047
STRONG = 12*2
K.Iohn. Our strong possession, and our right for vs.   45
Eli. Your strong possessio(n) much more then your right,   46
Till your strong hand shall helpe to giue him strength,   326
His forces strong, his Souldiers confident: 355
In any breast of strong authoritie,   410
Our former scruple in our strong barr'd gates: 684
Thou euer strong vpon the stronger side;   1043
So newly ioyn'd in loue? so strong in both,   1171
Pand. Before the curing of a strong disease,   1497
And picke strong matter of reuolt, and wrath   1552
Dol. Strong reasons makes strange actions: let vs go,   1567
I haue possest you with, and thinke them strong.   1758
And more, more strong, then lesser is my feare   1759
Iohn. We cannot hold mortalities strong hand.   1800

STRONGER = 2
Thou euer strong vpon the stronger side;   1043
Be stronger with thee, then the name of wife?   1247
STRONGEST = 1
The fit is strongest: Euils that take leaue   1499
STRONGLY = 2
Which was so strongly vrg'd past my defence.   271
So strongly guarded: Cosen, looke not sad,   1300
STRUCK = *1
*Deepe shame had struck me dumbe, made me break off,   1960
STRUGGLE = 1
I will not struggle, I will stand stone still: 1653
STRUMPET = 1
That strumpet Fortune, that vsurping *Iohn*:   982
STUBBORNE = 2
Are you more stubborne hard, then hammer'd Iron?   1644
Vpon your stubborne vsage of the Pope: 2185
STUCKE = 1
There stucke no plume in any English Crest,   628
STUDIES = 1
Bend their best studies, heartily request   1768
STUFFE = 1
To your proceedings? Do not seeke to stuffe   1854
STUFFES = 1
Stuffes out his vacant garments with his forme;   1482
STUFT = 1
My armes, such eele skins stuft, my face so thin,   149
STUMBLING = 1
The stumbling night did part our wearie powres?   2544
SUBIECT = 4
Philip. Your faithfull subiect, I a gentleman,   58
But we will make it subiect to this boy.   336
A widdow, husbandles, subiect to feares,   935
O, let me haue no subiect enemies,   1893
SUBIECTED = 1
Subiected tribute to commanding loue,   277
SUBIECTION = 1
I do bequeath my faithfull seruices | And true subiection euerlastingly.   2715
SUBIECTS = 2*1
Iohn. England for it selfe: | You men of Angiers, and my louing
subiects.   508
Fra. You louing men of Angiers, *Arthurs* subiects,   510
**Cit.* In breefe, we are the King of Englands subiects   573
SUBMISSION = 1
To whom with all submission on my knee,   2714
SUBMIT = 2
Then ere the coward hand of *France* can win; | Submit thee boy.   458
Vnlesse he doe submit himselfe to *Rome*.   1122
SUCH = 31*1
And if my legs were two such riding rods,   148
My armes, such eele skins stuft, my face so thin,   149
But who comes in such haste in riding robes?   227
In such a iust and charitable warre.   329
Such as she is, in beautie, vertue, birth,   747
Left to be finished by such as shee,   753
O two such siluer currents when they ioyne   756
And two such shores, to two such streames made one,   758

SUCH *cont.*

Two such controlling bounds shall you be, kings,	759
In such a loue, so vile a Lout as he.	826
Make such vnconstant children of our selues	1174
When such profound respects doe pull you on?	1251
So hot a speed, with such aduice dispos'd,	1393
Such temperate order in so fierce a cause,	1394
There was not such a gracious creature borne:	1466
Fareyouwell: had you such a losse as I,	1484
When there is such disorder in my witte:	1487
Exec. I am best pleas'd to be from such a deede.	1662
*Ioh. Why do you bend such solemne browes on me?	1808
Mes. From France to England, neuer such a powre | For any forraigne preparation,	1828
That such an Army could be drawne in France, | And she not heare of it?	1836
Forme such another? This is the very top,	2044
For villanie is not without such rheume,	2111
Enough to stifle such a villaine vp.	2137
I am not glad that such a sore of Time	2263
But such is the infection of the time,	2271
But this effusion of such manly drops,	2300
And such as to my claime are liable,	2354
We hold our time too precious to be spent | with such a brabler.	2415
After such bloody toile, we bid good night,	2530
And brings from him such offers of our peace,	2694

SUCKE = 1

Why then I sucke my teeth, and catechize	202

SUDDEN *see* sodaine

SUDDENLY *see* sodainly

SUFFER = 1

Go we as well as hast will suffer vs,	880

SUFFISD = 1

And when my knightly stomacke is suffis'd,	201

SUGGESTION = 1

Of *Arthur*, whom they say is kill'd to night, on your | (suggestion.	1886

SUGGESTIONS = 1

Against these giddy loose suggestions:	1223

SUIT = 1

By long and vehement suit I was seduc'd	267

SUITE = 2

To grace occasions: let it be our suite,	1779
The suite which you demand is gone, and dead.	1802

SULLEN = 1

And sullen presage of your owne decay:	33

SUMME = 1

King *Iohn*, this is the very summe of all:	451

SUMMER = 1

There is so hot a summer in my bosome,	2637

SUMMES = 1

The summes I haue collected shall expresse:	1863

SUMMON = 2

Some Trumpet summon hither to the walles	501
What lusty Trumpet thus doth summon vs?	2370

SUN = *1

*Dol. The Sun of heauen (me thought) was loth to set;	2525

SUNDER = 1
 They whurle a-sunder, and dismember mee.   1263
SUNG = 2
 To whom he sung in rude harsh sounding rimes,   1871
 Pem. He is more patient | Then when you left him; euen now he sung. 2617
SUNKE = 1
 Are cast away, and sunke on *Goodwin* sands.   2539
SUNNE *see also* sonne = 4
 That yon greene boy shall haue no Sunne to ripe   788
 To solemnize this day the glorious sunne   1002
 The Sunne is in the heauen, and the proud day,   1333
 Of the old, feeble, and day-wearied Sunne,   2496
SUNS = 1
 Bla. The Sun's orecast with bloud: faire day adieu,   1259
SUN-SET = 1
 Weare out the daies in Peace; but ere Sun-set,   1035
SUPERFLUOUS = 2
 With this abundance of superfluous breath?   448
 Was once superfluous: you were Crown'd before,   1721
SUPERNAL = *1
 **Fra.* Fro(m) that supernal Iudge that stirs good thoughts   409
SUPPER = 1
 It drawes toward supper in conclusion so.   214
SUPPLY = 2
 Mes. Be of good comfort: for the great supply   2449
 And your supply, which you haue wish'd so long,   2538
SUPPORTER = 1
 That no supporter but the huge firme earth   994
SUPPOSE = 3
 Borne in *Northamptonshire*, and eldest sonne | As I suppose, to *Robert*
 Faulconbridge,   59
 I did suppose it should be on constraint,   2195
 (Which some suppose the soules fraile dwelling house)   2607
SUPREAME = 1
 But as we, vnder heauen, are supreame head,   1082
SUPREMACY = 1
 So vnder him that great supremacy   1083
SURE = 1
 There is no sure foundation set on blood: 1822
SURELY = 1
 For by this knot, thou shalt so surely tye   786
SURETIE = 1
 And mak'st an oath the suretie for thy truth,   1213
SURETY = 1
 What surety of the world, what hope, what stay,   2678
SURLY = 1
 Or if that surly spirit melancholy   1341
SUSPECT = 1
 I do suspect thee very greeuously.   2138
SUSPECTED = 1
 Makes sound opinion sicke, and truth suspected,   1743
SUSPIRE = 1
 To him that did but yesterday suspire,   1465
SWAIES = 1
 Which swaies vsurpingly these seuerall titles,   18
SWALLOWING = 1
 With open mouth swallowing a Taylors newes,   1920

SWAN = 1
I am the Symet to this pale faint Swan,   2627
SWART = 1
Lame, foolish, crooked, swart, prodigious,   967
SWAY = 1
This sway of motion, this commoditie,   899
SWAYES = 1
That swayes the earth this Climate ouer-lookes,   658
SWEARE = 8*1
Rather lost more. And by this hand I sweare   657
*Con. Gone to be married? Gone to sweare a peace?   922
A ramping foole, to brag, and stamp, and sweare,   1048
Vn-sweare faith sworne, and on the marriage bed   1176
To sweare, sweares onely not to be forsworne,   1215
Else what a mockerie should it be to sweare?   1216
But thou dost sweare, onely to be forsworne,   1217
And most forsworne, to keepe what thou dost sweare,   1218
And Noble Dolphin, albeit we sweare   2260
SWEARES = 1
To sweare, sweares onely not to be forsworne,   1215
SWEARING = 1
Swearing Allegiance, and the loue of soule   2177
SWEARST = 2
By what thou swear'st against the thing thou swear'st,   1212
SWEAT = 2
With burden of our armor heere we sweat: 389
Sweat in this businesse, and maintaine this warre?   2355
SWEET = 9*1
No sir, saies question, I sweet sir at yours,   209
Sweet, sweet, sweet poyson for the ages tooth,   223
*Bast. Hang nothing but a Calues skin most sweet lout.   1151
And bitter shame hath spoyl'd the sweet words taste,   1495
The foule corruption of a sweet childes death.   1799
To hug with swine, to seeke sweet safety out   2396
Hub. O my sweet sir, newes fitting to the night,   2576
And happily may your sweet selfe put on   2712
SWEETE = 3
Kneeling before this ruine of sweete life,   2064
My date of life out, for his sweete liues losse.   2109
Be guiltie of the stealing that sweete breath   2140
SWELL = 1
Shall leaue his natiue channell, and ore-swell   651
SWELLING = 2
Did neuer flote vpon the swelling tide,   368
The vn-owed interest of proud swelling State: 2152
SWIFT = 1
Fore-wearied in this action of swift speede,   539
SWIFTER = 1
With swifter spleene then powder can enforce   763
SWINDGD = 1
Bast. Saint George that swindg'd the Dragon,   595
SWINE = 1
To hug with swine, to seeke sweet safety out   2396
SWINSTED = 1*1
*Iohn. Tell him toward Swinsted, to the Abbey there.   2448
Set on toward Swinsted: to my Litter straight,   2456

SWORD = 3
Desiring thee to lay aside the sword   17
Bast. Your sword is bright sir, put it vp againe.   2079
Ile strike thee dead. Put vp thy sword betime,   2100
SWORDS = 4*1
Aust. The peace of heauen is theirs y lift their swords   328
Lest vnaduis'd you staine your swords with bloud,   338
With vnhack'd swords, and Helmets all vnbruis'd,   560
The swords of souldiers are his teeth, his phangs,   667
By heauen, I thinke my sword's as sharpe as yours.   2082
SWORE = 1
Euen on that Altar, where we swore to you | Deere Amity, and
euerlasting loue.   2480
SWORNE = 9
Beene sworne my Souldier, bidding me depend   1051
Was deepe-sworne faith, peace, amity, true loue   1162
Vn-sweare faith sworne, and on the marriage bed   1176
What since thou sworst, is sworne against thy selfe,   1199
For that which thou hast sworne to doe amisse,   1201
But thou hast sworne against religion: 1211
Hub. I haue sworne to do it: 1635
Yet am I sworne, and I did purpose, Boy,   1703
By cutting off your heads: Thus hath he sworne,   2477
SWORST = 1
What since thou sworst, is sworne against thy selfe,   1199
SWOUND = 1
I am no woman, Ile not swound at it.   2579
SYMET = 1
I am the Symet to this pale faint Swan,   2627
TABLE = 2
Drawne in the flattering table of her eie. | *Whispers with Blanch.*   819
Bast. Drawne in the flattering table of her eie,   821
TACKLE = 1
The tackle of my heart, is crack'd and burnt,   2662
TAKE = 18*3
Chat. Then take my Kings defiance from my mouth,   26
Bast. Brother, take you my land, Ile take my chance;   159
That will take paines to blow a horne before her?   229
Const. O take his mothers thanks, a widdows thanks,   325
But Asse, Ile take that burthen from your backe,   445
Which heauen shall take in nature of a fee: 472
Bast. Speed then to take aduantage of the field.   605
Makes it take head from all indifferency,   900
With my vext spirits, I cannot take a Truce,   938
The fit is strongest: Euils that take leaue   1499
Hub. His words do take possession of my bosome.   1605
By slaues, that take their humors for a warrant,   1934
*Heauen take my soule, and England keep my bones. *Dies*   2006
How easie dost thou take all *England* vp,   2147
Pan. Take againe | From this my hand, as holding of the Pope   2169
To cudgell you, and make you take the hatch,   2392
He meanes to recompence the paines you take,   2476
Bast. How did he take it? Who did taste to him?   2585
Nor let my kingdomes Riuers take their course   2646
As we with honor and respect may take,   2695
TAKEN *see also* tane = 1
Passing these Flats, are taken by the Tide,   2598

TAKES = 1
That takes away by any secret course | Thy hatefull life.   1105
TAKING = 1
But taking note of thy abhorr'd Aspect,   1949
TALE = 9
Your tale must be how he employ'd my mother.   106
Be well aduis'd, tell ore thy tale againe.   926
Then speake againe, not all thy former tale,   946
But this one word, whether thy tale be true.   947
Tell him this tale, and from the mouth of *England*,   1079
Life is as tedious as a twice-told tale,   1493
This acte, is as an ancient tale new told,   1735
Cuts off his tale, and talkes of *Arthurs* death.   1927
As bid me tell my tale in expresse words: 1959
TALKE = 2
Hub. If I talke to him, with his innocent prate   1598
And when they talke of him, they shake their heads,   1913
TALKES = 3
Talkes as familiarly of roaring Lyons,   775
Const. He talkes to me, that neuer had a sonne.   1476
Cuts off his tale, and talkes of *Arthurs* death.   1927
TALKING = 1
And talking of the Alpes and Appenines, | The Perennean and the riuer
Poe,   212
TAME = 2
And make them tame to their obedience.   1987
And tame the sauage spirit of wilde warre,   2327
TANE = 3
My Mother is assayled in our Tent, | And tane I feare.   1291
Arthur tane prisoner? diuers deere friends slaine?   1389
By some damn'd hand was rob'd, and tane away.   2209
TAPER-LIGHT = 1
Vnto the Raine-bow; or with Taper-light   1731
TARRE = 1
Snatch at his Master that doth tarre him on.   1696
TASKE = 1
And stirre them vp against a mightier taske: 349
TAST = 1
Can tast the free breath of a sacred King?   1075
TASTE = 3
And bitter shame hath spoyl'd the sweet words taste,   1495
Neuer to taste the pleasures of the world,   2067
Bast. How did he take it? Who did taste to him?   2585
TAUGHT = 1
You taught me how to know the face of right,   2341
TAYLORS = 1
With open mouth swallowing a Taylors newes,   1920
TEACH = 5*1
Teach vs some sence. Sirrah, were I at home   597
Con. Oh if thou teach me to beleeue this sorrow,   950
Teach thou this sorrow, how to make me dye,   951
To teach thee safety: thou art periur'd too,   1046
Bast. The spirit of the time shall teach me speed. *Exit*   1898
Or teach thy hastie spleene to do me shame,   2099
TEACHES = 1
And teaches mee to kill or hang my selfe: 1440

TEARE = 1
I am not mad: this haire I teare is mine,   1429
TEARES = 6*1
Much worke for teares in many an English mother,   613
Out at mine eyes, in tender womanish teares.   1609
*Approaching neere these eyes, would drinke my teares,   1639
Presented to the teares of soft remorse.   2049
My heart hath melted at a Ladies teares,   2298
Hen. Oh that there were some vertue in my teares, | That might releeue
you.   2652
And knowes not how to do it, but with teares.   2720
TEDIOUS = 1
Life is as tedious as a twice-told tale,   1493
TEETH = 3
Why then I sucke my teeth, and catechize   202
The swords of souldiers are his teeth, his phangs,   667
To tug and scamble, and to part by th'teeth   2151
TEL = *1
P. There tel the king, he may inquire vs out. *Ex. Lords.*   2118
TELL = 18*1
That marry wiues: tell me, how if my brother   128
There's toyes abroad, anon Ile tell thee more. | *Exit Iames.*   244
Then tell vs, Shall your Citie call vs Lord,   569
Where is she and her sonne, tell me, who knowes?   863
Be well aduis'd, tell ore thy tale againe.   926
Tell me thou fellow, is not France forsworne?   983
Tell him this tale, and from the mouth of *England,*   1079
So tell the Pope, all reuerence set apart | To him and his vsurp'd
authoritie.   1086
And tell me how you would bestow your selfe?   1156
On yon young boy: Ile tell thee what my friend,   1360
As bid me tell my tale in expresse words: 1959
Returne, and tell him so: we know the worst.   2025
Hub. Do but heare me sir. | *Bast.* Ha? Ile tell thee what.   2122
And come ye now to tell me *Iohn* hath made   2344
Iohn. How goes the day with vs? oh tell me *Hubert.*   2440
Iohn. Tell him toward *Swinsted,* to the Abbey there.   2448
Hub. A Monke I tell you, a resolued villaine   2586
Ile tell thee *Hubert,* halfe my power this night   2597
Fore-tell the ending of mortality.   2609
TELS = 2
Gracing the scroule that tels of this warres losse,   662
He tels vs *Arthur* is decreas'd to night.   1803
TEMPER = 1
Dolph. A noble temper dost thou shew in this,   2291
TEMPERATE = 2
Fra. Peace Lady, pause, or be more temperate,   498
Such temperate order in so fierce a cause,   1394
TEMPEST = 4
Fra. So by a roaring Tempest on the flood,   1383
Hold out this tempest. Beare away that childe,   2161
Pand. It was my breath that blew this Tempest vp,   2184
This showre, blowne vp by tempest of the soule,   2301
TEMPLES = 1
When liuing blood doth in these temples beat   405
TEMPORIZE = 1
And will not temporize with my intreaties: 2379

TEMPT = 2
Nor tempt the danger of my true defence;	2084
And tempt vs not to beare aboue our power.	2596

TEMPTS = 1
| | |
| *Con.* O *Lewis*, stand fast, the deuill tempts thee heere | 1138 |

TEN = 2
Euen to that drop ten thousand wiery fiends	1448
To traine ten thousand English to their side;	1560

TEND = 1
| | |
| *Bast.* Who didst thou leaue to tend his Maiesty? | 2589 |

TENDER = 3
Out at mine eyes, in tender womanish teares.	1609
Your tender kinsman, and to choake his dayes	1775
Sal. And the like tender of our loue wee make	2717

TENDS = 1
| | |
| And being not done, where doing tends to ill, | 1203 |

TENT = 1*1
Dol. She is sad and passionate at your highnes Tent.	864
My Mother is assayled in our Tent, | And tane I feare.	1291

TERRITORIES = 2
To this faire Iland, and the Territories:	15
From out the circle of his Territories.	2390

TERROR = 1
| | |
| Thou hate and terror to prosperitie, | 1411 |

TERTIA *l.*1381 1995 2438 = 3
TERTIUS *l.*997 = 1
TH *see also* i'th = 10*1
Th'aduantage of his absence tooke the King,	110
Bast. Brother by th'mothers side, giue me your hand,	172
And all th'vnsetled humors of the Land,	360
Against th'involnerable clouds of heauen,	558
Without th'assistance of a mortall hand:	1085
Holding th'eternall spirit against her will,	1401
Doth make the fault the worse by th'excuse:	1748
Th'infranchisement of *Arthur*, whose restraint	1769
And finde th'inheritance of this poore childe,	1815
Th'vncleanly sauours of a Slaughter-house,	2115
To tug and scamble, and to part by th'teeth	2151

THAN *see* then
THANKD = 1
| | |
| But (heau'n be thank'd) it is but voluntary. | 2196 |

THANKE = 2
With all my heart I thanke thee for my father:	283
Art. O heauen! I thanke you *Hubert*.	1713

THANKES = 2
I giue heauen thankes I was not like to thee.	91
Hen. I haue a kinde soule, that would giue thankes,	2719

THANKS = *2
| | |
| *Const.* O take his mothers thanks, a widdows thanks, | 325 |

THAT *see also* y *l.*38 53 *64 65 68 69 71 75 84 85 86 101 103 109 119 128
139 150 205 218 229 *233 234 236 237 *255 270 281 295 296 306 314
316 319 320 322 340 342 385 386 388 392 398 401 404 406 *409 412 420
*429 431 435 441 442 445 446 *447 466 487 495 496 506 513 523 546
553 554 561 570 576 577 581 591 595 626 629 631 658 662 678 679 702
711 719 735 *738 740 751 757 772 *774 788 789 *798 800 804 *825 828
829 834 835 838 841 855 857 *865 879 888 889 890 893 894 910 942 943
949 960 962 964 982 994 1006 1010 1015 1016 1018 *1041 1044 *1056

THAT *cont.*
   1071 1080 1083 1091 1094 1099 1101 1103 1105 1108 1114 1116 1120
   1124 1144 1145 1161 1192 1198 1201 1210 1231 1234 1239 1248 1260
   1264 1265 1268 1275 1278 *1280 1341 1344 1347 1355 1356 1366 1392
   1397 1407 1422 1424 1448 1454 1456 1462 1463 1465 1476 1496 1499
   1508 1517 1522 1524 1528 1532 1536 1548 1549 1565 1592 1595 1603
   1631 1633 1642 1665 1670 1672 1695 1696 1697 1699 1702 1711 *1720
   1722 1727 1734 1761 1764 1778 1780 1790 1812 1817 1824 1825 1833
   1836 1849 1868 1872 1875 1877 1915 1916 1925 1934 1988 *2011 2024
   2043 2048 2058 2059 2102 2132 2140 2161 2182 2184 2193 2210 2219
   2255 2263 2267 2272 2276 2284 2285 2297 2308 2314 2324 2328 2338
   2340 2345 2349 2353 2381 2391 2400 2401 2404 2426 2442 2450 2463
   2480 2490 2503 2522 2542 2556 2562 2569 2582 2608 2612 2614 2625
   2632 2638 2651 2652 2653 *2684 2707 2719 = 287*18

THATS = 2
   I am not worth this coyle that's made for me.   467
   Bla. That's the curse of *Rome.*   1137

THE *see also* th' = 656*31

THEATER = 1
   As in a Theater, whence they gape and point   689

THEE *l.*17 *72 91 *156 186 189 244 283 286 311 323 347 431 453 455 456
   457 459 480 660 849 919 928 930 958 970 973 976 984 *989 1046 1064
   1073 1138 *1153 1226 1244 1247 1248 *1253 *1277 1301 1302 1319 1320
   1327 1331 1353 1360 1372 1373 1376 1418 1712 1715 1814 1880 1950
   1952 1985 1991 1994 2077 2100 2123 2133 2134 2138 2285 2286 2287
   2414 2510 2519 2556 2597 2681 2682 = 73*6

THEIR *l.*274 281 307 *328 363 364 370 385 516 518 524 525 567 568 584
   591 626 634 646 688 696 697 727 791 1015 1016 1228 1262 1345 1455
   1457 1458 1459 1500 1535 1560 1564 1565 1698 1746 1765 1768 1888
   1889 1912 1913 1934 1986 1987 2174 2191 2219 2357 2410 2411 2527
   2592 2620 2625 2630 2646 = 63*1

THEIRS = 1*1
   Aust. The peace of heauen is theirs y lift their swords   328
   And made his Maiestie the bawd to theirs.   980

THEM *l.*54 98 349 359 378 454 502 631 701 719 730 757 760 791 948 1130
   1225 1227 1455 1459 1505 1542 1636 1704 1758 1766 1767 1831 1891
   1892 1897 1987 2593 2599 2622 2654 2728 = 37

THEMSELUES = 3*2
   *Though churlish thoughts themselues should bee your | Iudge,   836
   Doe glew themselues in sociable griefe,   1449
   The French fight coldly, and retyre themselues.   2453
   In their continuance, will not feele themselues.   2620
   *Counfound themselues. 'Tis strange y death shold sing: 2626

THEN *l.*26 *46 66 122 133 138 141 188 192 202 206 262 323 *330 341
   348 367 378 404 424 458 550 552 555 569 575 *590 605 656 673 674 682
   705 714 720 742 744 746 761 763 781 835 *843 847 916 946 955 969 970
   1099 1146 1165 1182 1192 1204 1222 1225 1247 1258 *1280 1351 1423
   1433 1483 1485 1524 1528 1549 1556 1604 1632 1644 1663 1673 *1745
   1751 1759 1764 1773 1782 1847 1857 1939 1942 1984 1991 2014 2015
   2016 2125 2181 2247 2303 2309 2330 2431 2489 2575 2584 2618 2667
   2682 2691 2711 = 97*7

THENCE = 1
   Pem. And when it breakes, I feare will issue thence   1798

THERE *l.*30 108 387 628 *738 800 *825 915 917 1111 *1271 1287 1320
   1466 1487 1559 1668 1670 1673 1688 1822 2029 2117 *2118 2126 *2198
   2226 2268 2316 *2413 *2448 *2551 2637 2652 2655 = 28*9

THEREBY = 1
Yet indirection thereby growes direct,   1207
THEREFORE = 12*1
We know his handy-worke, therefore good mother   251
To parlie or to fight, therefore prepare.   373
Iohn. For our aduantage, therefore heare vs first: 512
Opprest with wrongs, and therefore full of feares,   934
Therefore since Law it selfe is perfect wrong,   1117
Therefore to Armes, be Champion of our Church,   1186
Therefore thy later vowes, against thy first,   1219
I shall not know him: therefore neuer, neuer   1473
*Thy foote to Englands Throne. And therefore marke: 1515
Therefore I will be sodaine, and dispatch.   1600
Sal. Therefore, to be possess'd with double pompe,   1726
Therefore 'twere reason you had manners now.   2030
Therefore thy threatning Colours now winde vp,   2326
THERES = 4*3
There's toyes abroad, anon Ile tell thee more. | *Exit Iames.*   244
Queen. Theres a good mother boy, that blots thy fa-|(ther   429
Const. There's a good grandame boy | That would blot thee.   430
There's a good grandame.   464
Pan. There's Law and Warrant (Lady) for my curse.   1112
Dol. There's nothing in this world can make me ioy,   1492
There's few or none do know me, if they did,   1999
THESE *l.*18 23 252 397 405 473 500 502 513 520 548 567 660 670 *687 699
718 760 *839 848 945 1032 1036 1128 1170 1223 1414 1439 1456 1457
*1571 1633 *1639 1650 1655 1659 1709 1764 1853 *1928 2005 2014 2254
2256 2288 2307 2356 2367 2598 2599 *2675 2726 = 47*6
THEY = 33*2
THICKE = 1
Had bak'd thy bloud, and made it heauy, thicke,   1342
THIMBLES = 1
Their thimbles into armed Gantlets change,   2410
THIN *see also* thin-bestained = 1
My armes, such eele skins stuft, my face so thin,   149
THINE = 20*2
Doth he lay claime to thine inheritance?   80
*That for thine owne gaine shouldst defend mine honor?   255
This toyle of ours should be a worke of thine;   390
As thine was to thy husband, and this boy   422
Call not me slanderer, thou and thine vsurpe | The Dominations,
Royalties, and rights   477
What meanes that hand vpon that breast of thine?   942
Why holdes thine eie that lamentable rhewme,   943
Sh'adulterates hourely with thine Vnckle *Iohn,*   977
Bast. Wil't not be? | Will not a Calues-skin stop that mouth of thine?   1230
His Honor, Oh thine Honor, *Lewis* thine Honor.   1249
Father, I may not wish the fortune thine: 1266
Heare me without thine eares, and make reply   1348
Good *Hubert, Hubert, Hubert* throw thine eye   1359
Hub. Well, see to liue: I will not touch thine eye,   1701
For all the Treasure that thine Vnckle owes,   1702
Bast. Go, beare him in thine armes: 2144
That shall reuerberate all, as lowd as thine.   2426
(As lowd as thine) rattle the Welkins eare,   2428
Right in thine eye. Away, my friends, new flight,   2521
Why may not I demand of thine affaires, | As well as thou of mine?   2557

THINE *cont.*

  *Bast. With-hold thine indignation, mighty heauen,   2595

THING = 5

  That any thing he see's which moues his liking,   829
  Who hauing no externall thing to loose,   892
  By what thou swear'st against the thing thou swear'st,   1212
  Giue me thy hand, I had a thing to say,   1324
  I had a thing to say, but let it goe: 1332

THINGS = 3

  This day all things begun, come to ill end,   1019
  Then feeling what small things are boysterous there,   1673
  All things that you should vse to do me wrong   1697

THINK = 1

  Then was his will to get me, as I think.   141

THINKE = 22*2

  That is well knowne, and as I thinke one father: 68
  Will I not thinke of home, but follow Armes.   324
  My boy a bastard? by my soule I thinke | His father neuer was so true
  begot,   426
  Sal. As true as I beleeue you thinke them false,   948
  And by my troth I thinke thou lou'st me well.   1354
  Come, grin on me, and I will thinke thou smil'st,   1417
  Or madly thinke a babe of clowts were he;   1442
  'Tis strange to thinke how much King *Iohn* hath lost   1506
  Nay, you may thinke my loue was craftie loue,   1629
  I haue possest you with, and thinke them strong.   1758
  Thinke you I beare the Sheeres of destiny?   1809
  Bast. What ere you thinke, good words I thinke | were best.   2026
  *Sal. Sir *Richard*, what thinke you? you haue beheld,   2040
  Or haue you read, or heard, or could you thinke?   2041
  Or do you almost thinke, although you see,   2042
  By heauen, I thinke my sword's as sharpe as yours.   2082
  That you shall thinke the diuell is come from hell.   2102
  *Sal. I did not thinke the King so stor'd with friends.   2460
  Where I may thinke the remnant of my thoughts   2507
  I did not thinke to be so sad to night   2541
  Bast. Hubert, I thinke. | *Hub.* Thou hast a perfect thought: 2559
  Thou maist be-friend me so much, as to thinke   2565
  If you thinke meete, this afternoone will poast   2704

THINKES = 3

  Me thinkes I see this hurley all on foot;   1554
  Art. 'Mercie on me: | Me thinkes no body should be sad but I: 1585
  I am amaz'd me thinkes, and loose my way   2145

THINKING = 1

  Thinking this voyce an armed Englishman.   2399

THIN-BESTAINED = 1

  We will not lyne his thin-bestained cloake   2022

THIRTEENE = 1

  As maids of thirteene do of puppi-dogges.   776

THIRTY = 1

  Full thirty thousand Markes of English coyne: 850

THIS *l.*15 21 41 56 73 89 96 105 116 119 129 130 132 135 152 153 154 215
  228 253 256 272 298 312 313 331 334 336 348 354 374 390 398 400 402
  403 *407 412 422 *447 448 451 467 479 481 486 489 492 499 511 525
  539 542 545 547 551 554 574 612 625 656 657 658 662 682 694 698 709
  713 716 724 727 733 761 762 765 770 777 *784 786 792 797 799 801 804
  805 824 827 835 *843 849 860 861 *865 868 873 881 898 899 902 903

THIS *cont.*
  908 939 947 950 951 958 1000 1002 1006 1009 1012 1013 1015 1017 1018
  1019 1022 1031 1034 1060 1072 1079 1088 1090 1096 1144 1148 1157
  1164 1166 1172 1240 *1256 1274 *1285 1290 1296 1303 1319 1323 1339
  1362 1396 1397 1415 1429 1486 *1492 1501 1507 *1530 1534 1554 1637
  1640 *1675 1688 1704 1705 *1720 1735 1738 1752 1757 1771 1778 1787
  1807 1815 1817 1819 1842 1942 1948 1970 1971 1976 1979 1986 2000
  2010 2033 2035 2038 2043 2044 2046 2050 2051 2055 2064 2070 2106
  2116 *2119 2121 2127 2130 2141 2146 2148 2149 2161 2170 2179 2184
  2187 2189 2192 2246 2252 2267 2276 2277 2281 2291 2296 2300 2301
  2306 2322 2337 2338 2342 2343 2347 2352 2353 2355 2359 2362 2366
  2385 2386 2387 2389 2399 2430 2433 *2435 2442 2452 2454 2455 2475
  2482 2494 2497 2502 2504 2508 2512 2542 2578 2582 2584 2597 2627
  2640 2667 2679 2696 2704 2705 2723 = 265*15
THITHER = 1*1
  *Elinor. Nay, I would haue you go before me thither.   163
  Bast. Thither shall it then,   2711
THO = *1
  *Bast. Madam by chance, but not by truth, what tho;   178
THORNES = 1
  Among the thornes, and dangers of this world.   2146
THOSE *l.*471 522 585 *590 630 734 *924 985 1055 *1056 *1057 *1059
  1375 1445 1446 1825 1848 *1961 2110 2307 2492 2516 = 15*7
THOU see also y l.29 30 32 63 65 142 *156 169 170 *185 190 238 239 240
  241 254 256 264 284 288 315 391 392 404 406 *407 415 417 420 424 428
  434 454 475 476 477 494 *648 653 655 715 717 786 *811 851 925 927
  932 937 940 941 950 951 955 964 970 972 974 983 *989 1040 *1041 1042
  1043 1044 1046 1047 1049 1050 1053 1054 1058 1060 1068 1076 1100
  1109 *1123 1131 1142 *1153 1154 1189 1192 1194 1199 1201 1211 1212
  1214 1217 1218 1221 1225 1227 1234 1244 *1253 1264 1265 *1277 1279
  1305 1329 1330 1340 1347 1354 1358 1363 1364 1409 1411 1417 1428
  1436 *1571 1824 1849 1852 1874 1881 1902 *1928 1929 1931 1945 1953
  *1956 1962 1991 2077 *2087 2090 2097 2098 2103 2121 2125 2127 2129
  2131 2134 2147 2246 2284 2291 2311 2414 *2436 2553 2555 2558 2560
  2562 2563 2564 2565 *2567 2589 2661 2667 2680 = 151*19
THOUGH = 8*2
  Which though I will not practice to deceiue,   224
  Though all these English, and their discipline   567
  *Though churlish thoughts themselues should bee your | Iudge,   836
  And though thou now confesse thou didst but iest   937
  *Iohn. Though you, and all the Kings of Christendom   1089
  Though you, and al the rest so grossely led,   1095
  Is to mistake again, though indirect,   1206
  Though that my death were adiunct to my Act, | By heauen I would doe
  it.   1356
  The Iron of it selfe, though heate red hot,   1638
  Though to no vse, but still to looke on you.   1681
THOUGHT = 7*1
  Alter not the doome fore-thought by heauen.   1245
  And flye (like thought) from them, to me againe.   1897
  The dreadfull motion of a murderous thought,   1980
  That you do see? Could thought, without this obiect   2043
  Hub. If I in act, consent, or sinne of thought,   2139
  Be great in act, as you haue beene in thought: 2213
  *Dol. The Sun of heauen (me thought) was loth to set;   2525
  Bast. Hubert, I thinke. | Hub. Thou hast a perfect thought: 2559

THOUGHTS = 3*2
  Fra. Fro(m) that supernal Iudge that stirs good thoughts   409
  *Though churlish thoughts themselues should bee your | Iudge,   836
  I would into thy bosome poure my thoughts: 1352
  It makes the course of thoughts to fetch about,   1741
  Where I may thinke the remnant of my thoughts   2507
THOURT = 1
  Thou'rt damn'd as blacke, nay nothing is so blacke,   2124
THOUSAND = 8
  Twice fifteene thousand hearts of Englands breed. | *Bast.* Bastards and
  else.   582
  Full thirty thousand Markes of English coyne: 850
  And thou possessed with a thousand wrongs: 1340
  Euen to that drop ten thousand wiery fiends   1448
  To traine ten thousand English to their side;   1560
  Told of a many thousand warlike French,   1924
  Ile finde a thousand shifts to get away;   2003
  A thousand businesses are briefe in hand,   2163
THOUSANDS = 1
  To feast vpon whole thousands of the French.   2434
THREATEN = 1
  Threaten the threatner, and out-face the brow   2217
THREATNED = 2
  To saue vnscratch'd your Citties threatned cheekes: 531
  This friendly treatie of our threatned Towne.   797
THREATNER = 1
  Threaten the threatner, and out-face the brow   2217
THREATNING = 2
  Shee lookes vpon them with a threatning eye: 1505
  Therefore thy threatning Colours now winde vp,   2326
THREATS = *1
  *Iohn. No more then he that threats. To Arms let's hie. | *Exeunt.*   1280
THRED = 2
  And if thou want'st a Cord, the smallest thred   2131
  Are turned to one thred, one little haire: 2664
THREE = 5
  Lest men should say, looke where three farthings goes,   151
  Three foot of it doth hold; bad world the while: 1818
  Three dayes before: but this from Rumors tongue   1842
  Are wrack'd three nights ago on *Goodwin* sands.   2451
  Come the three corners of the world in Armes,   2727
THRILL = 1
  In vaults and prisons, and to thrill and shake,   2397
THRIUE = 2
  Grandam, I will not wish thy wishes thriue: 1267
  So thriue it in your game, and so farewell.   1813
THRONE = 1*1
  Heere is my Throne bid kings come bow to it.   996
  *Thy foote to Englands Throne. And therefore marke: 1515
THRONG = 1
  Which in their throng, and presse to that last hold,   2625
THROUGH = 2
  But as I trauail'd hither through the land,   1864
  Through my burn'd bosome: nor intreat the North   2647
THROUGHOUT = 1
  To any Soueraigne State throughout the world.   2335

THROW = 3
Good *Hubert, Hubert, Hubert* throw thine eye   1359
To throw a perfume on the Violet,   1729
Throw this report on their incensed rage,   1986
THRUST = 6
Thrust but these men away, and Ile forgiue you,   1659
Iohn. Gentle kinsman, go | And thrust thy selfe into their Companies,   1887
Had falsely thrust vpon contrary feete,   1923
Come, come; for thou shalt thrust thy hand as deepe   2311
Yea, thrust this enterprize into my heart,   2343
To thrust his ycie fingers in my maw;   2645
THUNDER = 4
The thunder of my Cannon shall be heard.   31
Fran. Our Thunder from the South, | Shall raine their drift of bullets on
this Towne.   726
Hast thou not spoke like thunder on my side?   1050
And mocke the deepe mouth'd Thunder: for at hand   2429
THUNDERS = 1
O that my tongue were in the thunders mouth,   1422
THUS = 12
Chat. Thus (after greeting) speakes the King | of France,   6
Thus leaning on mine elbow I begin,   204
Why stand these royall fronts amazed thus: 670
Thou shalt be punish'd for thus frighting me,   932
Adde thus much more, that no *Italian* Priest   1080
This must not be thus borne, this will breake out   1819
I saw a Smith stand with his hammer (thus)   1918
K.Iohn. Thus haue I yeelded vp into your hand | The Circle of my glory.   2167
What lusty Trumpet thus doth summon vs?   2370
For thus his Royaltie doth speake in me: 2383
By cutting off your heads: Thus hath he sworne,   2477
My Liege, my Lord: but now a King, now thus.   2676
THY *l.*13 20 *72 143 145 *156 157 165 177 *185 *233 254 264 266 295 301
303 312 344 396 401 408 413 418 419 421 422 *429 454 460 479 481 484
495 650 652 664 717 787 800 852 926 928 940 945 946 947 957 965 971
972 1052 1058 1060 1106 *1123 1196 1199 1200 1213 1219 1220 1222
1233 1246 1267 1270 *1277 1279 1301 1302 1321 1322 1324 1342 1352
1412 1413 1414 1416 1418 *1515 1827 1844 1888 1896 1930 1949 *1956
*1961 1964 1965 1989 *2072 2098 2099 2100 2134 2286 2292 2297 2305
2311 2326 *2413 2424 2540 2569 2666 2683 = 107*13
THYSELFE *see* selfe
TICKLING = 2
That smooth-fac'd Gentleman, tickling commoditie,   894
Which else runnes tickling vp and downe the veines,   1343
TIDE = 3
Did neuer flote vpon the swelling tide,   368
Vnder the tide; but now I breath againe   1859
Passing these Flats, are taken by the Tide,   2598
TIDES = 2
Whose foot spurnes backe the Oceans roaring tides,   317
Among the high tides in the Kalender?   1011
TIDINGS *see* tydings
TIE *see* tye
TIGER *see* tyger
TILL = 20
Till she had kindled *France* and all the world,   39
Till *Angiers*, and the right thou hast in *France*,   315

TILL *cont.*

Euen till that *England* hedg'd in with the maine,	319
Euen till that vtmost corner of the West	322
Salute thee for her King, till then faire boy	323
Till your strong hand shall helpe to giue him strength,	326
To him will we proue loyall, till that time	577
Cit. Till you compound whose right is worthiest,	588
The others peace: till then, blowes, blood, and death.	674
And till it be vndoubted, we do locke	683
Till their soule-fearing clamours haue braul'd downe	697
Euen till vnfenced desolation | Leaue them as naked as the vulgar ayre:	700
Till now, infixed I beheld my selfe,	818
Till this aduantage, this vile drawing byas,	898
Which till this time my tongue did nere pronounce;	1240
O make a league with me, 'till I haue pleas'd	1845
Till I haue set a glory to this hand,	2070
Sal. Not till I sheath it in a murtherers skin.	2080
Till my attempt so much be glorified,	2364
Which holds but till thy newes be vttered,	2666

TIME = 21*3

To treat of high affaires touching that time:	109
And in the meane time soiourn'd at my fathers;	111
Full fourteene weekes before the course of time:	121
For he is but a bastard to the time	217
Whose leisure I haue staid, haue giuen him time	352
Which died in *Geffrey*: and the hand of time,	399
By this time from their fixed beds of lime	525
To him will we proue loyall, till that time	577
Which till this time my tongue did nere pronounce;	1240
Bast. Old Time the clocke setter, y bald sexton Time:	1257
But thou shalt haue: and creepe time nere so slow,	1330
Still and anon cheer'd vp the heauy time;	1623
Being vrged at a time vnseasonable.	1737
I shall indue you with: Meane time, but aske	1760
Bast. The spirit of the time shall teach me speed. *Exit*	1898
This gentle offer of the perillous time.	2010
Be stirring as the time, be fire with fire,	2216
Iohn. Haue thou the ordering of this present time.	2246
I am not glad that such a sore of Time	2263
But such is the infection of the time,	2271
We hold our time too precious to be spent | with such a brabler.	2415
The better arme you to the sodaine time,	2583
Bast. Oh let vs pay the time: but needfull woe,	2721

TIMES = 4

Iohn layes you plots: the times conspire with you,	1531
That the times enemies may not haue this	1778
To the yet vnbegotten sinne of times;	2053
Then pause not: for the present time's so sicke,	2181

TIS *l.*161 198 230 507 565 927 1000 1433 1506 1563 1792 1811 2032 2107 2339 *2626 2699 = 16*1

TITHE *see* tythe

TITLE = 6

A Will, that barres the title of thy sonne.	495
Whose title they admit, *Arthurs* or *Iohns*.	503
Iohn. To verifie our title with their liues.	584
Iohn to stop *Arthurs* Title in the whole,	883
Ar. As little Prince, hauing so great a Title	1582

TITLE *cont.*
To guard a Title, that was rich before;   1727
TITLES = 2
Which swaies vsurpingly these seuerall titles,   18
In titles, honors, and promotions, | As she in beautie, education, blood,   808
TO *see also* too = 484*19, 1
He is prepar'd, and reason to he should,   2384
TODAY *see* day
TOGETHER = 4
Together with that pale, that white-fac'd shore,   316
Married in league, coupled, and link'd together   1159
Iohn. Cosen, goe draw our puisance together,   1272
Like true, inseparable, faithfull loues, | Sticking together in calamitie.   1450
TOILE = 1
After such bloody toile, we bid good night,   2530
TOKENS = 1
Doe you not read some tokens of my sonne   95
TOLD = 6
Life is as tedious as a twice-told tale,   1493
And told me *Hubert* should put out mine eyes,   1646
This acte, is as an ancient tale new told,   1735
For when you should be told they do prepare,   1832
Told of a many thousand warlike French,   1924
Iohn. That villaine *Hubert* told me he did liue.   2210
TOLL = 1
Shall tythe or toll in our dominions: 1081
TOMORROW *see* morrow
TONGUE = 22*1
The accent of his tongue affecteth him: 94
He giues the bastinado with his tongue: 779
There is no tongue hath power to curse him right.   1111
How can the Law forbid my tongue to curse?   1118
France, thou maist hold a serpent by the tongue,   1189
Thy tongue against thy tongue. O let thy vow   1196
Which till this time my tongue did nere pronounce;   1240
Did with his yron tongue, and brazen mouth   1337
Without a tongue, vsing conceit alone,   1349
O that my tongue were in the thunders mouth,   1422
*I would not haue beleeu'd him: no tongue but *Huberts.*   1647
Let me not hold my tongue: let me not *Hubert*,   1678
Or *Hubert*, if you will cut out my tongue,   1679
Pem. Then I, as one that am the tongue of these   1764
Three dayes before: but this from Rumors tongue   1842
To any tongue, speake it of what it will.   1861
Yet I am none. Whose tongue so ere speakes false,   2092
My tongue shall hush againe this storme of warre,   2187
And warrant limited vnto my tongue.   2377
Strike vp the drummes, and let the tongue of warre   2420
Thou art my friend, that know'st my tongue so well: 2562
That any accent breaking from thy tongue,   2569
TONGUES = 3
Abbortiues, presages, and tongues of heauen,   1543
Art. Hubert, the vtterance of a brace of tongues,   1676
The deed, which both our tongues held vilde to name.   1966
TONIGHT *see* night
TOO *see also* to = 20*1
'Tis two respectiue, and too sociable   198

243

TOO *cont.*

Lady. Hast thou conspired with thy brother too,	254
Fran. As many and as well-borne bloods as those. | *Bast.* Some Bastards too.	585
Aust. And your lippes too, for I am well assur'd,	854
To teach thee safety: thou art periur'd too,	1046
Cons. And for mine too, when Law can do no right.	1113
Is all too wanton, and too full of gawdes	1335
I am not mad: too well, too well I feele	1443
Pand. You hold too heynous a respect of greefe.	1475
Ar. Too fairely *Hubert,* for so foule effect,	1611
What euer torment you do put me too.	1660
*Hub. Is this your promise? Go too, hold your toong.	1675
Found it too precious Princely, for a graue.	2039
I am too high-borne to be proportied	2332
And now 'tis farre too huge to be blowne out	2339
Pand. The *Dolphin* is too wilfull opposite	2378
We hold our time too precious to be spent | with such a brabler.	2415
If they miscarry: we miscarry too.	2462
Hen. It is too late, the life of all his blood	2605

TOOKE = 5

(Faire fall the bones that tooke the paines for me)	86
Th'aduantage of his absence tooke the King,	110
His lands to me, and tooke it on his death	118
Who as you say, tooke paines to get this sonne,	129
May know wherefore we tooke the Sacrament,	2257

TOONG = *1

*Hub. Is this your promise? Go too, hold your toong.	1675

TOOT = 2*1

Pembroke looke too't: farewell *Chattillion.* | *Exit Chat. and Pem.*	35
Sirra looke too't, yfaith I will, yfaith.	440
*Hub. Vncleanly scruples feare not you: looke too't.	1577

TOOTH = 2

Sweet, sweet, sweet poyson for the ages tooth,	223
A fasting Tyger safer by the tooth,	1191

TOOTH-PICKE = 1

Hee and his tooth-picke at my worships messe,	200

TOP = 2

Forme such another? This is the very top,	2044
Then had I seene the vaultie top of heauen	2303

TOPFULL = 1

Now that their soules are topfull of offence,	1565

TORAINE = 3

England and *Ireland, Angiers, Toraine, Maine,*	452
For *Angiers,* and faire *Toraine Maine, Poyctiers,*	803
Iohn. Then I doe giue *Volquessen, Toraine, Maine,*	847

TORAYNE = 1

To *Ireland, Poyctiers, Aniowe, Torayne, Maine,*	16

TORE = 1

I tore them from their bonds, and cride aloud,	1455

TORMENT = 1

What euer torment you do put me too.	1660

TORTURE = 2

Turning dispitious torture out of doore?	1607
Let hell want paines enough to torture me:	2142

TOSTING-IRON = 1

Or Ile so maule you, and your tosting-Iron,	2101

TOTTRING = 1
And woon'd our tott'ring colours clearly vp,   2531
TOUCH = 2
Dol. May be he will not touch yong *Arthurs* life,   1545
Hub. Well, see to liue: I will not touch thine eye,   1701
TOUCHD = 2
Resembling Maiesty, which being touch'd and tride,   1025
Is touch'd, corruptibly: and his pure braine   2606
TOUCHING = 1
To treat of high affaires touching that time: 109
TOWARD = 4*1
It drawes toward supper in conclusion so.   214
With al true duetie: On toward *Callice*, hoa. | *Exeunt.*   1379
Big. Away, toward *Burie*, to the Dolphin there.   2117
*Iohn. Tell him toward *Swinsted*, to the Abbey there.   2448
Set on toward *Swinsted*: to my Litter straight,   2456
TOWNE = 13
Against the browes of this resisting towne,   331
Wee'll lay before this towne our Royal bones,   334
His marches are expedient to this towne,   354
Before the eye and prospect of your Towne,   514
In warlike march, these greenes before your Towne,   548
Which heere we came to spout against your Towne,   562
For him, and in his right, we hold this Towne.   574
We hold our Towne for neither: yet for both.   645
Your sharpest Deeds of malice on this Towne.   694
Being wrong'd as we are by this peeuish Towne: 716
Fran. Our Thunder from the South, | Shall raine their drift of bullets on
this Towne.   726
This friendly treatie of our threatned Towne.   797
And Earle of Richmond, and this rich faire Towne   873
TOWNES = 2
When aduerse Forreyners affright my Townes   1894
Viue le Roy, as I haue bank'd their Townes?   2357
TOWNESMEN = 1
Iohn. Whose party do the Townesmen yet admit?   675
TOWRES = 2*1
*Hubert. Heralds, from off our towres we might behold   636
Bast. Ha Maiesty: how high thy glory towres,   664
And like an Eagle, o're his ayerie towres,   2403
TOYES = 1
There's toyes abroad, anon Ile tell thee more. | *Exit Iames.*   244
TOYLE = 1
This toyle of ours should be a worke of thine;   390
TRADED = 1
And he, long traded in it, makes it seeme   2112
TRAINE = 2
To traine ten thousand English to their side;   1560
Enter Dolphin, and his Traine.   2524
TRANSGRESSION = 1
Heauen lay not my transgression to my charge,   269
TRANSLATE = 1
I can with ease translate it to my will: 830
TRAUAILD = 1
But as I trauail'd hither through the land,   1864
TRAUELLER = 1
For your conuersion, now your traueller,   199

TRAYTOR = 1
Himselfe loues traytor, this is pittie now;   824
TREACHEROUS = 1
Euen with a treacherous fine of all your liues: 2499
TREACHERY = 1
Paying the fine of rated Treachery,   2498
TREAD = 4
For this downe-troden equity, we tread   547
To tread downe faire respect of Soueraigntie,   979
O then tread downe my need, and faith mounts vp,   1146
And wheresoere this foot of mine doth tread,   1362
TREADING = 1
With many hundreds treading on his heeles: 1870
TREASURE = 1
For all the Treasure that thine Vnckle owes,   1702
TREAT = 1
To treat of high affaires touching that time: 109
TREATIE = 1
This friendly treatie of our threatned Towne.   797
TREMBLE = 3
Aust. Peace, no more. | *Bast.* O tremble: for you heare the Lyon rore.   601
But they will quake and tremble all this day.   939
And fright him there? and make him tremble there?   2226
TRESSES = 1
Fra. Binde vp those tresses: O what loue I note   1445
TRIALL = 2
In dreadfull triall of our kingdomes King.   593
In this hot triall more then we of France,   656
TRIBUTE = 1
Subiected tribute to commanding loue,   277
TRICKE = 1
Elen. He hath a tricke of *Cordelions* face,   93
TRIDE = 1
Resembling Maiesty, which being touch'd and tride,   1025
TRIPPING = 1
Like *Amazons*, come tripping after drummes: 2409
TRIUMPHANTLY = 1
Who are at hand triumphantly displayed   619
TRODDEN = 1
Keepe my need vp, and faith is trodden downe.   1147
TRODEN = 1
For this downe-troden equity, we tread   547
TROOPE = 2
And like a iolly troope of Huntsmen come   632
Is not the Ladie *Constance* in this troope?   860
TROOPES = 1
This vn-heard sawcinesse and boyish Troopes,   2387
TROTH = 2
And by my troth I thinke thou lou'st me well.   1354
Loe, by my troth, the Instrument is cold,   1682
TROUBLED = 3
Fresh expectation troubled not the Land   1724
Do shew the mood of a much troubled brest,   1791
Iohn. This Feauer that hath troubled me so long,   2442
TROUBLESOME = 1
And, in the last repeating, troublesome,   1736

TRUCE = 3
    With my vext spirits, I cannot take a Truce,   938
    And euen before this truce, but new before,   1164
    Send fayre-play-orders, and make comprimise, | Insinuation, parley, and
    base truce   2236
TRUE = 24
    Chat. Philip of *France*, in right and true behalfe   12
    But where I be as true begot or no,   83
    Con. My bed was euer to thy sonne as true   421
    My boy a bastard? by my soule I thinke | His father neuer was so true
    begot,   426
    But this one word, whether thy tale be true.   947
    Sal. As true as I beleeue you thinke them false,   948
    That giue you cause to proue my saying true.   949
    Fran. 'Tis true (faire daughter) and this blessed day,   1000
    Was deepe-sworne faith, peace, amity, true loue   1162
    And make a ryot on the gentle brow | Of true sincerity? O holy Sir   1178
    With al true duetie: On toward *Callice*, hoa. | *Exeunt.*   1379
    But that which ends all counsell, true Redresse: 1407
    Like true, inseparable, faithfull loues, | Sticking together in calamitie.   1450
    If that be true, I shall see my boy againe;   1463
    For he that steepes his safetie in true blood,   1532
    I idely heard: if true, or false I know not.   1843
    Bast. 'Tis true, to hurt his master, no mans else.   2032
    Nor tempt the danger of my true defence;   2084
    Sal. May this be possible? May this be true?   2482
    Why should I then be false, since it is true   2489
    Mes. Who euer spoke it, it is true my Lord.   2545
    Should scape the true acquaintance of mine eare.   2570
    I do bequeath my faithfull seruices | And true subiection euerlastingly.   2715
    If England to it selfe, do rest but true. *Exeunt.*   2729
TRUELY = 2
    Is not amisse when it is truely done: 1202
    Not truely speakes: who speakes not truly, Lies.   2093
TRULY = 2
    To pay that dutie which you truly owe,   553
    Not truely speakes: who speakes not truly, Lies.   2093
TRUMPET = 6
    So hence: be thou the trumpet of our wrath,   32
    Some Trumpet summon hither to the walles   501
    Trumpet sounds. | *Enter a Citizen vpon the walles.*   504
    Our Trumpet call'd you to this gentle parle.   511
    Enter English Herald with Trumpet.   622
    What lusty Trumpet thus doth summon vs?   2370
TRUMPETS = 2
    Heere after excursions, Enter the Herald of France | *with Trumpets to
    the gates.*   608
    Shall braying trumpets, and loud churlish drums   1236
TRUNCKS = 1
    To lye like pawnes, lock'd vp in chests and truncks,   2395
TRUST = 5
    Which trust accordingly kinde Cittizens,   537
    To our solemnity: I trust we shall,   876
    I trust I may not trust thee, for thy word   928
    Sal. Trust not those cunning waters of his eyes,   2110
TRUSTING = 1
    (Not trusting to this halting Legate heere,   2430

KING JOHN

TRUTH = 11*1
But for the certaine knowledge of that truth,   69
But truth is truth, large lengths of seas and shores   113
*Bast. Madam by chance, but not by truth, what tho;   178
The truth is then most done not doing it: 1204
And mak'st an oath the suretie for thy truth,   1213
Against an oath the truth, thou art vnsure   1214
Makes sound opinion sicke, and truth suspected,   1743
That thou for truth giu'st out are landed heere? | Mes. Vnder the
Dolphin.   1849
Pet. Fore-knowing that the truth will fall out so.   1875
The life, the right, and truth of all this Realme   2149
That I must dye heere, and liue hence, by Truth?   2490
TRY = 1
To try the faire aduenture of to morrow. Exeunt   2548
TUG = 1
To tug and scamble, and to part by th'teeth   2151
TUMBLED = 1
Or, as a little snow, tumbled about,   1561
TUMULT = 1
Hostilitie, and ciuill tumult reignes   1972
TUNE = 1
But I will fit it with some better tune.   1325
TUNED = 1
It ill beseemes this presence to cry ayme | To these ill-tuned repetitions: 499
TURN = *1
*Dol. There end thy braue, and turn thy face in peace,   2413
TURND = 2
Which we God knowes, haue turn'd another way, | To our owne
vantage.   869
Or turn'd an eye of doubt vpon my face;   1958
TURNE = 4*1
Chat. Then turne your forces from this paltry siege,   348
Turne face to face, and bloody point to point: 704
Turne thou the mouth of thy Artillerie,   717
Nay, rather turne this day out of the weeke,   1012
*Fra. Thy rage shall burne thee vp, & thou shalt turne   1277
TURNED = 1
Are turned to one thred, one little haire: 2664
TURNING = 2
Turning with splendor of his precious eye   1004
Turning dispitious torture out of doore?   1607
TWAS = 1
Who sayes it was, he lyes, I say twas not. | Exeunt.   289
TWERE = 1
Therefore 'twere reason you had manners now.   2030
TWICE = 1
Twice fifteene thousand hearts of Englands breed. | Bast. Bastards and
else.   582
TWICE-TOLD = 1
Life is as tedious as a twice-told tale,   1493
TWILL = 1
Sal. Or rather then set forward, for 'twill be   2016
TWISTED = 1
That euer Spider twisted from her wombe   2132
TWIXT = 2*1
Set armed discord 'twixt these periur'd Kings,   1036

248

TWIXT *cont.*

Like Heralds 'twixt two dreadfull battailes set:	1796
Ioh. Oh, when the last accompt twixt heauen & earth	1941

TWO = 14

Which now the mannage of two kingdomes must	43
And if my legs were two such riding rods,	148
'Tis two respectiue, and too sociable	198
Enter the two Kings with their powers, | *at seuerall doores.*	646
O two such siluer currents when they ioyne	756
And two such shores, to two such streames made one,	758
Two such controlling bounds shall you be, kings,	759
To these two Princes, if you marrie them:	760
As doth the furie of two desperate men,	953
Like Heralds 'twixt two dreadfull battailes set:	1796
Two long dayes iourney (Lords) or ere we meete.	2017
Where these two Christian Armies might combine	2288
King *Iohn* did flie an houre or two before	2543

TYDINGS = 2

The tydings comes, that they are all arriu'd.	1833
With these ill tydings: Now? What sayes the world	1853

TYE = 1

For by this knot, thou shalt so surely tye	786

TYGER = 1

A fasting Tyger safer by the tooth,	1191

TYRANNIZE = 1

Is, as a fiend, confin'd to tyrannize,	2656

TYRANT = 1

Iohn. Aye me, this tyrant Feauer burnes mee vp,	2454

TYTHE = 1

Shall tythe or toll in our dominions:	1081

VACANT = 1

Stuffes out his vacant garments with his forme;	1482

VAINE = 2

Is but the vaine breath of a common man:	929
The bloud of malice, in a vaine of league,	2289

VAINLY = 1

Our Cannons malice vainly shall be spent	557

VALIANT = 2

Thou little valiant, great in villanie,	1042
Mes. My Lord: your valiant kinsman *Falconbridge,*	2445

VALOUR = 1

Whose valour plucks dead Lyons by the beard;	438

VALUED = 1

The blood and deerest valued bloud of *France.*	1276

VALUELESSE = 1

Proues valuelesse: you are forsworne, forsworne,	1026

VANITY = 1

Hen. Oh vanity of sicknesse: fierce extreames	2619

VANTAGE = 1

Which we God knowes, haue turn'd another way, | To our owne vantage.	869

VAST = 1

Meet in one line: and vast confusion waites	2157

VAULTIE = 2

And put my eye-balls in thy vaultie browes,	1413
Then had I seene the vaultie top of heauen	2303

VAULTS = 1
In vaults and prisons, and to thrill and shake,   2397
VEHEMENT = 1
By long and vehement suit I was seduc'd   267
VEINE *see* vaine
VEINES = 4
Whose veines bound richer blood then Lady *Blanch*?   746
Within the scorched veines of one new burn'd: 1209
Which else runnes tickling vp and downe the veines,   1343
That whiles warme life playes in that infants veines,   1517
VENGEANCE = 1
Plainly denouncing vengeance vpon *Iohn*.   1544
VENTURE = 1
I am afraide, and yet Ile venture it.   2001
VERIE = 1
The Dolphine rages at our verie heeles.   2690
VERIFIE = 1
Iohn. To verifie our title with their liues.   584
VERTUE = 5
Vpon the maiden vertue of the Crowne: 395
If zealous loue should go in search of vertue,   743
Such as she is, in beautie, vertue, birth,   747
And being rich, my vertue then shall be,   916
Hen. Oh that there were some vertue in my teares, | That might releeue
you.   2652
VERTUOUS = 1
I doe pray to thee, thou vertuous *Daulphin*,   1244
VERY = 13
This might haue beene preuented, and made whole | With very easie
arguments of loue,   41
Ele. The very spirit of *Plantaginet*:   176
King *Iohn*, this is the very summe of all: 451
Will giue her sadnesse very little cure: 866
Which in the very meeting fall, and dye.   954
But on my Liege, for very little paines | Will bring this labor to an
happy end. *Exit*.   1295
He is a very serpent in my way,   1361
With this same very Iron, to burne them out.   1704
Forme such another? This is the very top,   2044
I do suspect thee very greeuously.   2138
We cannot deale but with the very hand   2273
Dol. Ah fowle, shrew'd newes. Beshrew thy very | (hart: 2540
Bast. Shew me the very wound of this ill newes,   2578
VEXING = 1
Vexing the dull eare of a drowsie man;   1494
VEXT = 3
And with a blessed and vn-vext retyre,   559
Whose passage vext with thy impediment,   650
With my vext spirits, I cannot take a Truce,   938
VGLY = 3
This newes hath made thee a most vgly man.   958
Vgly, and slandrous to thy Mothers wombe,   965
There is not yet so vgly a fiend of hell   2126
VICE = 1
To say there is no vice, but beggerie: 917
VICTORIE = 1
And victorie with little losse doth play   617

VICTORIOUS = 1
Shall that victorious hand be feebled heere,   2400
VICTORS = 1
Open your gates, and giue the Victors way.   635
VICTORY = 1
And kisse him with a glorious victory: 708
VIEW = 1
Mel. Haue I not hideous death within my view,   2483
VIGOR = 1
The grapling vigor, and rough frowne of Warre | Is cold in amitie, and
painted peace,   1029
VILDE = 5
And by the merit of vilde gold, drosse, dust,   1092
In the vilde prison of afflicted breath: 1402
Makes nice of no vilde hold to stay him vp: 1523
Your vilde intent must needs seeme horrible.   1674
The deed, which both our tongues held vilde to name.   1966
VILDEST = 1
The wildest Sauagery, the vildest stroke   2047
VILE = 2
In such a loue, so vile a Lout as he.   826
Till this aduantage, this vile drawing byas,   898
VILE-CONCLUDED = 1
To a most base and vile-concluded peace.   907
VILLAIN = 1
Auant thou hatefull villain, get thee gone.   2077
VILLAINE = 6
Aus. Thou dar'st not say so villaine for thy life.   1058
Hu. I am no villaine. *Sal.* Must I rob | (the Law?   2078
Second a Villaine, and a Murtherer? | *Hub.* Lord *Bigot*, I am none. 2104
Enough to stifle such a villaine vp.   2137
Iohn. That villaine *Hubert* told me he did liue.   2210
Hub. A Monke I tell you, a resolued villaine   2586
VILLANIE = 3
Thou little valiant, great in villanie,   1042
Finding thee fit for bloody villanie: 1950
For villanie is not without such rheume,   2111
VIOLENT = 1
Bast. Oh, I am scalded with my violent motion   2659
VIOLET = 1
To throw a perfume on the Violet,   1729
VIRTUE *see* vertue
VIRTUOUS *see* vertuous
VISAGD = 1
For your owne Ladies, and pale-visag'd Maides,   2408
VISITED = 1
Thy sinnes are visited in this poore childe,   481
VIUE = 1
Viue le Roy, as I haue bank'd their Townes?   2357
VNACQUAINTED = 2
And kisse the lippes of vnacquainted change,   1551
And follow vnacquainted colours heere: 2283
VNADUISD = 1
Lest vnaduis'd you staine your swords with bloud,   338
VNADUISED = 2
Que. Thou vnaduised scold, I can produce   494
This harness'd Maske, and vnaduised Reuell,   2386

KING JOHN

VNATTEMPTED = 1
But for my hand, as vnattempted yet,   912
VNBEGOTTEN = 1
To the yet vnbegotten sinne of times;   2053
VNBRUISD = 1
With vnhack'd swords, and Helmets all vnbruis'd,   560
VNCKLE = 4
Sh'adulterates hourely with thine Vnckle *Iohn,*   977
My Vnckle practises more harme to me: 1593
For all the Treasure that thine Vnckle owes,   1702
Your Vnckle must not know but you are dead.   1708
VNCKLES = 2
Blan. My vnckles will in this respect is mine,   827
Oh me, my Vnckles spirit is in these stones,   2005
VNCLE = 3
And to rebuke the vsurpation | Of thy vnnaturall Vncle, English *Iohn,*   302
Vpon my knee I beg, goe not to Armes | Against mine Vncle.   1241
Vncle, I needs must pray that thou maist lose: 1265
VNCLEANLY = 1*1
Hub. Vncleanly scruples feare not you: looke too't.   1577
Th'vncleanly sauours of a Slaughter-house,   2115
VNCONSTANT = 1
Make such vnconstant children of our selues   1174
VNDER = 8
Shadowing their right vnder your wings of warre: 307
Vnder whose warrant I impeach thy wrong,   413
But as we, vnder heauen, are supreame head,   1082
So vnder him that great supremacy   1083
But in despaire, dye vnder their blacke weight.   1228
Vnder whose conduct came those powres of France,   1848
That thou for truth giu'st out are landed heere? | *Mes.* Vnder the
Dolphin.   1849
Vnder the tide; but now I breath againe   1859
VNDERGO = 1
Much danger do I vndergo for thee. *Exeunt*   1715
VNDERSTAND = 3
He lies before me: dost thou vnderstand me?   1363
And on the winking of Authoritie | To vnderstand a Law; to know the
meaning   1936
But, thou didst vnderstand me by my signes,   1962
VNDERTAKE = 1
Hub. So well, that what you bid me vndertake,   1355
VNDER-BEARE = 1
And leaue those woes alone, which I alone | Am bound to vnder-beare.   985
VNDER-GOE = 1
That vnder-goe this charge? Who else but I,   2353
VNDER-PROP = 1
To vnder-prop this Action? Is't not I   2352
VNDER-WROUGHT = 1
That thou hast vnder-wrought his lawfull King,   392
VNDESERUED = 1
In vndeserued extreames: See else your selfe,   1687
VNDETERMIND = 1
In vndetermin'd differences of kings.   669
VNDOUBTED = 1
And till it be vndoubted, we do locke   683

VNEXPECTED = 2
Aust. By how much vnexpected, by so much   375
Deuoured by the vnexpected flood.   2674
VNFAINEDLY = 1
For I doe loue her most vnfainedly.   846
VNFENCED = 1
Euen till vnfenced desolation | Leaue them as naked as the vulgar ayre: 700
VNFORTUNATE *see* infortunate
VNGODLY = 1
Let not the howres of this vngodly day   1034
VNGRATEFULL *see* ingratefull
VNHACKD = 1
With vnhack'd swords, and Helmets all vnbruis'd,   560
VNHEARD *see* vn-heard
VNION = 1
This Vnion shall do more then batterie can   761
VNITED = 1
That done, disseuer your vnited strengths,   702
VNKINDE = *1
Hub. Vnkinde remembrance: thou, & endles night,   2567
VNKLE = 1
Thy Grandame loues thee, and thy Vnkle will   1301
VNLESSE = 2
Vnlesse thou let his siluer Water, keepe | A peacefull progresse to the
Ocean.   653
Vnlesse he doe submit himselfe to *Rome*.   1122
VNLOOKD = 2
Kin. How much vnlook'd for, is this expedition.   374
To this vnlook'd for vnprepared pompe. *Exeunt.*   881
VNMANNERLY = 1
This apish and vnmannerly approach,   2385
VNMATCHEABLE = 1
And this so sole, and so vnmatcheable,   2051
VNMATCHED = 1
Against whose furie and vnmatched force,   278
VNNATURALL = 1
And to rebuke the vsurpation | Of thy vnnaturall Vncle, English *Iohn*,   302
VNNEIGHBOURLY *see* vn-neighbourly
VNOWED *see* vn-owed
VNPLEASING = 1
Full of vnpleasing blots, and sightlesse staines,   966
VNPREPARED = 1
To this vnlook'd for vnprepared pompe. *Exeunt.*   881
VNREPREEUABLE = 1
On vnrepreeuable condemned blood.   2657
VNREUEREND = 1
Lady. Sir *Roberts* sonne, I thou vnreuerend boy,   238
VNRULY = 1
A Scepter snatch'd with an vnruly hand,   1520
VNSCRATCHD = 1
To saue vnscratch'd your Citties threatned cheekes: 531
VNSEASONABLE = 1
Being vrged at a time vnseasonable.   1737
VNSETLED = 1
And all th'vnsetled humors of the Land,   360
VNSTAINED = 1
But with a heart full of vnstained loue,   309

VNSURD = 1

Thy now vnsur'd assurance to the Crowne,   787

VNSURE = 1

Against an oath the truth, thou art vnsure   1214

VNSWEARE *see* vn-sweare

VNTHRED = 1

Vnthred the rude eye of Rebellion,   2472

VNTILL = 1

Kings of our feare, vntill our feares resolu'd   685

VNTO = 8

Madam, Ile follow you vnto the death.   162

To speake vnto this Cittie: what say you?   799

Looke who comes heere? a graue vnto a soule,   1400

Vnto the Raine-bow; or with Taper-light   1731

And like a shifted winde vnto a saile,   1740

The heighth, the Crest: or Crest vnto the Crest   2045

And cripple thee vnto a Pagan shore,   2287

And warrant limited vnto my tongue.   2377

VNTOWARD = 1

What meanes this scorne, thou most vntoward knaue?   256

VNTREAD = 1

We will vntread the steps of damned flight,   2513

VNTRIMMED = 1

In likenesse of a new vntrimmed Bride.   1139

VNTRUE = 1

Shall finde but bloodie safety, and vntrue.   1533

VNUEXT *see* vn-vext

VNWARILY = 1

Were in the *Washes* all vnwarily,   2673

VNWASHD = 1

Another leane, vnwash'd Artificer,   1926

VNWORTHY = 1

So slight, vnworthy, and ridiculous   1077

VNYOKE = 1

Vnyoke this seysure, and this kinde regreete?   1172

VN-HEARD = 2

Then let the worst vn-heard, fall on your head.   1857

This vn-heard sawcinesse and boyish Troopes,   2387

VN-NEIGHBOURLY = 1

And not to spend it so vn-neighbourly.   2290

VN-OWED = 1

The vn-owed interest of proud swelling State: 2152

VN-SWEARE = 1

Vn-sweare faith sworne, and on the marriage bed   1176

VN-VEXT = 1

And with a blessed and vn-vext retyre,   559

VN-URGD = 1

A voluntary zeale, and an vn-urg'd Faith   2261

VOLLEY = 1

When with a volley of our needlesse shot,   2529

VOLQUESSEN = 1

Iohn. Then I doe giue *Volquessen, Toraine, Maine,*   847

VOLUME = 1

Shall draw this breefe into as huge a volume: 400

VOLUNTARIES = 1

Rash, inconsiderate, fiery voluntaries,   361

VOLUNTARY = 3

And my good friend, thy voluntary oath	1322
But (heau'n be thank'd) it is but voluntary.	2196
A voluntary zeale, and an vn-urg'd Faith	2261

VOUCHSAFE = 3*1

Behold the French amaz'd vouchsafe a parle,	532
*Hub. Heare vs great kings, vouchsafe awhile to stay	731
What you in wisedome still vouchsafe to say.	842
If thou vouchsafe them. But if not, then know	1225

VOW = 4

That dayly breake-vow, he that winnes of all,	890
Thy tongue against thy tongue. O let thy vow	1196
The Incense of a Vow, a holy Vow:	2066

VOWD = 1

Is most diuinely vow'd vpon the right	543

VOWES = 3

With all religous strength of sacred vowes,	1160
It is religion that doth make vowes kept,	1210
Therefore thy later vowes, against thy first,	1219

VOYCE = 2

Which cannot heare a Ladies feeble voyce,	1425
Thinking this voyce an armed Englishman.	2399

VP = 51*2

That holds in chase mine honour vp and downe.	234
And stirre them vp against a mightier taske:	349
They shoote but calme words, folded vp in smoake,	535
Saue in aspect, hath all offence seal'd vp:	556
Haue we ramm'd vp our gates against the world.	578
Iohn. Vp higher to the plaine, where we'l set forth	603
Fra. Know him in vs, that heere hold vp his right.	678
I know she is not for this match made vp,	861
Iohn. We will heale vp all,	871
(If not fill vp the measure of her will)	877
Can hold it vp: here I and sorrowes sit,	995
And our oppression hath made vp this league:	1031
And sooth'st vp greatnesse. What a foole art thou,	1047
Aust. Well ruffian, I must pocket vp these wrongs,	1128
O then tread downe my need, and faith mounts vp,	1146
Keepe my need vp, and faith is trodden downe.	1147
To clap this royall bargaine vp of peace,	1166
France, I am burn'd vp with inflaming wrath,	1273
Fra. Thy rage shall burne thee vp, & thou shalt turne	1277
Iohn. Hubert, keepe this boy: *Philip* make vp,	1290
Which else runnes tickling vp and downe the veines,	1343
Fra. Binde vp those tresses: O what loue I note	1445
Fra. Binde vp your haires. | *Con.* Yes that I will: and wherefore will I do it?	1453
Con. Greefe fils the roome vp of my absent childe:	1478
Lies in his bed, walkes vp and downe with me,	1479
Makes nice of no vilde hold to stay him vp:	1523
Of all his people, and freeze vp their zeale,	1535
Still and anon cheer'd vp the heauy time;	1623
The steppes of wrong, should moue you to mew vp	1774
Your Highnes should deliuer vp your Crowne.	1873
I shall yeeld vp my Crowne, let him be hang'd	1878
Bast. Your sword is bright sir, put it vp againe.	2079
Ile strike thee dead. Put vp thy sword betime,	2100

VP *cont.*

Enough to stifle such a villaine vp.	2137
How easie dost thou take all *England* vp,	2147
K.Iohn. Thus haue I yeelded vp into your hand | The Circle of my glory.	2167
Pand. It was my breath that blew this Tempest vp,	2184
And wilde amazement hurries vp and downe	2203
Vpon her gentle bosom, and fill vp	2279
This showre, blowne vp by tempest of the soule,	2301
Lift vp thy brow (renowned *Salisburie*)	2305
Therefore thy threatning Colours now winde vp,	2326
That like a Lion fostered vp at hand,	2328
To lye like pawnes, lock'd vp in chests and truncks,	2395
You bloudy Nero's, ripping vp the wombe	2406
Strike vp the drummes, and let the tongue of warre	2420
* Dol. Strike vp our drummes, to finde this danger out.	2435
Iohn. Aye me, this tyrant Feauer burnes mee vp,	2454
Pem. Vp once againe: put spirit in the French,	2461
And woon'd our tott'ring colours clearly vp,	2531
The day shall not be vp so soone as I,	2547
That all my bowels crumble vp to dust:	2638
Vpon a Parchment, and against this fire | Do I shrinke vp.	2640

VPHOLD = 1

Where we doe reigne, we will alone vphold	1084

VPHOLDETH = 1

Con. That which vpholdeth him, that thee vpholds,	1248

VPHOLDS = 2

Con. That which vpholdeth him, that thee vpholds,	1248
In spight of spight, alone vpholds the day.	2464

VPON = 62

Vpon the right and party of her sonne.	40
That still I lay vpon my mothers head,	84
Vpon his death-bed he by will bequeath'd	117
Vpon good Friday, and nere broke his fast:	248
Aust. Vpon thy cheeke lay I this zelous kisse,	312
King. A wonder Lady: lo vpon thy wish | Our Messenger *Chattilion* is arriu'd,	344
Did neuer flote vpon the swelling tide,	368
Vpon the maiden vertue of the Crowne:	395
Looke heere vpon thy brother *Geffreyes* face,	396
As great *Alcides* shooes vpon an Asse:	444
Con. Now shame vpon you where she does or no,	469
And all for her, a plague vpon her.	493
Trumpet sounds. | *Enter a Citizen vpon the walles.*	504
Is most diuinely vow'd vpon the right	543
Vpon the dancing banners of the French,	618
I'de play incessantly vpon these Iades,	699
Make worke vpon our selues, for heauen or hell.	721
Is neere to England, looke vpon the yeeres	739
And all that we vpon this side the Sea,	804
Made to run euen, vpon euen ground;	897
Since Kings breake faith vpon commoditie,	918
What meanes that hand vpon that breast of thine?	942
Thou euer strong vpon the stronger side;	1043
Vpon my partie: thou cold blooded slaue,	1049
Vpon thy starres, thy fortune, and thy strength,	1052
And raise the power of *France* vpon his head,	1121
Vpon which better part, our prayrs come in,	1224

VPON *cont.*

Daul. Father, to Armes. | *Blanch.* Vpon thy wedding day?	1232
Vpon my knee I beg, goe not to Armes | Against mine Vncle.	1241
Const. O, vpon my knee made hard with kneeling,	1243
Pand. I will denounce a curse vpon his head.	1252
Must by the hungry now be fed vpon:	1308
I will not keepe this forme vpon my head,	1486
Shee lookes vpon them with a threatning eye:	1505
And he that stands vpon a slipp'ry place,	1522
Plainly denouncing vengeance vpon *Iohn.*	1544
Vpon the bosome of the ground, rush forth	1573
Nor looke vpon the Iron angerly:	1658
And look'd vpon, I hope, with chearefull eyes.	1719
As patches set vpon a little breach,	1749
Do prophesie vpon it dangerously:	1911
Had falsely thrust vpon contrary feete,	1923
More vpon humor, then aduis'd respect.	1939
Or turn'd an eye of doubt vpon my face;	1958
Vpon thy feature, for my rage was blinde,	1989
Hub. Vpon my soule.	2128
And heauen it selfe doth frowne vpon the Land. *Exit.*	2164
Vpon your stubborne vsage of the Pope:	2185
Vpon your oath of seruice to the Pope,	2190
Shall we vpon the footing of our land,	2235
Sal. Vpon our sides it neuer shall be broken.	2259
Cries out vpon the name of *Salisbury.*	2270
Vpon her gentle bosom, and fill vp	2279
Vpon the spot of this inforced cause,	2281
To feast vpon whole thousands of the French.	2434
Vpon the Altar at S.(aint) *Edmondsbury,*	2479
I will on all hazards well beleeue	2561
Death hauing praide vpon the outward parts	2621
To set a forme vpon that indigest	2632
Vpon a Parchment, and against this fire | Do I shrinke vp.	2640
As I vpon aduantage did remoue,	2672
Shall waite vpon your Fathers Funerall.	2708

VPPON = 1

For bloody power to rush vppon your peace.	527

VRGD = 2

Which was so strongly vrg'd past my defence.	271
A voluntary zeale, and an vn-urg'd Faith	2261

VRGE = 3

That right in peace which heere we vrge in warre,	340
Marke how they whisper, vrge them while their soules | Are capeable of this ambition,	791
Doth lay it open to vrge on reuenge.	2037

VRGED = 1

Being vrged at a time vnseasonable.	1737

VRGEST = 1

Why vrgest thou so oft yong *Arthurs* death?	1929

VS *see also* let's *l.**5 45 88 *92 241 502 506 512 528 538 541 569 597 678 679 *731 805 *853 880 *1567 1780 1803 1943 2015 2021 *2118 2242 2318 2370 2414 2440 2596 2689 2721 2728 = 30*6

VSAGE = 1

Vpon your stubborne vsage of the Pope:	2185

VSD = 2

Being create for comfort, to be vs'd	1686

VSD *cont.*
Whom he hath vs'd rather for sport, then neede)   2431
VSE = 7
Vse our Commission in his vtmost force.   1309
If heauen be pleas'd that you must vse me ill,   1631
Though to no vse, but still to looke on you.   1681
All things that you should vse to do me wrong   1697
For I must vse thee. O my gentle Cosen,   1880
And from his holinesse vse all your power   2173
Since I must loose the vse of all deceite?   2488
VSEFULL = 1
Or vsefull seruing-man, and Instrument   2334
VSES = 1
Creatures of note for mercy, lacking vses.   1700
VSING = 1
Without a tongue, vsing conceit alone,   1349
VSURPATION = 1
And to rebuke the vsurpation | Of thy vnnaturall Vncle, English *Iohn,*   302
VSURPD = 1
So tell the Pope, all reuerence set apart | To him and his vsurp'd
  authoritie.   1086
VSURPE = 2
K.Iohn. Alack thou dost vsurpe authoritie.   415
Call not me slanderer, thou and thine vsurpe | The Dominations,
  Royalties, and rights   477
VSURPER = 1
Queen. Who is it thou dost call vsurper *France*?   417
VSURPING = 3
Fran. Excuse it is to beat vsurping downe.   416
Const. Let me make answer: thy vsurping sonne.   418
That strumpet Fortune, that vsurping *Iohn:*   982
VSURPINGLY = 1
Which swaies vsurpingly these seuerall titles,   18
VTMOST = 2
Euen till that vtmost corner of the West   322
Vse our Commission in his vtmost force.   1309
VTTER = 1
Pand. Lady, you vtter madnesse, and not sorrow.   1427
VTTERANCE = 1
Art. Hubert, the vtterance of a brace of tongues,   1676
VTTERED = 1
Which holds but till thy newes be vttered,   2666
VULGAR = 1
Euen till vnfenced desolation | Leaue them as naked as the vulgar ayre: 700
WADE = 1
Wade to the market-place in *French*-mens bloud,   335
WAFT = 1
Then now the *English* bottomes haue waft o're,   367
WAGE = 1
The awlesse Lion could not wage the fight,   279
WAIST *see* waste
WAITE = 2
And then my soule shall waite on thee to heauen,   2682
Shall waite vpon your Fathers Funerall.   2708
WAITES = 1
Meet in one line: and vast confusion waites   2157

WALKE = 1*1
Who dares not stirre by day, must walke by night,   181
*Hub. Why heere walke I in the black brow of night | To finde you out.   2573
WALKES = 3
Lies in his bed, walkes vp and downe with me,   1479
How wildely then walkes my Estate in France?   1847
That leaues the print of blood where ere it walkes.   2024
WALL = 2
We owe thee much: within this wall of flesh   1319
Ar. The Wall is high, and yet will I leape downe.   1997
WALLED = 1
That Water-walled Bulwarke, still secure   320
WALLES = 9
Some Trumpet summon hither to the walles   501
Trumpet sounds. | Enter a Citizen vpon the walles.   504
Cit. Who is it that hath warn'd vs to the walles? | Fra. 'Tis France, for
England.   506
Their Iron indignation 'gainst your walles: 518
To make a shaking feuer in your walles,   534
Craues harbourage within your Citie walles.   540
'Tis not the rounder of your old-fac'd walles,   565
As we will ours, against these sawcie walles,   718
Enter Arthur on the walles.   1996
WALL-EYD = 1
That euer wall-ey'd wrath, or staring rage   2048
WANDERING = 1
A graine, a dust, a gnat, a wandering haire,   1671
WANT = 5
And she againe wants nothing, to name want,   750
If want it be not, that she is not hee.   751
Doth want example: who hath read, or heard   1395
Must needes want pleading for a paire of eyes: 1677
Let hell want paines enough to torture me: 2142
WANTON = 2
Is all too wanton, and too full of gawdes   1335
A cockred-silken wanton braue our fields,   2239
WANTONNESSE = 1
Onely for wantonnesse: by my Christendome,   1589
WANTS = 1
And she againe wants nothing, to name want,   750
WANTST = 1
And if thou want'st a Cord, the smallest thred   2131
WAR = 2*2
*K.Io. Heere haue we war for war, & bloud for bloud,   24
Const. War, war, no peace, peace is to me a warre: 1039
WARD = 1
Bast. The Dolphin is preparing hither-ward,   2669
WARLIKE = 3
In warlike march, these greenes before your Towne,   548
Told of a many thousand warlike French,   1924
Is warlike Iohn: and in his fore-head sits   2432
WARM = 1
Full warm of blood, of mirth, of gossipping: 2310
WARME = 1
That whiles warme life playes in that infants veines,   1517

WARND = 1
  Cit. Who is it that hath warn'd vs to the walles? | *Fra.* 'Tis France, for
  England.   506
WARRANT = 7*1
  Vnder whose warrant I impeach thy wrong,   413
  * *Pan.* There's Law and Warrant (Lady) for my curse.   1112
  Exec. I hope your warrant will beare out the deed.   1576
  I warrant I loue you more then you do me.   1604
  He shew'd his warrant to a friend of mine,   1788
  By slaues, that take their humors for a warrant,   1934
  To giue vs warrant from the hand of heauen,   2318
  And warrant limited vnto my tongue.   2377
WARRE = 18*1
  * *Chat.* The proud controle of fierce and bloudy warre,   22
  Shadowing their right vnder your wings of warre: 307
  In such a iust and charitable warre.   329
  That right in peace which heere we vrge in warre,   340
  Fran. Peace be to *England,* if that warre returne   386
  Can hide you from our messengers of Warre,   566
  From a resolu'd and honourable warre,   906
  The grapling vigor, and rough frowne of Warre | Is cold in amitie, and
  painted peace,   1029
  Const. War, war, no peace, peace is to me a warre: 1039
  And like a ciuill warre setst oath to oath,   1195
  Doth dogged warre bristle his angry crest,   2154
  My tongue shall hush againe this storme of warre,   2187
  Away, and glister like the god of warre   2222
  And tame the sauage spirit of wilde warre,   2327
  Sweat in this businesse, and maintaine this warre?   2355
  Before I drew this gallant head of warre,   2366
  To whip this dwarfish warre, this Pigmy Armes   2389
  Strike vp the drummes, and let the tongue of warre   2420
  With purpose presently to leaue this warre.   2696
WARRES = 3
  And fought the holy Warres in *Palestine,*   297
  Gracing the scroule that tels of this warres losse,   662
  Your breath first kindled the dead coale of warres,   2336
WARRE-LIKE = 1
  And flesh his spirit in a warre-like soyle,   2240
WAS *see also* twas = 54*1
WASH = 1
  No longer then we well could wash our hands,   1165
WASHES = 2
  These Lincolne-Washes haue deuoured them,   2599
  Were in the *Washes* all vnwarily,   2673
WAST *l.190* = 1
WASTE = 1
  That as a waste doth girdle you about   523
WASTEFULL = 1
  Is wastefull, and ridiculous excesse.   1733
WATCH = 2
  Fast to the chaire: be heedfull: hence, and watch.   1575
  That I might sit all night, and watch with you.   1603
WATCHFULL = 2
  Then, in despight of brooded watchfull day,   1351
  And like the watchfull minutes, to the houre,   1622

WATER = 3
  As raine to water, or deuill to his damme;   425
  Vnlesse thou let his siluer Water, keepe | A peacefull progresse to the
  Ocean.   653
  Put but a little water in a spoone,   2135
WATERS = 2
  Sal. Trust not those cunning waters of his eyes,   2110
  Commend these waters to those baby-eyes   2307
WATER-WALLED = 1
  That Water-walled Bulwarke, still secure   320
WAXE = 1
  Which bleeds away, euen as a forme of waxe   2485
WAY = 10
  Bast. Our Country manners giue our betters way.   164
  For thou wast got i'th way of honesty. | *Exeunt all but bastard.*   190
  Open your gates, and giue the Victors way.   635
  Is the yong Dolphin euery way compleat,   748
  Which we God knowes, haue turn'd another way, | To our owne
  vantage.   869
  He is a very serpent in my way,   1361
  I haue a way to winne their loues againe: 1889
  I am amaz'd me thinkes, and loose my way   2145
  And send him word by me, which way you go.   2447
  I come one way of the *Plantagenets.*   2566
WE = 97*7
WEAKE = 2
  With that same weake winde, which enkindled it: 2340
  Out of the weake doore of our fainting Land: 2688
WEAKNESSE = 1
  Weaknesse possesseth me, and I am faint. *Exeunt.*   2457
WEALE = 2
  Then, whereupon our weale on you depending,   1782
  Counts it your weale: he haue his liberty.   1783
WEALTH = 1
  That *Hubert* for the wealth of all the world, | Will not offend thee. 1711
WEARE = 2
  Weare out the daies in Peace; but ere Sun-set,   1035
  Thou weare a Lyons hide, doff it for shame,   1054
WEARIE = 1
  The stumbling night did part our wearie powres?   2544
WEARIED = 2
  Fore-wearied in this action of swift speede,   539
  Of the old, feeble, and day-wearied Sunne,   2496
WEATHER = 2
  Poure downe thy weather: how goes all in France?   1827
  And make faire weather in your blustring land: 2188
WEDDING = 1
  Daul. Father, to Armes. | *Blanch.* Vpon thy wedding day?   1232
WEDLOCKE = 1
  Your fathers wife did after wedlocke beare him: 125
WEE *l.*660 2717 = 2
WEEKE = 1
  Nay, rather turne this day out of the weeke,   1012
WEEKES = 1
  Full fourteene weekes before the course of time: 121
WEEL = 2
  Wee'l put thee downe, 'gainst whom these Armes wee | (beare,   660

WEEL *cont.*
For wee'l create yong *Arthur* Duke of Britaine   872
WEELL = 1
Wee'll lay before this towne our Royal bones,   334
WEEPE = 2
I honour'd him, I lou'd him, and will weepe   2108
Her Enemies rankes? I must withdraw, and weepe   2280
WEEPES = 1
Qu.Mo. His mother shames him so, poore boy hee | (weepes.   468
WEIGH = 2
One must proue greatest. While they weigh so euen,   644
Her Dowrie shall weigh equall with a Queene: 802
WEIGHT = 1
But in despaire, dye vnder their blacke weight.   1228
WEL = 1*1
Iohn. Vp higher to the plaine, where we'l set forth   603
Pem. When Workemen striue to do better then wel,   1745
WELCOME = 6
Embrace him, loue him, giue him welcome hether.   304
I giue you welcome with a powerlesse hand,   308
Welcome before the gates *Angiers* Duke.   310
Let them be welcome then, we are prepar'd.   378
And will not let me welcome this good newes.   2455
And welcome home againe discarded faith,   2473
WELKIN = 1
But staid, and made the Westerne Welkin blush,   2526
WELKINS = 1
(As lowd as thine) rattle the Welkins eare,   2428
WELL = 48*5
That is well knowne, and as I thinke one father: 68
But that I am as well begot my Liege   85
K.Iohn. Mine eye hath well examined his parts,   97
Phil. Well sir, by this you cannot get my land,   105
Elinor. I like thee well: wilt thou forsake thy fortune,   156
Neere or farre off, well wonne is still well shot,   183
Well, now can I make any *Ioane* a Lady,   194
Sir *Robert* could doe well, marrie to confesse   249
Who liues and dares but say, thou didst not well   284
Lewis. Before *Angiers* well met braue *Austria*,   294
King. Well, then to worke our Cannon shall be bent   330
Blan. O well did he become that Lyons robe,   441
I like it well. France, shall we knit our powres,   712
Fra. It likes vs well young Princes: close your hands   853
Aust. And your lippes too, for I am well assur'd,   854
Go we as well as hast will suffer vs,   880
The world, who of it selfe is peysed well,   896
Well, whiles I am a begger, I will raile,   914
Be well aduis'd, tell ore thy tale againe.   926
Aust. Well ruffian, I must pocket vp these wrongs,   1128
Con. O be remou'd from him, and answere well.   1149
No longer then we well could wash our hands,   1165
Is it as he will? well then, *France* shall rue.   1258
But (ah) I will not, yet I loue thee well,   1353
And by my troth I thinke thou lou'st me well.   1354
Hub. So well, that what you bid me vndertake,   1355
Well, Ile not say what I intend for thee: 1373
Remember: Madam, Fare you well,   1374

WELL   *cont.*
  Pand. Courage and comfort, all shall yet goe well.   1386
  Fra. What can goe well, when we haue runne so ill?   1387
  Fra. Well could I beare that *England* had this praise,   1397
  I am not mad: too well, too well I feele   1443
  Hub. Well, see to liue: I will not touch thine eye,   1701
  Sal. In this the Anticke, and well noted face   1738
  To ouer-beare it, and we are all well pleas'd,   1754
  What you would haue reform'd, that is not well,   1761
  And well shall you perceiue, how willingly   1762
  *Bast. Once more to day well met, distemper'd Lords,   2019
  Big. Who kill'd this Prince? | *Hub.* 'Tis not an houre since I left him
  well: 2106
  I left him well.   2143
  On this Ascension day, remember well,   2189
  Our Partie may well meet a prowder foe. *Exeunt.*   2248
  The youth saies well. Now heare our *English* King,   2382
  The King doth smile at, and is well prepar'd   2388
  We grant thou canst out-scold vs: Far thee well,   2414
  *Dol. Well: keepe good quarter, & good care to night,   2546
  Why may not I demand of thine affaires, | As well as thou of mine?   2557
  I will vpon all hazards well beleeue   2561
  Thou art my friend, that know'st my tongue so well: 2562
  My selfe, well mounted, hardly haue escap'd.   2600
  Our selues well sinew'd to our defence.   2698
WELLES = 1
  To diue like Buckets in concealed Welles,   2393
WELL-BORNE = 1
  Fran. As many and as well-borne bloods as those. | *Bast.* Some Bastards
  too.   585
WERE *see also* 'twere *l.*89 120 133 148 152 272 397 466 568 597 1167 1339
  1356 1422 1432 1441 1442 1459 1559 1590 1597 1602 1670 1706 1721 1752
  1906 1925 2027 2468 2652 2673 = 31
WERT *l.*428 964 2097 = 3
WEST = 3
  Euen till that vtmost corner of the West   322
  By East and West let France and England mount.   695
  Iohn. We from the West will send destruction | Into this Cities bosome.   723
WESTERNE = 1
  But staid, and made the Westerne Welkin blush,   2526
WHAT *l.**5 21 37 56 63 *92 99 122 165 *178 210 228 231 256 258 346 434
  *447 449 777 795 799 *811 *839 842 940 942 956 959 1009 1047 1074
  1131 1132 1152 *1153 1185 1199 1212 1216 1218 1235 1246 1327 1355
  1360 1373 1387 1392 1434 1445 1501 1512 1526 1555 1564 1624 1625
  1652 1660 1673 1755 1756 1761 1772 1786 1793 1846 1853 1861 1867
  1940 1957 2026 2033 2036 *2040 2060 2103 2123 2225 2284 2294 2345
  2350 2351 2370 2487 2535 2553 *2571 2678 = 87*10
WHATERE *see* ere
WHATS = 2
  Bast. Whether doest thou go? | *Hub.* What's that to thee?   2555
  Bast. Breefe then: and what's the newes?   2575
WHEN *l.*103 116 175 201 285 287 405 541 631 665 *677 719 756 855 911
  1045 1113 1202 1251 1311 1387 1472 1487 1504 1547 1572 1587 1616
  *1745 1798 1832 1894 1913 1938 *1941 1957 2038 2223 2468 2527 2529
  2618 2679 2697 2725 = 42*3
WHENCE = 1
  As in a Theater, whence they gape and point   689

WHERE *l.*112 151 *233 603 722 742 744 863 955 1084 1168 1203 *1271
1339 1447 1624 1824 1834 1835 2024 2208 2269 2288 2317 2480 2507
2534 2670 *2685 = 27*4, 2

But where I be as true begot or no,	83
Con. Now shame vpon you where she does or no,	469

WHEREFORE = 4

Fra. Binde vp your haires. | *Con.* Yes that I will: and wherefore will I do it?	1453
Iohn. Thou idle Dreamer, wherefore didst thou so?	1874
But wherefore doe you droope? why looke you sad?	2212
May know wherefore we tooke the Sacrament,	2257

WHEREIN = 1

Wherein we step after a stranger, march	2278

WHEREOF = 1

In lieu whereof, I pray you beare me hence	2505

WHEREON = 1

And on that day at noone, whereon he sayes	1877

WHERESOERE = 1

And wheresoere this foot of mine doth tread,	1362

WHEREUPON = 1

Then, whereupon our weale on you depending,	1782

WHEREWITH = 1

And all the shrowds wherewith my life should saile,	2663

WHERE-ERE *see* ere

WHET = 1

For England go; I will whet on the King.	1566

WHETHER *see also* where = 4

Eli. Whether hadst thou rather be a *Faulconbridge,*	142
And so am I whether I smacke or no:	219
But this one word, whether thy tale be true.	947
Bast. Whether doest thou go? | *Hub.* What's that to thee?	2555

WHICH *l.*18 43 49 76 127 139 224 271 340 399 406 472 537 553 562 570
815 829 857 869 954 961 985 1025 1143 1192 1201 1224 1240 1248 1260
1343 1407 1425 1426 1507 1514 1574 1599 1699 1767 1773 1781 1802
1817 1922 1966 1982 2141 2340 2391 2447 2485 2512 2538 2607 2614
2623 2625 2633 2666 = 61

WHILE = 8

Bast. Iames Gournie, wilt thou giue vs leaue a while?	241
One must proue greatest. While they weigh so euen,	644
Be friends a-while, and both conioyntly bend	693
Marke how they whisper, vrge them while their soules | Are capeable of this ambition,	791
Con. O lawfull let it be | That I haue roome with *Rome* to curse a while,	1107
While *Philip* breathes.	1289
Art. O now you looke like *Hubert.* All this while | You were disguis'd.	1705
Three foot of it doth hold; bad world the while:	1818

WHILES = 3

Whiles we Gods wrathfull agent doe correct	384
Well, whiles I am a begger, I will raile,	914
That whiles warme life playes in that infants veines,	1517

WHILST = 2

Whilst he that heares, makes fearefull action	1916
The whilst his Iron did on the Anuile coole,	1919

WHIP = 1

To whip this dwarfish warre, this Pigmy Armes	2389

WHIRLE = 1
Foure fixed, and the fift did whirle about   1907
WHISPER = 2
Marke how they whisper, vrge them while their soules | Are capeable of
this ambition,   791
And whisper one another in the eare.   1914
WHISPERS = 2
So much my conscience whispers in your eare,   48
Drawne in the flattering table of her eie. | *Whispers with Blanch.*   819
WHITE-FACD = 1
Together with that pale, that white-fac'd shore,   316
WHITHER *see* whether
WHO *l.*129 181 227 263 284 289 311 417 496 506 529 612 619 714 863 892
896 1094 1395 1400 1881 1921 *2011 2093 2106 2285 2353 2542 2545
2563 2564 2585 2589 2628 2693 = 34*1
WHOLE = 4
This might haue beene preuented, and made whole | With very easie
arguments of loue,   41
Iohn to stop *Arthurs* Title in the whole,   883
A whole Armado of conuicted saile   1384
To feast vpon whole thousands of the French.   2434
WHOM *l.*252 *407 437 660 707 886 1869 1871 1886 2431 2703 2714 = 11*1
WHOSE = 31*1
K.Iohn. From henceforth beare his name | Whose forme thou bearest: 168
Against whose furie and vnmatched force,   278
Whose foot spurnes backe the Oceans roaring tides,   317
Whose leisure I haue staid, haue giuen him time   352
Vnder whose warrant I impeach thy wrong,   413
And by whose helpe I meane to chastise it.   414
Whose valour plucks dead Lyons by the beard;   438
Whose title they admit, *Arthurs* or *Iohns*.   503
And let vs in. Your King, whose labour'd spirits   538
Loe in this right hand, whose protection   542
Cit. Till you compound whose right is worthiest,   588
Whose sonnes lye scattered on the bleeding ground: 614
Of both your Armies, whose equality   638
Whose passage vext with thy impediment,   650
Iohn. Whose party do the Townesmen yet admit?   675
Fra. Speake Citizens for England, whose your king.   676
Whose veines bound richer blood then Lady *Blanch*?   746
Whose fulnesse of perfection lyes in him.   755
And France, whose armour Conscience buckled on,   885
A rage, whose heat hath this condition;   1274
Th'infranchisement of *Arthur*, whose restraint   1769
Vnder whose conduct came those powres of France,   1848
Whose priuate with me of the Dolphines loue,   2013
From whose obedience I forbid my soule,   2063
Yet I am none. Whose tongue so ere speakes false,   2092
Away with me, all you whose soules abhorre   2114
Now happy he, whose cloake and center can   2160
A bare-rib'd death, whose office is this day   2433
But euen this night, whose blacke contagious breath   2494
Hub. Whose there? Speake hoa, speake quickely, or | I shoote.   2551
Whose Bowels sodainly burst out: The King   2587
At whose request the king hath pardon'd them,   2593
WHO-EUER *see also* euer = 1
Who-euer wins, on that side shall I lose: 1268

WHURLE = 1
They whurle a-sunder, and dismember mee. 1263
WHY *l.*79 81 *92 202 239 670 720 796 908 941 943 1068 1632 1773 *1808
*1928 1929 *1932 2212 2489 2557 *2573 2590 = 17*6
WICKED = 3
Con. I who doubts that, a Will: a wicked will, 496
Const. A wicked day, and not a holy day. 1008
The image of a wicked heynous fault 1789
WIDDOW = 3
This widdow Lady? In her right we came, 868
A widow, husbandles, subiect to feares, 935
A widow cries, be husband to me (heauens) 1033
WIDDOWES = 1
Many a widdowes husband groueling lies, 615
WIDDOWS = *1
Const. O take his mothers thanks, a widdows thanks, 325
WIDDOW-MAKER = 1
To be a widdow-maker: oh, and there 2268
WIDE = 3
Had bin dishabited, and wide hauocke made 526
F.Her. You men of Angiers open wide your gates, 610
The mouth of passage shall we fling wide ope, 764
WIDOW-COMFORT = 1
My widow-comfort, and my sorrowes cure. *Exit.* 1490
WIERY = 1
Euen to that drop ten thousand wiery fiends 1448
WIFE = 5
Your fathers wife did after wedlocke beare him: 125
Be stronger with thee, then the name of wife? 1247
And busse thee as thy wife: Miseries Loue, | O come to me. 1418
My name is *Constance*, I was *Geffreyes* wife, 1430
Pan. You, in the right of Lady *Blanch* your wife, 1527
WIL *l.*435 *1153 *2422 = 1*2
WILDE = 3
How like you this wilde counsell mighty States, 709
And wilde amazement hurries vp and downe 2203
And tame the sauage spirit of wilde warre, 2327
WILDELY = 1
How wildely then walkes my Estate in France? 1847
WILDEST = 1
The wildest Sauagery, the vildest stroke 2047
WILFULL = 1
Pand. The *Dolphin* is too wilfull opposite 2378
WILFULLY = 1
So wilfully dost spurne; and force perforce 1069
WILL *see also* hee'll, Ile, 'twill, wee'l, wee'll, we'l *l.*30 224 229 286 314
324 336 440 462 561 577 659 718 722 723 831 832 833 866 871 880 914
919 939 *989 990 1084 1231 1252 *1253 1258 1267 1296 1301 1303 1312
1325 1353 1412 1417 1421 1452 1454 1459 1467 1469 1486 1537 1541
1545 1566 1568 1576 1599 1600 1614 1615 1630 1632 1653 1656 1657
1679 1692 1694 1701 1712 1756 1763 1798 1819 1861 1875 1892 1997
2008 2022 2108 2133 2201 *2331 2363 2379 2418 2419 2455 2513 2561
2602 2620 2644 2697 2704 = 93*3, 14
Vpon his death-bed he by will bequeath'd 117
My fathers land, as was my fathers will. 123
Rob. Shal then my fathers Will be of no force, 138
Then was his will to get me, as I think. 141

WILL *cont.*

A Will, that barres the title of thy sonne.   495
Con. I who doubts that, a Will: a wicked will,   496
A womans will, a cankred Grandams will.   497
Blan. My vnckles will in this respect is mine,   827
I can with ease translate it to my will: 830
(If not fill vp the measure of her will)   877
Holding th'eternall spirit against her will,   1401
Good Lords, although my will to giue, is liuing,   1801

WILLD = 1

Hen. At Worster must his bodie be interr'd, | For so he will'd it.   2709

WILLINGLY = 2

Hath willingly departed with a part,   884
And well shall you perceiue, how willingly   1762

WILT *l.**156 241 454 2103 2564 = 4*1, 1

Bast. Wil't not be? | Will not a Calues-skin stop that mouth of thine?   1230

WIN = 4

Then ere the coward hand of *France* can win; | Submit thee boy.   458
Win you this Citie without stroke, or wound,   733
I say againe, if *Lewis* do win the day,   2491
If *Lewis*, by your assistance win the day.   2500

WINCH = 1

I will not stirre, nor winch, nor speake a word,   1657

WINDE = 5

No common winde, no customed euent,   1540
And like a shifted winde vnto a saile,   1740
Therefore thy threatning Colours now winde vp,   2326
With that same weake winde, which enkindled it: 2340
Against the winde, the which he prickes and wounds   2623

WINDES = 2

Hath put himselfe in Armes, the aduerse windes   351
To make his bleake windes kisse my parched lips,   2648

WINDIE = 1

Least zeale now melted by the windie breath   793

WINDOW = 1

In at the window, or else ore the hatch: 180

WINDOWES = 1

It would not out at windowes, nor at doores,   2636

WINGS = 1

Shadowing their right vnder your wings of warre: 307

WINKING = 2

Comfort your Citties eies, your winking gates: 521
And on the winking of Authoritie | To vnderstand a Law; to know the
meaning   1936

WINNE = 5

May easily winne a womans: aye my mother,   282
Husband, I cannot pray that thou maist winne: 1264
I haue a way to winne their loues againe: 1889
To winne this easie match, plaid for a Crowne?   2359
To out-looke Conquest, and to winne renowne   2368

WINNES = 1

That dayly breake-vow, he that winnes of all,   890

WINS = 1

Who-euer wins, on that side shall I lose: 1268

WINTER = 1

And none of you will bid the winter come   2644

WIPE = 1
   Let me wipe off this honourable dewe,   2296
WISEDOME = 1
   What you in wisedome still vouchsafe to say.   842
WISH = 5
   Madam I would not wish a better father: 273
   King. A wonder Lady: lo vpon thy wish | Our Messenger *Chattilion* is
   arriu'd,   344
   Father, I may not wish the fortune thine: 1266
   Grandam, I will not wish thy wishes thriue: 1267
   To wish him dead, but thou hadst none to kill him.   1931
WISHD = 1
   And your supply, which you haue wish'd so long,   2538
WISHES = 1
   Grandam, I will not wish thy wishes thriue: 1267
WITCHCRAFT = 1
   This iugling witchcraft with reuennue cherish,   1096
WITH = 196*8
WITHALL = 2
   Phillip of France, if thou be pleas'd withall,   851
   Which is the side that I must goe withall?   1260
WITHDRAW = 1
   Her Enemies rankes? I must withdraw, and weepe   2280
WITHIN = 12*1
   Craues harbourage within your Citie walles.   540
   Con. Which harme within it selfe so heynous is,   961
   Within the scorched veines of one new burn'd: 1209
   Eng. France, y shalt rue this houre within this houre.   1256
   We owe thee much: within this wall of flesh   1319
   Within the Arras: when I strike my foot   1572
   Hub. Go stand within: let me alone with him.   1661
   To breake within the bloody house of life,   1935
   Within this bosome, neuer entred yet   1979
   Mel. Haue I not hideous death within my view,   2483
   Stoope lowe within those bounds we haue ore-look'd,   2516
   Within me is a hell, and there the poyson   2655
   The Cardinall *Pandulph* is within at rest,   2692
WITHOUT = 14
   Win you this Citie without stroke, or wound,   733
   And giue you entrance: but without this match,   765
   Sal. Pardon me Madam, | I may not goe without you to the kings.   987
   Without th'assistance of a mortall hand: 1085
   To my keene curses; for without my wrong   1110
   Or if that thou couldst see me without eyes,   1347
   Heare me without thine eares, and make reply   1348
   Without a tongue, vsing conceit alone,   1349
   Without eyes, eares, and harmefull sound of words: 1350
   So foule a skie, cleeres not without a storme,   1826
   Yea, without stop, didst let thy heart consent,   1964
   That you do see? Could thought, without this obiect   2043
   For villanie is not without such rheume,   2111
   To rest without a spot for euermore.   2718
WITH-HELD = 1
   To inforce these rights, so forcibly with-held,   23
WITH-HOLD = 1*1
   Iohn. With-hold thy speed, dreadfull Occasion: 1844
   Bast. With-hold thine indignation, mighty heauen,   2595

WITNESSE = 1
Witnesse against vs to damnation.   1943
WITNESSES = 1
And if not that, I bring you Witnesses   581
WITTE = 1
When there is such disorder in my witte: 1487
WIUES = 4
That marry wiues: tell me, how if my brother   128
Philip, good old Sir *Roberts* wiues eldest sonne.   167
And leaue your children, wiues, and you in peace.   563
Or if it must stand still, let wiues with childe   1014
WOE = 1
Bast. Oh let vs pay the time: but needfull woe,   2721
WOES = 2
And leaue those woes alone, which I alone | Am bound to vnder-beare.   985
How I may be deliuer'd of these woes.   1439
WOMAN = 3
What woman post is this? hath she no husband   228
A woman naturally borne to feares;   936
I am no woman, Ile not swound at it.   2579
WOMANISH = 1
Out at mine eyes, in tender womanish teares.   1609
WOMANS = 2
May easily winne a womans: aye my mother,   282
A womans will, a cankred Grandams will.   497
WOMBE = 4
Being but the second generation | Remoued from thy sinne-conceiuing
wombe.   483
Vgly, and slandrous to thy Mothers wombe,   965
That euer Spider twisted from her wombe   2132
You bloudy Nero's, ripping vp the wombe   2406
WOMEN = *1
Lew. Women & fooles, breake off your conference.   450
WON = 2
Dol. What he hath won, that hath he fortified: 1392
Pan. If you had won it, certainely you had.   1503·
WONDER = 2
King. A wonder Lady: lo vpon thy wish | Our Messenger *Chattilion* is
arriu'd,   344
A wonder, or a wondrous miracle,   813
WONDERFULL = 1
Go with me to the King, 'tis wonderfull,   1563
WONDROUS = 2*1
A wonder, or a wondrous miracle,   813
Bast. Now by my life, this day grows wondrous hot,   1285
The other foure, in wondrous motion.   1908
WONNE = 3
Neere or farre off, well wonne is still well shot,   183
She is corrupted, chang'd, and wonne from thee,   976
In this which he accounts so clearely wonne: 1507
WOOED = 1
But for because he hath not wooed me yet: 909
WOOND = 1
And woon'd our tott'ring colours clearly vp,   2531
WORD = 8*1
Our eares are cudgel'd, not a word of his   780
But the word Maid, cheats the poore Maide of that.   893

WORD *cont.*

This Bawd, this Broker, this all-changing-word,   903
I trust I may not trust thee, for thy word   928
But this one word, whether thy tale be true.   947
And nere haue spoke a louing word to you: 1627
I will not stirre, nor winch, nor speake a word,   1657
Iohn. Now keep your holy word, go meet the *French,*   2172
And send him word by me, which way you go.   2447

WORDE = 1

Ele. Come hether little kinsman, harke, a worde.   1317

WORDS = 11*2

They shoote but calme words, folded vp in smoake,   535
Zounds, I was neuer so bethumpt with words,   782
Be these sad signes confirmers of thy words?   945
Envenom him with words, or get thee gone,   984
Aus. O that a man should speake those words to me.   1056
The latest breath that gaue the sound of words   1161
Without eyes, eares, and harmefull sound of words: 1350
Puts on his pretty lookes, repeats his words,   1480
And bitter shame hath spoyl'd the sweet words taste,   1495
Hub. His words do take possession of my bosome.   1605
As bid me tell my tale in expresse words: 1959
Bast. What ere you thinke, good words I thinke | were best. 2026
Pem. Big. Our soules religiously confirme thy words.   2072

WORK = *1

Ba. Here's a good world: knew you of this faire work?   2119

WORKE = 9*1

We know his handy-worke, therefore good mother   251
King. Well, then to worke our Cannon shall be bent   330
This toyle of ours should be a worke of thine;   390
Much worke for teares in many an English mother,   613
Make worke vpon our selues, for heauen or hell.   721
Bast. It is a damned, and a bloody worke,   2056
If that it be the worke of any hand.   2058
Sal. If that it be the worke of any hand?   2059
It is the shamefull worke of *Huberts* hand,   2061
Pand. You looke but on the out-side of this worke.   2362

WORKEMEN = *1

Pem. When Workemen striue to do better then wel,   1745

WORLD = 25*3

Till she had kindled *France* and all the world,   39
And if he were, he came into the world   120
This Calfe, bred from his Cow from all the world: 132
That thou maist be a Queen, and checke the world.   420
Haue we ramm'd vp our gates against the world.   578
Holdes hand with any Princesse of the world.   810
Bast. Mad world, mad kings, mad composition: 882
Commoditie, the byas of the world,   895
The world, who of it selfe is peysed well,   896
Attended with the pleasures of the world,   1334
Then with a passion would I shake the world,   1423
My life, my ioy, my food, my all the world: 1489
Dol. There's nothing in this world can make me ioy,   1492
Pan. How green you are, and fresh in this old world?   1530
That *Hubert* for the wealth of all the world, | Will not offend thee. 1711
Three foot of it doth hold; bad world the while: 1818
With these ill tydings: Now? What sayes the world   1853

WORLD *cont.*

Neuer to taste the pleasures of the world,	2067
Ba. Here's a good world: knew you of this faire work?	2119
Among the thornes, and dangers of this world.	2146
Let not the world see feare and sad distrust	2214
That neuer saw the giant-world enrag'd,	2308
To any Soueraigne State throughout the world.	2335
And cull'd these fiery spirits from the world	2367
Bast. According to the faire-play of the world,	2372
What in the world should make me now deceiue,	2487
What surety of the world, what hope, what stay,	2678
Come the three corners of the world in Armes,	2727

WORMES = 1

And ring these fingers with thy houshold wormes,	1414

WORSE = 2

But many a many foot of Land the worse.	193
Doth make the fault the worse by th'excuse:	1748

WORSHIP = 2

Gaine be my Lord, for I will worship thee. *Exit.*	919
By giuing it the worship of Reuenge.	2071

WORSHIPD = 1

Canonized and worship'd as a Saint,	1104

WORSHIPFULL = 1

But this is worshipfull society,	215

WORSHIPS = 1

Hee and his tooth-picke at my worships messe,	200

WORST = 3

Bast. But if you be a-feard to heare the worst,	1856
Then let the worst vn-heard, fall on your head.	1857
Returne, and tell him so: we know the worst.	2025

WORSTER = 1

Hen. At Worster must his bodie be interr'd, | For so he will'd it.	2709

WORTH = 2

I am not worth this coyle that's made for me.	467
Your Worth, your Greatnesse, and Nobility.	2086

WORTHIE = 1

That all I see in you is worthie loue,	834

WORTHIEST = 2

Cit. Till you compound whose right is worthiest,	588
We for the worthiest hold the right from both.	589

WOULD *see also* I'de *l.**5 38 101 153 154 155 *163 210 273 311 431 466 599 862 911 969 1145 1156 1352 1357 1423 1432 1559 1588 1592 1596 1597 1602 1626 1637 *1639 *1647 1683 1755 1761 2060 2083 2205 2286 2613 2636 2719 = 39*4

WOULDST *l.*1358 2134 = 2

WOUND = 5

And wound her honor with this diffidence.	73
Win you this Citie without stroke, or wound,	733
And heale the inueterate Canker of one wound,	2265
Bast. Shew me the very wound of this ill newes,	2578
But when it first did helpe to wound it selfe.	2725

WOUNDED = 2

Enter Meloon wounded.	2466
Pem. It is the Count *Meloone.* | *Sal.* Wounded to death.	2469

WOUNDS = 1

Against the winde, the which he prickes and wounds	2623

WRACKD = 1
Are wrack'd three nights ago on *Goodwin* sands.   2451
WRACKE = 1
But (on this day) let Sea-men feare no wracke,   1017
WRAPT = 1
And now insteed of bulletts wrapt in fire   533
WRASTLING = 1
And great affections wrastling in thy bosome   2292
WRATH = 5
So hence: be thou the trumpet of our wrath,   32
The Canons haue their bowels full of wrath,   516
France, I am burn'd vp with inflaming wrath,   1273
And picke strong matter of reuolt, and wrath   1552
That euer wall-ey'd wrath, or staring rage   2048
WRATHFULL = 1
Whiles we Gods wrathfull agent doe correct   384
WRESTED = 1
The iminent decay of wrested pompe.   2159
WRETCH = *1
*That bloudy spoyle: thou slaue, thou wretch, y coward,   1041
WRINKLE = 1
Hang'd in the frowning wrinkle of her brow,   822
WRINKLED = 1
With wrinkled browes, with nods, with rolling eyes.   1917
WRIST = 1
And he that speakes, doth gripe the hearers wrist,   1915
WRIT = 1
Can you not reade it? Is it not faire writ?   1610
WRITTEN = 1
That hauing our faire order written downe,   2255
WRONG = 8
Or else it must go wrong with you and me,   47
Vnder whose warrant I impeach thy wrong,   413
To my keene curses; for without my wrong   1110
Let it be lawfull, that Law barre no wrong: 1114
Therefore since Law it selfe is perfect wrong,   1117
All things that you should vse to do me wrong   1697
The steppes of wrong, should moue you to mew vp   1774
Of sterne Iniustice, and confused wrong: 2274
WRONGD = 1
Being wrong'd as we are by this peeuish Towne: 716
WRONGS = 4
His grandames wrongs, and not his mothers shames   470
Opprest with wrongs, and therefore full of feares,   934
Aust. Well ruffian, I must pocket vp these wrongs,   1128
And thou possessed with a thousand wrongs: 1340
WROUGHT = 3*1
That thou hast vnder-wrought his lawfull King,   392
What may be wrought out of their discontent,   1564
(The best I had, a Princesse wrought it me)   1619
*And those thy feares, might haue wrought feares in me.   1961
Y = 1*6
Eli. Out on thee rude man, y dost shame thy mother,   72
Aust. The peace of heauen is theirs y lift their swords   328
*That bloudy spoyle: thou slaue, thou wretch, y coward,   1041
Eng. *France*, y shalt rue this houre within this houre.   1256
Bast. Old Time the clocke setter, y bald sexton Time: 1257

Y *cont.*
(If thou didst this deed of death) art y damn'd *Hubert*.   2121
*Counfound themselues. 'Tis strange y death shold sing: 2626
YARD = 1
If this same were a Church-yard where we stand,   1339
YCE = 1
To smooth the yce, or adde another hew   1730
YCIE = 1
To thrust his ycie fingers in my maw;   2645
YE *l.*2344 = 1
YEA = 3
Yea, faith it selfe to hollow falshood change.   1020
Yea, without stop, didst let thy heart consent,   1964
Yea, thrust this enterprize into my heart,   2343
YEARELY = 1
The yearely course that brings this day about,   1006
YEELD = 2
Arthur of *Britaine*, yeeld thee to my hand,   456
I shall yeeld vp my Crowne, let him be hang'd   1878
YEELDED = 2*1
K.Iohn. Thus haue I yeelded vp into your hand | The Circle of my glory.   2167
Bast. All Kent hath yeelded: nothing there holds out   2198
And shall I now giue ore the yeelded Set?   2360
YEELDING = 1
1 see a yeelding in the lookes of France: 790
YEELDS = 1
That it yeelds nought but shame and bitternesse.   1496
YEERE = 3
At least from faire fiue hundred pound a yeere: 77
A halfe-fac'd groat, fiue hundred pound a yeere?   102
Your face hath got fiue hundred pound a yeere,   160
YEERES = 1
Is neere to England, looke vpon the yeeres   739
YES = 1
Fra. Binde vp your haires. | *Con.* Yes that I will: and wherefore will I
    do it?   1453
YESTERDAY = 1
To him that did but yesterday suspire,   1465
YET = 28*2
Yet sell your face for fiue pence and 'tis deere: 161
Yet to auoid deceit I meane to learne;   225
We hold our Towne for neither: yet for both.   645
Iohn. France, hast thou yet more blood to cast away?   648
Iohn. Whose party do the Townesmen yet admit?   675
Yet in some measure satisfie her so,   878
But for because he hath not wooed me yet: 909
But for my hand, as vnattempted yet,   912
Yet I alone, alone doe me oppose   1097
Yet indirection thereby growes direct,   1207
Iohn. Good friend, thou hast no cause to say so yet,   1329
Yet it shall come, for me to doe thee good.   1331
But (ah) I will not, yet I loue thee well,   1353
Pand. Courage and comfort, all shall yet goe well.   1386
Yet I remember, when I was in France,   1587
Yet am I sworne, and I did purpose, Boy,   1703
Pem. Stay yet (Lord Salisbury) Ile go with thee,   1814
Is yet a maiden, and an innocent hand.   1977

YET *cont.*

Within this bosome, neuer entred yet	1979
Is yet the couer of a fayrer minde,	1983
Ar. The Wall is high, and yet will I leape downe.	1997
I am afraide, and yet Ile venture it.	2001
To the yet vnbegotten sinne of times;	2053
Hub. Not for my life: But yet I dare defend	2088
Yet I am none. Whose tongue so ere speakes false,	2092
There is not yet so vgly a fiend of hell	2126
Bast. Away then with good courage: yet I know	2247
To your proceedings: yet beleeue me Prince,	2262
Yet speakes, and peraduenture may recouer.	2588
* Pem. His Highnesse yet doth speak, & holds beleefe,	2611

YFAITH = 2

Sirra looke too't, yfaith I will, yfaith.	440

YIELD *see* yeeld
YIELDED *see* yeelded
YIELDING *see* yeelding
YIELDS *see* yeelds
YON = 2

That yon greene boy shall haue no Sunne to ripe	788
On yon young boy: Ile tell thee what my friend,	1360

YONG = 19*1

And put the same into yong *Arthurs* hand,	19
Of him it holds, stands yong *Plantagenet,*	544
To him that owes it, namely, this yong Prince,	554
And let yong *Arthur* Duke of Britaine in,	611
Is the yong Dolphin euery way compleat,	748
For wee'l create yong *Arthur* Duke of Britaine	872
Of kings, of beggers, old men, yong men, maids,	891
Yong *Arthur* is my sonne, and he is lost:	1431
Dol. But what shall I gaine by yong *Arthurs* fall?	1526
Dol. May be he will not touch yong *Arthurs* life,	1545
If that yong *Arthur* be not gone alreadie,	1548
Yong Lad come forth; I haue to say with you.	1578
Yong Gentlemen would be as sad as night	1588
*Reade heere yong *Arthur.* How now foolish rheume?	1606
Hub. Yong Boy, I must. | *Art.* And will you? | *Hub.* And I will.	1613
Yong *Arthurs* death is common in their mouths,	1912
Why vrgest thou so oft yong *Arthurs* death?	1929
Yong *Arthur* is aliue: This hand of mine	1976
After they heard yong *Arthur* was aliue?	2206
After yong *Arthur,* claime this Land for mine,	2347

YONGER = *1

* K.Iohn. A good blunt fellow: why being yonger born	79

YONG-ONES = *1

*Iohn. What saie these yong-ones? What say you my | Neece?	839

YOU = 208*16
YOUNG = 1*1

* Fra. It likes vs well young Princes: close your hands	853
On yon young boy: Ile tell thee what my friend,	1360

YOUR *l.*33 *46 48 58 87 99 104 106 124 125 130 131 134 136 137 160 161
*172 199 207 208 275 276 307 326 327 337 338 348 350 436 439 445 446
*450 514 515 518 521 527 528 530 531 534 536 538 540 548 562 563 565
569 598 599 610 *623 624 635 638 676 690 691 694 702 703 815 816
*836 *853 854 856 *864 1130 1156 1181 1183 1250 1299 1312 1314 1328
1366 1375 1378 1404 1453 1477 1510 1527 1547 1576 1597 1616 1618

YOUR *cont.*
  1621 1624 1628 1667 1669 1674 *1675 1687 1693 1694 1708 *1720 1734
  *1753 1756 1763 1767 1773 1775 1783 1786 1813 1831 1840 1854 1857
  1873 1886 1940 1974 1975 2020 2029 2079 2083 2085 2086 2101 2167
  2171 *2172 2173 2185 2188 2190 2201 2202 2204 2220 2243 2262 2314
  *2331 2336 2391 2394 2398 2401 2407 2408 *2422 2441 2445 2446 2477
  2497 2499 2500 2501 2538 2642 2660 *2684 *2685 2703 2708
  2712 = 166*18

YOURS = 10

My father gaue me honor, yours gaue land:	173
No sir, saies question, I sweet sir at yours,	209
And so doth yours: your fault, was not your follie,	275
Arthur of Britaine, Englands King, and yours.	621
But now in Armes, you strengthen it with yours.	1028
Fra. Good reuerend father, make my person yours,	1155
Let him come backe, that his compassion may | Giue life to yours.	1665
Art. O heauen: that there were but a moth in yours,	1670
By heauen, I thinke my sword's as sharpe as yours.	2082
He is forsworne, if ere those eyes of yours	2492

YOURSELFE *see* selfe

YOUTH = 3

With barbarous ignorance, and deny his youth	1776
Iohn. Let it be so: I do commit his youth	1785
The youth saies well. Now heare our *English* King,	2382

YOUTHFULL = 1

Pan. Your minde is all as youthfull as your blood.	1510

YRON = 1

Did with his yron tongue, and brazen mouth	1337

YT *l.*461 463 = 2

ZEALE = 5

Being no further enemy to you | Then the constraint of hospitable zeale,	549
Least zeale now melted by the windie breath	793
Whom zeale and charitie brought to the field,	886
Of all his people, and freeze vp their zeale,	1535
A voluntary zeale, and an vn-urg'd Faith	2261

ZEALOUS = 1

If zealous loue should go in search of vertue,	743

ZELOUS = 1

Aust. Vpon thy cheeke lay I this zelous kisse,	312

ZOUNDS = 1

Zounds, I was neuer so bethumpt with words,	782

&*l.**24 *450 *1277 *1310 *1941 2007 *2034 *2546 *2567 *2611 = 1*9

F5